MAKING AND UNMAKING NATIONS

MAKING AND UNMAKING NATIONS

War, Leadership, and Genocide in Modern Africa

SCOTT STRAUS

CORNELL UNIVERSITY PRESS

Ithaca and London

First published 2015 by Cornell University Press

First printing, Cornell Paperbacks, 2015

Printed in the United States of America

Library of Congress Cataloging-in-Publication Data

Straus, Scott, 1970– author.
    Making and unmaking nations : war, leadership, and genocide in modern Africa / Scott Straus.
        pages cm
    Includes bibliographical references and index.
    ISBN 978-0-8014-5332-8 (cloth : alk. paper)
    ISBN 978-0-8014-7968-7 (pbk. : alk. paper)
    1. Africa, Sub-Saharan—Politics and government—1960–
2. Genocide—Africa, Sub-Saharan.   3. Nation-building—
Africa, Sub-Saharan.   4. Political leadership—Africa,
Sub-Saharan.   I. Title.
    DT352.8.S76 2015
    364.15'10967—dc23   2014035618

Cornell University Press strives to use environmentally responsible suppliers and materials to the fullest extent possible in the publishing of its books. Such materials include vegetable-based, low-VOC inks and acid-free papers that are recycled, totally chlorine-free, or partly composed of nonwood fibers. For further information, visit our website at www.cornellpress.cornell.edu.

Cloth printing   10 9 8 7 6 5 4 3 2 1
Paperback printing   10 9 8 7 6 5 4 3 2 1

For Sadie and Solomon, Dad and Bruce

CONTENTS

PREFACE

To my surprise, this book is about the legacy of ideas and the ways in which ideas about politics and political community sometimes make the unimaginable seem righteous.

Ever since I was a journalist covering the aftermath of the Rwandan genocide in the mid-1990s, I have sought to understand how and why states and citizens dedicate themselves to mass violence against human populations.

In my book on the Rwandan genocide, I investigated the question at the local level. What drove perpetrators? How did mobilization to commit violence occur? With answers to those questions, I sought to build an explanation of how and why the Rwandan genocide happened. Ideology was not a big part of my story. I found that war mattered a huge amount, as did the strength of Rwanda's state and widespread awareness of ethnic categories.

In this book, however, I ask different questions. The main one is: Why do some major crises, usually involving armed conflict, escalate to genocide, while other, similar crises do not? To my mind, asking the negative question of why genocide does *not* happen is essential to answering the positive question of why genocide does happen.

The question requires a shift of focus from local actors to national ones. To that end, I have investigated the question in two main ways. First, I isolate a "logic" of genocide and seek to distinguish it from the logics of other forms of political violence. Why would state leaders ever think that genocide is the right course of action? Second, I compare five countries in depth—Rwanda, Sudan, Mali, Côte d'Ivoire, and Senegal—and multiple other countries more superficially. In both instances, my main purpose is to build, rather than to test, theory. I want to understand how such violence became possible, and I had no *a priori* answer.

My conclusions are nonetheless unexpected. I come away convinced that the key to solving the puzzle is how leaders frame threats and define goals. Leaders in different crises employ different constructs about whom they are fighting and what they are fighting to achieve. Those ideas in turn shape leaders' strategies of violence, making a logic of genocide imaginable in some cases and less imaginable in others.

The origins of genocide are, to be sure, a lot more complicated than leaders' mental constructs. Genocide is an extreme form of violence that becomes a reality only during deep crises, especially wars, and only after a process of escalation. Leaders need to galvanize and sustain far-flung operations of violence involving multiple actors. These and other factors matter, as I discuss in the book. But I conclude that to explain variation—to explain why countries with similar crises experience different outcomes—the role of ideology is essential.

The sources of ideology are notoriously difficult to pin down. I take a view that history delivers a package of available ideas and that material conditions constrain the range of available options but also that prominent leaders have some autonomy in synthesizing and developing particular ideologies. In that way, I assign importance to leaders, and, as far as Africa is concerned, I place particular emphasis on the lasting legacy of the first generation of leaders.

For genocide, the key issue is how leaders define the primary political community and the main project of the state. Ideologies that identify a specific category of people as the main population whose interests the state promotes are the ideologies that are most prone to genocide. I call these ideas "founding narratives" in that they tell a fundamental story about the character and purpose of a state.

The risk of genocide increases when state leaders associate a significant material threat, generally a military one, with a category of people that differs from the primary political community. In such situations, state leaders are more likely to define the enemy as a social category and victory over the enemy as destruction of that social category. By contrast, in places where the primary political community is not defined in terms of one social category over another, that logic is difficult to imagine and sustain.

My story about the origins of genocide assigns importance to political agency. Leaders make crucial decisions at critical historical junctures about how to frame the founding narratives of the state. Moreover, elites in later time periods face the same choice—they can choose to abandon, challenge, or follow the founding narratives that precede them. Every choice is not equal. Moving away from a founding narrative can be politically costly, but nonetheless there is a degree of autonomy in decision-making.

My explanation is elite-centric. However, genocide is not just an elite story. Genocide requires local-level actors to identify, sort, and often inflict violence against civilian groups. Some joint coordination between national and local actors—whether in a formal, centralized way or in a more informal, decentralized way—is necessary for large-scale violence against civilians to take place.

The book has some other, related implications. For example, I come away unconvinced that genocide is a fully conceived strategy. To be sure, there are exceptions, such as the later stages of the Holocaust where detailed planning to exterminate the Jews and other groups took place. But in most cases genocide is the expression of a particular logic of violence. Leaders typically do not sit down and map out extermination as the best way to retain power. Rather, they say, in effect: "We face a major threat from some malicious group, and we have to do whatever it takes to defeat them." In other words, the search for a genocide "plan" or "conspiracy"—as scholars and international criminal justice lawyers frequently do—is likely to mislead. I am not saying that the violence in these cases is not deliberate, systematic, widespread, organized, and exterminatory. It is genocide. But the end goal may be vague even to those who unleash the violence.

Finally, this is a book not only about genocide and political violence but also about Africa. Pairing violence with Africa might seem to reinforce a stereotype of a continent where atrocity and conflict run amok. But Africa is not exceptionally violent, and there is significant variation across the continent in terms of the frequency and intensity of violence. Africa is not monolithic.

More importantly, I credit the visions of some leaders who crafted ultimately positive paths for their countries. Contemporary scholars and policymakers tend to downplay leadership and ideology as vacuous or superficial; given the generally poor outcomes across the continent in the 1970s and 1980s many now disparage the first three decades of African political development. Even though this is a book about genocide, I beg to disagree.

I have worked on this book for a long time, and I have incurred many debts as a result. I start by acknowledging how much I learned from those I interviewed in the field. I took several trips to Côte d'Ivoire, especially, but also to Mali and Senegal, and I tried to take seriously what smart Ivoirians, Malians, and Senegalese told me. I can remember one interview in particular with a since-deceased Ivoirian intellectual, Bernard Zadi, in which he told me that genocide would never happen in Côte d'Ivoire. Why, I pressed? Because, he said, the country's first president had over and over again emphasized the values of tolerance, and those values had permeated the country's political culture. At the time—on one of my first visits to Côte d'Ivoire—I thought that Professor Zadi's ideas were interesting but old-fashioned. But I kept thinking about it; I kept interviewing more Ivoirians; I came back to speak with him; I traveled to other countries; I thought about my experiences in Rwanda and Sudan and my knowledge of other cases, such as the Armenian genocide, the Holocaust, the former Yugoslavia, and Cambodia. In the end, I have come to believe that Professor Zadi was incredibly insightful. And I'd like to recognize not only his wisdom but also the wisdom of all those who answered my many questions.

Along the various stages of this project, I have been extremely fortunate to receive funding to support the work. I thank the Harry Frank Guggenheim Foundation for supporting the project at its early stages, the Committee on Conscience at the United States Holocaust Memorial Museum for supporting the conceptual work in chapter 1, and the United States Institute of Peace, which supported the final stages of the project. The Graduate School at the University of Wisconsin also has been a terrific source of support. I spent six months at the Centre d'études et de recherches internationales (CERI) at Sciences Po in Paris while on sabbatical and during a critical phase of the writing. My hosts, especially Jacques Sémelin, were welcoming and gracious.

I have presented various stages of the project in several venues, including, in chronological order, Yale University's Order, Conflict, and Violence Seminar, the University of Notre Dame, Vanderbilt University, the University of Cambridge, the University of London, Colgate University, the University of Michigan, CERI, Simon Fraser University, the African Studies Center at the University of Florida, Clark University's Strassler Center for Holocaust and Genocide Studies, the Comparative Politics Workshop at the University of Illinois, the Johns Hopkins School of Advanced International Studies, Princeton University's Comparative Politics Workshop, the African Studies Program at the University of Wisconsin–Madison, the Comparative Politics Colloquium at the University of Wisconsin–Madison, the Program on International Security and Policy at the University of Chicago, the United States Holocaust Memorial Museum, the Comparative Politics Workshop at Yale University, and finally the Africa Working Group of the University of Notre Dame. I have benefited enormously from the comments and suggestions that I received during these presentations.

Along the way, many colleagues made terrific suggestions, including Claire Andrieu, Nick Barnes, Tom Bassett, Mark Beissinger, Dorina Bekoe, Max Bergholz, Rikhil Bhavnani, Jaimie Bleck, Jeff Checkel, Thierry Cruvellier, Rafaela Dancygier, Jim Delehanty, Jo Ellen Fair, Vincent Foucher, Lee Ann Fujii, Bernadette Graves, Yoi Herrera, Stathis Kalyvas, Andy Kydd, Brett Kyle, René Lemarchand, Peter Lewis, Evan Lieberman, John Mearsheimer, Matthew Mitchell, Tamir Moustafa, Steve Ndegwa, Bob Pape, Chris Price,

Matthew Scharf, Michael Schatzberg, Gay Seidman, Jacques Sémelin, Nadav Shelef, Erica Simmons, Dan Slater, Ben Smith, Nick Smith, Stephen Smith, Aliko Songolo, Carol Spindel, Paul Staniland, Aili Tripp, Ben Valentino, Leo Villalon, Sam Vorthoerms, Lars Waldorf, Leonard Wantchekon, Lisa Wedeen, Andreas Wimmer, Susanna Wing, and Libby Wood, among others. I thank them all.

In my final revisions, my extraordinary colleague Crawford Young read the entire manuscript and offered eleven pages of detailed, single-spaced comments. Crawford is an inspiration not only for his intellectual gifts and legacy but also for his generosity. Roger Haydon of Cornell University Press also read each chapter, and his sharp, careful, thoughtful, and usually encouraging comments were simply wonderful. An enormous thank you to Roger, a true editor. Matthew Mitchell also read half of the manuscript and offered many terrific suggestions.

Matthew Scharf has been a wonderful research assistant on the project. He labored to find, digitize, and upload years and years of presidential speeches that are now available on a website (http://users.polisci.wisc.edu/straus/speech/). Brett Kyle and Cassidy Sandoval also contributed research to the book.

The book cover is based on an extraordinary painting by the Ivoirien artist, Aboudia. Thanks to him and to Cécile Fakhoury for permission.

My work builds on the research of many scholars. In particular, this book is a long and appreciative engagement with some of the work of Stathis Kalyvas, Michael Mann, Jacques Sémelin, Jay Ulfelder, Ben Valentino, Eric Weitz, and Libby Wood. In researching the case studies, I sought to read widely and deeply in the existing literature, and my work is thus indebted to a wide range of scholars who write on Côte d'Ivoire, Mali, Rwanda, Senegal, Sudan, and other places. I learned a great deal from the scholarly record.

During the course of researching and writing this book, my two wonderful children, Sadie and Solomon, were born. I dedicate the book to them. They give me joy and make me proud every day. Going from the office where I study genocide to home, where a different logic reigns, was often jarring. But that change was so vital as I struggled for many years to make sense of my subject. During the course of writing the book, I lost my two fathers. I have been lucky in life to have been parented by two remarkable and very different men. I miss them every day. I also thank my mother, Leila, Dan and Cheryl, Jane and John, Alex and Ben, Erica, Jonathan, and Danny for their continuing support and encouragement. And, finally, to Sara, my love, who makes it all work.

Introduction
The Puzzle of Genocide

Genocide and similar forms of mass violence are among the most devastating of all human phenomena. Genocide extinguishes masses of lives; it scars societies and families for generations.[1] No society should ever experience it. Genocide is also the ultimate failure in politics. Genocide reflects a decision to reject accommodation, to inflict maximum violence, and to extinguish future social interaction in a shared territory. Rather than manage a social contract, negotiate difference, devolve power, distribute goods, and compromise through accommodation or negotiation—the promise of politics, however flawed in all its myriad applications and however constrained by limited means—genocide is about destroying human populations so that they can and will not make demands or pose threats.

Genocide is hard to explain. Genocide is "atrocity by policy."[2] Genocide is therefore deliberate and strategic.[3] Genocide requires planning and perseverance. It is both costly and difficult to sustain violence against unarmed citizens for long periods of time across multiple locations. Leaders who choose to commit such violence invite ethical dissension from within their

---

1. I discuss the concept of genocide at length in the next chapter. In essence, by genocide I mean sustained large-scale violence against a social category that aims at that group's destruction.

2. Browning 1991.

3. Fein 1979; Valentino 2004.

organizations and from their own supporters, international condemnation and material sanctions, greater resolve and recruitment from their opponents, and opportunity costs—committing genocide saps resources from other vital programs. The leaders who choose, orchestrate, and implement such violence must be committed to such policies. They must believe in the righteousness of such actions. Why would any leader consider such radical violence against unarmed people legitimate? Why choose such a policy over many less violent and less costly alternatives? How and why can such leaders sustain violence over long periods of time?

Scholars have made great progress in studying these and other questions during the past forty years. We know a great deal more about individual cases, and we have identified important commonalities among otherwise diverse genocide cases. However, key questions still remain. In this book, I focus on two. First, what is the logic of violence that drives genocide? Why would political leaders foment genocide over a range of other policies? Second, what constellation of conditions gives rise to that logic? What must be present for genocide to occur? And why do those conditions give rise to genocide?

My approach to answering those questions departs from most previous studies. Rather than focus primarily on genocide cases, I emphasize the importance of studying nongenocides. To know why and when genocide occurs, we need to know why and when genocide does *not* occur, especially when our existing explanations tell us it *should* occur. If the big question of this book is what drives genocide, the more specific empirical question is why does genocide happen in some situations but not in other, similar situations?

My arguments are ultimately about the legacies of political ideas, the nature of threat usually in warfare, the ways in which states mobilize, and the conditions that favor moderation. The book speaks not only to those interested in genocide and how to prevent it but also to those interested in political violence more generally, the role of ideology in shaping outcomes, the challenges of managing diversity, and the maintenance of coalitions of actors at the national and local levels. The book is also about political leadership and about leadership in sub-Saharan Africa. Readers interested in these subjects will, I hope, find much to ponder in these pages.

What We Know about the Origins of Genocide

For many years the study of genocide was reducible to the study of the Holocaust. Genocide was not a political phenomenon per se, an outcome to be studied comparatively, but a singular, aberrational perversion. Such was not the view of a relatively small group of dedicated scholars, who argued, as Raphael Lemkin did when he coined the term, that the crime was ancient and more common than most had appreciated.[4]

Political events in the 1990s changed how many thought about genocide. In particular, the state-perpetrated mass violence in the Balkans and Central Africa garnered a great deal of international attention, and the failure to stem those atrocities shaped a generation of citizens and policymakers. The cases also prompted and legitimized comparative questions—about examining the common causal factors that diverse genocide cases might share. The comparative questions in turn revitalized the study of other twentieth-century cases of mass violence, including Southwest Africa, the Armenians in the late Ottoman empire, Burundi, Bangladesh, Indonesia, Cambodia, Guatemala, Iraq, East Timor, and others.[5] Some historians took an even further look back, writing, in the case of Ben Kiernan, a world history of the phenomenon.[6] Some social scientists pioneered quantitative cross-national studies of the phenomenon.[7]

The new research added considerable scope and rigor to the study of genocide. We now have studies linking genocide to more ubiquitous social phenomena, such as ethnic nationalism,[8] colonialism,[9] the modern nation-state,[10] strategic concerns,[11] and war.[12] These studies have contributed to the "normalization" of the study of genocide, to the point that we are now able to consider genocide as an outcome that exhibits patterns that social scientists can examine and explain.[13]

What, then, has been learned about the factors that drive genocide? No consensus reigns, but I would identify five main clusters of theory. One cluster revolves around intergroup animosity and discrimination. Some argue that widespread, preexisting attitudes of hatred, denigration, dehumanization, distrust, and fear between groups in a society drive genocide.[14] Others focus on more vertical relationships of exclusion, whereby practices

---

4. Lemkin 1944.
5. Bloxham and Moses 2010; Gellately and Kiernan 2003; Totten and Parsons 2009.
6. Chalk and Jonassohn 1990; Kiernan 2007.
7. Butcher et al. 2012; Harff 2003; Krain 1997; Ulfelder and Valentino 2008; Valentino et al. 2004; Wayman and Tago 2010.
8. Mann 2005.
9. Moses 2008.
10. Levene 2005.
11. Valentino 2004.
12. Shaw 2003.
13. Bloxham 2005; Shaw 2007.
14. Goldhagen 2009; Kuper 1981; Staub 1989; Wilshire 2006.

of official and institutional discrimination create the conditions for dehumanization, hatred, and violence to succeed.[15] The essential ideas are that genocide is rooted in preexisting, pejorative mass beliefs or discriminatory institutional practice.

Another cluster focuses on the characteristics of a political system—on regime type. Genocide is possible when power is concentrated in the hands of few decision-makers, when there is a history of political repression of alternative political ideas, and when a political system and civil society lack the checks and balances that restrain extreme measures.[16]

A third cluster highlights the importance of stress and upheaval. The main argument is that highly traumatic periods create hardship and stress in populations. The central mechanism is frustration-aggression: People channel social stress into blame and then scapegoat certain social groups.[17] Another model is that, in periods of great change and uncertainty, populations are more receptive to extreme policies. Whether located at the elite or mass level, the main claim is that social stress and upheaval create conditions in which genocide succeeds.[18]

A fourth cluster of arguments places ideology at the center of the analysis. The authors who make this argument typically emphasize a need to understand what Jacques Sémelin calls the "political imaginary."[19] The specific ideological constellations vary. Eric Weitz, for example, emphasizes racial utopia.[20] Sémelin focuses on purification efforts in the midst of perceived threat.[21] Michael Mann argues that organic nationalist projects— when a legitimate political community is defined as a unified whole, as an "ethnos"—lay the foundation of mass violence against groups defined as outside that organic whole.[22] Robert Melson argues that revolutions create similar legitimate and illegitimate communities.[23] Kiernan argues there are four ideological paths to mass violence.[24]

---

15. Fein 1979; Harff 2003; Staub 1989; Ulfelder and Valentino 2008.

16. Horowitz 1976; Rummel 1994.

17. Staub 1989; Wilshire 2006. Midlarsky's emphasis on territorial and socioeconomic loss, in particular in wartime, as triggering the emotions and policies that lead to genocide, represents a similar causal logic. See e.g. Midlarsky 2005: 88–89.

18. Harff 1987, 2003.

19. Semelin 2007.

20. Weitz 2003.

21. Semelin 2007.

22. Mann 2005.

23. Melson 1992.

24. That is, racism, territorial expansionism, agrarianism or "cults of cultivation," and the desire for to restore purity and order based on imagined antiquity.

A fifth cluster of arguments emphasizes the strategic origins of genocide, which builds on a robust empirical finding between genocide and war.[25] The mechanisms remain disputed. Some see mass killing and genocide as tactics to fight insurgencies, in particular when governments do not have the information, professionalism, will, or capacity to separate civilians from combatants.[26] Others see genocide as an extension of modern, "degenerate" warfare in which civilians are routinely targeted to defeat adversaries.[27] Still others claim that wars of attrition lead to greater civilian destruction.[28]

This categorization into five theoretical clusters is not exhaustive. Other important empirical regularities exist. One is that the decision to commit genocide emerges from a dynamic process of escalation.[29] Genocide is a product of events, contingencies, unforeseen actions, failures, and successes. Another is that, while perpetrators of genocide range from senior officials to ordinary peasants, genocide consistently involves specialized, generally state-funded paramilitary or organized militia groups.[30] A third is that previous, unpunished atrocities predate future ones. The point is explicit in some analyses[31] and implicit in others.[32]

A final issue concerns the nature of control. Do strong institutions with effective control commit mass violence or do weak states with minimal control perpetrate the act? Some argue that states lacking in capacity, control, and information use indiscriminate, rather than targeted or selective, violence.[33] By contrast, regime-oriented arguments about autocratic states suggest that states with excessive power and control commit genocide. Case studies of the Holocaust where the role of bureaucracy, as well as of Rwanda with its strong local institutions, imply that state domination is a necessary ingredient.

Throughout the book, I shall return to these various arguments, weighing their strengths and weaknesses.

---

25. Butcher et al. 2012; Krain 1997; Melson 1992; Midlarsky 2005; Shaw 2003, 2007; Straus 2006b, 2007; Ulfelder and Valentino 2008; Valentino 2004; Valentino et al. 2004. Moreover, though not the main focus of their arguments, that genocide tends to occurs in wartime are points made in Mann 2005, Weitz 2003, and Sémelin 2007. Harff 2003 emphasizes "political upheaval," which can be caused by armed conflict.

26. Kalyvas 2006; Ulfelder and Valentino 2008; Valentino et al. 2004.

27. Shaw 2003.

28. Downes 2005.

29. Bloxham 2005, 2009; Browning 2004; Mann 2005; Straus 2006b; Valentino 2004.

30. Alvarez 2010; Mann 2005.

31. Harff 2003; Midlarsky 2005.

32. Bloxham 2005; Valentino 2004.

33. Kalyvas 2006; Ulfelder and Valentino 2008.

Unanswered Questions

While much has been gained in the study of genocide, several problems and unanswered questions remain. For one, as this brief review suggests, there remains significant theoretical disparity in the literature.[34] Consensus is not common in most academic fields of inquiry, and disagreement fuels innovation and progress. Still, the theoretical disparity is striking, and the priority now is to develop arguments and clarify the causal mechanisms at work.

Another, related concern is that arguments do not distinguish well enough between places and times that will likely escalate to genocide from those that will not. In statistical terms, existing theory produces too many "false positives"—cases that should result in genocide but do not. One quantitative study using state-of-the-art forecasting techniques at best yielded a false positive to true positive rate of 30:1.[35] In the course of researching and writing this book, I watched leading international analysts warn that multiple crises would or could result in genocide—in places such as the Central African Republic, Côte d'Ivoire, Guinea, Iraq, Kenya, Mali, Myanmar, South Sudan, and Sudan—yet genocide has occurred in none of those locations, at least as of this writing.

The problem is not the analysts; it is the theory. If the clusters of arguments identified above were individually or, in some combination, jointly sufficient explanations, genocide would be much more common than it is. Take any of the clusters of arguments—intergroup antipathy, authoritarianism, acute deprivation, nationalist/transformative ideologies, or armed conflict—those conditions are considerably more widespread than genocide is.[36] In other words, we do not live in an "age" or "century" of genocide, as some scholars claim.[37] The phenomenon is and has been uncommon, and that reality should be central to any analysis.

The "logic" of genocide is also poorly understood. Genocide is a deliberate, sustained policy that stems from a process of decision-making. But what

---

34. For a different set of labels on the genocide literature than I present in this chapter but one that effectively shows how broad the range of existing theories are, see Hiebert 2008.

35. Valentino and Hazlett 2012; see also Ulfelder 2011.

36. Genocide is thankfully uncommon. How uncommon depends on how the phenomenon is measured. Manus Midlarsky (2005) argues for three twentieth-century cases; Ben Kiernan (2007) highlights fourteen cases in the twentieth century; Barbara Harff (2003) identifies thirty-seven cases of genocide and politicide—measured by as few as 1,000 deaths in a conflict cycle—between 1955 and 2000; in their study of "mass killing," defined as 1,000 civilian deaths or more, Jay Ulfelder and Benjamin Valentino (2008) identify ninety cases between 1955 and 2007. In an updated study, Valentino and Chad Hazlett (2013) find that mass killing occurs in about 1% of all the possible years in which it could have occurred in countries around the world.

37. Goldhagen 2009: 33; Monroe 2011; Totten and Parsons 2009; Weitz 2003.

is that process? What drives leaders to choose such a costly, extreme policy orientation over the alternatives? Is that logic different from other forms of political violence? If so, how? Answering these questions is critical for understanding why genocide, versus other violent outcomes, might occur.[38]

How genocide happens also matters. Specifically, how do national actors interact with local ones to form and execute genocide? Existing studies typically bifurcate the question. Some studies focus on macro-level, structural conditions, but other studies focus on micro dynamics of genocide in localities and among perpetrators. Missing from many comparative studies is an account of how subnational coalitions matter and how those coalitions interact with national actors. Are alliances between national and local actors necessary for genocide to occur? If so, how? Understanding those alliances, and how they are forged or not forged, should help explain variation among genocide and nongenocide cases.

Research Design

My research design builds from these concerns. In the next chapter, I analyze genocide conceptually and deductively to isolate how the logic of genocide differs from other forms of political violence. I also use that analysis to make predictions about the nature of local-national interactions.

But the core of the book is a controlled, qualitative comparison between genocide and nongenocide cases. Cross-national quantitative studies are especially strong at identifying empirical relationships. In the case of genocide, the most consistent finding is that genocide typically takes place during an armed conflict. Yet we know much less about why that is the case and, more importantly, why some armed conflicts escalate to genocide while others do not. Qualitative studies can shed light on the dynamics and causal mechanisms in the genocide cases and how they differ from the dynamics and causal mechanisms in the nongenocide cases.[39]

The emphasis on negative cases is essential. The main approach in existing cross-national studies is to compare similar-outcome cases. Some studies

38. In recent pieces, Ernesto Verdeja and I have argued for the importance of linking the study of genocide to the study of other kinds of political violence. See Straus 2007, 2012a, b; Verdeja 2012.

39. The methodological studies that influenced my approach are George and Bennett 2004; Gerring 2007; Lieberman 2005; and Sambanis 2004a. For a recent statement about the utility of controlled comparisons, see also Slater and Ziblatt 2013. The claims about the quantitative findings stem from Butcher et al. 2012; Harff 2003; Krain 1997; Ulfelder and Valentino 2008; Valentino et al. 2004; Wayman and Tago 2010.

include a discussion of negative cases, but they are often peripherally included as shadow cases.[40] While that method of agreement was worthwhile as the field of comparative genocide research established itself, scholars should now explore negative cases to understand what distinguishes them from genocide ones.

In practice, I sampled negative cases from those that had ex-ante similar probabilities of escalating to genocide, given existing theory.[41] The approach follows the logic of a "possibility principle" advocated by case-study methodologists—these were cases where genocide seemed possible, even probable, again given existing theory.[42] The analysis then seeks to understand what was commonly different among the nongenocide cases from what was commonly present among the genocide cases.

My universe of "genocide possible" cases had the following conditions present: the country was experiencing an ongoing internal armed conflict; the insurgent group was seen to represent or claimed to represent a social identity group; there was a history of discrimination or unpunished violence against that group; and the country had experienced some additional upheaval in the form of significant political change or economic decline (or both). In some cases, the political authorities supported or condoned irregular armed forces in addition to formal militaries to combat the insurgents, and in some cases the political authorities defending the state invoked a form of ethnic nationalism in their effort to retain power. No two countries were identical on each of these dimensions—in some situations, for example, the armed conflict was more intense than in others—but in general I looked for cases that embodied the empirical conditions that theory tells us should have led to genocide.[43]

I also narrowed the universe of cases to a similar time period and similar geographic region.[44] The typical comparison in genocide studies includes some combination of the Armenian genocide, the Holocaust, Cambodia

---

40. Kuper 1981; Mann 2005; Midlarsky 2005; Valentino 2004. An exception is Chirot and McCauley 2006.

41. The method follows the logic of a most-similar or matching design. See Seawright and Gerring 2010.

42. Mahoney and Goertz 2004.

43. The case selection focuses on state actors. As I discuss, non-state actors and organizations could commit genocide and similar forms of mass violence. But theoretically speaking, state actors are the more likely perpetrators; at the very least, mass violence is very difficult to sustain without support or acquiescence from the political authority that exercises territorial control. That is borne out empirically in the book.

44. This is inspired by Sambanis 2004a which criticizes the unit heterogeneity between cases in comparisons of conflict.

under the Khmer Rouge, Bosnia, Rwanda, and Darfur. These cases are all plausibly considered cases of genocide, but they take place in different time periods, on different continents, in different economies, in different regimes, and so forth. The many moving parts make the comparison unwieldy. Instead, I sampled from sub-Saharan Africa after the Cold War. By holding the region and the time period relatively constant, I hold certain variables steady in order to isolate the factors that drive the escalation or non-escalation toward genocide.

In the end, I selected the following negative cases: Côte d'Ivoire from 2002 to 2011, Mali from 1990 to 1995 (and again from 2011 to 2012), and Senegal from the late 1980s to 2011. For positive cases, I selected Sudan, in particular Darfur in the 2000s, and Rwanda in 1994. To research these cases, I conducted field research in Côte d'Ivoire, Mali, and Senegal over a six-year period. My field research centered on elite interviews with then-current or former political and military officials—as well as academics, journalists, and diplomats. In addition, I sought to obtain original data from ministries or other country-based sources. For Rwanda, I built on previous field research in that country as well as a raft of new material that emerged from the international court established to try high-level perpetrators, the International Criminal Tribunal for Rwanda. For Sudan, I relied principally on secondary sources. In addition, for all five countries, I constructed an original dataset of presidential speeches given on official holidays or at the height of the crises in question. The source materials were principally in-country, state-run newspapers; these were supplemented with foreign-country news reporting where possible.[45]

The Argument in Brief

Genocide is a distinctive form of political violence. Genocide is an attempt to destroy or inflict maximum damage upon a civilian category within a territory. Genocide is therefore different conceptually and logically from armed conflict, in which the violence is directed against an opponent's institutional war-making capacity. Genocide is also distinctive from other forms of political violence, including terrorism, rioting, electoral violence, and limited violence against noncombatants in war. Typically such violence is organized

---

45. Matthew Scharf provided essential research assistance on the project. The speeches database is available at http://users.polisci.wisc.edu/straus/speech/. The logic of choosing holidays (generally New Year's Day and Independence Day) was that I wanted to examine consistent times across years when heads of states made major speeches. Then in crises, I looked to see if the themes of prior speeches reappeared.

around a logic of intimidation and communication. The violence is designed to shape and change the behavior of those who survive it. By contrast, in genocide, from the perpetrators' perspective, the purpose of violence is not only to contain a present danger but also to preempt a regenerated one. Genocide is therefore a form of future-oriented, anticipatory violence in which perpetrators imagine a recurrent threat from, or permanent incompatibility with, a specific social category.

To be executed, genocide requires that the perpetrating organization exercise effective domination over a territory in which the target group resides. As I underline in the next chapter, this is different from indiscriminate violence. Genocide is group-selective violence that requires coordination and the sustained application of violence against an identified population. What is therefore paradoxical about genocide is that the conditions favoring genocide are an unusual mixture of intense fears of vulnerability and danger combined with effective domination. That combination is empirically rare.

Genocide, furthermore, requires a period of extended collaboration between national and subnational actors. Genocide is sustained violence across time and territory. Although its specific iteration—shooting, gassing, knifing, drowning, burning, poisoning, or destroying the means of survival—may vary across and within cases, genocide requires the sustenance of a similar character of targeted violence for periods of time and in multiple locations. National actors are necessary to coordinate, authorize, and plan as well as to provide a level of overwhelming force. But local actors are necessary to identify, separate, and attack the targets of the violence. Local actors also invent policies as they implement occasionally vague orders from national authorities, leading to a feedback mechanism in which national authorities in turn condone local iterations of violence.

My study confirms that genocide is a dynamic product of fluid decision-making, but I emphasize that that process is subject to mechanisms of both escalation *and* restraint. In any given situation, there will be factors that push perpetrators toward the use of extreme, genocidal violence but also factors that push leaders to limit or moderate violence. Restraint may be material: Perpetrators who want to commit genocidal violence may lack the material capacity to maintain coalitions of violence or access to target populations to execute mass violence. But restraint may be more political: leaders may find genocide unthinkable; they may face lateral pressure from elites in their society who argue that the costs of mass violence are too great or from their military officers who refuse to participate in massacres of civilians; or regional or international actors may successfully intervene and change the dynamics.

The main causal claim that I advance is a synthesis between strategic and ideological arguments. Preexisting ideological frameworks—what I call "founding narratives"—shape how elites understand and respond to threats in acute crises, especially war.[46] Leaders typically predicate genocide on the idea of countering a grave, imminent, and irreversible danger. Material conditions, such as the military balance of power and battlefield dynamics, matter for how threat is experienced, but ideological frames shape how elites understand the terms and stakes of a conflict. In the end, those who pursue policies of mass civilian destruction believe in the righteousness of such decisions. They believe that the course of events binds them, even requires them, to carry out drastic measures in order to save their core political communities and most treasured political projects. Ideas and beliefs are fundamental to that process.

Genocide is like a race war. According to perpetrators, the fight is between peoples, not between militaries, states, or political parties. That frame depends on how leaders have defined the core political community and shared goals prior to the onset of a military crisis. Where leaders have isolated one civilian group as the legitimate, rightful bearers of state power in whose interests the state serves, it is more likely that once in a crisis such leaders will define the fight for state power as a fight between that category and a different category that is contesting power. In those circumstances, leaders claim that the state legitimately represents, even expresses, a specific category of people, and therefore armed challenges to the state are equivalent to armed challenges to that people.[47]

Ideological frames also serve to coordinate coalitions of violence, both at the elite and subnational level. Genocide involves abhorrent violence against categories of people. Actors need to be convinced of the righteousness of their actions, and the rationales that elites provide must resonate with other influential actors in the society. War is surely a powerful convincer, because fear motivates people to defend themselves with violence. So too are opportunity and in-group coercion. But I also attribute a role to ideological frameworks: The idea that the state belongs to a category of people helps to convince others that challengers who do not belong to the in-group do not have a right to control the state.

---

46. In invoking ideology, which can have many meanings (Gerring 1997), I follow Stephen Hanson's notion of "formal, explicit, and relatively consistent definitions of political community articulated by political elites" (2003: 372). To this, I would add the idea of formal, explicit goals that political elites seek to accomplish.

47. My argument resonates with Mann 2005; Melson 1992; Weitz 2003.

Putting these points together, I emphasize the concept of "founding narratives" as central to the causal structure of genocide. These are ideological frames and stories that political leaders craft at critical junctures in the histories of countries. When they are first articulated, such founding narratives have little to nothing to do with genocide or the use of violence. But the narratives become reference points that in turn shape how political elites define their strategies and win support for extreme policies during acute crises.

Finally, restraint matters. I find that "counternarratives" can deescalate violence, especially those that emphasize accommodation and tolerance. Another source of restraint is economic—where the main sources of revenue would be devastated through genocide, elites have an incentive to moderate violence. Capacity also is significant. Without the capacity to identify, access, and inflict violence on large numbers of civilians, genocide is difficult to accomplish. External actors can impose costs on would-be perpetrators or position themselves militarily between perpetrators and victims. These too serve as mechanisms of restraint.

Practical Implications

The book is not policy-oriented, but the arguments have implications for policy. I hope that the analysis will help policymakers design better predictive tools, in particular ones that have fewer false positives. In the appendix, I develop a qualitative diagnostic tool that should aid policymakers and genocide prevention advocates to identify risks and indicators of genocide.

Genocide prevention is complicated and difficult. My book does not offer any magic bullets, and it did not attempt to evaluate different prevention methods. Nonetheless, the analysis suggests certain principles that should guide external prevention and response policies.

One is that conflict management should be integral to genocide prevention. Threat typically animates genocide, and wherever possible international actors should look to diminish threat. That could take multiple forms, such as pressuring belligerent actors to stop fighting, creating a separation force and demilitarized zone in order to keep warring sides apart, and providing information through a nominally neutral third party in order to make transparent the actions of armed opponents. Diminishing the prospect of serious war is probably the single best method to reduce the likelihood of genocide.

But genocide prevention is greater than conflict management. International actors should impose costs on perpetrators of atrocities without materially assisting one side or the other in a military conflict. My study finds that decision-makers are indeed sensitive to costs. They make strategic decisions, even if nonstrategic ideas shape how they understand the terms and stakes of the conflict. Whether through public denunciations, investigative commissions that name and shame, targeted sanctions, threats of prosecution, or other means, external actors should look to signal and impose costs on perpetrators.

Where possible, international actors should enhance domestic restraint mechanisms. In many circumstances there will be influential elites who argue through business associations, religious networks, civil society organizations, speeches, back channel connections, and even political parties that escalation is wrong or will be damaging. Where such domestic actors exist, external actors should encourage and support them. International actors can also encourage defection from violence coalitions, seeking to split off subnational collaborators from those who would encourage such violence.

The book is ultimately about how nations are made or unmade. "Unmaking" nations starts when political leaders craft visions of their states as belonging to a primary political community that differs on some fundamental basis from another human community that shares the same territory. The ultimate unmaking of nations is genocide. "Making" nations is the opposite—it involves articulating visions of the state and nation in inclusive terms that recognize diversity as core to the identity of the state. The responsibility of making nations is ultimately a domestic one; it is the purview of leaders in particular countries. External actors may not be able to engineer such narratives, but they can look for ways to encourage or support them.

None of this will be easy, and each approach has pitfalls, but the study provides a theoretical foundation for why these prevention and response strategies should work.

PART I

Concepts and Theory

CHAPTER 1

The Concept and Logic of Genocide

Writing a book about genocide requires a clear operationalization of the term. Unfortunately, the meaning of genocide remains contested, the essential differences between genocide and other forms of political violence remain unclear, and the term remains embedded in a legal framework. For these reasons, some social scientists balk at studying genocide as a distinct, explainable phenomenon.

This chapter addresses these definitional problems. I argue that genocide is a form of large-scale, group-selective violence, or what I term "mass categorical violence." In addition, I argue that a logic of group destruction animates genocide. Both of these qualities distinguish genocide from other types of political violence and generate a series of theoretical propositions.

In particular, group-selective violence typically requires perpetrators to command effective territorial domination over target populations. Local actors in general possess the information necessary to identify and sort target populations. Local actors are thus key to most forms of group-selective violence. Furthermore, given the widespread, sustained nature of genocide, perpetrators typically need to mount large operations that involve multiple agencies. There are exceptions. In particular, where a target population is highly spatially concentrated, perpetrators can attack that population aerially or through a blockade, diminishing the need for local information or multi-agency coalitions of violence. But such circumstances are empirically rare.

These dimensions—territorial domination, local actor integration, and large, multi-agency operations—suggest that national state involvement and capacity are nearly necessary for genocide and extreme forms of mass categorical violence to occur. National states have the institutional foundation to dominate territory, though not all states do, and states have the authority and hierarchy to incorporate local actors and command coalitions of violence over space and time. Nonstate actors, such as rebel organizations, *could* execute genocide and mass categorical violence, but they would need to dominate territory where target populations exist and possess enough internal organization to command sustained, far-flung coalitions of violence. That scenario is possible but empirically rare. Coalitions of local actors could commit violence against target groups, but on balance the scale of such violence should be lower than national-local coalitions of violence because of the difficulty of local actors to coordinate and sustain operations of group-selective violence in the absence of a central authority.

The chapter also focuses on the purpose of violence. Most political violence conforms to a logic of coercion and communication where the purpose is to force a change in behavior or policy. The premise of such violence is built on an expectation of future interaction. The logic of genocide is different. The signature of genocide is crushing opponents in the short term *and* destroying their ability to pose a long-term challenge. Genocide is therefore about extinguishing human interaction, not seeking to shape it. For this logic to operate, I hypothesize that perpetrators are likely to see target groups as inherently dangerous, uncontainable, and unwinnable (in the sense that they cannot be coopted or cowed; they cannot be won over). Putting these two sets of points together, I propose that the conditions most likely to give rise to genocide entail the unlikely combination of territorial domination and organizational capacity, on the one hand, and a profound sense of danger associated with a civilian group, on the other. Most states or organizations that possess the capacity to manage large-scale, multi-actor operations of violence do not simultaneously experience great vulnerability and a sense of threat emanating from civilian populations.

Unpacking Genocide

The original author of the term *genocide*, jurist Raphael Lemkin, provides a useful and succinct starting point for any conceptual analysis. His invention combines the Greek word for "race," nation, or tribe (*genos*) with the Latin word for killing (*cide*). In an efficient and enduring conceptualization,

Lemkin writes that genocide is the "destruction of a nation or of an ethnic group."[1] He claims:

> Generally speaking, genocide ... signif[ies] a coordinated plan of different actions aiming at the destruction of essential foundations of the life of national groups, with the aim of annihilating the groups themselves.... Genocide is directed against the national group as an entity, and the actions involved are directed against individuals, not in their individual capacity, but as members of the national group.[2]

Similarly, Lemkin wrote:

> The crime of genocide involves a wide range of actions ... to cripple permanently a human group. The acts are directed against groups, as such, and individuals are selected for destruction only because they belong to these groups.[3]

After rounds of negotiations, in which certain political forces came to bear on the exact wording, the United Nations in 1948 adopted the United Nations Convention on the Prevention and Punishment of the Crime of Genocide.[4] That Convention defines genocide as the "intent to destroy, in whole or in part, a national, ethnical, racial, or religious group, as such." The Convention in turn specifies five methods of genocide: (1) killing members of the group; (2) causing serious bodily or mental harm to members of the group; (3) deliberately inflicting on the group conditions of life calculated to bring about its physical destruction in whole or in part; (4) imposing measures intended to prevent births within the group; and (5) forcibly transferring children of the group to another group.

None of these definitions is completely satisfactory to most scholars who devote themselves to the study of genocide, and many have sought to redefine the concept of genocide or to develop cognate concepts.[5] The main points of disagreement are the nature of the groups and the nature of the violence. On the former, many scholars seek to broaden the concept to include political, class, or gender groups.[6] Others argue that Lemkin's genocide definitions and the United Nations Convention imply an essentialist reading of "groups"

---

1. Lemkin 1944: 79.
2. Lemkin 1944: 79.
3. Lemkin 1947: 147.
4. Kuper 1981; Schabas 2000.
5. For a review of genocide definitions, see Shaw 2007; Straus 2001. For a review of some alternative terms, see Alvarez 2010.
6. Chalk and Jonassohn 1990; Jones 2004.

as real definable entities, rather than as socially constructed categories and in particular categories that perpetrators create.[7]

The second major debate concerns how much and what kind of violence constitutes "genocide." Does a group need to be physically exterminated? How much "partial" destruction, as the UN Convention implies, is needed? Is cultural destruction genocide? Lemkin himself was not always clear on these questions; his formulations varied across his written work, and there is debate about what Lemkin meant and about the quality of Lemkin's historical understanding.[8]

These debates matter, but regardless of one's conclusions, it is still possible to distill a core meaning of genocide, and that is intentional group destruction. Etymologically, that is the central idea—the killing of groups. Lemkin's core formulations are simply that, such as "the destruction of a nation or of an ethnic group."

Group-Selective Violence

Working from this core meaning, I propose that one key empirical property of genocide is that it is group-selective, or categorical, violence. Lemkin's formulations are clear: "The acts [of genocide] are directed against groups, as such, and individuals are selected for destruction only because they belong to these groups."[9] Much scholarship recognizes the fundamental group orientation of genocide,[10] and most subsequent scholarly definitions retain some focus on groups—or "collectivities" or "social categories"—as fundamental to genocide.[11]

Group selection is frequently a central organizing principle of violence. In many circumstances, perpetrators attack, maim, punish, and kill individuals not because of actions those individuals have taken but because of their categorical associations, whether those associations are ethnic, religious, racial, clan, political, gender, regional, and so forth.[12] The point is not that such groupings are real phenomena; they are constructed categories.[13] But in the minds of the perpetrators and according to the logic and patterns of violence, the violence is directed against categories of people.

---

7. Bloxham and Moses 2010; Chalk and Jonassohn 1990; May 2010; Mazower 2009.
8. Schaller and Zimmerer 2009.
9. Lemkin 1947.
10. May 2010.
11. For example, see the definitions in Chalk and Jonassohn 1990: 23; Fein 1990: 24.
12. Horowitz 2001.
13. Brubaker 2006.

Stathis Kalyvas has influentially introduced the distinction between selective violence and indiscriminate violence.[14] For many analysts, genocide is a form of indiscriminate violence. My argument is different. Genocide is *discriminate* violence that exhibits strong group selection.[15]

The group-selective aspect of genocide has several empirical implications. Such violence will be against civilians.[16] By definition, social groups encompass noncombatants (unless somehow every single person in a said social category is a fighter, which would be highly unlikely). Furthermore, mechanisms to identify and sort groups are necessary. In some locations, there will be latent mechanisms for group identification, such as family name, phenotype, dress, religious practice, national identity cards, and even neighborhood. In other locations, the mechanisms for group identification will have to be created or newly emphasized through the passage of national laws, dress requirements, or other means that would establish boundaries between groups.

In addition, attacks will likely target not only persons but also the symbols, markers, and indicators of social categories. This might include mosques, synagogues, churches, graves, bakeries, butchers, or specific retail outlets. In short, the logic of group-selective violence should translate into attacks on the symbolic markers of the social category and other forms of "extra-lethal" violence.[17]

Group-selective violence also implies that perpetrating authorities exercise territorial domination over target populations. Group-selective violence involves sorting using information; it involves distinguishing between those who are said to belong to a targeted category and those who are not. All this implies a degree of territorial control—the ability to identify, locate, and separate people on the basis of their social categories. Such circumstances are different from typical cases of indiscriminate violence. In those cases, perpetrating authorities lack control and information, so they target indiscriminately.[18]

Moreover, identification and sorting into groups is most likely to come from local actors—from actors who live in proximity to the target populations

---

14. Kalyvas 2006.

15. My argument resonates with Steele 2009, which discusses "collective targeting."

16. In his conceptual analysis, Martin Shaw (2007) rightfully insists that civilian targeting is the essential characteristic of genocide. I agree, but I argue that the reason why is because of the group-oriented nature of the violence.

17. Fujii 2013.

18. Kalyvas 2006; Ulfelder and Valentino 2008.

and who have information about who is who. National actors typically lack the information necessary to find, and sometimes identify, target populations.

The one exception to both of these conditions is when a target population is so geographically concentrated that a perpetrating authority could simply bomb or blockade that territory. In that case, neither territorial domination nor local actor participation would be as necessary.

Large-Scale—"Mass"—Violence

A second major characteristic of genocide is its extent. As an effort to destroy a human group within a specific territory, genocide implies a large scale. Genocide is about sustained violence that is repeated across time and space against a substantial part of a target group.[19] The recurring, repetitive, *systematic* nature distinguishes genocide from a massacre or a riot, which are more one-off events. Genocide is sustained and widespread. The violence will not be restricted to one neighborhood, one town, or one city; it will exhibit a pattern of target selection and civilian destruction that is repeated across those spaces where the group is located.

Those qualities have implications. For example, such violence is deliberate. The question of deliberateness is often self-evident, especially when individuals are killed. But in genocide, those in the target group sometimes die from indirect causes associated with displacement, such as lack of food, water, health care, or shelter. The question to ask is whether the displacement and deprivation are the result of deliberate actions by the perpetrator against the civilian members of the target group.

But the key theoretical implication is that scale requires a significant degree of organization and coordination. Genocide is about the destruction of human groups within territories. In most circumstances, the targeted human population will live in multiple localities across a national territory. To mount operations large enough and long enough to attack the targeted group, perpetrators need to manage broad coalitions of actors. Those actors typically include local collaborators and civilian officials who identify, sort, and sometimes attack groups. They also typically include national agencies whose role is to manage public security or defend territory, such as the police, army, or sometimes paramilitaries. Those agencies are the ones who

---

19. Determining how much violence is necessary for genocide is difficult to pin down. A helpful guide is spelled out in the appeals court decision from the International Criminal Tribunal for the former Yugoslavia (ICTY) in the Krstić case. In that decision, the court argued that genocide entailed destruction of a "substantial" part of a targeted group. See ICTY 2004; Schabas 2006.

control violence in national territory and have the capacity to inflict or prevent such violence. Genocide therefore implies at a minimum the tacit approval and support of national agencies and more typically their active participation.

Putting these characteristics together, I propose that genocide requires some capacity to organize and sustain multi-agency, multi-level coalitions of violence across time and space. These coalitions are necessary to inflict violence against a target group on a large scale and in a consistent fashion across multiple locations.

Establishing and sustained coalitions of violence is likely achieved in two ways.

The most common scenario is vertical coordination by the territorially sovereign state, which centralizes orders and planning across multiple agencies and across multiple locations. States are hardwired to perform this task, even if some states lack the capacity for effective coordination. States have the authority to command and coordinate local civilian administrations and national agencies of violence, especially military, police, or paramilitary units.

The other scenario is decentralized coordination through alignments of interests. This can be achieved through informal coalitions between national officials and agencies, on the one hand, and local actors on the other.

It is conceivable that coalitions of violence could be achieved through horizontal coordination between local actors without the participation of a national actor. But such coalitions are unlikely to achieve the scale necessary to commit genocide. Horizontal, decentralized coalitions may commit group-selective violence, but their ability to mount a national or even regional campaign of such violence is unlikely without the participation and coordination of a central, national body.[20]

These claims about the group-selective and extensive qualities of genocide lead to a prediction: States are likely to be the primary perpetrators of such violence, but states will require some alliance with local actors.

Genocide requires territorial domination and sustained coalitions of actors to commit violence in a regular way across time and space. Genocide also requires identifying and sorting groups. National states are the most likely institutions to have that capacity for domination and coordination. Local actors are the most likely to have the information to find target

---

20. In 2014, at the time of writing, the violence sweeping the Central African Republic is a good example of horizontal, local actor, group-selective violence, primarily against Muslims. However, the scale of such violence is limited by the absence of national actor coordination.

groups. Group-selective violence without national actor participation will likely have a limited scale, and national actor involvement without local actor participation will likely not be group-selective. Nonstate actors *could* exercise territorial domination over a target population and sustain a multi-agency coalition, but empirically—at least in the contemporary world—nonstate actors infrequently have such capacity.

Group Destruction

The final major characteristic of genocide, group destruction, is the hardest to demonstrate empirically. In theory, what distinguishes genocide from other forms of large-scale violence is the overall intent or purpose of violence. Genocide is about the destruction of human groups or, as Lemkin wrote, to "cripple permanently" a group. That implies that genocide entails sustained violence not only against those who present an immediate threat—say, adult men and sometimes women—but also against the people and things essential for the constitution and reconstitution of a group. Genocide is designed to destroy the ability of a group to survive and reproduce in a territory. One should thus observe attacks on group survival (in terms of attacks on shelter, food, water sources, and medical centers) and on group reproduction (in terms of violence against children as a future generation and against women and others who could reconstitute a group).

The Logic of Genocide

The last point requires some elaboration. The deliberate use of most political violence assumes a period of future group interaction on the part of perpetrators. The logic of violence is coercive—to change attitudes and power—in order to assert control, and the use of violence is demonstrative or communicative. Violence signals costs; it is meant to show target audiences what would happen to them if they do not change course. "Violence," Kalyvas argues, "is intended to shape the behavior of the targeted audience by altering the expected value of particular attitudes. Put otherwise, violence performs a communicative function with a clear deterrent dimension."[21]

---

21. Kalyvas 2006: 26.

Such political violence rests on an assumption of the adaptability, win-nability, and controllability of target populations—that with the right mix of coercion, incentives, and persuasion, individuals in target populations will be contained or won over.

There are situations in which violence conforms to this logic, namely as a tool that shapes behavior and preferences by imposing costs. Kalyvas himself focuses on the use of violence in civil war, arguing that selective violence is a tool to punish collaborators and to deter defections. The logic is clearly at work in other situations of violence as well, including, for example, electoral violence. In his analysis of election-related violence in India, Steven Wilkin-son shows how riots are designed to raise the salience of ethnicity in close contests in order to secure electoral victory.[22] As such, electoral violence is communicative.[23] Terrorist violence is perhaps the best example of com-municative, coercive violence. By targeting a more or less random sample of civilians, terrorist violence sends a message to other civilians, to governments, and to potential recruits.[24]

In war, the general objective is to contain, bargain with, coopt, or defeat an enemy. A strategy of containment assumes a future period in which groups will share the same territory, but where the containing side will remain dominant. A strategy of cooption and bargaining—offering rewards in the form of territorial concessions, ministerial posts, regional autonomy, new political rights, and even money often through peace deals—similarly assumes a period of shared space. A strategy of defeat is consistent with the logic of genocide. But classically defeat in war focuses on destroying the institutional military capacity of one's opponents, not the population itself.

The logic of genocide differs. The premise of genocide is to destroy group interaction. In that sense, genocidal violence is not coercive but rather terminal. Genocide is also not principally communicative; the idea of genocide is to destroy interaction, not to signal the high costs of certain behaviors. The logic of genocide is not primarily to change the behavior of others by altering expected costs. In Lemkin's language, the idea is to "change permanently the population balance."[25] Genocide thus

---

22. Wilkinson 2004.
23. Klopp and Zuern 2005.
24. Richardson 2006.
25. Lemkin 1947: 147.

differs fundamentally from the logic of bargaining, containment, and deterrence.[26]

I suggest three further propositions based on this analysis. First, the rationale for genocide requires that organizing-level perpetrators conclude that future cooperation with the target group is impossible. In the minds of perpetrators, the target population is unwinnable, in the sense that it cannot be persuaded to change its behavior. The population cannot be deterred, coopted, wooed, or changed; it cannot be won over.

Second, the rationale for genocide requires that organizing-level perpetrators calculate that the target population is uncontrollable and uncontainable. In theory, a group for which cooperation is not forthcoming could still be contained. Where a group is contained, the rationale for destroying the group diminishes—unless the perpetrating agent believes it must repopulate the territory the group inhabits. But in most cases where uncooperative groups can be controlled and contained, the rationale for genocide dissipates.

Third, the rationale for genocide requires that organizing-level perpetrators posit a present and persistent threat from the target group. An uncontrolled and unwinnable population could, in the minds of perpetrators, simply be a nuisance. They might be unseemly, even embarrassing to the nation. But the rationale for destroying the group strongly increases where the organizing-level perpetrators believe that the uncooperative and uncontrollable group is committed to harming, even destroying, the perpetrator group and can act on such intentions. Acute threat is therefore essential to the logic of this type of violence.

Empirically, however, a different logic could generate similar patterns of violence. In this other scenario, the logic of violence is coercive but the idea is that perpetrators impose maximal damage on a civilian social category in order to force a change in behavior from the ostensible representatives of that category. A strategy of imposing maximal damage on a social category in order to coerce an enemy looks empirically similar to a strategy of group destruction. Both entail inflicting large-scale, group-selective violence over time and space. Both entail typically tens and even hundreds of thousands of civilian lives lost. The purpose may be different—one is destruction, the other coercion—but the practice is similar. I refer to the former as genocide, the latter as mass categorical violence.

---

26. Other scholars recognize similar points though they express them differently. Helen Fein (1979:7), for example, wrote: "While collective violence often serves to put (or keep) a subjugated group in its place, genocide eliminates the group." Arman Grigoryan (2010) similarly argues for two distinctive strategies violence in wartime—between coercive and what he calls "eliminationist," which includes ethnic cleansing and genocide. I do not disagree with these formulations; I seek to explicate them.

The question is why would perpetrators use mass categorical violence, as opposed to some other form of violence. If perpetrators have the objective of forcing a change in behavior from their armed opponent, why would they kill large numbers of civilians to achieve that goal? Two conditions are likely. One is that the perpetrators construct the civilian population and the enemy party as intrinsically linked. By committing atrocities against the population, therefore, perpetrators believe that they will pressure their enemy to desist. Two is that perpetrators believe that they need a very high level of violence in order to force a change of behavior. Perpetrators therefore construct the enemy both as highly committed and as highly dangerous; in those circumstances, perpetrators conclude that they need to impose maximal violence in order to achieve their objectives. These conditions are similar to those that I hypothesize give rise to genocide. The key difference is that, in using mass categorical violence, perpetrators conclude that with excessive brutality they can contain a motivated and dangerous enemy; by contrast, with genocide, perpetrators conclude that their enemies are unwinnable.

Theoretical Implications

How does the existing literature hold up in light of this analysis? Consider, for example, arguments about intergroup prejudice and hatred in a society. There are two plausible versions of the argument. The first is an active or hard version of the argument in which the main drivers of genocide are widespread and harshly negative attitudes of a dominant population toward the targeted population. The alternative, more passive version of the argument is that antipathy or even apathy in the general population facilitates group destruction. Only the first really provides a theory of genocide, namely that genocide occurs because the general population despises an out-group and wants to rid society of it. The latter argument is a claim for why there would be no strong social objections to genocide.

However, a theory that emphasizes hatred does not answer the question of why perpetrators do not ignore, coopt, or contain the despised group. Why would hateful perpetrators see a need to destroy future interaction rather than simply isolate and control the outcast group? If the argument essentially equates genocide with eliminationist hatred, the claim becomes tautological; it risks confusing the act with the cause—a common problem in studies of violence.[27]

---

27. See Kaylyvas 2006.

Similarly, a theory that emphasizes deprivation or authoritarianism cannot sufficiently account for the rationale to commit genocide. The idea behind a frustration–aggression mechanism is that perpetrators turn on target groups in order to scapegoat groups. The idea behind authoritarianism is that absolute power leads to a deeply violent form of politics without institutional checks and balances. But neither theory accounts for the fundamental problem of why perpetrators would choose a logic of perpetrating group destruction or imposing maximum costs versus other types of violence. Why would a scapegoating state not use the alternative of episodic violence to let off steam? Why would an authoritarian state conclude that target populations cannot be controlled?

Like hatred arguments, ideological arguments address the question of group selection in genocide. However, on their own, ideological arguments do not answer the question of why (or when) group destruction is the choice over an alternative strategy. Most ideological arguments pivot on a mechanism of exclusion.[28] But different versions of nationalism do not necessarily answer why the strategic choice is not group isolation, group cooption, or group containment. Indeed, most nationalists create and seek to live with hierarchies of social identity groups. They do not move to destroy the lower-status groups; rather, they exclude them or relegate them to an inferior status.

That said, an ideological framework that emphasizes transformation works.[29] The more that leaders seek to renew their society on the basis of some exclusionary mechanism, the more destruction of the other takes place. To destroy a group is to purify, and to purify will be, in the minds of perpetrating authorities, the key to transformation. A plausible argument for this mechanism could be made for the Holocaust and for Cambodia under the Khmer Rouge. But the argument has limited empirical applications to the in-depth cases that ground this book, including Rwanda and Sudan but also other cases of genocide or extreme mass categorical violence, such as in Burundi, the Democratic Republic of Congo, Uganda, and Nigeria. The argument is also a stretch for other twentieth-century genocide and extreme mass categorical violence cases, such as Southwest Africa, Guatemala, and Indonesia, where an ideological commitment to social transformation is absent.

These points bring us to the question of strategic arguments, namely that genocide is a wartime tool to achieve military victory. The most consistent empirical finding is that genocide occurs in wartime. But given that most

---

28. Mann 2005; Melson 1992; Sémelin 2007; Weitz 2003.
29. Kiernan 2007; Semelin 2007; Weitz 2003.

wars do not produce genocide, any strategic argument needs to answer the question of why genocide or mass categorical violence is the strategic choice rather than a whole range of other approaches, such as conventional (combatant on combatant) warfare, negotiations and accommodation, containment, or divide and conquer.

Surveying the literature, I isolate four plausible mechanisms. One is tactical: genocide is a counterinsurgency measure to defeat rebels who are ensconced in a civilian population. The argument is most developed in the work of Ben Valentino and several coauthors.[30] The main claim is that states choose mass killing when they lack the means and interest to separate civilians from insurgents. Such militaries might lack the professionalization or capacity to isolate rebels; lacking information and not caring about an excluded group, they target rebels and civilians indiscriminately. If, by Mao's analogy, rebel soldiers are like fish that swim in a sea of civilians, then mass killing is a tactic to "drain the sea"—that is, to destroy the rebels by destroying their environs and their means of survival.[31] Similarly, Kalyvas argues that indiscriminate mass killing that targets insurgents and civilians is most likely in conditions where armed actors do not have enough control and information to deploy selective violence.[32] When actors in war cannot know who is a collaborator and who is not, they target suspect populations indiscriminately.

As I argue above, however, genocide (and mass categorical violence) is conceptually and empirically distinguishable from indiscriminate violence. Genocide and mass categorical violence entail group-selective violence, which requires enough control and information to sort populations into targeted and not-targeted groups. Such a theory also does not explain why perpetrators actively seek to destroy groups or impose maximal damage. In short, while a counterinsurgency tactical logic works well to explain indiscriminate mass killing, the argument works less well for explaining genocide and mass categorical violence.

A second mechanism is the logic of a "final solution," a term that Valentino insightfully borrows from the Holocaust to apply generally to cases of mass killing and genocide.[33] The main intuition is that genocide and mass killing are part of a cycle of past attempts to rectify a problem. When leaders judge that more moderate policies failed in previous instances of conflict or

---

30. Ulfelder and Valentino 2008; Valentino et al. 2004 ; see also Sullivan 2012.
31. Valentino et al 2004.
32. Kalyvas 2006.
33. Valentino 2004.

crisis, they escalate in later crisis rounds in order to achieve a more durable solution.

The logic behind the argument makes sense, and the intuition captures the idea that genocide is part of a long-run conflict between groups and not the first choice of perpetrators. But why would genocide be the choice over another option? In theory, if previous efforts failed, a perpetrating authority could try a more moderate solution or an entirely different solution. Based on my analysis above, I hypothesize that perpetrating authorities must make judgments about the target populations and in particular that the would-be perpetrators must hold three characteristics to be true. First, that the target population is unwinnable. That is, for strategic escalation and group destruction to be the choice rather than strategic deescalation, the authors of genocide must believe that they cannot persuade the target populations. Second, perpetrating authorities must believe that the target population cannot be contained. There is no strategic reason to escalate violence against a group if the group can be contained. Third, the perpetrating authorities must believe that the target population is inherently dangerous. If they are not inherently dangerous, then there is not a strategic reason to solve the problem through violence. In sum, the idea behind a final solution provides insight into these questions but does not satisfy them.

A different strategic argument is that genocide follows a coercive bargaining logic. In this case, the violence is designed to raise the costs of war continuation by maximally punishing the supporters of opponents. Perpetrators in effect leverage the fate of civilian populations in order to force a change of behavior from their armed opponents. They use mass categorical violence to impose maximal costs on their enemy, as I described at the end of the previous section.

To assess which logic is at work, one could ask whether perpetrators calibrate their behavior based on the actions of their opponents. If a coercive logic was operative, perpetrators should update their information; perpetrators should assess whether their violence was effective or, if the strategic environment changes, perpetrators should alter the level of violence against civilians. If not—if large-scale, group-selective violence continues even if it does not appear to change opponents' behavior or even if the strategic environment changes—then that scenario would suggest a group-destructive logic is operative.

Some well-known cases strongly suggest that a coercive logic is *not* operative. In the Armenian case, there seems little evidence that the violence slowed because of the military actions of the Russians or the general dynamics of World War I. Similarly, in the Holocaust there is little evidence that the extermination of the Jews, as well as Roma and Sinti, diminished as the Germans defeat in the war looked more inevitable. The same is true in Rwanda. In places such as Southwest Africa in 1905, Indonesia in 1965, Burundi in 1972, and the Democratic Republic of Congo (DRC) in 1996–97, perpetrators sought to destroy populations after insurgencies were largely defeated—in those places, perpetrators seem to be anticipating future threats more than fighting present threats, which conforms to the logic of genocide spelled out in this chapter.

At the same time, we lack information about counterfactuals: What would have happened if the Russians had surrendered in World War I, the Soviets and Americans had surrendered in World War II, or the Rwandan Patriotic Front had decided to negotiate rather than win militarily? What would have happened if opponents had waved a white flag in Southwest Africa, Indonesia, Burundi, and the DRC?

In other cases, it would seem that battlefield dynamics do shape killing rates. In places like Nigeria, Guatemala, and Darfur, state violence against populations associated with insurgents diminished as states gained the upper hand militarily. That pattern is at least consistent with the logic of imposing maximal violence for coercive purposes. At the same time, reasons other than coercion may have prompted perpetrators to diminish violence. It is also possible that both logics operate simultaneously or at least that one may give rise to the other.

In sum, it is probably unwise to distinguish overly between genocide (as conforming to a logic of group destruction) and mass categorical violence (conforming to a coercive logic of imposing maximal costs on civilian populations from a particular social category). Empirically, both entail group-selective violence on a very large scale. What is distinctive about genocide is the specific purpose of group destruction, irrespective of the short-term strategic value of such violence, but observationally it can be difficult to know for certain that such a logic is at work.

Finally, there might be a preemptive strategic logic in genocide.[34] The main idea would be that perpetrating authorities fear that a target population will cause massive damage should the perpetrating authorities not act. Thus,

---

34. This argument is similar, though more specific, than a security dilemma (as developed by Posen 1993) in which the idea is that one side does not have sufficient information about the other side's objectives in the context of anarchy. René Lemarchand (2009) perceptively applies the logic to the Rwandan genocide, in which the argument is that the Hutu-led regime in Rwanda preemptively killed Tutsi civilians as the Tutsi-led RPF advanced. Similarly, the argument resonates with Manus Midlarsky (2005), who argues that genocide emerges from "imprudent realpolitik," which is brought on by perceptions of vulnerability in the context of loss.

the authors of genocide would act before, preemptively, in order to prevent a catastrophic outcome to themselves. The perpetrating authorities must perceive a grave threat, and they must perceive that the target population—not just their armed enemies—as integral to the threat. The perpetrating authorities must also believe that they are vulnerable or at least that they should expect that in a future round of confrontation they would reasonably expect to be in a weaker position, vulnerable to the grave threat that the target population would pose. The question then becomes under what circumstances such a set of calculations are at work. Why would perpetrators experience a threat and see the civilian population as integral to that threat?

A last consideration, which surprisingly receives little attention in the existing literature, is an economic logic of genocide. The main intuition would be that a target population should be removed or destroyed because they inhabit highly desirable land. Thus, genocide is a choice in order to gain access to vital resources. In this case, the analysis would need to explain why alternative choices were not possible. Why could a group not be relocated? Why could a group not be incorporated or coopted? Here again, the logic of the violence would suggest that the perpetrating authorities either perceived bargaining as unacceptable because of a fundamental incompatibility with the target population, because the target population was inherently dangerous (and thus no compromise was feasible), or because the target population was unwinnable—they would never relinquish their demands on vital territory. And the logic of genocide, as opposed to the logic of group removal, would be more probable when the above were true and either when the target population posed some imminent threat or when removal was not practically feasible.

The most likely scenario in which an economic logic of genocide would hold is during imperial expansion into areas controlled by indigenous populations. The location of the violence could be the United States, Latin America, Australia, and parts of Africa—locations where an indigenous population was seen to inhabit land that was vital to imperial expansion or to imperial wealth. The theoretical expectation would be that when indigenous populations were characterized as inherently unchangeable, uncontainable, and dangerous and when they posed some imminent threat, then genocide would be the strategic choice over group removal and group cooption.

To conclude, genocide is a form of mass categorical violence, which is defined by large-scale, group-selective violence. Such violence will depend on the ability of perpetrators to dominate the territory where target populations reside and to sustain multi-agency, multi-level coalitions of violence over space and time. States are the most likely actors to have that capacity. But local actors are usually necessary to identify and find perpetrators, suggesting that genocide and mass categorical violence require an alliance between national and local actors.

Genocide conforms to a logic of group destruction. Extreme mass categorical violence conforms to a logic of imposing maximal violence on target groups in order to force a change in behavior. Any theory should explain why perpetrators would choose group destruction or the infliction of maximum violence on groups over alternatives.

For genocide, the chapter developed four probable conditions: (1) that a target population is viewed as unwinnable; (2) that a target population is viewed as uncontainable; (3) that a target population is viewed as inherently dangerous with interests that are inimical to those of the perpetrator; and (4) that perpetrators experience themselves as vulnerable to the threat from the target group. For mass categorical violence, perpetrators believe that they can coerce a change but only through imposing extremely high costs on a population associated with a committed, dangerous enemy.

Putting these sets of points together, genocide and extreme mass categorical violence are most likely in the unusual circumstance when perpetrators possess significant capacity for coordination and control over the target group while calculating that they face some immediate threat from a dangerous enemy and, in the case of genocide, unwinnable and uncontainable group.

When are these conditions likely to be present? In the remainder of the book, I shall endorse a synthesis between ideological and strategic arguments. Ideology helps to explain why perpetrating authorities come to locate some social categories as dangerous, uncontainable, and unwinnable. Strategic arguments bring the importance of imminent threat and vulnerability into focus. Strategic arguments also place an emphasis on dynamic circumstances, in particular war, that intensify threats. To these, I add the general question of restraint, a topic I take up in the next chapter.

CHAPTER 2

Escalation and Restraint

Most theories of genocide focus on why leaders opt for such violence and why societies accept it. In this chapter, I turn that question around.[1] Instead of asking what drives genocide, I ask what restrains it. Focusing on restraint is important for explaining variation among genocide and nongenocide cases, as well as for explaining variation among other types of violence. This chapter therefore sets up the explanation advanced in the next chapter and the empirical analyses of African cases in the second half of the book.

My claim about restraint is based on two consistent empirical findings. First, genocide is a nonteleological outcome. Genocide emerges from a process that is shaped by events, interests, actors, and interactions. Genocide is also usually a phase within a longer, broader pattern of conflict. In other words, genocide reflects a policy choice at one point along a continuum of decision-making, not a predetermined or inexorable outcome. Second, genocide is rare. If one considers the number of conflicts, intergroup or majority-minority interactions, and other circumstances in which genocide could occur, then the simple but powerful conclusion must be that genocide is, thankfully, the exception rather than the norm.

---

1. This chapter draws on Straus 2012b.

The two points matter on their own terms, but they also matter for rethinking the causal process that leads to or away from genocide. If genocide is the outcome of fluid decision-making, then a key question becomes what pushes decision-makers toward or—more frequently—away from genocide. For genocide to occur, the factors of escalation should be considerably stronger than the factors of restraint. We have many theories about what drives genocide but few on what restrains it.

In this chapter, I develop these claims. I show how genocide should be conceptualized as the outcome of a dynamic process, and I illustrate the point in relation to key genocide cases. I also mine the existing literature on political violence and genocide to develop some hypotheses about restraint at the micro, meso, macro, and international levels. I reach a conclusion consistent with the claims in the previous chapter: The most important sources of restraint occur at the national level. Meso-level restraint matters but primarily in the early stages of escalation or when coalitions of violence are decentralized. Micro-level factors shape who commits violence but generally will not explain whether genocide happens.

The Process of Genocide

No two genocides are likely to unfold in precisely the same manner or in the same causal sequence, a point made equally in relation to other complex macro-social outcomes.[2] The Armenian genocide took place after earlier measures of persecution and exclusion, in the context of World War I, and after a failed Ottoman advance in Russia. The genocide also took shape in a rapid sequence of escalation in the spring of 1915.[3] Rooted in anti-Semitism, the Nazi Holocaust took shape after a decade of Jewish persecution by the National Socialists; the specific policy of extermination came into existence over time, in the context of World War II and multi-country territorial conquest and after earlier policies of radical segregation proved inadequate, according to Nazi leaders.[4] Following earlier violence against Tutsis, a sharp escalation in anti-Tutsi discourse, and wartime self-defense, Rwanda experienced a rapid escalation of exterminatory violence following a presidential assassination and resumption of a rebel offensive.[5] In each of these cases, the

---

2. Kuper 1981; McAdam and Tarrow 2010.
3. Bloxham 2005; Ungor 2006.
4. Longerich 2010.
5. Straus 2006b.

coalitions of actors, the means of violence, and the locations of violence differed—even if, as I shall document in a subsequent chapter, there are identifiable common patterns among these and other cases.

Nonetheless, one consistent finding across these cases is that the outcome occurred after a process of escalation. That is, the policy and practice of group destruction was the product of decisions made over time; genocide was not the initially envisaged choice. Donald Bloxham argues that the Armenian genocide "emerged, like many other governmental policies in a spectrum of regimes, often piecemeal, informed by ideology but according to circumstance."[6] The literature on the Holocaust is vast, but major studies claim that the policy of extermination emerged over time, after a series of escalations.[7] Scholars differ on the causal roles of the Nazi leadership and anti-Semitism as well as the exact timing of the decision (or how to conceptualize a "decision" in the first place), but the idea that physical extermination "became imaginable little by little" is well established.[8] Comparative studies reach similar conclusions. Valentino's conceptualization of genocide and mass killing as "final solutions" after earlier more limited policies have failed encapsulates this idea.[9] So does Michael Mann's argument that murderous cleansing is analogous to a "Plan C" that emerges after other plans fail.[10]

These points may seem straightforward enough to observers of other social and political outcomes, but in the context of genocide studies, which is often informed by legalistic and normative approaches, the implications are wide-ranging and counterintuitive. In particular, they require taking seriously the circumstances, actors, institutions, interests, and ideas that shape the process of escalation leading to the outcome of genocide—or, by contrast, the process of deescalation leading to the avoidance of genocide. In genocide studies, such an approach is unusual in part because the legal definition of genocide distinguishes the outcome by the *intent* to destroy groups. By implication, many observers emphasize moments in time prior to the mass violence to demonstrate an intentional plan or conspiracy to commit genocide. The result is an often static, teleological paradigm for understanding the way in which genocide comes about, a paradigm that views acts or statements of persecution, preparations for violence, and other institutions that might eventually contribute to genocide as originally designed for that purpose.

---

6. Bloxham 2005: 69; see also Naimark 2011: xvii.
7. Browning 2004; Gerlach 2000; Kershaw 2000; Longerich 2010.
8. Gerlach 2000: 139.
9. Valentino 2004.
10. Mann 2005: 7.

But a more dynamic, gradualist, nonteleological account of how a policy of group destruction emerges implies that institutions that were not initially designed for genocide may come to be used for that purpose. For example, in the Armenian genocide, the Special Organization was a paramilitary unit initially designed to protect the interests and vision of the Committee on Union and Progress (CUP) party against foreign interference and Armenian political restiveness. But in 1915, once the state issued a deportation order, the Special Organization became a key agency responsible for the forced removal and killing of Armenians.[11] The existence of the Special Organization facilitated and ultimately was central to the implementation of genocide, but its initial creation is not evidence that a decision to destroy the Armenians of Anatolia had been made. The same is true for the Holocaust and Rwanda.

Ideology works in much the same way. The CUP's pan-Turkic nationalism shaped the path toward genocide, as did the Nazi's ideological commitment to racial homogeneity. But many outcomes besides genocide were consistent with the promulgation of Turkification in the late Ottoman Empire. In Germany, where the Nazi worldview was more coherent, Aryanization did not necessarily determine genocide. And in Rwanda, the anti-Tutsi-ism at the heart of Hutu nationalism that ultimately shaped genocide was consistent with other outcomes, including containing Tutsis and limiting their advancement. Indeed, those were the principal strategies for thirty years prior to the genocide.

The same is true about pre-genocide violence. In the Armenian genocide, there were multiple massacres of Armenians before the deportation order of 1915.[12] In the Holocaust, there was Kristallnacht and acts of violence against political prisoners and the disabled prior to the onset of policies of killing and extermination in 1941 and 1942. In Rwanda, there were a series of anti-Tutsi massacres from 1990 to 1992 as well as in the 1960s and 1970s. These are not "dress rehearsals," as some claim, because they were not undertaken with the objective of extermination in mind. Yet, once committed, the pre-genocide violence created expectations or generated outcomes that later had consequences. Early massacres and the reaction to them, for example, allowed elite decision-makers to imagine larger-scale violence; early massacres prompted new actors to arise in their standing and power, and they in turn become spearheads of violence and escalators of larger-scale violence; and early massacres in the Armenian and Rwandan cases failed to deter restiveness, prompting decision-makers to conclude that target populations were unwinnable and uncontrollable.

---

11. Bloxham 2005.
12. Suny 2011; Ungor 2006.

The point is crucial to the arguments that I develop in the book. I contend that we should see genocide as the outcome of a crystallization of forces whose ultimate expression may not have been previously imaginable even to those who ultimately order, organize, and carry out genocide. The idea of a crystallization of forces suggests that in any given moment decision-makers are subject to various influences and incentives, ranging from ideas about ways of doing things and ideas about the nature of a legitimate political community, to ideas about the nature of the threat and the expected costs or gains from pursuing certain policies, to questions of tactical advantage or disadvantage in wartime. The question then becomes what pushes key decision-makers toward a trajectory of escalation or away from it. Said differently, genocide should not be considered a two-stage outcome (of policy conception and implementation) but rather as a multi-stage process of escalation over time subject to a variety of influences, both escalatory and restraining.

To illustrate the argument about the dynamic nature of the path to genocide, I turn to the Rwandan genocide, the Holocaust, and the Armenian genocide, each of which now represent canonical cases in the emerging comparative literature on genocide. The Rwandan genocide of 1994 was an exceptionally swift case in which the acting authorities ordered and legitimized the systematic and widespread killing of the resident Tutsi civilian population. The swift execution was facilitated by steps taken before the onset in 1994. Those steps included a military statement defining the "enemy"; the formation of a civil defense force, which entailed training of civilians and the distribution of weapons; the promulgation of propaganda that stereotyped Tutsis and stimulated fear; the creation of political party youth wings and eventually militias; mass ethnic arrests and some ethnic killing; and the creation of lists of rebel supporters and sympathizers, among other issues. When the genocide started on the night of April 6/7, many of these elements became integral to the process of destruction—they crystallized into a coherent order. Civilian defense weapons were used to hunt and kill Tutsis who became equated with the enemy, the extremist radio station became a tool for naming individuals suspected of being "accomplices" to the enemy, many militia members became leading killers, and those actors who were instrumental in the original promulgation of these institutions became key actors in the violence.

But are the militia, the civil defense, the radio propaganda, and other bodies that became integral to the genocide evidence of a plan to commit genocide well before April 1994? In most interpretations of the genocide, the answer is yes, and they amount to evidence of a conspiracy to plan to commit genocide in advance of the assassination of President Juvénal Habyarimana and the renewed

onset of war in April 1994.[13] Indeed, the approach was the essence of the prosecution's case at the most important trial at the International Criminal Tribunal
for Rwanda, the court established to prosecute the high-level architects of the
Rwandan genocide. The case in question is known colloquially as "Military
I" because it tried the military elites allegedly most responsible for committing
Rwanda to genocide, notably Théoneste Bagosora.[14] The prosecutor charged
that the defendants "conspired . . . to work out a plan with the intent to exterminate the civilian Tutsi population . . . this plan consisted of, among other things,
recourse to hatred and ethnic violence, the training and distribution of weapons
to militiamen as well as the preparations of lists of people to eliminated."[15]

However, in a subtle, thoughtful decision reached after ten years of research
and trial—a decision subsequently upheld in the Appeals Chamber and reinforced in later decisions—the ICTR trial chamber judges found that none of
the documents that alleged a prior plan to commit genocide could be unequivocally proven to have been initially designed for that purpose. The Tribunal
thus acquitted the alleged masterminds of the Rwandan genocide of conspiracy, even while finding them guilty of genocide and other crimes. Throughout
the long decision, the judges discuss how civil defense, militia creation, forming
lists, and even death squads are consistent with various outcomes, including
preparations for war. There is no question in the decision that after April 6
genocide took place and, the judges argue, the defendants had command or
superior responsibility. There is also clear evidence of genocide—a practice of
exterminatory violence against Tutsis in Rwanda.

The court is careful to note that they are ruling simply in relation to the
evidence. Nonetheless, the court's detailed judgment demonstrates how an
infrastructure of violence and a polarized environment may exist but how
genocide was not necessarily the only possible outcome:

> After the death of President Habyarimana, these tools were clearly put to
> use to facilitate killings. When viewed against the backdrop of the targeted
> killings and massive slaughter perpetrated by civilian and military assailants
> between April and July 1994, as well as earlier cycles of violence, it is under-
> standable why for many this evidence takes on new meaning and shows a
> prior conspiracy to commit genocide. Indeed, these preparations are com-
> pletely consistent with a plan to commit genocide. However, they are also
> consistent with preparations for a political or military power struggle.[16]

---

13. Melvern 2004, for instance.
14. Dallaire and Beardsley 2005; Des Forges 1999.
15. ICTR 1999: para 5.1.
16. *ICTR vs Bagosora et al.* 2008, p. 539.

The court's motivation is not social science, but its findings resonate with what close observers have found about the nature of this and other genocides.[17]

A different study by Vladimir Solonari of Romania's policy of ethnic purification during World War II reveals similar processes.[18] Solonari traces the way in which an ideal of Romanian ethnic nationalism ultimately shaped and motivated Romanian national and local authorities to pursue violent policies of population transfer and deportation, which led to large-scale massacres of Jews and Roma. His emphasis is on the ideological origins of the policy, what he labels a dream of achieving ethnic purity based on an ahistorical imagining of the country's past in which non-Romanians were considered anomalous and of second class.[19]

But he also shows that the same ideology in different circumstances could produce varying outcomes. When the Romanians collaborated with the Nazis in the earlier stages in the war, in part to counter the Soviet Union and Hungary, the Romanians accelerated deportation and killing; they pursed a policy of ethnic purification. By contrast, as the international circumstances shifted and as the Nazis gradually lost power during the war, the Romanians chose other international allies and the same ideology led to the promotion of minority rights in a Romanian-majority state. The nationalist ideal of a Romania for Romanians remained, but the circumstances changed.[20]

The evolution of the persecution of the Jews in the Holocaust was exceptionally complex and has been the subject of a vast amount of scholarship. Solonari's study effectively shows how the policy emerged in one occupied state, Romania. But many scholars of the Holocaust recognize that phases of radicalization were essential to the outcome of a Europe-wide extermination attempt. For example, in one of the more thoughtful recent accounts, Peter Longerich identifies four major periods of escalation.[21] He starts by showing how a policy of systematic exclusion of Jews from German society was central to the National Socialist's ideological vision of restoring an Aryan community. Many policy choices flowed logically from that position, as well as from Hitler's maniacal obsession with the Jews, but along the way several factors shaped the process of escalation. These include the onset of war in 1939; the capture of territory in Poland and the Soviet Union that held very large numbers of Jews; the promulgation and failure of

---

17. Guichaoua 2010; Mann 2005; Straus 2006b; Valentino 2004.
18. Solonari 2010.
19. Solonari 2010: 333.
20. Solonari 2010: 333–36.
21. Longerich 2010.

deportation plans, including sending Jews to Madagascar or Eastern Europe; the improvisations on the periphery of particular local potentates; the design and completion of a gassing "euthanasia" program; the bogging down of the German army in the Soviet Union; and the eventual entry of the United States into the war. All of these elements were crucial accelerators of violence, especially war.[22]

In short, even in the highly unusual case of a political leader committed and obsessed with anti-Semitism and racial nationalism and a case on a continental scale—*the* exemplar of genocide—there are still key periods of escalation and radicalization that were shaped by a variety of circumstances, influences, inventions, and interests.

In a thoughtful summary of scholarship, Ronald Suny concludes that several influences also shaped the Armenian genocide. These include a turn toward modernizing Turkish nationalism, a hardening of negative interethnic attitudes between Turks and Armenians, and finally the outbreak and conditions of war. But like other recent scholarship, he argues that the genocide was not a foregone conclusion but rather emerged as a response to events and was fed by underlying ideological and attitudinal orientations. The genocide, he concludes, was a "pathological response of desperate leaders who sought security against a people they had both constructed as enemies and driven into radical opposition."[23]

Factors of Restraint

If we accept that the orchestration of genocide is the end product of a process of escalation, that supposition raises the question of what drives the process. Most theory, including that which I summarized in the introduction, puts forth claims about why decision-makers pursue policies of genocide and why publics accept them. That too was the line of argument I implied in the conclusion of the previous chapter. Thus, with some exceptions,[24] it is fair to claim that existing theory focuses on drivers of escalation.

But the presence or absence of escalatory factors neither suffices theoretically nor accounts empirically for the variation observed across cases. Alongside drivers of escalation are ideas, incentives, events, institutions, and outside actors that could prompt the moderation or non-escalation of violence. The question is what they are.

---

22. Longerich 2010: 132; see also Bergen 2009; Browning 2004.
23. Suny 2011: 41.
24. Chirot and McCauley 2006; Kuper 1981; Lynch 2013.

Micro-Level Sources of Restraint

At the individual level, many people have values and morals that lead them not to commit violence. Many individuals find violence against innocents or noncombatants, especially their neighbors, abhorrent. Few are good at it, and committing violence runs contrary to "basic mechanisms of emotional entertainment and interactional solidarity."[25] Kristen Renwick Monroe explains variation among rescuers, bystanders, and Nazi supporters during World War II as a function of personal, moral choice driven by self-identity.[26] Violence can also be detrimental to one's self-interest: Violence invites revenge and disrupts interpersonal systems of mutual benefit. These arguments are the inverse of group animosity theory or group envy theory prominent in ethnic conflict and genocide studies. Rather than holding sharply negative views of others or being resentful of their accomplishments, many individuals in a society harbor life-affirming values and cherish cooperation, and these personal values in turn may serve as a restraint on violence.

These approaches clearly have merit. If one considers the volume of human interaction across global space and over time, nonviolence is almost infinitely more common than violence. People do not regularly kill or physically harm others. The frequency of nonviolence is surely partly due to institutions, rather than only to personal values; nonetheless, most people prefer to interact with other people without violence. This dimension must be theorized in explaining how and why violence succeeds, suggesting more specifically that for violence to succeed on a large and sustained scale, micro-level sources of restraint must be overcome.

Indeed, studies of violence show precisely how such a process occurs. Collins's research shows that in situations of "confrontational fear," individuals commit violence.[27] Stanley Milgram's social psychology experiments of the 1960s demonstrate that persuasion from a "legitimate authority" suffices for ordinary individuals to commit serious harm against people like themselves and against whom they have no prior hatred. The Stanford prison experiments by Philip Zimbardo similarly show that students who were given excessive power over more vulnerable students quickly and willingly inflicted harm. Multiple studies of armed conflict and other highly tense scenarios show how individuals, when they fear for their lives or when they face horizontal peer or vertical coercive pressure, willingly commit harm against other

25. Collins 2008: 25.
26. Monroe 2011.
27. Collins 2008.

civilians.[28] In short, micro-level, personal values are real sources of restraint, but in particular situations—notably danger often in the context of fear and war, horizontal or vertical intragroup pressure, or unrestricted power and impunity—and with high-level political authorities committed to violence, such values are comparatively weak bulwarks against the escalation of violence. Theories focusing on such micro-level values are thus probably best at explaining variation among individuals in the context of the commission of violence rather than explaining variation among cases of violence.[29]

Meso-Level Sources of Restraint

Empirically, the meso level clearly matters. In the previous chapter, I argued that a nearly necessary condition for genocide to succeed is a sustained collaboration between national and local actors. Empirically, in the most studied major cases—the Armenian genocide, the Holocaust, and Rwanda—local actors are critical in the identification and sorting of target populations as well as in the infliction of violence against them. We also know that in each of these cases subnational actors (or, in the case of the Nazis, non-German actors) at times resisted violence. Moreover, the Nazi case clearly shows, and the Armenian and Rwandan cases strongly imply, an interplay between national and local actors in how the strategy of genocide is ultimately promulgated. Local actors sometimes improvise or invent violence, which high level authorities in turn support, condone, or oppose, which in turn shapes the trajectory of violence. So the middle or "meso" level—by which I mean sets of actors who operate between the national and the individual at the level of inter-group relations, subnational organizations, subnational governmental institutions, and civil society—is clearly very important in how policies of genocide take shape and are implemented. In theory, then, meso-level restraint could serve as a major source of restraint and explain variation across genocide cases.

An important game theoretic insight is that groups interact with other groups repeatedly. Over time, it is in the interest of groups to develop formal and informal institutions to facilitate intercommunal, mutually beneficial cooperation.[30] Daniel Chirot and Clark McCauley emphasize intergroup codes of conflict, exogamous marriage practices, commercial exchanges, and ritualized gift giving that foster cooperation or limit violence.[31] Saumitra Jha

28. Browning 1991; Costa and Kahn 2008; Straus 2006b.
29. Monroe 2011.
30. Fearon and Laitin 1996.
31. Chirot and McCauley 2006.

argues that interethnic commercial complementarities are a source of tolerance between Hindus and Muslims in India.[32] In effect, Hindus and Muslims in some towns relied on each other in order for their trades and livelihoods to thrive; they in turn developed institutions that survived over time to provide incentives for continued cooperation.[33]

Beyond groups, civil society organizations can foster intergroup dialogue and understanding in crisis periods.[34] In her analysis of variation in Jewish victimization rates in the Holocaust, Helen Fein argues that when the Catholic Church and other churches actively opposed the persecution of Jews, the level of violence diminished compared to places where the those religious institutions were quiescent or supported such violence, in particular in places that were not under the direct SS control of the Nazis.[35] Tim Longman similarly shows that in Rwanda Catholic and Presbyterian churches, which are highly influential in that country's society and politics, acted to facilitate and legitimize genocide in Rwanda through practicing ethnic politics, promoting subservience to state authorities, and failing to condemn previous periods of ethnic violence before the 1994 genocide in Rwanda.[36] Longman provides evidence of religious dissent and noncooperation that served to slow and displace genocidal violence in local communities in western Rwanda. These church leaders did not stop the violence, but their opposition yielded some effect, which Longman interprets as evidence of what could have happened had the churches in Rwanda not, on average, condoned the violence.

Though the mechanisms differ, modern domestic nongovernmental organizations, which in turn are plugged into international networks, also serve as a buffer against the escalation of violence. Two recent studies from different parts of the globe make the point. In East Timor, a careful study by historian Geoffrey Robinson shows that a robust network of nongovernmental organizations with ties to national and international policymakers was established in the late 1990s.[37] When East Timor looked to be on the verge of rapidly escalating violence in 1999, the network of NGOs broadcast the dangers at hand. Robinson argues that they became conduits to policymakers and, together with international journalists, telegraphed to the world that there was a risk of genocide in East Timor.[38] As envisioned in other work on transnational

---

32. Jha 2008.
33. Jha 2008: 4.
34. Varshney 2002.
35. Fein 1979: 67, 94–99.
36. Longman 2010.
37. Robinson 2010.
38. Robinson 2010: 19, 236–37.

advocacy networks, a key mechanism is information exchange.[39] Externally funded NGOs may not have shaped public attitudes on violence, but they effectively transmitted information to international actors who could and did take forceful action to halt the violence. Studying ethnic peace in Eastern Europe in the 1990s, Patrice McMahon reaches similar conclusions.[40] She argues that a network of transnational organizations took root in the 1990s. These organizations emphasized cooperation and information exchange. More specifically, she argues that the network provided a common "message" of ethnic peace, a "motivation" (transnational actors could credibly offer incentives to states that avoided violence or sanctions to states that did not), and the "means" (financial, technical, and moral assistance for dialogue, education, and training).[41] Eventually, these paid off in changes in policies and social behavior.[42]

Another organizational-level source of restraint is identified in the work of Jeremy Weinstein.[43] His analysis focuses on the different initial "endowments" of rebel organizations. Dividing rebels into "activist" and "opportunistic" rebellions, Weinstein argues that the initial endowments of each shape the institutional makeup and strategies of civilian interaction. Because of their common political and social commitments, activist rebellions tend to develop shared identities and ideologies, which lead to norms of cooperation with civilians. Crucially, activist rebellions also depend on civilian support; they need civilians for provisions, shelter, and recruitment. As such, activist rebellions have an interest in restraining violence; if they alienate the civilians on whom they depend, activist rebellions risk their own future. By contrast, Weinstein argues, opportunistic rebellions that rely on cash-flowing resources, like diamonds or gold, attract recruits who have an interest in making money and gaining power. The institutional structures that opportunistic rebellions build are weaker and are thus less able to police its members; crucially, because of their resource endowment, opportunistic rebellions do not require as much civilian support. Opportunistic rebellions thus tend toward greater use of indiscriminate violence.[44] Whether the empirical world of rebellions can be divided neatly in this way,[45] Weinstein provides a compelling argument for why organizations have incentives for restraint, namely

---

39. Keck and Sikkink 1998.
40. McMahon 2007.
41. McMahon 2007: 180–81.
42. McMahon 2007: 183.
43. Weinstein 2007.
44. Weinstein 2007: 204–7.
45. Reno 2011.

where their own survival depends on cooperative interaction. In its implications, Weinstein's argument resonates with Jha's—certain political economies can create powerful commercial or organizational incentives for moderation.

A structurally similar argument is found in Steven Wilkinson's analysis of riots in India. Unlike Jha and Varshney, who locate sources of restraint at the group level, Wilkinson focuses on political parties and the ways in which electoral calculus creates incentives for violence or the restraint of violence. Wilkinson argues that when regional or national parties rely on the votes of minorities to form minimum winning coalitions, they will act to prevent political violence against those minorities.[46] By contrast, where parties need the support of a dominant ethnic or religious group to win, they may stimulate violence in order to raise the salience of identity and trigger bloc voting. Here again, we see a strategic argument for why restraint would be in the interest of political elites, in particular when their own electoral success depends on peaceful, cooperative relations.

The review of meso-level mechanisms suggests a series of avenues of restraint: group-level formal and informal mechanisms that foster cooperation (sanctions, codes of conduct, and marriage pacts); group-level and organization-level incentives for moderation based on a recognition of mutual dependence; organization-level mechanisms that shape public and elite attitudes; and organization-level mechanisms that supply information to influential actors via transnational networks. While the discussion has focused on certain types of organizations (democracy-supporting NGOs, churches, rebels, and political parties), the theoretical implications apply to other types of organizations, including media institutions, business lobbies, and other organized actors.

The question is, do they work for restraining genocide? The answer is subject to empirical testing, but nonetheless even judging from the above discussion a series of observations is possible. The first concerns the model of violence. If genocide takes the form of top-level, state-enforced violence in the context of strong state control, then group-level and organization-level mechanisms are likely to be relatively weak bulwarks against the escalation of violence. Fein's work, which shows that where Nazis exerted direct control churches had less autonomy and power, suggests as much. Even in Longman, the holdout churches did not stop the genocide in their communities; they just changed how and where the violence occurred. Other case-study evidence from Rwanda shows that interethnic ties and intermarriage were high before the genocide; there was a great deal of neighborhood interdependence;

---

46. Wilkinson 2004.

farmers cooperated and mutually assisted one another in planting and harvesting crops. Yet those group-level sources of moderation were weak bulwarks against state and paramilitary-backed violence.[47] Similar points apply to rural Bosnia-Herzegovina and Croatia, where preexisting intergroup marriage, interaction, and other forms of cooperation were easily overpowered when organized military and state actors promulgated interethnic violence in the context of war.[48] But a different model of genocide might have different theoretical implications. If genocide occurs in the context of a weaker, non-centralized state, the authorities must win local cooperation through selective incentives, ideological persuasion, or other means rather than coerce cooperation. In those cases, meso-level actors and institutions should have greater autonomy and therefore should be a greater potential source of restraint.

A second observation concerns periodization. Informal exchange mechanisms are likely to be weak at the moment when mobilization and coordination to commit mass violence occur. But group-level and organizational-level sources of restraint should have more bite at earlier stages of escalation, as national and local elites craft a response to perceived threats. Even if the initial response is one of repression—for example, arresting leaders or violently breaking up protests—strong meso-level mechanisms of restraint create pressure on the authorities to avoid further escalation or to tone down the response. By contrast, where meso-level mechanisms for restraint are weak, then political authorities are more unconstrained in their decision-making as they continue to confront a perceived threat in a crisis. Such is one implication of Longman's research; he argues that over decades the Catholic Church's embrace of racialist policies, its emphasis on subservience, and its failure to denounce pre-genocide violence accustomed the faithful in Rwanda to accept practices of violence, which in turn facilitated political elites' ultimate escalation. But the opposite should also be true: Namely, where there is an active challenge to violent practices, elites should have a harder time gaining public acceptance and should face a higher hurdle to the promulgation of such policies.

A third observation is that civil society institutions cannot be assumed to exercise a peaceful, moderating influence. As Fein and Longman argue explicitly, civil society institutions can contribute to a genocidal consensus or at least to forming worldviews that are consistent with ethnic violence against a target population. In the Rwanda case, the Catholic Church in

---

47. Fujii 2009; Straus 2006b.
48. Bringa 1995; Gagnon 2004.

particular was deeply entangled in the history of colonial and postcolonial state-building; the Church was hardly an ideal-typical autonomous institution, independent of the state. But similar arguments are applicable to nominal civil society institutions, such as the media. In the Holocaust, the former Yugoslavia, and Rwanda, some media institutions actively promoted leaders who advocated genocide or pejorative views of minorities that were consistent with genocide. Civil society can act in illiberal ways.[49]

Finally, organizations' ability to restrain violence will depend on their power. Here again, we have another source of variation. In some locations, such as Rwanda before the genocide and Europe during wartime, institutions such as the Church wielded significant social and political influence. But for other locations or for other types of organizations in the same states, civil society institutions may be less socially and politically embedded. In McMahon's and Robinson's analysis, the power of local NGOs depended on their preexisting effective placement in transnational networks. But in other locations, the human rights NGOs may have little domestic embeddedness and weak transnational connections. Thus, the presence of peace or tolerance promoting civil society institutions is not sufficient to act as a source of deescalation; one must know the extent of their power.

In short, meso-level mechanisms—from group-level informal mechanisms of cooperation to key civil society organizations—in theory *can* serve as important restraints against the escalation of violence of persecuted groups. They can reinforce incentives to cooperate, provide information, turn public or elite opinion away from violence, articulate more moderate visions, and leverage international actors. But in assessing the power of such institutions, one must consider the model of violence and the institutional setting, the period when the restraint mechanism would be effective, the nature of civil society institutions, and the relative power of such institutions.

Macro-Level Sources of Restraint

The political economy perspective introduced above points to an often-overlooked dimension of extreme violence: namely, that such violence carries high costs. While the genocide studies literature now recognizes the ways in which leaders sometimes view the commission of mass violence as in the interests of the state and thus strategically valuable,[50] there is little attention paid to when and why political and military elites would view

---

49. Chambers and Kopstein 2001.
50. Midlarsky 2005; Valentino 2004.

the commission of such violence as highly costly to state interests. Some research recognizes that repressive violence is costly,[51] but the insight has not, surprisingly, filtered strongly into existing models of genocide and political violence.

There are multiple ways in which the practice of genocide could be costly. Most obviously, genocide invites international condemnation and carries significant reputational costs. In the presence of increasingly common judicial mechanisms of accountability, the commission of large-scale human rights abuses will now likely trigger international arrest warrants, as the twenty-first-century cases of Kenya, Sudan, Côte d'Ivoire, and the Democratic Republic of Congo make clear. In situations of armed conflict, genocide likely has opportunity costs: The resources devoted to violence against civilians cannot be used in broader military campaigns against an opposing military. To be sure, genocidal leaders almost always view killing civilians as integral to a war effort; nonetheless, cooler military heads often recognize the costs of resource diversion.

But there are other domestic costs, in particular economic costs of committing large-scale violence. There is some discussion of the economic sources of restraint in the existing genocide studies literature. Reminiscent of Jha, one argument is that mutually beneficial commercial exchange between potentially conflicting groups establishes incentives to limit damage.[52] Another finding by Barbara Harff is that low trade openness is a significant risk factor for the onset of genocide or politicide.[53] Harff argues that the mechanism is international interdependence (as opposed to costs); where more interdependence exists, state elites that would commit genocide are more exposed and sensitive to international condemnation. The implicit argument is one of socialization and reputational costs; states that are more exposed to and more dependent on international markets will be more sensitive and reluctant to incur those costs.[54] A third argument is the inverse of the prominent arguments that economic loss creates frustration and that poverty lowers the opportunity costs for recruitment for violence.[55] The inverse of those arguments suggest that economic gains and prosperity could create well-being

---

51. Acemoglu and Robinson 2006: 29.

52. Chirot and McCauley 2006: 133.

53. Harff 2003; see also Ulfelder and Valentino 2008; Valentino and Hazlett 2013.

54. Harff also argues that trade openness in and of itself does not constrain violence, but rather that openness is an "indicator of state and elite willingness to maintain the rules of law and fair practices" in the economic sphere (2003: 65).

55. Staub 1989; Miguel et al. 2005.

and instill attitudes of generosity; growth could also create higher costs to recruitment for violence.

But economic-oriented analysis should go further. Here, drawing on political economy insights discussed earlier, I propose on additional economic source of restraint stemming from a revenue mechanism. Genocide entails large-scale human destruction; it is sustained violence committed over time and space. Such violence in general is likely to trigger significant population upheaval, which in turn could significantly disrupt an economy. If a state depends on tax revenue from sectors that would be highly sensitive to such disruption, then the state would have an incentive for restraint. There are likely to be industries that are highly sensitive to violence, such as manufacturing that requires skilled labor or agriculture that requires skilled labor, long planting seasons, or stable spaces to transport inputs and goods to market. By contrast, some industries are likely to be insulated from disruption and violence, such as (offshore) petroleum or high-value minerals and metal, such as diamond or gold. If oil wells or diamond mines are protected geographically from the disruption and provide large revenue streams to states, there would be fewer incentives to avoid a sharp escalation of violence. There is some limited empirical evidence found in recent forecasting models that find high oil exports to be associated with greater risk of mass killing.[56]

Another macro-level source of restraint concerns formal political institutions. An argument prominent in some early comparative research is that democratic institutions establish constraints on executive power that theoretically serve to limit escalation and restrain the execution of highly violent policies.[57] Harff's study endorses that view, adding that democratic states also recognize minority rights protection, and she finds strong empirical support for the claim. A related argument is that international human rights laws are more effective in the presence of political competition, independent judiciaries, and private media—all indicators of democratic polities.[58] These domestic democratic institutions serve as multiplier effects and increase the costs of noncompliance; in their absence, autocratic states may simply ignore previous commitments to international human rights. All of these accounts suggest that democratic institutions constrain escalation.

Ideology could also be a source of restraint. Most scholars of genocide conceptualize ideology as a factor of escalation, but again the opposite could hold. In crises, national political culture or explicit ideologies that either

56. Valentino and Hazlett 2013.
57. Horowitz 1976; Rummel 1994.
58. Hathaway 2003.

promote multiethnic cooperation or eschew exclusivist conceptions of the national community could serve as a check on the escalation of violence. In one of the few existing claims along these lines, Chirot and McCauley argue that an embrace of Enlightenment individualism (as opposed to emphasizing ethnic or categorical solidarity) and of modesty and doubt (as opposed to arrogance and certitude) serve as sources of nonviolence.[59]

In the end, I conclude that macro-level sources of restraint are most consequential. Because in most cases national authorities are the most influential decision-makers when it comes to genocide, the factors that influence them have the greatest impact on the likelihood of genocide or nongenocide. Of the various influences listed in this section, and as I elaborate in later chapters, I find that ideology matters most, followed by the economic structure of the state.

International Sources of Restraint

Finally, at the international level, several arguments are apparent. One is an interventionist claim. In the right circumstances, swift international intervention in the form of coercive diplomacy or military action may deter or prevent an escalation of violence. In other cases, international allies may exert a restraining influence over client states. The argument would be the converse of claims that international or diplomatic support or acquiescence facilitates genocide.[60]

There is some empirical support for these claims. Robinson's careful study of East Timor argues that in 1975 the United States and other major international actors tacitly endorsed Indonesian violence in East Timor; by contrast, in 1999, swift international intervention short-circuited quickly escalating dynamics of violence. In the aftermath of electoral violence in Kenya in early 2008, many observers feared that the tense situation and ethnic violence would escalate sharply. Yet swift and coercive diplomatic multilateral and bilateral action by key actors, notably United Nations Secretary General Kofi Annan, the African Union, Great Britain, and the United States, influenced Kenyan political actors to moderate their claims.[61] Solonari's study of Romanian ethnic nationalism in the 1940s shows that such ideational predispositions could escalate to mass ethnic deportation and killings under Nazi influence but could also deescalate toward minority rights protection

---

59. Chirot and McCauley 2006: 139–45.
60. Midlarsky 2005.
61. Cohen 2008.

under the influence of the Allies.[62] The intuition is that international engagement, influence, and pressure can act as a restraint. That claim seems to be an
assumption in the recent upsurge of policy pressure to develop an atrocities
prevention policy in domestic and international settings.[63]

Critics hold a different view. One argument is that, by promising intervention, international actors unleash a "moral hazard" by encouraging
weaker parties in a conflict to provoke atrocities by stronger actors. In so
doing, weaker actors trigger third-party intervention, which they calculate
will increase their chances of winning. In this way, international promises
to intervene perversely stimulate atrocities, rather than prevent them.[64] This
view has been challenged empirically and theoretically.[65]

Peacekeeping may matter too. In her comprehensive study of peacekeeping, Virginia Page Fortna identifies multiple ways that peacekeeping affects
the prospects for a stable peace, including by deterrence (threatening to punish defectors to an agreement), by increasing benefits (signaling to donors the
good behavior of belligerents), by reducing uncertainty and retaliatory cycles
through monitoring and providing information, and by strengthening moderates through providing information, among other mechanisms.[66] As applied to
potential situations of genocide, the mechanisms that Fortna identifies could
have a deescalating effect. Indeed, if, as discussed in the previous chapter, exag-
gerated fears are a central mechanism of escalation, then through providing
information to both sides, through monitoring, and through separating would-
be combatants, a credible and neutral third-party peacekeeping force could
have a constraining effect. The imposition of costs through threatened judicial
action or sanctions could also create incentives for leaders to moderate violence.

The review is not exhaustive. Rather, the main point is that existing
research points to plausible sources of restraint that explain why strategies of
increasing levels of violence are avoided or tried and then abandoned. New
research may well point to other factors.

What can be concluded from this discussion? First, the most general point is
that we should approach genocide not as a foregone conclusion but rather as an
outcome that is subject to a variety of causal influences. Those influences are
not only factors that cause escalation but also factors that restrain escalation or

---

62. Solonari 2010.
63. Evans 2008; GPTF 2008.
64. Kuperman 2008.
65. Kydd 2010; Kydd and Straus 2013.
66. Fortna 2008: 87–98.

encourage moderation. Restraint factors are not insurmountable obstacles; rather, they create mechanisms and incentives to moderate the use of violence. As such, these factors may explain variation in genocide and nongenocide outcomes.

Second, seeing genocide in this way opens the causal framework to agency and contingency. In any given situation, there will always be room for maneuver. Certain conditions will make certain strategies of violence more likely, but outcomes are fluid. Leaders' decisions, nondecisions, and emphases will have an important influence on events, both toward escalation and away from it. Similarly, unforeseen events may change dynamics on the ground, pushing trajectories of violence in one way or another.

Third, macro-level national factors are likely to be the most consequential for shaping the process of violence toward or away from genocide. Genocide is a form of large-scale, widespread, sustained, and coordinated violence. In most cases, such violence requires organization from the supreme authority in the land, generally the state. States have the theoretical capacity to coordinate multiple agencies, such as the army, the police, paramilitary units, and the civilian administration. Even in decentralized states where there exists much local autonomy, national states serve as the coordinating institution. This implies that the most important decision-makers are at the national level and therefore that the most important sources of escalation and restraint will occur at that level. In theory, an insurgent or criminal organization that exercised territorial control over a large space could also be the key actor. However, even in that case, the most consequential actor will be the supreme, central one that is equivalent to a national state.

But local actors matter too. Empirically, local actors are essential for the identification and sorting of victims; local actors are also often key perpetrators of violence. Thus, genocide requires sustained coordination between national and local actors. In a centralized state, in particular during periods of mobilization to commit violence, meso-level actors are weak bulwarks against the coercive pressure of national authorities. But meso- or local-level restraint will be most consequential (1) for containing escalation during early stages in the process of violence and (2) in decentralized states where local actors enjoy a degree of autonomy.

Finally, the review of restraint mechanisms implies one further observable implication. In any society, there is always likely to be some restraint. The strength of those factors will vary. But for genocide to succeed there must be some mechanism to overpower or marginalize the restraints that exist, whether at a micro, meso, national, or international level. A theory of genocide should account for that process of overcoming restraints, and that process should be observable to outsiders looking to understand when and where genocide is likely to happen.

CHAPTER 3

A Theory of Genocide

Genocide and mass categorical violence are about sustained, coordinated, group-selective, widespread violence, primarily orchestrated or at least condoned by states. Such outcomes are happily rare. Most armed conflicts end through negotiation, stalemate, or military victory. Most violence against civilians is coercive and communicative, designed to shape future behavior with the expectation that the targeted group can be contained or persuaded. By contrast, genocide and mass categorical violence occur when authorities claim that persuasion, accommodation, containment, and conventional military victory are neither possible nor desirable. Genocide is about destroying future interaction, not shaping it; genocide therefore follows a preventive, future-oriented logic. Such violence requires the capacity to identify and sort populations and the capacity to inflict significant violence across time and space. Such violence also requires the removal or overriding of restraints. Genocide and mass categorical violence are the outcome of a process, one subject to the medium- and short-term dynamics of escalation and deescalation. These are the central points I have sought to establish in the previous two chapters.

The key question that this chapter addresses is: Under what constellation of conditions does this process occur? Why do some elites favor strategies of mass violence against civilians while other elites, facing similar crises, choose other strategies? Why and when do elites conclude that target populations are

dangerous and unwinnable? How do national elites sustain violence coalitions across time and space? What sustains the process of escalation, leading,
ultimately, to the destruction of large numbers of civilians?

I propose a synthesis that affords a central role to the interaction between
national-level security concerns, usually in wartime and following a period
of unsettled politics, and pre-crisis ideational frameworks. The empirically
consistent rationale for genocide is that extreme violence is necessary to
protect one's country, one's core political project, and one's primary political community against a fundamental, imminent, and, usually, future danger.
Perpetrating authorities in turn define that danger as a social category. To
understand that process—of how that rationale develops over time—we need
to examine the interaction between ideology and security.

Certain material conditions aggravate threat. Genocide and mass categorical
violence typically occur in wartime, and wars are the most important material
condition shaping the perception of danger. The severity of wars in turn varies. I disaggregate along two dimensions: the strength of an opponent's military
capability, including its alliances, and the vulnerability of one's own side. In
some cases, armed opponents are weak. They can be militarily divided; they
can be geographically contained; they can have low fighting capacity; they can
be unable to mount a direct challenge to capturing the central state. They may
not have a powerful ally. In short, they pose a minimal threat. By contrast, in
other locations, opposing armies pose a serious material threat. The militaries
are well structured, with effective command and control, good discipline, and
good equipment. In these cases, threat perception is likely to be higher.

The same is true about vulnerability. To the extent that authorities are confident in their internal strength and ability to withstand attack, then the degree
of vulnerability is diminished and the perception of grave danger decreases.
But in other cases, authorities may be militarily weak, unprepared, internally
divided, and outgunned. They may also face large demographic imbalances
when, for example, an authority represents a small ethnic or religious minority fighting an enemy who represents a much larger population. Moreover,
particular battlefield events may crystallize vulnerability—a surprise attack, an
assassination, some unexpected advance, or some key defection. All of these
acts in the course of an armed conflict can spark the perception of danger.

On balance, the perception of acute danger that drives genocide and mass
categorical violence will more likely be present when the material threat is
greater.

But to understand how and why perpetrating authorities frame the threat
so intensely and why they locate the threat as a social category, we need to
look beyond material threat and thus beyond the uniquely strategic origins of

genocide and mass categorical violence. Ideas about who is fighting whom, and for what purpose, shape how perpetrating authorities frame threat and develop responses; those ideas in turn derive, I argue, from pre-crisis ideological constructs about a state's core mission and the identity of its core political community.

Deductively, a unique focus on material conditions is insufficient for two reasons. First, genocide requires some leap of imagination. Such violence involves by definition attacks against unarmed civilians, against whole groups of people who are not directly involved in creating threat. In genocide, per-petrators construct the civilian social category as dangerous, linking it to armed threat. That process necessarily involves imagination; genocide neces-sitates a social construction of threat.

Second, genocide entails a domination-vulnerability paradox. On the one hand, genocide requires the capacity to inflict violence across time and space using multi-agency coalitions. Such violence requires physical domination over target groups. On the other hand, such groups are constructed as a dangerous, imminent, and future threat, which suggests that the perpetrating authorities consider themselves not to have effective control over the popula-tions in question. That domination-vulnerability paradox suggests again an element of imagination to how the threat is constructed.

Empirically—as the case-study structure of this book makes plain—material military conditions cannot alone explain variation in threat percep-tion and in turn variation in strategies of violence. In this book, I examine how elites facing objectively similar military confrontations construct threats in very different ways.

Consider Rwanda and Côte d'Ivoire. A uniquely strategic or infor-mational approach would emphasize that threat perception was deeper in Rwanda because the state crisis was deeper, the military enemy was stronger in Rwanda, and the state lacked information about who was who, prompting the state to target an ethnic category indiscriminately. But that was not the case. Rwanda was in a deep political and military crisis in the early 1990s. But so was Côte d'Ivoire from the late 1990s until 2011. The Rwandan rebels were clearly strong in 1994, and they ultimately overthrew government forces. But the same can be said of Côte d'Ivoire, where rebels quickly advanced on gov-ernment forces in 2002 and then ultimately unseated the government with international support in 2011. True, Ivoirians settled into a "no peace, no war" equilibrium for periods, as discussed in chapter 5, but at key moments the rebels threatened the state and in 2011 they defeated government forces. In terms of information, Rwanda had excellent information-gathering mecha-nisms. The state was strong at the local level. By contrast, despite the general bureaucratic capability in Côte d'Ivoire, the state was more dispersed and exercised weaker control over civilian populations than in Rwanda. Yet in Rwanda the authorities constructed the Tutsi enemy as a mortal danger to the nation and the goals of the Republic while in Côte d'Ivoire they did not.

Now consider Sudan (Darfur), Mali, and Senegal, where insurgencies persisted in peripheral regions where the state exercised minimal control. In each case, the central state faced informational limits about who was in the rebellion and who was not. In each case, as a general statement, the insurgents were considerably weaker than the state's military forces. In each case, the insurgencies were confined to one region with little military likelihood of defeating those in control at the center. Yet the framing of the threat and the strategies of violence that were developed in response differed significantly across the cases.

These observations extend beyond the principal cases discussed in the second half of the book. Threat construction clearly varies across military confrontations, and that variance cannot be explained by the severity of a military crisis, military capabilities, battlefield dynamics, and information asymmetries alone. Nor can variation in material military threats explain variation in target selection and why some leaders pursue policies of genocide and mass categorical violence while others do not.

International Relations scholars have developed a variety of approaches to examine the nonmaterial sources of threat perception.[1] Evan Lieberman has shown how variations in ethnic boundaries shape how elites perceive the risk from AIDS to their societies.[2] Some recent experimental evidence shows how the identity and perceived intentions of an opponent shape how individuals perceive threat and develop wartime loyalty.[3] These and other studies provide further evidence that pre-crisis psychological, emotional, and ideational constructs affect how threat is experienced and how responses to threat develop.

The specific argument that I advance is that pre-crisis "founding narratives" shape how elites understand and respond to threat. Some founding narratives identify a core population in whose name the state is said to serve. Such narratives in turn create an implicit moral hierarchy between, on the one hand, a primary population whom the state should benefit and protect and, on the other hand, secondary populations to whom the state should pay less attention and who should not rule.[4] Many political processes are

---

1. For a helpful review, see Herrmann 2013 and Stein 2013.
2. Lieberman 2009.
3. Lyall, Blair, and Imai 2013; Tomz and Weeks 2013.
4. This conceptualization is similar to Mylonas's (2012) notion of "core" and "non-core" groups and to that of organic nationalism in Mann 2005. However, in my formulation the primary population need not be a national type or an ethnic group, as implied in these studies.

possible downstream of the formation of such a narrative. But the typical scenario in genocide cases is that members of the inferior category seek to change the political dispensation, which in turn cements the perception of the narrative's defenders that the interests of the two populations are inherently antagonistic and zero-sum. Then in wartime, in particular in wars that present a serious military risk to those in power, the defenders of the core population define the antagonistic population as an unwinnable threat, given their persistent resistance. Such a process rests on seeing social categories as the principal historical actors, thereby suggesting that struggles for state power are really struggles for the dominance of one identity group over another.

On balance then, genocide will be more likely where there exists a pre-crisis founding narrative that constructs an implicit hierarchy between a primary citizen class, defined as a social identity group, whom the state serves and a secondary citizen class whom the state should not serve. Genocide is less likely where the founding narrative is inclusionary or pluralistic, where the state is not said to rule in the name of one group over another.

I discuss details and permutations below, including how such narratives are crafted and sustain policies of genocide. I also discuss who subscribes to such ideas and the idea of counternarratives. But the argument boils down to the over-time interaction between founding narratives that define the identity of political community and the dynamics of threat, especially in war.

The theory explains outcomes (or non-outcomes) better than leading strategic alternatives, such as military capabilities, informational dynamics, type of war, the duration of war, the actions or inactions of military opponents, or even bargaining failures. Military dynamics matter, but underlying the dynamics are interpretations of events, which in turn are shaped by ideological frameworks. Those frameworks in turn prime elite decision-makers to frame threat and respond in specific ways. The theory also explains outcomes in question better than classic arguments about intergroup hatred, regime type, hardship, or even the demographic nature of the society, none of which hold up empirically and which, as I discussed in chapter 1, do not provide a clear theory of genocide.

In addition, I find that some sources of restraint shape outcomes. I emphasize four. First is the strength of a counternarrative to one that supports violence. Second is the capacity to inflict violence and to dominate target groups. Lacking such capacity, perpetrating authorities are restrained in their ability to carry out their policies. Third are economic incentives. In some cases, elites would face sharply negative economic consequences for the use of mass violence, given the disruption to state revenue sources it would cause.

Finally, external actors can impose costs on decision-makers or successfully interpose themselves so as to reduce threat perception.

Security and Ideology

Across a variety of cases, the most consistent rationale that national leaders cite to justify genocide or mass categorical violence is grave danger. Perpetrating authorities consistently predicate the use of violence as a last-ditch measure to protect a fundamental but jeopardized political project. They claim there exists a major threat to themselves, their core political community, and their national agendas. They in turn plan and promote large-scale violence as a measure for safety, protection, and survival in the face of a significant threat from an implacable enemy. Nearly every leader who defends his or her policy of genocide or mass categorical violence says, in effect, "We were in danger, and we had to defend ourselves from a group that was bent on destroying us."

Consider, for example, the 2013 closing statement of Guatemalan former head of state Rios Montt, who was accused of orchestrating mass killings of Mayan Indians during a counterinsurgency campaign in the early 1980s. Even while proclaiming his innocence, he claimed: "My work as head of state was to take the reins of the country that was on the edge. Guatemala had failed. And forgive me, Your Honor, the guerrillas were at the door of the presidential palace."[5] Whether one considers the Guatemalan case one of genocide or mass categorical violence—there are strong arguments for both—the rationale that Montt provides is strikingly similar to other cases of large-scale, group-selective violence.

Consider the Armenian case. In a remarkable set of comments, the interior minister at the time, Tâlât Pasha, justified the deportation and massacres of Armenians to U.S. Ambassador Henry Morgenthau. In essence, Tâlât claimed that the actions were necessary in the face of defeat and danger. He told the ambassador: "There is only one way in which we can defend ourselves against them in the future, and that is just to deport them."[6] In a later meeting, Tâlât went on to elaborate why he considered the Armenians a dangerous and ultimately unwinnable enemy:

> I have asked you to come today . . . so that I can explain our position on the whole Armenian subject. We base our objections to the Armenians

---

5. "Despite Evidence of Massacres, Former Guatemalan Dictator Proclaims Innocence at Genocide Trial," Democracy Now!, available at www.democracynow.org/2013/5/10/despite_evidence_of_massacres_former_guatemalan, accessed June 20, 2014.

6. Suny 2011: 19.

on three distinct grounds. In the first place, they have enriched themselves at the expense of the Turks. In the second place, they are determined to domineer over us and to establish a separate state. In the third
place, they have openly encouraged our enemies. They have assisted
the Russians in the Caucasus and our failure there is largely explained
by their actions.[7]

The Armenians, in other words, were framed as a present, future, and unwinnable threat—one linked to the real material military threat that the Ottomans faced in World War I.

Consider Rwanda. As in the Armenian case, perpetrators predicated
destroying a target population on the idea of self-survival *and* on the idea that a
group is inherently unwinnable, uncontrollable, and dangerous. The rationale for
genocide thus conformed to a logic of existential preemption—destroy them
to save us.[8] A pamphlet from April 12, 1994—the day that the mass killing
shifted to an exterminatory campaign, as I discuss in chapter 9—remarkably
demonstrates that logic. In it, a high-ranking official in the ruling party decreed
a "call for resistance":

> Rwandans, all citizens of Rwanda, be reassured, protect the Republic
> and Democracy, which you achieved with the 1959 "Popular Revolu-
> tion;" the *Inkotanyi* want to erase your achievements and return you
> to servitude.
>
> You, commune leaders, heads of political parties, you, heads of com-
> munal councils and members of cell committees, be active, organize
> meetings, warn the population, a great danger is at its gates.
>
> Rwandans, put aside your divisions, unite your forces so that you can
> face the grandchildren of UNAR that have decided to submit you once
> again to servitude.[9]

As in Guatemala and the late Ottoman period, the tract's central message is to
mobilize the population because a "great danger is at your gates." In this case,
the tract additionally claims that the enemy wants to "erase your achievements and return you to servitude." The danger is fundamental. The threat
would destroy the Revolution, and even worse, the enemy were said to be the

---

7. Quoted in Suny 2011: 19–20.
8. See Sémelin 2007 for further discussion of the idea of "destroy them to save us."
9. Drawn from Guichaoua 2010, online annexes, Annex 74, available at http://rwandadelaguer-
reaugenocide.univ-paris1.fr/wp-content/uploads/2010/01/Annexe_74.pdf, accessed June 20,
2014. Translation by author.

"grandchildren" of "UNAR"—the Party that had fought against the Revolution. In other words, the current enemy to which the pamphlet makes reference is inherently unwinnable and uncontrollable because they keep returning.

Finally, consider Cambodia. When the Khmer Rouge state orchestrated the mass violence against several categories of citizens ("new" people, Chinese, Vietnamese, Muslims, and Buddhist monks in particular), the party was not technically at war—at least not until 1978 when the war with Vietnam started. But the leaders of the Communist Party of Kampuchea (DPK, a synonym for the Khmer Rouge) came to power through insurgency, and once in power they considered themselves at war with Vietnam and much of the world. Indeed, the Extraordinary Chambers in the Courts of Cambodia, which was tasked with trying high-level perpetrators, concluded that the Khmer Rouge experienced itself as at war with Vietnam. There is "ample evidence," the court concluded, to show that the atrocities were "closely related to the armed conflict between DK [Democratic Kampuchea] and Vietnam."[10]

Indeed, Khmer Rouge official documents are replete with references to unseen enemies that threaten their project to transform Cambodian society.[11] Leaders displayed intense paranoia about enemies from within and without. In a remarkable interview, Nuon Chea, the second in command, explained: "Our project was to transform the nature of society. ... Ours was a clean regime. ... That was our aim, but we failed because the enemy's spies attacked and sabotaged us from the start."[12] In other words, Cambodia faced a grave danger. Pushed by the videographer to explain why the DPK enemies were not just imprisoned, rather than killed, Nuon Chea emphatically said: "The country was in danger of being taken over by Vietnam."[13] Once again, the logic of danger and being "taken over" provide the rationale for killing.

Versions of this "logic" are present in the other major twentieth-century cases of mass categorical violence and genocide that I studied for this book, including Southwest Africa, Nazi Germany, Nigeria, Burundi, Indonesia, the former Yugoslavia, and others. National-level elites claim that they had to take extraordinary measures to save the state, their fundamental political projects, and their primary political communities in the face of an extraordinary danger. Such threat perception constitutes the fundamental

---

10. ECCC 2010: 145, 147.
11. Chandler 1992, 1999; Kiernan 1996.
12. Lemkin and Thet 2009: 13:55–14:10.
13. Lemkin and Thet 2009: 49:22.

rationale that high-level authorities cite to explain their decision-making and policies.

But why do decision-makers experience such intense threat? And why do they locate the threat as a civilian category? Part of the story is material. In each of these cases, save perhaps Cambodia, the state was engaged in a war against a dangerous military opponent, and the state had significant internal vulnerability. In Southwest Africa, the Herero started an uprising against a small band of German colonialists. In the late Ottoman Empire, the Ottomans faced Russia and Britain in World War I. In Nazi Germany, the Germans faced the Soviet Union and eventually the United States (as well as Britain and other Allied states) in World War II. In Cambodia, the Khmer Rouge were a highly inexperienced and internally divided party, and Vietnam had a much stronger military. In Guatemala in the early 1980s, the central state had been facing an insurgency rooted in the indigenous population, and the central state had been facing a series of battlefield setbacks.

In the making of a rationale for mass categorical violence and genocide, these wars are front and center in the strategic calculations of the highest-level, decision-making elites. That is one central reason why armed conflict is so correlated to these outcomes of violence, as the qualitative and quantitative literature show and as my African sample demonstrates (in the next chapter).[14]

Indeed, there are good reasons to see why threat increases and killing becomes easier in war. First, wars are often dangerous. States face armed opponents who wish to use violence to take power or secede. In that way, wars crystallize uncertainty and fear. Second, wars create emergencies in which "normal" rules are often suspended, thereby weakening micro and meso sources of restraint. Third, wars formally legitimize killing: In war, the opposing sides seek to destroy each other. Fourth, wars prompt the involvement of institutions that are designed and have the capacity to inflict violence, in particular militaries and paramilitaries.

But, as I argue above, a unique focus on material dangers in wartime cannot alone explain why some conflicts result in genocide or mass categorical violence and others do not. To understand that process, I argue that we need to examine the long-run influence of ideological constructs about to whom the state belongs and whom the state serves, which in turn shape how elites perceive threat, construct enemies, and develop responses.

---

14. Harff 2003; Krain 1997; Melson 1992; Midlarsky 2005; Naimark 2010; Sémelin 2007; Shaw 2003, 2007; Straus 2007; Ulfelder and Valentino 2008; Valentino et al. 2004; Valentino and Hazlett 2013; Weitz 2003.

I advance the concept of a founding narrative to capture this intuition. Such narratives are foundational in that they define the identity of a primary national political community and the core values and goals of the nation and state. They are narratives in that they craft a story about the state and nation—what it is, where it comes from, what it stands for, what it should achieve, who should captain it, and whom it serves. Over time, founding narratives confer political legitimacy on certain courses of action and illegitimacy on other courses of action. They are akin to a political grammar or a cognitive map that guide decision-making in conscious and unconscious ways. They make, I believe, certain ways of processing political and military developments thinkable and other ways unthinkable.[15]

High-level leaders, especially heads of state, fashion founding narratives at critical junctures. The narratives are not invented from whole cloth. They are derivative of the past and the social conditions in a country; they synthesize historical elements and then current political and cultural ideas. But these narratives are not inevitable. The narratives do not simply reflect ethnic distributions or other material conditions in a country, though again, those conditions are part of the raw materials that shape founding narratives. Rather, leaders make choices about what to emphasize and what not to emphasize; they create new syntheses. In these ways political agency matters to the formation and nurturing of certain founding narratives.

The most typical period in which to fashion a founding narrative is a change in regime. When states emerge from colonialism, monarchy, dictatorship, or even democracy, high-level authorities, especially heads of state, have windows of opportunity to define and recast their mission, the characteristics of the nation, and the goals of the state. Party-level change provides a less powerful but possible window of opportunity. In the sub-Saharan African cases that form the empirical core of this book, the most common critical junctures occur around independence and the end of one-party systems.

Once articulated, to be impactful, the founding narratives must be repeated and stressed by leaders in public events and inculcated through education and public media. To be effective, the narratives also must resonate with core cultural orientations and values in a society. The stories that elites tell about their nation and state must in some ways synthesize and frame cultural elements that people in society accept as part of their cultural universe.[16]

---

15. My claims thus endorse those of other social scientists who emphasize the role of ideology and political culture in shaping outcomes: Berman 1998; Hanson 2003, 2010; Lakoff 2002; Ross 1997; Schatzberg 2001; Swidler 1986; Wedeen 2002.

16. This section borrows from other work that takes ideas seriously: Glassman 2011; Goddard 2010; Hanson 2010; Ross 1993

Founding narratives by definition are not immutable.[17] They found the goals of a regime, but leaders in new regimes often seek to recast the purpose of state and the contours of nation. Old founding narratives, once stressed and inculcated, carry a political residue into the future that in turn may compete with new founding narratives. That competition between founding narratives and counternarratives in turn has implications, which I discuss later.

Some countries and administrations have founding narratives that have little to do with primary political communities. Elites may take and justify power in the name of development or other somewhat bland goals. They do not seek to inculcate a vision of state and nation or to legitimate their rule on the basis of a grander story about what the state stands for or whom it serves.

For explaining the specific outcome of mass categorical violence and genocide, or why such outcomes do not occur, the key dimensions are how founding narratives define (1) the primary national political community; (2) the main goals and principles of the state, that is, the core mission of the political project; and (3) who should rule.

As a general statement, mass categorical violence and genocide are more likely in those places where founding narratives establish a primary identity-based population whom the state serves. Such narratives thereby construct a group or groups within a territorial space that should not be dominant and in whose hands power should not reside. In a crisis, political elites are more likely to take actions that conform to the protection of the group that defines the nation and to construct the excluded group as having interests that are inimical to the primary group. As the military crisis escalates, so do the fears that a victory for the group representing the excluded group will result in devastation for the primary group. In military crises, moreover, state elites are more likely to associate the military enemy with the dangerous social group such that winning the war becomes synonymous with destroying the threatening social group.

By contrast, some founding narratives do not lend themselves to the escalation of violence along group identity lines. Some narratives stress that the nation is fundamentally mixed or non-identity based. Some narratives explicitly value multiethnic cooperation, pluralism, dialogue, and cosmopolitanism. Some narratives are explicitly inclusionary or integrationist. In these situations, faced with a crisis, political elites do not move to protect their own community and attack those whose interests are defined as antagonistic to the primary community. Such ideas would be foreign; they are not thinkable

---

17. Shelef 2010 shows how nationalism evolves.

or legitimate to the decision-makers. In military crises, state elites in turn are more likely to distinguish between armed opponents and their supporters, on the one hand, and social categories of civilians, on the other. They will not define their fight as *against a social category*.

How and why certain founding narratives emerge is a complicated process, as students of nationalism know. I find the process is not simply the function of structure. It is not the case, for example, that hierarchical nationalism emerges when there are two primary ethnic groups. One of the central insights from constructivist accounts of social identity is that there is a range of identities in a society that could become politically relevant. While in Rwanda and Burundi, the political landscape centers around two groups, Hutus and Tutsis, other major cleavages were possible—such as region, class, or clan. In Sudan, while a dominant cleavage emerged between Arab/northern/Muslim and black/southerner/Christian-animist, given the extensive ethnic and linguistic heterogeneity in that country, many other formulations were possible.

By contrast, in places such as Côte d'Ivoire, Mali, and Senegal, where explicit hierarchical nationalisms could have occurred—around, say, religion, region, or ethno-linguistic identities—such cleavages did not occur. They did not occur in part because of history, in particular under colonialism, but I also attribute significant impact to influential leaders, such as Félix Houphouët-Boigny, Alpha Oumar Konaré, and Léopold Senghor.

My claim is not that in places where founding narratives exist the elite is univocal. There is always contestation, always hardliners and moderates, true believers and opportunists, loyalists and opponents, who propose different solutions to crises. Founding narratives can also be strategically emphasized or deemphasized at different times. But all the same, founding narratives are deeply resonant among elites, and as such they can become focal points for generating elite consensus. Such narratives make it likely or unlikely for certain responses to crises to develop and be sustained. In other words, the idea of destroying significant numbers of civilians from another social category to protect one's own becomes much more easily imagined and sustained where nationalist narratives that establish one group as the primary political community preexist a crisis. In the absence of such narratives, or where founding narratives explicitly reject the idea of core identity groups and foster inclusion or pluralism, fashioning a strategy of genocide or mass categorical violence and obtaining a degree of elite consensus around that strategy are much more difficult.

I contend in this chapter that some elite consensus, cooperation from local actors, and popular compliance are necessary to sustain violence across space and time. The material conditions of a crisis affect the capacity to sustain violence coalitions. So do the institutional capabilities of states when states are perpetrators or, less frequently, insurgent organizations when insurgents are perpetrators. But a legitimating framework is central for winning support for extreme policies and developing and sustaining a policy of mass violence against civilians. In that way, founding narratives serve as coordinating mechanism, or center of gravity, around which elites build violence coalitions.

Founding narratives matter in descending order for these three sets of actors. At the senior elite level, one needs a vanguard of actors who drive—by designing and authorizing—the policies of violence. They in turn assess and reassess the violence, opting to maintain, moderate, or intensify violence. Among these elites, the regime's founding narrative is a center of gravity that facilitates consensus that a policy of extreme violence is warranted. Among these elites, one finds the greatest degree of self-conscious ideological commitments. Most are invested in a specific vision of the state, and they are committed to the policies of extreme violence as a necessary measure to safeguard the state and their vision for it. Some are opportunists, but if so they are familiar with the ideological vision. Without these leaders, designing and sustaining genocide and mass categorical violence is very difficult, if not impossible. By elite decision-makers, I should clarify that I mean heads of state, cabinet-level officials, generals and colonels, and other highly influential actors in the policy-making process.

Below the decision-making elite are a range of more meso-level actors—from majors and lieutenants, to governors, mayors, and councilmen, to paramilitary leaders and police captains, to local businessmen and youth leaders. Their participation is necessary to commit and sustain violence at the local level—to identify, sort, and inflict violence on target populations across space and time. Some are ideological warriors or rabid racists. But most are loyalists who cooperate with national authorities for a variety of reasons, including opportunistic ones. For them, a founding narrative that is consistent with policies of mass violence works to sustain cooperation and prevent defection. A founding narrative in that way decreases the need to generate support based on coercion alone. In short, such actors need not be convinced of the righteousness of the cause, but they are likely to have a latent familiarity and acceptance of the legitimating framework. Among these actors, the impact of education and propaganda is most likely greatest—to help develop a general sense that the policies of mass violence are grounded in a broad vision of state and society.

Finally, different cases vary in the degree of ordinary citizen participation, but for all cases the senior elites need popular compliance—they need citizens not to mobilize to resist violence. In the language of genocide studies, national-level and meso-level elites need "bystanders." Authorities rely on coercion to ensure quiescence, and a general climate of fear and uncertainty that typically operates in periods of crisis and conflict decreases the likelihood of some protest movement. But a founding narrative whose general terms are familiar to and resonant with ordinary citizens will increase the likelihood of compliance. The point here is different from arguments about how a culture of hatred and prejudice breeds genocide and mass categorical violence. Rather, in most cases, popular compliance will be more likely if the justifications for public mass violence are resonant with the public.

This set of claims about the importance of ideational frameworks is not tautological. The argument does not hold that founding narratives that create core and secondary categories of citizens are inherently genocidal. Such ideological frameworks predispose some societies to genocide and mass categorical violence. They are a "risk factor" that make such outcomes more likely than when such narratives are not present. But many nongenocide outcomes are consistent with such a founding narrative, including forms of regional autonomy, practices of discrimination and containment, assimilation, accommodation, and simple neglect. Genocide and mass categorical violence become imaginable little by little, after patterns of interaction and other measures have failed. Much must happen—including downstream crisis, especially war—for the perception of acute threat and the development of a policy of violence to develop.

Founding narratives also can be measured well before the onset of genocide and mass categorical violence. Indeed, in the case-study sections of the book, I set out to measure states' founding narratives at independence through the crisis periods. I identify differences in how first presidents defined the core political community and how they articulated the core mission of the state. I trace the development of those narratives into the future, and then I assess whether and how the narrative influenced decision-making and threat construction during the crisis.

Brief Case Illustrations

The dynamic that I have just described plays out in the major cases of genocide and mass categorical violence in the twentieth century that I have studied. In this section, I briefly illustrate some of the central causal claims in relationship to four "out of sample" cases that are not discussed in detail later, in particular the Armenian genocide, the Holocaust, Southwest Africa, and Burundi in 1972. Although I do not show every process just described, I shall demonstrate three points: (1) the existence of a founding narrative that predates a military crisis and that establishes a core political community in whose name the state serves; (2) the entrance into a dangerous military conflict; and (3) the ways in which the founding narrative interacted with the military crisis, leading elites to claim that a non-core identity group posed a grave danger to the state and the core political community and how winning the war became synonymous with destroying the non-core population.

For some three centuries prior to the genocide, the Armenian population generally maintained a distinctive social identity vis-à-vis the Ottoman state. Armenians were Christian and Armenian speakers; the Ottoman leaders were mostly Muslim and Turkish speakers. However, throughout much of the history of Armenian-Ottoman interactions, the equilibrium was accommodation, in this case represented by the "millet" system. The Ottoman Empire was explicitly a multinational, multiethnic empire in which distinct communities were ruled as semiautonomous provinces. Like other minorities in the Empire, the Armenian population was treated as a separate "millet" in which they were allowed to practice their own religion, to maintain their language, to run their own education system, and to establish marriage laws. Under this system, Armenians did not have the same citizenship rights as Turks; Armenians were subject to distinctive taxes; they could not freely bear arms; and they were vulnerable to Turks and other Muslims in courts.[18]

However, the second half of the nineteenth century led to increased confrontation. There were three driving factors: the contraction of the Empire, increasing confrontation with Russia, and growing political restiveness of the Armenian population. The shrinking of the Empire was primarily due to growing nationalist self-determination movements throughout Eastern Europe, particularly in the Balkans. The Ottoman Empire also grew increasingly confrontational with Russia, which had a sizable Armenian population. In the negotiations to end the 1877 Russo-Turkish War, the so-called "Armenian Question" featured prominently. Indeed, following promised reforms, the domestic Armenian population became increasingly demanding of greater political rights. Thus, throughout the second half of the nineteenth century, there is a long process of imperial decline, increased vulnerability, and greater threat from a powerful external state (Russia) coupled with growing demands from a historically subordinate group.

In response, the Sultan of the Ottoman Empire created militias on the border areas with Russia. The Sultan raised taxes against the Armenian population, prompting a revolt in 1894, which prompted Ottoman soldiers

---

18. Balakian 2003: 41.

to be deployed to the region. Together with some militias, they attacked Armenians in the places where they had refused to pay taxes. The massacres triggered further protests, triggering more massacres. By 1896, tens of thousands of Armenian civilians had been killed; some estimates range as high as two hundred thousand.[19] The central change was political protest from a group to which the empire's founding narrative allocated an inferior status— protest that in the general context of decline and confrontation with Russia increased a sense of vulnerability and danger.

But a crucial change occurred at the beginning of the early twentieth century with a new articulation of Turkish nationalism in the form of the Committee on Union and Progress (CUP) or "Young Turk" movement. The CUP was a modernizing nationalist movement whose core vision was pan-Turkic renewal in the face of a depleted and contracting empire. In this new founding narrative, one built on the ideational residue of the past, Muslim Turkish-speaking groups were posited as the core of the revolution and nation, and their core territory was defined as Anatolia, that is, where many Armenians resided.[20] In other words, the founding narrative created a primary, pan-Turkic political community and a vision of creating a renewed Turkic space. In 1908, CUP officers deposed the Sultan in a coup, marking a change in regime.

After the rise of the CUP, there was an initial decline of violence. For Armenians, despite the CUP's nationalism, the Young Turks overthrew the hated Sultan and the party represented modernity. But the new regime quickly entered into a crisis. For one, the empire continued to contract following defeats in the Balkans. Armenian activists protested when they did not receive promised reforms, prompting a new round of persecution. The regime itself was split, and in 1913 divisions between moderate reformers and hardliner nationalists emerged, with the CUP hardliners murdering or forcing out the moderates.

The start of World War I, and in particular the dynamics of the war in late 1914 and 1915, crystallized a connection between an acute sense of military threat and a founding narrative that emphasized a core Turkish, Muslim community. The Ottoman's main enemy in the war was Russia, a state that CUP leader Cemal Pasha described as the Ottomans' "hereditary enemy." The Ottomans were also at war with Britain, which had significant assets in the region. In December 1914, the Ottomans launched a disastrous attack in the mountains of Russia, prompting massive losses. The Ottoman army retreated through Armenian territories, and state leaders blamed Armenian

---

19. Balakian 2003.
20. Mann 2005; Melson 1992.

nationalists for allying with Russia, which in turn launched an offensive against the Ottoman state with some Armenian volunteers. In spring 1915, the British also threatened Ottoman territory, in particular through the British landing at Gallipoli. In short, in early 1915, the state faced significant material military threats, and indeed those threats followed more than a decade of territorial contraction in which the Ottoman Empire lost more than a third of its territory, in particular territories in Eastern Europe, where Christians were said to have committed atrocities against Muslims.

In the face of military defeat and vulnerability, CUP leaders linked the Armenian civilian population to its presumed external allies, in particular the Russian state. Then came a crystallizing moment in late April or early May 1915, following the Armenian uprising in Van, which was a strategic area that the Ottomans feared the Russians would exploit.[21] After the uprising the logic of violence against Armenians shifted from large-scale repression and containment to destruction—the risks in the Ottomans' minds were too great and the Armenians too committed to resistance to chance a strategy of containment. The Ottomans concluded that the Armenians as a group were unwinnable and had to be removed then and for the future.

As indicated earlier in the chapter, CUP leaders claimed that their actions against the Armenian population were a measure of self-protection in the context of war. Tâlât Pasha described the actions as a national "necessity"[22] that were in the "vital" interests of the state,[23] for which the "idea of guaranteeing the existence of Turkey must outweigh every other consideration."[24] Similarly, Minister of War Enver Pasha defended the actions as a military necessity committed by a vulnerable state that nonetheless exercised control. "Our situation is desperate," he said in justifying the actions.[25] In sum, perceptions of threat in the context of World War I and of an Armenian enemy made more powerful through its external alliance provided the rationale for the violence. As Ronald Suny argues, the CUP leaders felt that their state was in a "mortal" danger and that the "survival of their state and 'race' required ... greater homogenization."[26] The violence claimed between 600,000 and 1.5 million civilian lives, according to different estimates.[27] Michael Mann estimates that two-thirds of the Armenian population under

---

21. Akçam 2006: 160; Bloxham 2005: 95.
22. Bloxham 2005: 95.
23. Akçam 2006: 155.
24. Mann 2005: 155.
25. Mann 2005: 155.
26. Suny 2011: 34–35.
27. Balakian 2003; Mann 2005.

Ottoman control perished.[28] In sum, the dynamics of the First World War interacted with the founding narrative of a Turkish primary political community to push elites towards greater escalation.[29]

Turning to the Holocaust, which I discuss in greater detail below, the founding narrative of the Nazi leadership before World War II emphasized racial purity. That narrative claimed danger in the form of a worldwide Jewish conspiracy. Jews were presented as parasites who wanted to destroy Germany, who had stabbed Germany in the back during World War I, and who were in league with the Nazi's archenemies, the Bolsheviks. As World War II began, the empirical threats that the Germans faced increased, and German vulnerability deepened as Germany got bogged down in the Soviet Union and after the United States entered the war. In the Nazi framework, the Jews were linked to their wartime external enemies, and destroying Jews became a way to save the German nation and win the war. To understand how the Nazi leaders made that calculation, it is essential to consider the ideological constructs that shaped their decision-making.

The Holocaust is the subject of a vast amount of historical scholarship, but I rely again on a compelling recent synthesis by Peter Longerich.[30] He presents the steps leading to the "final solution" as an outcome of a complex decision-making process that was coordinated from the center but met with enthusiasm and assisted by innovation on the periphery. For Longerich, a *judenpolitik* or Jewish policy was absolutely central to the philosophy that guided Nazi decision-making in several different dimensions. The Nazis were committed to the utopian dream of creating a "racially homogenous national community"—in my terms, that was its founding narrative.[31]

But only little by little did that founding narrative escalate to genocide. In a first phase, between 1933 and 1939, according to Longerich, the Jews were subject to policies of systematic discrimination, harassment, exclusion, and eventually the Kristallnacht pogrom in 1938. The preparations and onset of war escalated the violence to a new phase of destruction. In a famous speech in January 1939, Hitler ominously warned: "Today I will be a prophet again: if international Jewish financiers within Europe and abroad should succeed once more in plunging the nations into a world war, then the consequence will be not the Bolshevization of the world and therewith a victory of Jewry, but on the contrary, the annihilation of the Jewish race in Europe."[32] Here is

---

28. Mann 2005: 140.
29. Bloxham 2005: 94–96; Mann 2005: 137–39; Suny 2011: 34–35.
30. Longerich 2010.
31. Longerich 2010: 4.
32. Longerich 2010: 124.

a linkage between a war enemy and the internal social category. Indeed, once the war began, the Nazi policies of eradication entered a new phase of massive deportation and resettlement. For Longerich, the war provided the Nazis with the opportunity to reorder territory according to their racial views and to create an "unparalleled break with the humanitarian tradition."[33]

When the war expanded, in particular into the Soviet Union, Nazi policies toward Jews also reached a different phase of escalation. In the summer of 1941, Nazi policies extended to murdering tens of thousands of Jewish men in Soviet territories. This was in turn followed by a new phase in the fall of 1941 in which Nazi agents killed Jewish women and children in the Soviet Union and in Poland by shooting. In Longerich's account, the last phase was the spring of 1942 in which the policy became mass, industrialized extermination of the European Jewish population. These last two phases are examples of genocide; they represent a move from logics of repression to logics of group destruction. The key question is what escalated the policy.

For Longerich, there is a consistency of anti-Jewish policy, in particular from 1939 forward. Although extermination policies were implemented in the war, he argues that the original Nazi intention was for a final solution of the Jewish problem once the war ended. From the perspective of my theory, the Nazis' racist nationalist ideology was extreme, in particular in the way that it demonized an unarmed group as existentially dangerous to the German nation and the Nazi political project. But it is also not incidental that escalation from persecution and repression to destruction took place in the context of an expanding and ultimately quite dangerous war for Germany. In the Nazi worldview, the external enemies of the Soviet Union and the United States were linked to the Jews. Thus, as the war expanded and as the material military threats to the regime increased, so did the intensification of the exterminatory policies. Writes Longerich: "The longer the war lasted, the more completely what was originally a fairly abstract idea of the Jews as the pillars of the Bolshevist regime was replaced by a concept whereby the Jews were endowed with the capacity to present a variety of concrete threats."[34] The Nazi claim of course is one of fiction. Jewish civilians were not a military threat. But what made the fiction real to the Nazis—what allowed a civilian social category to be equated with a wartime enemy—is the ideological framework that animated the Nazi elite, what I am calling its founding narrative.

---

33. Longerich 2010: 423.
34. Longerich 2010: 210.

The same linkage between founding narratives and war applies to other major cases of mass categorical violence, in particular in the former Yugoslavia, Guatemala, and Cambodia. In these cases, founding narratives established core political communities and specific visions of states whose projects were threatened in war. The escalation of violence against civilian categories took place as elites forged a link between the military threats and the vulnerabilities they faced, on the one hand, and the non-core identity groups, on the other.

The same structure that links material military threat to a non-core civilian social category also takes place in minority-led states. In these cases, the founding narrative is counter-majoritarian—the idea that a regime exists as a bulwark against a majority whose own political vision fundamentally threatens the existence of the minority group.

Consider two cases: the annihilation of the Herero in the Germany colony of Southwest Africa in 1904 and mass categorical violence against elite Hutus in Burundi in 1972. In the Southwest Africa case, the German colonial army laid waste to the Herero and Nama communities. But here again the violence was triggered after an armed uprising on the part of the Herero, which the Germans interpreted as posing a grave danger. Why did they?

On the one hand, the German military forces were clearly significantly superior in battlefield terms. However, on the other hand, the Germans experienced several sources of vulnerability. First, the German settlers were badly outnumbered in the colony.[35] Second, the German colonial army was a volunteer one.[36] In terms of the nature of the threat, the Herero were constructed as innately ruthless, atrocity-committing savages.[37] When the Herero attacked and killed German settlers, the German colonial authorities and settlers feared the worst. In the words of one observer, they were "afraid to lose their existence."[38] Yet the Germans believed they were, and they were in fact, militarily superior.[39] As such, the Germans pursued a policy of annihilation to destroy a highly dangerous enemy while they held a window of opportunity to destroy their unwinnable enemy. In the words of a Germany military captain, "The strictest punishment is necessary to atone for the countless cruel murders and as a guarantee for a peaceful future."[40]

---

35. Zimmerer 2008a: 30.
36. Hull 2005: 132.
37. Hull 2005: 11, 135, 155; Steinmetz 2007.
38. Schaller 2008: 311.
39. Hull 2005.
40. Zimmerer 2008b: 44.

The 1972 campaign of violence in Burundi follows a similar logic. In Burundi, at independence, the ruling Tutsi elite watched neighboring Rwanda, where a violent revolution by Hutus was disastrous for Tutsis. The founding narrative of the Tutsi elite in Burundi was thus to protect Tutsis and specifically to protect them from a Rwandan-style revolution. Tutsi elites fended off a series of Hutu-led coup attempts in the 1960s, but in 1972 an armed attack from two parts of the country rattled the Tutsi authorities, who feared a revolution by the majority. Once they quelled the violence, the Tutsi-dominated authorities set out to eliminate systematically educated and elite Hutus, ultimately killing as many as two hundred thousand Hutu civilians.[41] Here the sense of threat was animated by the demographic imbalance of an 85 percent Hutu population and Tutsi elite perceptions of what Hutus wanted—a revolution, Rwanda-style.

The founding narrative shaped how Tutsi military and political elites responded to an ultimately weak insurgency. State leaders set out to protect their core group from a population judged to be unwinnable. Indeed, this is how Tutsi state leaders saw the violence. A leading scholar of the period, René Lemarchand, writes that for the perpetrators "extreme threat required extreme violence."[42] Lemarchand and a coauthor similarly claim that the violence was "prophylactic" with the aim of "decapitat[ing] not only the rebellion but Hutu society as well, and in the process lay the foundation of an entirely new order."[43]

Diplomats in Burundi describe in cables how both the foreign minister and the president separately justified the violence as protection against the "genocide" that the Hutu rebels intended. The former claimed they were in the "most difficult period in Burundi's history."[44] Here is how a U.S. diplomat based in Bujumbura summed up the first two weeks of the violence:

As we approach the second week of the insurrection, I would like to submit my third personal evaluation of this situation:

A) The Hutu-led coup involving Mulelist elements was well planned. It came closer to success than the preceding 3 Hutu lead coup attempts. Moderate Tutsis like the Bishop of Bujumbura and the rector of the University are convinced there was a coup designed to eliminate Tutsi control.

---

41. Lemarchand 2008.
42. Lemarchand 2008.
43. Lemarchand and Martin 1974: 18.
44. Hoyt 1972, cables "Burundi Foreign Ministry Briefs Ambassadors in Insurrection," May 2, 1972, and "Ambassador Meets with President," May 5, 1972.

B) This has energized the age-old Tutsi fear of extermination and, as the Bishop of Bujumbura said, "we almost had another Rwanda," (i.e. elimination of Tutsis from the country by killing or exile).

C) The Tutsi killed April 29–30 weekend were revenged with Hutus killed. Figures are not yet sure. The numbers on both sides are in the thousands. One thing is clear: hatred on both sides has been intensified. Efforts by moderates on both sides of the past years to promote a greater dialogue have been negated.[45]

Again, we can see how the main rationale for genocide is grave danger. The diplomat spoke of the fear of Tutsi elimination—of fear of "another Rwanda" and "an age-old Tutsi fear of extermination." which animated the threat perception and ultimately the violence. In these cables, we also see how war and threat overrode restraint, how the fears "negated" moderate voices.

Sources of Restraint

Factors of restraint can temper the dynamics that I have just described. Based on my study, I conclude that four sources of restraint are most consequential: counternarratives, capacity, economic incentives, and external conflict-mediation forces.

To be successful, those elites who foment genocide and mass categorical violence must consolidate at least a narrow coalition of influential, senior-level figures. A founding narrative that is consistent with the threat construction and policies of mass violence serves to coalesce influential elites around a policy of extreme public violence. But the reverse is also true. A strong counter-argument rooted in a counternarrative about the purpose of the state and the nature of political community can interrupt or at least render much more difficult the formation of an elite coalition committed to genocide.

There are multiple potential sources of a counternarrative to genocide and mass categorical violence. For example, in a highly religious society, senior religious figures can promulgate a vision of peace or neighborliness that would run counter to escalation. More probable is the implantation of a political alternative to the one being promoted by violence escalators. That political alternative might hold that the political community is fundamentally multiethnic or is steeped in values of cooperation and economic development, not violence and zero-sum antagonisms between groups. To be

---

45. Hoyt 1972, cable "Bujumbura 05/11, 0472," May 11, 1972.

successful, those who promulgate a counternarrative must have the capacity to wield influence. They must be able to survive, for example, and to persuade, either privately or publicly. Here regime type comes into play. Highly authoritarian states that punish defection with death or permanent detention make the capacity to present a counternarrative highly unlikely.

The second potential source of restraint is capacity. An odd paradox is that mass categorical violence and genocide improbably yoke territorial domination and capacity with high threat perception. Mass categorical violence and genocide are major, usually far-flung operations. They require the capacity to identify, separate, and destroy a population within a particular territory. Perpetrating authorities must be capable of maintaining sufficient control across large spaces, usually over periods of time measured by months but sometimes weeks, and they must be able to maintain alliances with local actors where either a central state is weak or a state is decentralized. To identify, sort, and destroy target populations, perpetrating authorities must also have access to those populations. The general intuition is straightforward, but empirically some organizations lack such access.

Capacity is an aggregate concept, and I disaggregate it into four dimensions: coordination, identification, control, and infliction. Coordination—that is, the management of different agencies, institutions, and populations—is essential for the sustained infliction of targeted violence across time and space. Leaders need the compliance and participation of actors throughout a hierarchy and across different institutions. Militaries and usually paramilitaries are generally essential actors in the overall process of inflicting violence. Their actions must be coordinated. Target civilian populations must also be found. They must be detected, separated, and attacked. That process generally requires the support of local-level police, civilian administrations, and civilian populations who know and interact with the targeted group. Thus, in addition to horizontal coordination across national agencies, there must also be vertical coordination between national and local actors. In that sense, borrowing from Stathis Kalyvas, mass categorical violence and genocide entail a "joint production" of national and local actors.[46]

Identification is the ability to label, find, and separate target populations. The outcomes in question are categorical, discriminate violence; they are forms of group-selective violence. There is a need for information about who is who and about where the targeted group resides or is hiding. Perpetrators need to know how to distinguish populations and where to find

---

46. Kalyvas 2003.

them. There is frequently a need to move, transfer, and collect populations. There is a need to separate target populations from non-target populations. To be sure, all of these actions can be done in a low-tech fashion, as was the case in Rwanda. But the capacity to identify populations in these ways is still a necessary component, and not every state will wield such capacity.

Control is another dimension. Perpetrating authorities must have some degree of control over the movement of target populations. By extension, perpetrating authorities must have access to target populations. Victims naturally wish to escape violence, and many in fact do. Victims also wish to resist on occasion. But for there to be successful mass categorical violence and genocide, that is for target populations to be killed, poisoned, sterilized, removed, and so forth in large numbers, then perpetrating authorities must have the capacity to limit the ability of victims to escape, evade, and resist. In effect, in these cases, perpetrating authorities exercise territorial domination over the target populations.

Finally, infliction is the idea that the capacity to destroy must exist. Perpetrating authorities must have the ability to inflict violence across space and time. To an extent, the capacity to inflict is dependent on the ability to coordinate institutions and alliances as well as to identify and control target populations. But there must be some independent weaponry, such as guns, rockets, bombs, grenades, firepower, knives, machetes, and poison. The infliction of such violence in genocide is systematic, which requires some capacity for organization. Institutionally, organizations with the specialization, training, and equipment to inflict violence are necessary for the large-scale commission of such violence. In particular, militaries, paramilitaries, and police are most often the central actors in the commission of large-scale, sustained violence. Even if the causes of much death is through starvation and disease because of forced displacement, perpetrating authorities must have the ability to terrorize populations and restrict the flow of food and medicine.

Third, economic incentives may serve to restrain escalation, and here I emphasize the principal sources of revenue matter. More specifically, some economies are more violence-sensitive than others. In those locations, the costs of escalation of mass violence are greater. High costs of escalation in turn create incentives to moderate or avoid the use of such violence. By contrast, in other locations, the principal sources of revenue may be less sensitive to the escalation of violence, and the distribution of wealth may be more bimodal, as for example divided between a wealthy elite and a large, unorganized poor. In those cases, the costs of escalation are lower, and therefore the ex-ante incentives to moderate or avoid the use of large-scale violence against civilians are weak.

In general, violence-insensitive economies are those whose vital sources of revenue would not be substantially negatively affected by extensive violence against civilians. For example, economies that are highly dependent on oil exports or other forms of production that are geographically isolated can still function effectively even if large parts of a country are engulfed in highly disruptive violence. Such economies might be considered enclave economies, and they function nearly as well in times of war as in times of peace. In these cases, neither production nor the markets depend on stability or absence of violence in the country. In that sense, the sources of revenue are violence-insensitive, and the costs of escalation are comparatively low because the creation of rents and the creation of revenue for states are not substantially harmed by the disruption that large-scale organization and execution of violence entail.

By contrast are economies where the principal sources of production and revenue require stability, predictability, and labor. In these cases, the costs of escalation are high because the sources of rent and revenue depend on the absence of large-scale sustained disruption. Widespread smallholder agricultural production, manufacturing, and tourism are examples of violence-sensitive economies. Widespread agriculture requires stability over time. Fields must be tilled, seeds planted, crops harvested, and goods must be prepared for market. For such a system of agriculture, when many people are displaced or die, growers have difficulty letting products mature, obtaining inputs, maintaining labor, and getting goods to market. In general, manufacturing similarly requires time, inputs, skilled labor, and the capacity for trade (import and export) in most locations. Even if the manufacturing consists of simple textile production, the factory would require several different products consistently over time (chiefly cotton), semi-skilled labor to create the textiles, and finally the capacity to export these goods to market. Large-scale violence will disrupt the flow of labor and goods in a substantial war. Tourism is also highly sensitive; as soon as images of murder reach international audiences, tourism will dry up. The presence of a violence-sensitive economy creates incentives for political elites to moderate conflict. They are aware that state receipts depend on such exports; they also face lateral pressure from business owners and associations to minimize disruption. These incentives to limit or avoid violence function as restraints.

Finally, international and regional actors can impose costs on decision-makers through sanctions, travel bans, threats of prosecution, and other measures. They also can interpose peacekeeping forces that, if successful, can reduce threat perception or physically contain perpetrators so that they lack access to victim populations. I return to the role of international and regional actors in the book's conclusion, and I illustrate the dynamics of restraint empirically in chapters 5, 6, and 7.

Consolidating Genocide and Mass Categorical Violence

While the theory explains how decision-makers come to select strategies of genocide and mass categorical violence, the theory has not yet illustrated how that process unfolds. Yet in the same way that different factors of escalation must be present for the outcome to occur, there are also necessary steps in the process of committing mass violence. If these steps fail, then it will be very difficult, if not impossible, for a sustained policy of categorical mass violence to succeed. From a prevention perspective, understanding the steps in a process of consolidating a policy of genocide in turn provides opportunities to interrupt the process. The analysis in this section thus has theoretical and practical import.

I find there are three critical observable consolidation nodes during the process of violence: elite consensus, subnational (local) alliances, and popular compliance. Leaders typically invest in all three of these dimensions in order to execute mass violence.

A policy of genocide or mass categorical violence against civilians is extreme; as sustained targeted violence, it is also difficult to achieve. Such violence typically requires central coordination, organization, official resources, and the participation of multiple agencies, in particular those institutions that are specialized in the use of violence. In order for the policy to be successful, there must be a plurality of voices within an administrative framework that support the policy. That plurality of voices is what I call an elite consensus, one that is made.

The process of building an elite consensus around a policy of mass categorical violence and genocide will have different degrees of difficulty. In particular, in states where there exists a strong counternarrative among senior influential elites, elite consolidation is difficult. But beyond that, in most states there will be a plurality of voices about optimal strategy. In most states, professional soldiers and officers will almost certainly have reservations about deploying organized violence in a systematic, deliberate fashion against noncombatants. Even in locations with pronounced ethnic nationalism, the idea of a policy of extirpating a group from a territory will face important reservations within a regime. All of this suggests that there will be internal opposition within a regime that must be overcome for a policy of genocide or mass categorical violence to be consolidated.

The process of elite consensus-making has observational implications. In any given regime, one should observe those leaders committed to policies of escalating violence actively persuading, marginalizing, and eliminating key elite actors who control militaries, police, political parties, civilian administrations or who have influential national-level positions within a national government or legislature but who remain unconvinced. In many case studies of specific cases, analysts often reference divisions between "hardliners" or "loyalists" in a regime and "moderates" or "liberals."[47] In the process of escalation that leads to sustained, mass violence, one observes the former persuading or more often marginalizing and eliminating the latter.

Consider the major cases of the twentieth century. In the late Ottoman Empire, that process of elite consolidation occurred after the CUP came to power. In particular in 1913, after the military defeat in the Balkans, there was a key purging of moderates within the CUP. That paved the way for the government's involvement in the 1915 massacres and deportations, a process that ultimately included the War Ministry, the CUP Central Committee, the Interior Ministry, the Department of Public Security and Dispatches, and other top-level government agencies.[48] In Germany, the Nazi consolidation of power in the 1930s was accompanied by the removal of political opponents and the Nazification of all the major national institutions in the country. Rwanda was politically divided right until the eve of the genocide. But after the assassination of the president on April 6, the hardliners removed or killed moderates and opponents in government as their first order of business; within the army, more moderate voices were marginalized. In Serbia, Slobodan Milošević consistently outmaneuvered and sidelined the Communist officials loyal to the idea of multiethnic Yugoslavia in the late 1980s and early 1990s. In short, in each case, one can observe a process of consolidating an elite, "hardliner" consensus by removing moderates and other would-be opponents to a policy of genocide or mass categorical violence. That in turn has implications for observing indicators of escalation. By contrast, as long as opponents and plural voices are allowed to remain in a governing or military authority structure, the practice of mass categorical violence is more difficult to implement because such violence is a centrally coordinated, multi-agency, extreme policy.

The second crucial process of consolidation is that of an alliance between senior officials and a range of regional and local actors. These include governors, mayors, local police officers, organized youth or militias based

---

47. Mann 2005; Straus 2006b.
48. Akçam 2006: 161; Mann 2005: 156.

outside the capital city, and even some local civil society institutions, such as religious organizations. In general, the genocide literature has not sufficiently theorized the role of subnational actors in the process of genocide.[49] Yet we know from the recent literature on political violence and civil war that subnational dynamics are essential parts of the process,[50] and, as I argued in chapter 1, large-scale, group-selective violence typically requires sustained alliance between national and subnational actors.

But as with the process of forging an elite consensus, the adhesion of regional and local actors to a policy of extensive violence against civilians should not be assumed. In some states, there may be very little vertical penetration by the central state into regional or rural areas. In some states, the elites who control the center may come from a different ethnic, religious, or political background from the elites who control local or regional areas. In some locations, local actors may have strong affective, commercial, or mutually beneficial bonds with the targeted group, and they may not wish to adhere to a policy of violence against them. To be sure, national actors may deploy the coercive apparatus of a state to overwhelm or destroy local opposition where it exists; they may politicize local institutions in order to engineer a coalition between local and national actors; they may use other means. But the ability to engineer that coalition should not be taken for granted.

Consider again major cases. In the Armenian case, regional and local civilian administrations (in particular governors and prefects), political party networks, paramilitaries (Special Organization), local militias (çetes), and local gendarmes were all key actors in the process of identifying, separating, killing, and removing Armenians civilians (and Greeks).[51] In addition, where there was active, open opposition and defiance—such subnational actors were removed or killed.[52] In the Nazi case, there were layers of local participation within Germany but also especially in the occupied areas of Western and Eastern Europe where Nazi officials relied on non-German authorities and institutions to sort, identify, kill, or deport massive numbers of Jews between 1941 and 1945. In Rwanda, local and regional administrators were essential to the process of identifying and attacking Tutsi civilians. During and also before the genocide, national authorities invested in winning the support of compliant officials, local political party leaders, social elites, and local organized youth. Even so, as of April 1994, there were also swaths of territory in

---

49. Finkel and Straus 2012.
50. Kalyvas 2003.
51. Akçam 2006: 159–66; Gerlach 2010: 96.
52. Akçam 2006: 166–67; Bloxham 2005: 93; Mann 2005: 159.

the southern parts of the country where local and even regional administrators opposed the violence, in particular in Butare and Gitarama prefectures. But national authorities and committed *génocidaires* sidelined, killed, or overwhelmed the opponents.[53]

In short, the adhesion of subnational actors is an essential dimension of the process of committing genocide, but that adhesion should not be taken for granted. A key observable implication is that national elites will have to forge alliances with local actors, a process that could include the removal or marginalization of those who actively oppose a policy of violence. By consequence, where national authorities are unable to forge such alliances—where they do not have the coercive capacity, the legitimacy, the political support, or the ability to manage an opportunistic alliance—they will be unable to sustain a policy of extreme categorical violence.

The third critical dimension for consolidating a policy of mass categorical violence concerns the public realm, by which I mean the citizenry of the state in which leaders promote mass violence. For a policy to succeed, the critical threshold that must be achieved for leaders is popular compliance. It is often the case that ordinary citizens who are not active in political parties, in government, or even in key institutions, such as churches or mosques, play important roles in the process of genocide and mass categorical violence. They often participate in the process of marginalization, identification, and even the infliction of violence. But the quantity of ordinary citizens who actively and enthusiastically participate in the process of violence need not be very high. That is, contra Daniel Goldhagen, one does not need chomping-at-the-bit hatred to burn in a large majority of the population to succeed in genocide.[54] The key alliance is between national and subnational institutions. The vanguard institutions and individuals leading the violence are generally in military, police, and paramilitary organizations and in the subnational bureaucracy; they coordinate and lead the violence. At the level of the general citizenry, there will always be individuals who seize the moment to join the vanguard for a variety of reasons, from opportunism, material interests, fear, hatred, personal grievances, or perhaps even sadism. But given that some level of popular participation is inevitable in an overall operation of violence, such participation is not the central hurdle for authorities committing to mass violence.

Rather, the argument here is that the success of the overall operation of genocide and mass categorical violence depends on popular compliance,

---

53. Straus 2010.
54. Goldhagen 1996, 2009.

meaning that authorities must be successful in thwarting, preventing, or displacing active opposition to the process of group destruction. The population that is not a part of the targeted group needs to acquiesce. They must remain passively supportive or indifferent. Should they not, the authorities would face a substantial hurdle given that mass categorical violence is sustained over time and through space and given that within any regime there will be opposition to the policy. Without popular compliance, the authorities would face a significant obstacle that would limit their ability to extend the categorical violence across a large territory and over time.

Through the years, the literature on genocide has produced several compelling theories of micro-level motivation to explain why ordinary individuals (or even national and local officials) would participate or acquiesce to extreme violence. The theories encompass arguments about intergroup animus (hatred, prejudice, jealousy, distrust, or propaganda-induced animosity),[55] frustration-aggression (scapegoating a target group given frustration in the dominant group's life),[56] obedience (individuals comply because they find the authorities who promote the policy legitimate),[57] opportunism (individuals jump on a bandwagon or use the process of violence to profit materially), careerism (individuals comply in order to protect or advance their employment), group dynamics (individuals do in groups what they would not do normally for a variety of reasons, including peer pressure),[58] horizontal or vertical coercion (individuals participate because they are pressured to do so),[59] fear (individuals commit violence to protect themselves and their family in times of war and uncertainty),[60] personal connections (individuals participate because of social networks),[61] cultural frameworks of meaning,[62] and psychological predisposition (sadism, for instance).[63] Sometimes all that need be the case is indifference, in particular if the detention and killing centers are removed from plain sight, as in Nazi Germany.[64] The framework presented here is ultimately agnostic about which motivations prevail.

---

55. See, for instance, Chrétien 1995; Dumitru and Johnson 2011; Fein 1979; Goldhagen 2009.
56. See, for instance, Staub 1989.
57. See, for instance, Milgram 1966, Waller 2002.
58. See, for instance, Browning 1992.
59. See, for instance, Straus 2006b.
60. See, for instance, McDoom 2009; Straus 2006b.
61. See, for instance, Fujii 2009.
62. Hinton 2005; Taylor 1999.
63. For a review of theories of participation, see Finkel and Straus 2012; Humphreys and Weinstein 2006; Rule 1988; Waller 2002.
64. Bankier 1992.

This is the case for several reasons. First, mass categorical violence and genocide are large-scale processes that, if one considers a range of participation from killing to identifying to looting to passive acquiescence, incorporates a large number of individuals on the perpetrator side of the violence. That large number means that there will be multiple motivations present across the process. Second, individuals are complex. They may have multiple motivations at the same time; they may want to pursue their career, be afraid in a war, and have a general sense of dislike or distrust for the targeted group at the same time. Third, mass categorical violence and genocide are sustained over time, and individuals' motivations may change over time. Indeed, in interviews that I conducted with Rwandan perpetrators, many of those Rwandans who killed civilians said that their personal demeanor changed after they took another's life. In short, motivations are complex and heterogeneous, a point that scholars who have studied particular cases in depth often reach,[65] and popular participation and compliance may be achieved through a wide variety of means, including preexisting hatred, propaganda, frustration, legitimacy and obedience, group dynamics, coercion, fear, promise of rewards, and so forth.

Even though popular participation and compliance may be achieved through multiple ways, the fact of its achievement should not be assumed. Killing for non-specialists is physically and emotionally difficult.[66] But more generally, achieving popular compliance is a process of removing often significant moral restraints. At the micro level, there will be a great deal of interaction between those in the targeted group and the rest of the population. There will likely be professional interactions, business connections, family relations, and other ways in which lives are entangled. Individuals will have ethical restraints that would prevent them, all other things being equal, from accepting the slaughter or physical removal of their neighbors. To be sure, groups can live side by side and have distrustful, animus-filled relations. But even in the cases of large-scale killing genocide where such interactions are studied—for example, in prewar Germany, Rwanda, and Bosnia—there are substantial preexisting ties among the would-be perpetrator and victim communities. Rwanda and Bosnia were particularly integrated.[67] Nationalism, political and economic tumult, and war all weaken those ties. Coercion and political legitimacy can also weaken those ties. But in each case, what was essential was that the populations did not oppose the extent of

---

65. Browning 1992; Straus 2006b.
66. Collins 2008.
67. Bringa 1995; de Lame 2005.

the destruction. Where they did, for example in Germany with regard to the euthanasia program, the perpetrating authorities reacted by changing or relocating the program or, in the case of Rwanda in southern areas of the country, by using force against noncompliers.

In short, the main point is that achieving popular compliance is essential to the overall process of consolidating a policy of mass categorical violence and genocide. Where such compliance fails, the perpetrating authorities would have a hard time sustaining policies of mass categorical violence across time and space.

Case Illustration: Romania

Anti-Jewish violence in the early 1940s in Romania is an "out-of-sample" case that illustrates the process of violence. Empirically, the discussion here relies on an account by Vladimir Solonari. In terms of the causal model presented earlier in the chapter, Solonari traces the development of a strong national ideal on the right in Romania to purify the nation of non-Romanians. During the war, the Romanian dictator Ion Antonescu allied with Nazi Germany and against the Soviet Union. When the war with the Soviet Union started in June 1941, Romanians participated in the organization and massacre of Jews, a pattern that would be repeated until the Romanians feared that the Nazis would lose the war. In tracing the evolution of anti-Jewish violence by Romanians, three factors are key: (1) the commitment to ethnic nationalism as the ideal for which the nation should strive; (2) a formal alliance with Nazi Germany for which *judenpolitik* was central; and (3) the onset of war with a powerful state (the Soviet Union), which was conceptually linked in the minds of the Romanian right-wing political establishment with the internal Jewish population. Indeed, the war was presented as an urgent, apocalyptic war of races and ideology for the survival and health of the Romanian nation. Consistent with the story I have told so far, leaders of massacres used the perceived threat on occasion to provoke violence by claiming that "Jews and Bolsheviks are coming to kill Christians."[68] Added to these factors was the military capacity of the state as well as its ability to ally with local actors, which is the focus here.

Solonari's account provides some remarkable analysis of the consolidation and organization of large-scale violence. The general model that he presents—in particular for Bessarabia—is that of Romanian military, gendarmes, and paramilitary death squad forces as the central organizers, followed by the

---

68. Solonari 2010: 150–51, 195.

participation of local leaders and opportunists, all with the tacit compliance of the Romanian population. In the military and paramilitary, colonels and other senior-level elites were essential for the direction of the policy. Where they were not as forthcoming with purification orders, as in Bukovina, the extirpation of Jews was much less successful. Death squads carried out much of the violence, and local actors were critical to identifying, gathering up, and bringing Jews to the massacres.[69]

The role of the local population was especially critical in rural areas where small teams of gendarmes were sent to identify and escort Jews. Solonari provides an example on July 8 where the Army general headquarters issued an order to remove "Judaic element[s]" from Bessarabia. The local army officers replied that they had established teams of "reliable elements" of patriotic Romanians who spread the "idea of collective defense against the Judaic menace." In some places, gendarmes would appoint mayors who in turn would organize local helpers to find and escort Jews. Solonari argues that in the face of such violence, local Christians were generally indifferent, and their indifference allowed the policy to succeed. Where they protested, the violence would have been much more restrained or, in some cases, where opposition did manifest, Jews would be released or spared.[70]

In short, elite consensus, local participation, and popular compliance or indifference were necessary for the consolidation of a policy of mass categorical violence. I have examined Romania during World War II. But a similar type of process is observable in every major twentieth-century case.

Understanding consolidation is central to considering strategies of resistance. The flip side of my claim that such processes of consolidation are necessary for the execution of violence is the idea that if such processes can be interrupted—if national elite moderates can be bolstered, if meso-level actors do not sign on, and if citizens can resist—then the restraint on committing mass categorical violence and genocide increases. The same is true for capacity. This, I shall argue in the final chapter, is an important consideration for thinking about how external and internal actors can respond to the escalation of violence.

---

69. Solonari 2010: 170, 176.
70. Solonari 2010: 193, 194, 197, 199.

PART II

Empirics

CHAPTER 4

Mass Categorical Violence and Genocide in Sub-Saharan Africa, 1960–2008

Why focus on independent sub-Saharan Africa, as I do in the empirical sections of the book? One reason is to move away from the unit heterogeneity that marks existing comparative research on genocide. A standard study includes some mix of the Armenian genocide, the Holocaust, Cambodia under the Khmer Rouge, Rwanda in 1994, and Bosnia in the early 1990s. Such a different system/similar-outcome design makes sense at an early stage of theory development. But the cases are quite different on many dimensions, which limits the analysis.

Sub-Saharan Africa is, of course, not homogeneous. Nonetheless, African states share a great deal. They are relatively new states. With the exception of Ethiopia, colonialism shaped the borders, economies, political systems, and social identities of African states.[1] Contemporary African states are mostly low- to middle-income countries; most economies center on the export of commodities; many depend on donor support. African states also tend to influence one another. In the late 1960s, 1970s, and 1980s, most states had one-party systems; by the late 1990s, the new norm was multiparty electoral competition. These features do not make African states identical—there is a great deal of diversity between and within states, as this and other studies

---

1. Mamdani 1996; Young 1994.

make clear[2]—but the features establish some baseline historical and structural similarities.

The other reason is variation. Many African states have experienced political repression, in particular in the one-party era, but the extent of repression has varied. Most states have experienced a war since independence—about two-thirds have[3]—but many have not, and there is variation over time. Many states have experienced a mass killing episode (about 38%),[4] but again not all armed conflicts have led to such violence. So political violence is common—making the region a good candidate for the "possibility principle" I outlined in the introduction—but there exists a lot of variation in when and where mass violence against civilians occurs.

My point is *not* that sub-Saharan Africa is uniquely prone to violence. Sub-Saharan African states have had fewer numbers of wars per country than Asia, and the wars in Africa are less long on average than those in Asia and the Middle East. Africa is also not the leader in cases of mass killing and genocide.[5] Thus, neither in relative terms nor in absolute terms is sub-Saharan Africa the regional leader in terms of incidents of mass killing.

This chapter examines broad patterns in large-scale violence. The first section maps out different forms of political violence that occur in sub-Saharan Africa. The second compiles and recodes all cases of large-scale killing of civilians in sub-Saharan Africa from 1960 to 2008. From there, the chapter explores whether and how the theories advanced in the first section of the book fit the empirical patterns. I do so first through simple correlational analysis followed by brief case studies. I look at those cases that are "on the regression line" (that the theory predicts would result in mass categorical violence) and those that are "off the regression line" (that do not have the predictive factors but that still produce mass violence).

The main finding is that the onset of mass violence strongly correlates with armed threats. The most common scenario is a group-selective counterinsurgency campaign in a region where rebels, or a social identity group seen to be supporting rebels, are concentrated. In these cases, states establish a

---

2. Boone 2003; Young 2012.

3. Straus 2012c.

4. Below I define such incidents as organized, systematic mass violence against civilians that claims at least 1,000 annualized deaths. If one relaxes that definition and includes any countries mentioned in the three main existing datasets on mass killing and genocide (Bellamy 2011; Harff 2003; Ulfelder and Valentino 2008), only one additional county (Malawi) would be added to table 4.2, making it 40% of African states with an incident of mass killing.

5. Straus 2012c using data from the Ulfelder and Valentino dataset, compares numbers of mass killing cases per region.

collective category as the enemy, and they target civilians associated with that category as a way of defeating insurgents. These empirics lend strong support to strategic arguments that emphasize security as an organizing principle for genocide and mass categorical violence. The chapter also shows that states are the main perpetrators of mass categorical violence, which is consistent with the propositions I advanced in chapter 1, which hold that territorial domination and the capacity to manage multi-agency violence coalitions are integral to the execution of mass violence.

The broad-gauge analysis lacks the detail needed to evaluate some of the book's other variables, namely founding narratives and restraint. But the main patterns that emerge are that of a weakly consolidated, that is, vulnerable, state responding to an insurgency rooted in a distrusted category of people. In almost all cases, the distrusted category is a population whose social identity differs from those that control the state. It is unclear from the evidence in this chapter whether and how "founding narratives" play into the decision-making process, but the evidence is at least consistent with the claim that prior notions of whom the state represents in turn shape the logic and practices of violence.

Variations in Violence

There are many kinds of violence. This book focuses on public, usually political violence against civilians, as opposed to private or criminal violence or as opposed to wars between armies. Studying Africa, I have identified five principal logics of violence, which I hypothesize affect scale, target choice, and perpetrator. Table 4.1 organizes the expectations articulated in this section.

The first logic is "normative," by which I mean the violence is principally about enforcing a prevalent norm. One example is "necklacing" whereby

Table 4.1 Types of violence in sub-Saharan Africa

LOGIC	MAIN PERPETRATORS	DURATION	TARGET SELECTION	SCALE (LOCATION)	SCALE (MAGNITUDE)
Normative	Civilian	Short	Varies	Local	Low
Protective	Civilian	Cyclical	Varies	Local	Low
Predatory	State and non-state armed groups	Varies	Varies	Local or regional	Varies
Repressive	State or other sovereign	Sustained	Varies	National or regional	Varies
Destructive	State or other sovereign	Sustained	Group	National or regional	High

passersby identify, capture, and often lynch an alleged thief. Another example is rioting in relation to the alleged violation of a particular norm. A concrete case took place in 1995 when Zambians in the town of Livingstone accused Asian business owners of trafficking in body parts and attacked Asians for a couple days. Attacking suspected witches is another example. This form of violence is often expressive, motivated by hatred or resentment, and fueled by economic interest, but the logic of violence is to punish the violation of a perceived norm. The main perpetrators are civilians, the duration short, and the scale local. On balance, I expect the causal structure of normative violence to be very different from the causal structure of mass categorical violence because the threat is individualized.

The second logic is "property protective," by which I mean that armed actors use violence to protect their property from infraction or predation. In sub-Saharan Africa, the most common form is violence over access to vital resources, such as water, land, pasturage, and fishing zones. Among these clashes, the most common is between sedentary farmers and animal-husbanding pastoralists, who move their animals with the seasons in search of pasturage and water, in particular in the areas of the continent where those two livelihood systems frequently interact (such as across the Sahelian band). A frequent pattern is low-level crop or herd destruction, which, if not properly managed, leads local actors to organize to protect themselves and their property or to inflict reprisals, which in turn leads to similar acts from members of the attacked communities.

Natural resource conflicts have complex origins; they are not simply "resource conflicts." Politics, policy, and institutions such as land tenure matter greatly.[6] But the main logic is using violence to protect property. The main perpetrators are civilians (sometimes organized into self-defense groups), the violence short-lived, and the scale local. The violence is sometimes cyclical, in the sense of a series of attacks and counter-attacks, but given the local origins of threat and the resulting organizing logic of the violence, the scale should be systematically smaller than cases of mass categorical violence. Even if local groups experience an existential threat, without a national coordinating authority and a sense of threat to the broader political project, I expect the scale of violence to be limited.

A third logic is "predatory," in which the purpose of violence is to obtain resources illegally. Nonstate armed actors operating in the

---

6. Benjaminsen and Ba 2009; Turner 2004.

context of state collapse or on the peripheries of weak states often commit such violence. State security forces also commit predatory violence, as they seek bribes. The logic of such violence is similar to property protective violence, and I thus expect such violence to be local, episodic, and small-scale.

The fourth main logic is "repressive" and coercive: to counter and control opposition, armed or not, to existing power holders. In these cases, the main perpetrators are sovereign authorities in nominal control of a territory—generally states but not always.[7] Where authorities face what they consider intolerable opposition to their rule, they will employ violence to manage and control that opposition. Sometimes the opposition itself is nonviolent, for example opposition political parties or pro-democracy or pro-rights demonstrators. Sometimes the opposition is violent, in the form of rebellion. I expect threat perception and therefore levels of repressive violence to increase with an armed opposition. For example, repressive violence to control nascent opposition in the one-party era in sub-Saharan Africa should be systematically less extensive than violence to counter armed opposition in that era. In the multiparty era, repressive violence to defeat an electoral threat should be systematically less extensive than violence to defeat an insurgency. Overall, repressive violence should be more extensive than normative, property-protective, and predatory violence because the stakes are national and the threat deeper.

A key question is why authorities would target civilians or civilians of a certain category and on a large scale. A strategic argument would hold that perpetrators calculate that such violence will increase their chance of victory. Such violence could coerce the armed opposition into moderating their demands (saying, in effect, if you proceed, your people will face the consequences); prevent defection and new recruits for rebels (if you defect, your families will be killed); or weaken the rebellion because the insurgents rely on the civilian population for material and logistical support. An ideational argument would emphasize that how authorities frame the fight, in terms of who is fighting whom and for what purpose, will also affect target selection. If authorities frame the fight as between population categories, they would be more likely to distrust the loyalty of the opposing population and in general not make distinctions between the armed members of that group and unarmed members. Authorities would consider the enemy a social category.

---

7. Mamphilly 2011; Weinstein 2007.

The last logic of violence is group destructive. With repressive violence, as outlined in chapter 1, if the threat subsides (through military gains, through the opposition's change of tactics, or through population relocation), so too should the violence. For perpetrators, the enemy can be contained and controlled. With group destructive violence, perpetrators also define the enemy as a social category but in this case conclude that the enemy is unwinnable, uncontrollable, and inherently dangerous. The violence is designed, then, to destroy a present and anticipated threat; the violence is future-oriented with a goal of destroying a regenerated threat. Such calculations are more likely when threat is greater, so such violence should take place in the context of armed opposition. Moreover, the conflict will be framed as a fight between social categories. But there should be something additional that leads perpetrators to conclude that the enemy category is unwinnable, uncontrollable, and inherently dangerous.

One empirical implication is that large-scale repressive violence against population groups—what I call mass categorical violence—will co-vary with group destructive violence or genocide. They both should occur in environments of high threat to authorities and where the authorities define the fight as between social categories. Moreover, if the decision to commit genocide flows from a decision-making process, then the decision will probably occur after perpetrators conclude that group-repressive violence is no longer possible or effective.

Indeed, this chapter shows how empirically intertwined these logics are. In several cases, perpetrators exhibit a logic of repressive and group-destructive violence *at different periods* or *different perpetrators* exhibit different logics in the same period. Darfur is a case of the latter. National actors were fighting a counterinsurgency campaign through collective violence against the presumed supporters of the Darfur insurgents. That led to a policy of mass categorical violence, but the state also armed and empowered local militias. Those local actors sought to change the demography of the region and pushed the counterinsurgent campaign into something conforming more to a group-destructive logic. Biafra is an example of the former. The Biafran war primarily followed a logic of mass repressive violence against a group in which the objective was to defeat the rebellion. But at times and in locations, as discussed below, the anti-Ibo violence followed more of a group-destructive logic. In sum, there may be various logics of violence within the same case. While mass categorical violence and genocide are theoretically and in principle empirically distinctive, the evidence from this chapter suggests there may not be "pure" cases of one or the other. Cases are changing, dynamic, and complex.

Patterns of Mass Violence in Sub-Saharan Africa, 1960–2008

To compile a snapshot of African cases of large-scale violence against civilians, I synthesized three main publicly available and well-respected datasets on mass killing and genocide.[8] There are problems of comparability between these. Each dataset measures the outcome differently.[9] The authors agree on the start/end dates and levels of violence for only six cases in three countries.[10] Alex Bellamy's dataset has nearly three times as many sub-Saharan Africa cases (N = 37) as that of Barbara Harff (N = 14). The datasets also lump together quite heterogeneous cases, from those such as Malawi with comparatively low-level political repression (with a low-end death toll of 6,000 deaths for the period)[11] with cases such as Rwanda in 1994 or Sudan's second North-South civil war (with estimates of 500,000 to 1 million deaths). Given these discrepancies, some caution is in order.

To improve comparability, I take some additional steps. First, I provide a per annum threshold. In measuring the extent of violence, it is misleading to compare cases of 15 or 30 years to cases of one or two years. So I take an average of the high-end and low-end estimate of the number of civilians killed and then divide that sum by the number of years in which the atrocities occurred. This creates a problem of flattening out variation over time within a single case, but it has the advantage of annualizing the estimates.[12] Second, I limit the cases to those of 1,000 deaths per year. Any numerical threshold is arbitrary, and countries vary considerably in the baseline population sizes.

---

8. Bellamy 2011; Harff 2003; Ulfelder and Valentino 2008.

9. Jay Ulfelder and Ben Valentino detail cases of mass killing in which at least 1,000 civilian deaths took place and were committed by state forces. Alex Bellamy measures cases at 5,000 civilian deaths (by state and/or non-state actors). Barbara Harff counts cases of state-led group-selective violence (politicide, genocide, or both) but has no numerical threshold.

10. Rwanda 1963–1964; Rwanda 1994; Sudan first and second North-South wars; and Uganda under Idi Amin and the second term of Milton Obote.

11. Bellamy estimates 6,000–17,000 deaths from 1964 to 1994. But this estimate is too high. A comprehensive human rights report on Malawi under Banda portrays a "totalitarian" regime that engaged in widespread repression, dissent of speech, and other political and religious restrictions. But the report does not make reference to policies of widespread mass killings. The largest case listed is of 20 protestors killed, and even though there is talk of hundreds of possible Jehovah's witnesses being murdered, only five have been documented. The report lists other selective assassinations (Carver 1991: 46–53). In my discussion below, I do not consider the Malawi case to reach the threshold of mass violence, hence the case is not on my list.

12. Liberia is a good example of the problems of annualizing. The Liberian Truth Commission (2009) estimated that 250,000 people died between 1989 and 2003 in the country. Yet detailed analyses performed by three researchers showed clear peaks of violence in 1990, 1994, and 2003. In annualizing cases, I do not deny such variation over time, but I accept that weakness.

Table 4.2 Large-scale violence against civilians in sub-Saharan Africa, 1960–2008

COUNTRY	YEARS	ESTIMATE OF DEATHS	ANNUAL AVERAGE OF DEATHS	GROUP-SELECTIVE?	ARMED CONFLICT	ACTORS[i]	DATA SETS	NOTES
Angola	1975–2002	60–375K (UV)	7.8K	No	Yes	State; rebels	UV, BH	
Burundi	1972	200K (RL)	200K	Yes	Yes	State	All	
Burundi	1988	15K (RL)	15K	Yes	Yes	State	All	
Burundi	1993–2005	150–200K (UV)	13.5K	Yes	Yes	State; rebels; civilians	All	
Chad	1982–1990	37.8K	4.2K	Yes	Yes	State	AB, UV	
Congo-B	1964–1965	2–5K (UV)	1.8K	Yes	No	State	AB, UV	
Congo-B	1997–1999	5–11K (AB)	2.7K	Yes	Yes	State; rebels	AB, UV	
DRC	1964–1965	1–50K (AB, BH)	12.8K	Yes	Yes	State	AB, BH	
DRC	1977–1979	3–8K (AB, BH)	1.8	Yes	No	State	AB, BH	
DRC	1993–1996	8–10K	2.3K	Yes	No	Civilians	AB, UV	
DRC	1996–1997	200–230K[ii]	115K	Yes	Yes	State; rebels	ALL	
DRC	1998–2003	900K (HSR 2010)	150K	No	Yes	State; rebels; civilians	All	Deaths mainly by indirect causes
Equatorial Guinea	1969–1979	5–20K	1.1K	No	No	State	AB, UV	
Ethiopia	1961–1990	250K (AW)	8.3K	Yes	Yes	State		
Ethiopia	1977–1978	5–20K	6.8K	Yes	Yes	State	All	Red Terror
Ethiopia	1977–1985	40–60K (UV)	5.6K	Yes	Yes	State	AB, UV	Ogaden
Ethiopia	1983–1985	215–317K	90.3K	Yes	Yes	State	AB, UV	Tigray

Country	Years					Perpetrator		Notes
Guinea	1960–1984	3–50K	1K	No	No	State	AB, UV	
Liberia	1989–2003	250K (RLTRC)	16.7K	No	Yes	State, rebels, civilians	AB, UV	Peaks in 1990, 1994, 2003
Mozambique	1975–1992	100–200K (AB)	8.3K	No	Yes	Rebels	AB	
Nigeria	1966	7–30K	18.5K	Yes	No	Civilians; state	AB	North
Nigeria	1967–1970	1.0–1.5m	312.5K	Yes	Yes	State	AB, UV	Biafra
Rwanda	1963–1964	5–10K	3.75K	Yes	Yes	State	All	
Rwanda	1994	527.5K	527.5K	Yes	Yes	State, rebels[iii]	All	
Sierra Leone	1991–2002	50–100K (AB)	6.25K	No	Yes	State, rebels	AB, UV	
Somalia	1988–1989	50–60K	27.5K	Yes	Yes	State	All	
Sudan	1955–1972	400–600K (UV)	27.8K	Yes	Yes	State	All	1st N-S War
Sudan	1983–2005	1.5–2.0m(UV)	76.1K	Yes	Yes	State	All	2nd N-S War
Sudan	2003–2006	200–300K	62.5K	Yes	Yes	State	AB, UV	Darfur
Tanzania	1964	3–10K	6.5K	Yes	No	State	AB, UV	Zanzibar
Uganda	1971–1979	50–300K	19.4K	No	Yes	State	All	
Uganda	1981–1986	200–300K (UV)	41.7K	Yes	Yes	State	All	
Zimbabwe	1983–1985	3.8–6.0K	1.6K	Yes	No	State	UV	

Sources: AB = Alex Bellamy 2011; UV = Ulfelder and Valentino 2008; BF = Barbara Harff 2003; HSR = Human Security Report 2010; RL = René Lemarchand 1994; AW = Africa Watch 1991; RCTRC = Republic of Liberia Truth and Reconciliation Commission 2009, p. 61. Estimates without references are justified in this or later chapters.

[i] "State" refers to national and provincial level governmental authorities; "rebels" refers to armed non-state actors fighting the state; "civilians" refers to armed civilians acting not on behalf of the state or rebels.

[ii] See the discussion later in the chapter for these estimates. The "state" here is Rwanda who were the lead inflictor of violence in the DRC in this period.

[iii] The death toll estimates come from Des Forges 1999, in which the author calculates 500,000 mainly Tutsi civilians killed at the hands of state and pro-government forces and 25,000 to 30,000 mainly Hutu civilians killed at the hands of the rebel forces.

But the chosen threshold captures the concept of "mass" violence. Third, I improve the estimates through additional research on the cases. Fourth, I code whether the mass violence took place during an armed conflict, whether the violence was group-selective, and who the main perpetrators of civilian killing were.[13]

All told, the new dataset totals 34 cases. Of those, 25 cases have annualized averages of 5,000 deaths or more; 17 have annualized averages of 10,000 deaths or more; 8 have annualized averages of 50,000 deaths or more; and 5 have annualized deaths of 100,000 deaths or more.[14]

Using a standard armed conflict dataset from the PRIO/Armed Conflict database, the relationship between armed threats to states and the use of large-scale violence is strong: 24 of the 34 cases occurred during an armed conflict. But in fact, the relationship is even stronger. Careful study of the cases shows that even more occurred during an armed conflict, even if the UCDP/PRIO dataset did not code them that way. For example, in Burundi in 1972 state-led mass categorical violence occurred after the onset of an insurgency and a failed coup. In Rwanda in 1963, state-led mass categorical violence occurred after an invasion and insurgency. Both cases should be coded as occurring during an armed conflict even though the UCDP/PRIO dataset does not code them that way. In Burundi in 1988, armed Hutu agitators destroyed bridges and killed some Tutsi civilians, prompting large-scale reprisal violence by the state's armed forces. Indeed, the government claimed that it was fighting armed opponents who had support from outside the country.[15] Similarly, the 1980s Gukurahundi campaign in Zimbabwe took place in response to armed opposition, military sabotage, and assassination attempts. The Zanzibar violence against Arabs took place during an armed struggle for power.[16] The Equatorial Guinea and Guinea cases took place after a coup attempt or military invasion. In sum, qualitative analysis shows an even stronger association between the onset of mass violence against civilians and an armed attempt at regime change than the existing quantitative data suggest.

Equally revealing are the different *levels* of violence. Those cases that occur outside formal armed conflict (as defined by UCDP/PRIO with the

---

13. The armed conflict data come from the UCDP/PRIO dataset with armed conflict measured at the threshold of twenty-five battle deaths. Other coding is based on my reading of the cases.

14. Each of these thresholds (or others) could be cutoff points for defining "mass violence," but for now I include all cases at or above an annualized rate of 1,000 deaths.

15. Amnesty International 1992: 1–2; Harden 1988; Lewis 1988; see also Lemarchand 1994.

16. While the Bellamy dataset puts the high-end estimate at 17,000 deaths, the most consistent number in the literature is 5,000 killed (e.g., Lofchie 1970: 965). Jonathan Glassman (2011: 374) finds that most estimates range between 3,000 and 10,000 killed, which is the range adopted here.

two exceptions specified above of Burundi 1972 and Rwanda 1963), such as Guinea, Equatorial Guinea, Zanzibar, Zimbabwe, and Congo-Brazzaville, have systematically lower violence levels than those that occur during an armed conflict. Every case with an annualized rate of 10,000 civilian deaths or more took place during an armed conflict.

Furthermore, the state was the lead perpetrator in 24 cases. In another eight, the state was one of several actors initiating and committing atrocities against civilians. In only one case—Mozambique—were insurgents the lead perpetrator, and in only one other case were civilian actors committing atrocities not on behalf of or with support from state or rebel actors. That case is the violence against ethnic Tutsis in eastern Democratic Republic of Congo from 1993–1996. But even there, starting in 1994 the rump Hutu-led Rwandan state aided those killings.

Experts can quibble with one or two of the coding decisions, and certainly the numbers killed have to be taken with a note of caution given the poor quality of the data, but on the whole these correlations conform to the theoretical expectations I have advanced. First, most large-scale violence episodes occur in the context of armed conflict; those that do not typically occur in the context of violent challenges to the state, such as a coup attempt. Moreover, violence against civilians in wartime is of a significantly greater magnitude than violence outside warfare. Those relationships are consistent with the theoretical claims that material threat is a key driver of genocide and mass categorical violence and that the dominant logic of genocide and mass categorical violence is to contain or defeat armed challenges. There are no cases in this dataset where the primary logic of violence, as defined above, is normative, property-protective, or predatory. Second, the analysis shows that state actors are lead perpetrators in nearly every case. That provides face validity to the theoretical claim that organizational capacity and a coordinating sovereign authority are central to the commission of sustained, extensive violence against civilians.

Cases "On the Regression Line"

While indicative, the static correlational analysis only provides limited insight into the causal mechanisms. I turn now to broad-gauge qualitative analysis of cases that are "on the regression line."[17] These are among

---

17. The cases that I select in this section are those that have the highest levels of annualized violence, as reported in table 4.2, and that are not discussed in other parts of the book. The one exception is the case of Chad where I did fieldwork in the early stages of research for this book (which therefore provided me with a richer empirical understanding of the dynamics of the violence than I had for other "on the regression line" cases).

the highest-violence cases; they all take place during armed conflict; and, with one exception, they entail group-selective violence. Taken together, the cases clearly show that perpetrators kill civilians in large numbers in response to armed threats. Even for those cases that are "off the regression line," that is, cases that occur outside of armed conflict, security concerns drive the use of large-scale violence against civilians.

Nigeria: The Biafran Civil War

The Biafran civil war was a watershed event in African politics, one that divided diplomatic loyalties across the continent and led to a massive human-itarian crisis that was a precursor to similar crises in the 1990s and 2000s. In the end, more than a million civilians, primarily Ibo, lost their lives in the war due to the deliberate civilian-targeting policies of the Nigerian federal state. In addition, in the year before the war broke out, primarily Muslim local actors with army and some official support massacred thousands of Chris-tian Ibos in the north. Both cases are examples of large-scale, group-selective violence (and are included in table 4.2). The logic of violence is ultimately difficult to tease out. In the war, at different times, federal forces seemed to be pursuing a policy to destroy the Ibo population of Biafra. But at other times, and certainly in the second half of the war, the policy was primarily repressive, with greater survival rates for Ibo civilians and an eventual policy of integration once the Biafran secessionists ceded their cause.

Nigerian political history is complicated enough that I cannot do jus-tice to it in a few paragraphs. But in sum, colonial practice and institutions favored political mobilization along three ethnic-regional blocs in Nigeria: Hausa in the north, Yoruba in the center-west, and Ibo in the east.[18] At independence, Nigeria had a fragile equilibrium among the leaders of the three population blocs, one in which northerners had a marginal advantage. However, in January 1966 an Ibo-led coup took place and claimed the lives of several major northern politicians. That coup triggered generalized fear, especially in the north, of Ibo domination of independent Nigeria.[19] In May, there were anti-Ibo riots in several northern towns. In July, there was a counter-coup, led by northern officers, in which the initial intention was for the north to secede.[20] Ibo officers were massacred; in the east, the Ibo military leader, Lieutenant-Colonel C. Odumegwu Ojukwu, did not recognize the

---

18. Coleman 1958; Diamond 1988; Ekwe-Ekwe 1990; Horowitz 1985.
19. Dudley 1973; Panter-Brick 1970.
20. Forsyth 1969: 57.

new coup leaders, leading to a de facto divided state. In September and early October there was another round of murderous anti-Ibo riots, more violent than the May ones and in which army and police in the north participated.[21] The total sum of the 1966 anti-Ibo massacres is unclear. Some put the number at about 7,500,[22] others at 30,000.[23]

What followed the July coup and the massacres in the north were a set of complex negotiations over how Nigeria should be governed. The net effect was to further alienate the eastern region from the rest of the country.[24] On May 30, 1967, Ojukwu declared independence of the state of Biafra, and the Biafran war began in July. The federal government, which wanted to control Nigeria's oil in the east, was initially confident that the war would end quickly. But the Biafrans won the early battles. In August, they captured towns and gained control over the major oil reserves throughout the eastern and mid-western regions. By some accounts, they were in a position to march on the federal capital, Lagos, which one close observer described as being on the verge of collapse.[25] But soon the tide turned, in part because of a key defection among the Biafrans and because of international support for federal authorities. The war lasted into 1970 when the Biafran political and military leaders finally surrendered.

During the war, federal forces targeted eastern civilians in various ways. The key actions were (1) starvation, (2) aerial bombing of civilian targets, and (3) group-selective anti-Ibo massacres in some, but not all, areas that federal forces occupied or reoccupied. The Biafrans lost control of food-producing regions in 1967 and 1968, and the federal government imposed a blockade and refused relief supplies to the region. That triggered major starvation and malnutrition. At its height in August and September 1968, an estimated 5,000 civilians died daily, mostly children.[26]

Most observers conclude starvation was a deliberate government policy, given that the federal authorities in 1967 and 1968 refused relief entry or shot down relief planes.[27] Nigerian officials' statements lend support to this account. Said one: "Starvation is a legitimate weapon of war, and we have every intention of using it against the rebels."[28] Said another: "All is fair in

21. Forsyth 1969: 75.
22. Dudley 1973.
23. Cruise O'Brien 1967; Forsyth 1969: 81.
24. Forsyth 1969.
25. Forsyth 1969: 116–17.
26. Cruise O'Brien 1969; for higher numbers, see Jacobs 1987: 5.
27. Ekwe-Ekwe 1990: 87; Forsythe 1969: 175–82; Waugh and Cronjé 1969: 14.
28. Forsyth 1969: 217.

war, and starvation is one of the weapons of war.... I do not see why we should feed our enemy fat in order to fight us later."[29] In addition to the policy of starvation, federal forces also bombed civilian targets—hospitals, churches on Sundays, and residential neighborhoods. "Most of the air war was conducted against the civilian population," concluded one observer.[30] Finally, in areas that federal forces captured or recaptured, Ibos were systematically hunted down and killed in several locations.[31] Violence was particularly pronounced in Calabar, Benin City, and Asaba in August 1967, where men were often selected and killed.[32] At the same time, there were locations where federal forces did not kill Ibos.[33]

In terms of scale, the violence was massive. Most estimates place the cumulative civilian death toll between 1 million and 1.5 million.[34] Those numbers and the group-selective nature of the violence prompt some to label the case a genocide.[35] One insightful observer, who visited Biafra in late 1967, called the violence a "war waged in a genocidal spirit."[36] Some official statements suggest such a logic. One police officer claimed in November 1967, for example, that Ibos had to be "reduced considerably in number."[37]

However, all told, the violence seems to follow a more coercive, repressive logic as opposed to a group-destructive one: Starvation was designed to change the behavior of the rebels and their supporters as well as to weaken the rebellion itself. The violence was to "subdue the rebellion," as officials then claimed,[38] and to "crush the Ojukwu rebellion," as the federal leader General Gowon proclaimed.[39] In late 1968 and thereafter, as federal authorities gained the upper hand, the violence diminished; when the Biafrans finally lost, they were not massacred. These patterns are consistent with mass categorical violence, rather than genocide. In areas that federal forces recaptured in late 1968 and thereafter, there is international observer evidence of rehabilitation of the civilian population in terms of food, shelter, and health care.[40] Indeed, those observers argued that the genocide label was unwarranted, given their findings.[41]

---

29. Waugh and Cronjé 1969: 14; see also Ekwe-Ekwe 1990: 99.
30. Forsyth 1969: 216.
31. Forsyth 1969: 210–12.
32. Cruise O'Brien 1967, 1969; Okocha 1994: 24, 53–55.
33. Cruise O'Brien 1969; Okocha 1994: 1980: 27–28.
34. Cruise O'Brien 1969; Waugh and Cronjé 1969.
35. Forsyth 1969; Waugh and Cronjé 1969.
36. Cruise O'Brien 1967.
37. Cruise O'Brien 1967.
38. Cruise O'Brien 1967.
39. Okocha 1994: 23.
40. OAU 1968; Observer Team 1968.
41. OAU 1968: 28; Observer Team 1968: 6.

In short, this was a case that arguably had some elements of genocide, especially in the first half of the war, but on balance seems not to have been designed to destroy the Ibo population in areas under Nigerian territorial control.

Why did federal authorities target Ibo civilians in order to defeat the rebellion? Even this short synopsis suggests several reasons. First, the anti-civilian violence peaked in periods when federal forces were on the defensive or at least not yet in control of the war. In response to this military vulnerability, federal forces sought to impose very heavy costs on the rebels and their support base in order to gain the military upper hand. Second, the insurgents were strongly identified with a social category, Ibos; federal authorities framed the enemy and threat as an Ibo one. That is consistent with the then-dominant ideological narratives about post-independence politics: The fight for power was defined as a fight between Ibos, Hausas, and Yorubas. Federal authorities framed the fight in terms of population categories. Third, the rebels enjoyed wide support from Ibos in the east, and they recruited broadly from within the Ibo population. These patterns reinforced the federal idea that the fight was against Ibos and easterners. By punishing civilians, federal authorities calculated that they could weaken the rebellion. Finally, the federal government lacked control over the eastern areas; they therefore had incentives to target collectively rather than selectively. In this case, the concentration of Ibos in the east allowed the authorities to be group-selective while lacking local knowledge of who was who.

Rwandan Refugees in the Democratic Republic of Congo/Zaire

The second case I examine took place in Zaire, now (and hereafter in this book) the Democratic Republic of Congo (DRC), between 1996 and 1997. The main perpetrators were Rwandan forces associated with the Rwandan Patriotic Army (RPA), which invaded the DRC in October and spearheaded a Congolese rebellion. The RPA was the military wing of the Tutsi-dominated Rwanda Patriotic Front (RPF), the political movement that controlled the Rwandan state at the time. The main civilian targets were Rwandan Hutu refugees. While the numbers killed are contested, several serious estimates posit between 200,000 and 233,000 refugee deaths.[42] While details about what happened remain unclear, several high-quality studies are now available.[43] My discussion draws on these studies, as well as an extensive,

---

42. Emizet 2000: 179; Reyntjens 2011: 136.
43. Emizet 2000; Prunier 2009; Reyntjens 2010; Stearns 2011; Umutesi 2004.

nearly 500-page "mapping" report of human rights violations in Zaire/
DRC; that report was issued by the United Nations High Commissioner for
Human Rights.[44] I also draw on personal observations in the region, having
covered the war as a journalist.

The 1994 Rwandan genocide was committed during a civil war that
government forces lost. Following that loss, former government officials,
army personnel, militias, and more than two million refugees fled to neighboring Tanzania and the DRC. The latter received the overwhelming bulk
of militarized units and government officials as well as some 1.2 to 1.5 million refugees. Faced with a potentially enormous humanitarian catastrophe,
international humanitarian workers established a string of refugee camps
quite close to the Rwandan border. While some camps held ordinary refugees, several became militarized training and recruiting grounds for the
ex-regime to reinvade Rwanda. The new RPF-led government in Rwanda
warned that if the international community refused to right the problem, it
would do it on its own. In October 1996, frustrated with lack of change,
the RPA orchestrated an invasion under the banner of a Congolese-led
insurgency called the Alliance des forces démocratiques pour la libération du
Zaire-Congo (AFDL). RPA/AFDL forces first broke up the refugee camps
along Rwanda's border, allowing some 600,000 refugees to reenter Rwanda,
and then they succeeded in a remarkable and unlikely gambit to overthrow
the regime of Mobutu Sese Seko some 1,400 miles from Rwanda.

Along the way, the RPA/AFDL forces engaged in frequent, systematic
killing operations of Rwandan Hutu refugees who had fled westward after
the first camps were destroyed. The UN report concludes, "It was not a
question of people killed unintentionally in the course of combat, but people
targeted primarily by AFDL/APR/FAB forces and executed in their hundreds, often with edged weapons. The majority of the victims were children,
women, elderly people and the sick, who posed no threat to the attacking
forces."[45] The report details over and over again the group-selective, systematic, and widespread nature of the targeting, concluding, "The majority of
the incidents reported indicate that the Hutus were targeted as such, with
no discrimination between them."[46] The final report argues that the crimes
"may" constitute genocide but that the issue of intent remains unclear.[47]

---

44. UNHCHR 2010.
45. UNHCHR 2010: para. 513.
46. UNHCHR 2010: paras. 514, 515, 517.
47. UNHCHR 2010: paras. 518–21.

The question of genocide is difficult to parse. In the early stages of the war—in October and November—RPA/AFDL forces carried out indiscriminate shelling of camps as well as directed killings of refugees in certain locations. But on balance they allowed the overwhelming majority of Rwandan Hutu refugees to repatriate eastward. Starting in mid-December, however, there appeared to be a change in strategy, as the armed forces pursued fleeing armed Hutu groups and refugees further westward. In places such as Shabundu, Tingi-Tingi, Walikale, Kisesa, Biaro, Mbandaka, and Wendji there is evidence of a policy to murder Rwandan Hutu refugees—men, women, children, elderly, and the sick—wherever they were found. The UN report documents an "execution system" in which refugees were called to a meeting or herded into areas where they were subsequently massacred, often while RPA/AFDL forces deliberately kept out humanitarian workers and journalists.[48] The killings were systematic, under established chains of command and in the presence of high-ranking officers.[49] As in Nigeria during the Biafran war, the logic of violence is mixed. In the early stages, the violence in Congo was not group-destructive. But starting in December, the strategy became to eliminate the Hutu refugee population in the DRC—either through forced repatriation or through massacre.[50]

What drove the logic of violence? Here again, the violence took place during an armed conflict, actually two—RPA/AFDL forces were fighting the Congolese state and the rump ex-Rwandan one. However, in contrast to Nigeria but like Burundi in 1972, the perpetrating authorities had the military upper hand. The refugees and the rump Rwandan military forces were on the run starting in November 1996. If the book's arguments are correct, though, the perpetrators must have experienced some vulnerability and, given the group-destructive pattern of violence from December forward, concluded that the target population was unwinnable and dangerous.

Indeed, this was the case. Composed primarily of returning Tutsis, the RPF-led government represented a minority of 10 to 15 percent of the population. As such, they faced long-term demographic vulnerability, in particular if Hutu exiles could regroup and rearm in a neighboring state. Moreover, many of the Hutu political and military leaders in the DRC were implicated in the 1994 genocide; thus, RPF officials had good reason to fear the intentions of their adversaries. Both the RPF and the ex-genocidal leaders framed the fight as between population categories, as a long-term struggle between Hutu forces

48. UNHCHR 2010: para. 233; see also paras. 237, 238, 243, 245, 250, and 278, among others.
49. Stearns and Borello 2011: 155.
50. In 1997, some 240,000 refugees were repatriated. Emizet 2000: 178.

and Tutsi ones. RPF leaders also likely concluded that the Hutu population that fled westward was uncontrollable and unwinnable. From the RPF perspective, those who did not repatriate in October and November were either guilty of genocide or committed to overthrowing the new government. These elements—an armed threat, an ethnic framing of the war, and the RPA's military capacity—conform to the theoretical expectations I have advanced so far.

Ethiopia under Mengistu and Meles

Ethiopia has among the highest concentrations of armed conflicts and mass violence episodes in independent Africa. I focus on arguably the most violent period of post-1960 Ethiopian political history, between 1974 and 1991, when Ethiopia was under the authority of the Communist Party (the "Derg"), led by Mengistu Haile Mariam. After being ousted in 1991, Mengistu was subsequently tried by Ethiopian authorities in absentia and convicted of genocide. There are several different component parts to the political violence under Mengistu, chiefly (1) the "Red Terror" violence against rival political factions; (2) the counterinsurgency campaign in northern Ethiopia, primarily in Tigray; (3) the counterinsurgency campaigns in Eritrea, which began under Mengistu's predecessor, Emperor Haile Selassie; and (4) counterinsurgency campaigns in the south and southeast, principally in the Ogaden and Oromo regions, which spanned the rule of Haile Selassie, Mengistu, and Mengistu's successor, Meles Zenawi. For space reasons, I focus here on the cases associated with the worst violence under Mengistu—the Red Terror and counterinsurgency in Tigray—and I also make reference to counterinsurgency violence in the Ogaden, given the existence of a particularly detailed report on that region.

With a base of support among Amharas, the army, and the urban left, the Marxist-Leninist-inspired Derg took power through a military coup in 1974. Repressive violence against political opponents soon followed.[51] The peak violence years were in 1977 and 1978—the "Red Terror"—as the Derg leadership sought to eliminate rival Marxist factions, principally the Ethiopia People's Revolutionary Party (EPRP). The EPRP launched a campaign of targeted assassinations in 1976, including attempts on Mengistu's life.[52] That triggered a state-led campaign of violence first against the EPRP, its leadership and cadres, and other "enemies of the revolution."[53] The violence then extended in several waves to target other perceived dissidents, including those from another

---

51. Chege 1979; Tareke 2009.
52. Africa Watch 1991: 102.
53. Africa Watch 1991: 102.

Marxist faction, university students, and merchants.[54] The violence was initially concentrated in Addis Ababa but extended to other urban areas throughout the country. Reliable estimates put the death toll at between 5,000 and 20,000.[55]

The Red Terror also took place against the backdrop of four wars on the periphery. One was in the north, against the Tigray People's Liberation Front (TPLF), which formed in 1974. Another was against Eritrean separatists, who had been fighting since the 1960s. The others were in the Ogaden and Oromo regions, in the southern and southeastern parts of the country. Of those, the violence in Tigray and in Eritrea claimed the most lives.

The TPLF insurgency started small. In a first phase, the rebels sought to consolidate a foothold in the region, in particular while the Mengistu regime focused on the mostly urban political threat.[56] But the rebels grew in force. By 1980, they had established widespread territorial control in Tigray, and by 1982, they also controlled parts of Wollo.[57] The rebels' growing influence and territorial control, combined with the successful repression of the urban political threat, prompted the regime to focus more squarely on the Tigrayan insurgents. From 1980 onward, the state strategy became "counter-population warfare"—weakening the rebels by attacking their support base.[58] When drought hit in the early 1980s, the regime further restricted the population's mobility and access to food.[59] The dynamics of violence in northern Ethiopia thus resemble those in Biafra—state violence against a civilian category, including using food as a weapon, to defeat a growing insurgency with strong local support and regional territorial control.

In Ethiopia, as in Biafra, the violence entailed a series of military offensives, including ground and air military attacks, frequently against civilian populations and villages where food surpluses existed; starting in 1980, there were also nearly daily aerial bombing campaigns, often against market areas; and restrictions on trade in grain and population movement.[60] One air force commander, referring to similar attacks in the same period in Eritrea, said the policy was to "bomb everything that moves."[61] Coupled with a drop in rainfall in the mid-1980s, the counterinsurgency campaign set the stage for a massive famine in the region that claimed as many as 500,000 lives. Assessing the effects of

---

54. Africa Watch 1991; Halliday and Molyneux 1981.
55. Africa Watch 1991: 110; Keller 1988: 200.
56. Young 1997.
57. Africa Watch 1991: 139–40.
58. Africa Watch 1991: 141.
59. De Waal 1997: 117.
60. Africa Watch 1991: 141–54.
61. Africa Watch 1991: 123.

the government counterinsurgency campaign, Alex de Waal estimates between 225,000 and 317,000 of the half-million deaths were due to such government actions.[62] The bulk of those deaths took place between 1983 and 1985.

Another arena of large-scale violence against civilians in Ethiopia was the Ogaden region, which is predominantly populated by ethnic Somalis. Ethiopian Somalis distinguish themselves from the highlanders who controlled the central state, from Haile Selassie to Meles Zenawi. Somali insurgents fought both the Haile Selassie and Mengistu regimes, and in both cases Ethiopian government forces employed brutal counterinsurgency tactics, including population reloca-tion. Under Meles, who took power in 1991, the government initially sought to accommodate the demands of the Somali insurgents, but over time the main strategy was to divide the political leadership and isolate those leaders who wanted greater independence for the region. But the insurgencies persisted.

Detailed human rights reporting exists for the year 2007, when insurgents launched a series of attacks against local officials and military installations.[63] The most significant was an attack on a Chinese-run oil installation. From that point forward, the government engaged in more intensive counterinsur-gency offensive, which included recruiting local militias, public executions, destroying the means of survival (notably livestock), and forcible displace-ment into villages where the population could be monitored and controlled. Those who refused to move were sometimes killed. Human Rights Watch calls the violence "collective punishment" of Ogadeni for perceived support of the Ogadeni National Liberation Front (ONLF).[64]

To summarize, in each of the three examples, the Ethiopian state responded to armed threats through mass, usually group-selective violence. The urban violence in the Red Terror had a more limited extent, in part because the threat was more containable and did not involve a direct insurgency. That violence strongly resembles the political repression in Equatorial Guinea, Guinea, and even Chad, as described below. To respond to insurgencies, the state employed counterinsurgency strategies that consistently targeted and harmed civilians. In those cases, successive governments typically employed group-selective violence. They targeted distrusted populations, thought both to support the rebels and to be hostile to the center, as a way of weakening the rebels and scaring the civilians into submission. The tactics included forced displacement, destroying food stocks and shelter, indiscriminate bombing, and selective assassinations.

---

62. Africa Watch 1991: 176.
63. Human Rights Watch 2008b.
64. Human Rights Watch 2008b: 34.

By and large, the logic seems to be repressive. That is, there is not an apparent effort to destroy the long-term regenerative capacity of the targeted populations. Rather, the violence is a tactic designed to contain and control the armed threat, usually one that appears after previous strategies of accommodation or divide and rule have failed. The highest levels of violence took place where the threat to the regime was greatest—in Tigray and Eritrea— and indeed the Mengistu regime was toppled by a Tigrayan-Eritrean coalition in 1991. By contrast, the levels of violence have been more limited across time in the more peripheral areas of Oromo and Ogaden.

The short case summaries here continue to lend support the main hypothesis that the strategy of large-scale, group-selective violence is clearly causally related to containing or defeating armed threats; the greater the threat and the more vulnerable the regime, the more likely that states will employ greater levels of violence against civilians—in particular where they have the capacity to do so. On the latter point, the Ethiopian state and military fit the bill, given extensive development of the civilian administration, mass conscription, and heavy investments in the military apparatus under Mengistu and Meles. In both cases too, the insurgencies had a base of support in regions and from populations that differed in their ethnic identity from the core power base at the center.

Uganda under Amin and Obote

Like Ethiopia, Uganda has been one of the most violence-intensive countries in independent Africa. A battery of insurgencies from nearly every corner of the country has confronted successive governments. On occasion, state strategies to defeat those rebellions developed into mass categorical violence and political repression. Two periods stand out as the most violent: 1971 to 1979 under Idi Amin and 1980 to 1985 under Milton Obote. Amin's government committed widespread violence against suspected political opponents and civilians tagged as insurgent supporters. Amin also famously expelled the Asian community resident in Uganda in 1972 (and he likely expelled them, rather than killed them in general, because they were not involved in an armed challenge to the state). Under Obote, pro-government forces consistently used mass categorical violence to weaken and defeat rebellions. Detailed, reliable estimates on death tolls are difficult to obtain, and the existing ranges are large and unverified. For the Amin period, the estimate is 50,000 to 300,000 deaths;[65] for the Obote period, it is 300,000 to one million.[66] The latter

---

65. Amnesty International 1978: 13.
66. Kasozi 1994: 4.

figure is almost certainly too high and is politicized.[67] More conservative estimates, which I employ in table 4.2, estimate 200,000 to 300,000 deaths.[68] A State Department official, testifying in Congress, estimated that in 1984 alone, during the height of the civil war, government forces killed 100,000 to 200,000 civilians, most of whom were civilians.[69]

Amin was a mercurial head of state. He suspected and eliminated enemies throughout his rule. He distrusted and assassinated soldiers, officers, and elites associated with Obote (whom Amin had ousted in 1971). In general, they were Langi and Acholi speakers.[70] But the violence was not confined to those groups. Throughout his rule, prominent elites were tortured and killed.[71] Attempted coups or mutinies were met with brutal reprisals. Amin's military was given free license and frequently engaged in arbitrary, predatory violence.[72] One Ugandan analyst aptly describes the regime as insecure and ruling "by terror."[73] But the patterns of violence conform less to that seen in Ethiopia, Nigeria, and the DRC—namely, collective civilian targeting to weaken and defeat an insurgency with a large civilian support base from a distrusted identity group; it is much closer to randomized terror, including dragging judges from courtrooms, public executions, rounding up university students, shoot to kill orders for anyone suspected of a crime, disappearances, dumping of bodies in public spaces, and widespread torture.[74] The violence is that of a weak, vulnerable, and mercurial regime, one that more closely resembles the patterns of violence in Equatorial Guinea and Guinea.

Under Obote, the political violence was both more extensive and more group-selective than under Amin. Soon after taking power, Obote faced a series of rebellions, including the United National Rescue Front (with support from the West Nile areas); the Uganda Freedom Movement, which was primarily urban-based; and the National Resistance Movement (or NRM, with support in the southwest areas of the country). Of these, the first and third posed the gravest threat to Obote's state, and government forces responded much as other regimes detailed in this section did.

One major incident took place in the West Nile region in late 1980 in which government forces, responding to an assassination attempt on Obote, retaliated

---

67. Kasozi 1994: 289.
68. Ulfelder and Valentino 2008.
69. Kasozi 1994: 289.
70. Amnesty International 1978: 12; Omara-Otunno 1987: 104, 126.
71. Amnesty International 1978; Kasozi 1994.
72. Kasozi 1994; Omara-Otunno 1987.
73. Kasozi 1994: 104, 112.
74. Amnesty International 1978.

with a scorched-earth policy that claimed 3,000 to 30,000 lives.[75] The worst violence took place in the Luwero Triangle area, where the NRM was strongest. The violence was designed to "send a message" to the ethnic groups supporting the NRM, especially the Baganda and Banyarwanda, and government forces engaged in mass categorical violence against these groups.[76] Government forces also forcibly relocated those populations into "relief centers."

The patterns of violence under Obote conform to the emerging dominant scenario: a vulnerable government that employs mass categorical violence to contain and defeat an insurgency rooted in a distrusted population that differed from those controlling the central state. In this case, the violence is predominantly coercive and repressive, designed to weaken the military power of the rebels and to impose heavy costs on the insurgents and their supporters in areas where state forces have lost or are losing territorial control. The violence does not seem designed to destroy the distrusted population or its capacity to survive and reproduce, but rather to curtail the progress of a rebellion that cannot be contained through conventional military means.

Somalia under Siad Barre

The pattern is much the same under Siad Barre in Somalia. A military officer who took power in a 1969 coup, Barre ruled repressively under the banner of "scientific socialism" until he was ousted in 1991. As in the other cases, regime vulnerability stemming from gains by armed opposition groups triggered spikes in mass violence. In Somalia's political history, a key moment came in 1977. Looking to reunite ethnic Somalis in the Ogaden region of Ethiopia, Barre dispatched some 35,000 Somali troops alongside 15,000 troops from the Western Somali Liberation Front, an Ethiopian rebel group in the Ogaden.[77] But Ethiopian government forces, with Soviet and Cuban support, dislodged the Somalis, handing Barre a significant military and political defeat. Following the failed incursion, Barre faced a coup attempt in 1978 led by members of the Majeerteen clan. After the coup attempt, most of the mutiny's leaders were executed, but Colonel Abdullahi Yusuf Ahmed escaped to Ethiopia, where he founded the Somali Salvation Democratic Front (SSDF), which proceeded to make incursions into the country. Thereafter, Barre deployed a feared specialized military unit to punish Majeerteens from Yusuf's subclan.[78]

---

75. Kasozi 1994: 177.
76. Kasozi 1994: 180.
77. Samatar 1991: 18.
78. Africa Watch 1990: 29; Samatar 1991: 18.

Much worse followed in the mid-1980s. In 1981, leaders from the Isaak clan in the north formed the Somali National Movement (SNM). Throughout the mid-1980s, in particular following SNM attacks, Somali forces tended to target Isaaks collectively through assassinations, arrests, and destroying their means of survival—livestock, homes, and water.[79] Some of the worst violence occurred after significant SNM attacks on large cities in the north in May 1988, as the Barre regime grew progressively weaker. Thereafter the Barre regime collectively targeted Isaaks through indiscriminate aerial bombing; house-to-house searches; the destruction of wells, livestock, and shelter; and executions. A detailed report by Africa Watch estimated 50,000 to 60,000 civilian deaths over a nineteen-month period starting in May 1988.[80] In 1989, two more insurgent groups formed in the south and central regions, the Somali Patriotic Movement (with support from the Hawiye clan) and the United Somali Congress (with support from Ogadeen clan). Though less well documented, the Barre regime used mass categorical violence to fight the counterinsurgencies.[81]

The Somali cases qualify as examples of mass categorical violence. The violence was group-selective (first Majeerteen, then Isaak, then Hawiye and Ogadeen). Though not well documented for all groups, the violence was clearly of a large and systematic scale against the Isaak. The Isaak population was labeled as the enemy.[82] The logic of violence was primarily coercive: The main purposes were to punish civilian supporters and to impose heavy civilian costs in order to weaken support for the rebellion. Africa Watch concluded that the policy was "the outcome of a specific conception of how the war against the insurgents should be fought," and the logic was to "punish civilians for their presumed support for the SNM attacks and to discourage them from further assistance."[83]

Chad under Hissène Habré

That basic pattern is evident in Chad too. Chad is a fissiparous, large, and weak state that cuts across the Sahel in Central Africa. A product of French colonialism, Chad is home to hundreds of ethnic groups.[84] As in neighboring Sudan, one of the central cleavages is between a predominantly Muslim north and a predominantly non-Muslim south, a cleavage that is overlaid with perceived ethnic and racial divisions. (The north has a Sahelian/Arab

---

79. Africa Watch 1990: 9.
80. Africa Watch 1990: 3.
81. Africa Watch 1990: 11; Samatar 1991: 20.
82. Africa Watch 1990: 63.
83. Africa Watch 1990: 3–4.
84. Gatta 1985: 185.

orientation, and the south has a sub-Saharan, "black" orientation.) However, Chad is a quite heterogeneous and fractious state in which there exist major divisions and cleavages within the large regional blocs. Throughout Chadian postcolonial political history, there are many instances of north-north and south-south political rivalries and opportunistic alliances across the north-south divide. In short, the south and the north are not strongly coherent blocs.[85] Nevertheless, even if the cleavage is less coherent than in neighboring Sudan, Chadian political history is often narrated, both internally and externally, as being divided between the south and the north; the cleavage is a central recurring political theme in the country.[86]

As in other African states, the north-south cleavage is a direct product of colonialism. The French divided the country into a "useful" south and "not useful" north; French investments followed suit, with greater education, infrastructure, and agricultural production—notably cotton, the leading export until oil came on line in the 1990s—being directed toward the south. Upon independence in 1960, the French transferred power to a southern Christian, François Tombalbaye. He faced several difficulties. The new regime encountered open hostility in the north, riots in the capital, coup plots, and a series of defections in the south, the location of the president's nominal base of support.[87]

The first major rebellion broke out in the north in 1965, claiming unfair southern domination and discrimination against northerners.[88] But the rebellion itself was quite divided and fractured into several factions. In 1975, Tombalbaye was ousted and killed in a military coup, which saw another southerner come to power, Félix Malloum. His government continued to face rebellion and coup threats. In 1978, he persuaded one of the rebel faction leaders, a northerner named Hissène Habré, to join the government. But that government collapsed when Habré attempted a coup, which triggered massacres of southerners in N'Djamena, which were followed by massacres of northerners in the south.[89] There followed the capture of power by a Libyan-backed rebel faction, led by another northerner, Goukouni Oueddeï. His close relations with Libya—in 1980 he invited Libyan troops to defeat Habré's forces, and a year later he declared that the two countries would merge—prompted the United States and France to back Habré, who eventually came to power in 1982.[90]

---

85. Lemarchand 1986; Nolutshungu 1996: 34.
86. Buijtenhuijs 1987: 15.
87. Decalo 1987.
88. Gatta 1985: 176.
89. Lanne 1981.
90. Decalo 1987.

Habré's repressive rule from 1982 to 1990 is the main focus of my discussion, but the perennial weakness, instability, and internal divisions that characterize the Chadian state must be seen as an essential backdrop. Chad is variously characterized as a state of "total underdevelopment"[91] and a "fictive state."[92] By 1979, according to one Chadian observer, the state had "ceased to exist."[93] In any case, in coming to power, Habré had a fairly narrow band of domestic political support. He also faced a series of armed threats. Goukouni relocated to the north of the country, where with Libyan backing and eventually Libyan armed intervention, he fought Habré. Moreover, given the 1979 massacres and brutal measures that northern troops stationed in the south took, the south was quite negative toward Habré.[94] Habré's first move was to negotiate with some southern elites and incorporate southern soldiers and officers into a new national army, but by 1983 it was clear that Habré faced a budding insurgency in the south.[95] After initial military brutality, in which fifteen villages were attacked and civilians were killed indiscriminately, Habré chose negotiation. Through 1983 and the first half of 1984, a deal seemed within reach, but the rebels reneged and launched a surprise attack on a military base; some Muslim civil servants were also killed.[96]

The Chadian regime's reaction was swift and exceptionally violent. Deploying specialized security units into the south together with other armed units, state forces laid waste to whole swaths of southern areas; they burned villages; they committed massacres; they systematically targeted and killed southern elites in education and government sectors.[97] The period is sometimes called "Black September," but the violence lasted into 1985.[98] The results were catastrophic in the south, which was described at the time as a wasteland with a population terrorized by an occupation force.[99] Cotton production tumbled. Eventually, the pacification campaign would be replaced with calls for "reconciliation" in the south.[100] But in 1987 and 1989, as Habré's rule weakened, when the regime faced defections and then armed resistance from Hadjarai and Zaghawa leaders in other parts of the country, state forces exacted collective violence and torture against civilians associated

91. Bouquet 1982: 162.
92. Nolutshungu 1996: 2.
93. Gatta 1985: 167.
94. Buijtenhuijs 1987: 291; Nolutshungu 1996: 186.
95. Buijtenhuijs 1987: 291.
96. Buijtenhuijs 1987: 292–96.
97. Commission d'enquête nationale 1993: 83–84; Human Rights Watch 2005: 11–12
98. Commission d'enquête nationale 1992: 83–84.
99. Buijtenhuijs 1987: 296–97; Human Rights Watch 2005: 11.
100. Buijtenhuijs 1987: 433.

with those communities.[101] A national commission of inquiry established after his overthrow concluded the regime was guilty of "genocide."[102] The commission's final report estimated 37,800 deaths.[103] But the patterns of violence conform more to a repressive, coercive logic where the state responds to armed threats rooted in distrusted identity populations with mass categorical violence.

To summarize, among the cases of the highest violence in independent Africa, the principal pattern—evident in Chad, Ethiopia, Somalia, Uganda (under Obote), and Nigeria—is that internally weak, vulnerable governments face one or more insurgencies. In response to specific threats, often surprise assaults, national state leaders choose a strategy of sustained, large-scale violence against distrusted civilian populations associated with the armed resistance. In these cases, the government engages primarily in a coercive logic of punishing civilians for real or suspected collaboration, which is designed to weaken and impose costs on the armed opposition and its supporters. The campaigns are within a strategic logic of counterinsurgency, rather than the logic of group destruction. Where insurgencies are controlled or the military tide turns in favor of the state—as in Biafra, the Ogaden region, or the Chadian south—states lessen their practices of violence against civilians or allow relief supplies to penetrate.

But there are other cases where the violence appears to exceed a repressive logic of counterinsurgency, in which a deliberate effort is taken to destroy the foundations of a population irrespective of the actions of armed opponents and the evolution of the war. Here the cases of the Democratic Republic of Congo in 1996 and 1997, arguably elements of the Biafran civil war in the early parts of the war, as well as the cases discussed elsewhere in the book—Rwanda in 1994, Burundi in 1972, and aspects of Darfur from 2003 through 2005—fit the pattern. In these cases, there appear to be efforts to destroy populations, to change the demography of target populations by destroying their regenerative capacity.

In short, the case studies strongly support the relationship between mass categorical violence and genocide, on the one hand, and armed conflict and threat perception (as measured by the danger posed by rebels and internal vulnerability of divided, weak regimes), on the other. Group-selective violence is especially likely where the insurgents represent or claim to represent an identity population that is different from those that control the state and in whose name state leaders rule. While the boundary between large-scale, group-selective repressive violence and large-scale, group-selective

101. Commission d'enquête nationale 1993: 82; Human Rights Watch 2005: 12–14.
102. Commission d'enquête nationale 1993: 68.
103. Commission d'enquête nationale 1993: 69.

destructive violence is ambiguous, there do seem to be examples within and across cases of different logics of violence.

False Negatives: Cases "Off the Regression Line"

Not all cases of mass violence occur in the context of armed conflict. I call these cases "false negatives" in the sense that the theory would predict that they should not result in large-scale violence of civilians, but they do. The scale of violence is systematically lower than in the armed conflict cases; nonetheless, I examine the dynamics in these cases to see whether and how they would force a rethinking of the theory. In this section, I focus on three countries: Equatorial Guinea, Guinea, and Zimbabwe, which are chosen at random. The analysis reveals a connection between security fears and armed threats in vulnerable states and the strategic use of violence against civilians.

Equatorial Guinea under Macías Nguema

One of the most violent episodes in African political history to take place outside the context of armed conflict is that of Equatorial Guinea under Francisco Macías Nguema from 1968 to 1979. Macías's rule was highly repressive and unpredictable.[104] Several observers call it a "reign" or "machinery" of "terror," implicitly reminiscent of Amin.[105] His government engaged in selective assassinations, primarily of political elites; systematic attacks on organized religion, in particular the Catholic Church; and harassment of Spanish expatriates. Ideologically anti-imperialist, the government was "absolutist with a personality cult."[106] Equatorial Guinea became a one-party system in 1970, but in 1971 Macías engineered a constitution that accorded him direct control over all government institutions. In 1972, he was declared president for life, and his party awarded him several honorific titles, including that of the "only miracle."[107]

Against the backdrop of mercurial authoritarianism, enforced by a party youth wing, the regime increased its violent repression after an armed challenge. In March 1969, in response to fears about the safety of expatriates, Spanish troops took control of strategic points in the country; an apparent coup attempt followed shortly thereafter.[108] Those actions prompted a new

104. Cronjé 1976: 42.
105. Artucio 1979: 5; Fegley 1989: 64; Liniger-Goumaz 1988: 54.
106. Artucio 1979: 7.
107. Artucio 1979: 6.
108. Liniger-Goumaz 1988: 52.

level of selective assassinations, arrest, and torture of potential political rivals and what the regime deemed "intellectuals." On occasion, families and villages of origin were also targeted. Some data provide an illustration: About two-thirds of the political elites who attended the country's first (1967) constitutional conference or who were in the first (1968) national assembly were killed or "disappeared" by the time Macías was overthrown in a coup in 1979; of the twelve government ministers in the first cabinet, ten were murdered.[109] By 1979, between a third and a quarter of the population had fled.[110]

The final death toll is difficult to estimate. At Macías's trial in 1979, 474 names of victims were enumerated, but that sum was explicitly indicative rather than comprehensive.[111] One commentator, Max Linier-Goumaz, refers variously to "several thousands"[112] and "tens of thousands."[113] Another refers to 20,000 deaths "attributable" to the regime, of which only 514 are enumerated.[114] Based on these estimates, I advance an estimate range of 5,000 to 20,000 victims. In the terms of the book, the violence was not group-selective; multiple ethnic groups were targeted.[115] The primary selection mechanism seems to be that of political rivals or sources of a social challenge to the state, such as the Church. At his trial, the state prosecutor charged Macías with genocide, but the charge was not substantiated.[116]

A comparison between the Macías and Amin regimes is apt. In both cases, political repression and violence were the strategic responses to a weakly consolidated, vulnerable regime led by a mercurial figure. In Equatorial Guinea, the threat was diffuse and seemingly invented. But the logic of the violence was repressive, the intention to preempt any potential internal threat, a fear that was exacerbated by actions perceived as posing an armed challenge (that is, the 1969 coup attempt).

Guinea under Sékou Touré

In nearby Guinea, the first republic under the leadership of Ahmed Sékou Touré from 1958 to 1984 was a more structured, ideologically coherent polity. Pro-Communist and pro-revolutionary, Sékou Touré and the leadership of the

---

109. Artucio 1979: 11; Cronjé 1976: 21–22.
110. Artucio 1979: 2; Cronjé 1976: 42.
111. Artucio 1979: 32.
112. Liniger-Goumaz 1988: 164.
113. Liniger-Goumaz 1983: 11.
114. Fegley 1989: 266–67.
115. Fegley 1989: 266.
116. Artucio 1976: 31.

single party, the Parti démocratique de la Guinée (PDG), exercised authoritarian control over the political arena throughout the country's first twenty-seven years. The main justification for what one author calls "institutionalized terror" to repress real and imagined dissent was the threat of a "permanent plot."[117] First expressed in 1960, the idea behind the plot claim was that external imperialist forces, teaming up with local supporters who wished to overthrow Sékou Touré, constantly threatened the regime.[118] The worst repression took place in the wake of a failed coup in November 1970 in which Portuguese forces joined forces with Guinean dissidents to launch an attack on Conakry.[119] Another took place in 1976 after an assassination attempt led by a Peul man (the Peul are one of the main ethnic groups in Guinea).[120] The principal institutions committing violence were a secret police, a party militia, and a network of informants.[121] Political elites were common targets. Many were tortured using a variety of tactics, including a famous "black diet" of deprivation of food and water in the main detention center, Camp Boiro.[122] There were also show trials, public executions, and confessions broadcast over the radio.[123]

How many perished under Touré remains the subject of some speculation. In a 1982 report, Amnesty International identified 2,900 political prisoners who had been executed or "disappeared."[124] A report to the U.S. House of Representatives estimated 5,000 civilian deaths under Sékou Touré, again concentrated in the capital at Camp Boiro.[125] But victim groups claim that at least 50,000 perished or disappeared.[126]

The logic of political violence was repressive. Sékou Touré spoke of a devious "enemy" that was omnipresent.[127] His ministers warned of an enemy "vermin" who had to be crushed, and the president himself in the wake of the 1976 assassination attempt threatened to "annihilate" the Peul through revolutionary war.[128] Yet the violence was designed to eliminate potential rivals and to

117. Kaba 1988: 238.
118. MacDonald 2009: 235.
119. Adamolekun 1976: 164; Amnesty International 1982; Jeanjean 2005; MacDonald 2009: 235.
120. Amnesty International 1982: 4.
121. Human Rights Watch 2011c; Kaba 1988.
122. Amnesty International 1982: 5.
123. Human Rights Watch 2011c; MacDonald 2009.
124. Amnesty International 1982: 1; MacDonald 2012.
125. Cited in MacDonald 2009: 261.
126. See for example the Camp Boiro Memorial organization, with documentation at "Camp Boiro International Memorial," available at www.campboiro.org/bibliotheque/cbim-documents/cbim_intro.html, accessed June 20, 2014.
127. MacDonald 2009: 225.
128. Amnesty International 1982: 3–4.

signal to others the costs of dissent. The waves of arrests and party purges were not group-selective; they targeted all groups in the country, and Sékou Touré seemed committed to a founding narrative of anti-tribalism.[129]

As in other cases, the turn to large-scale political violence came in response to the perception of armed threat and the existence of a vulnerable regime that had defied its former colonial power in opting for early independence and actively supported freedom fighters from Guinea-Bissau (thereby triggering Portugal's intervention). Sékou Touré had weakened the armed forces as well, adding to a perception of vulnerability.[130] Thus, while the regime did not face an insurgency, the basic pattern holds, which is the use of large-scale violence against civilians by a vulnerable regime fearing some type of security threat.

Zimbabwe's Gukurahundi

The final case is the so-called Gukurahundi campaign in Zimbabwe. It took place shortly after that country's liberation war and transition to black rule in 1980. The main political background was twofold. On the one hand, the ruling ZANU-PF party and its guerilla wing were in a tense and at times violent rivalry with the main other party, ZAPU, which had its own guerrilla wing. On the other hand, white-ruled South Africa actively sought to destabilize and sabotage independent Zimbabwe. In that general context, and after a series of security incidents in the early 1980s, state forces used mass categorical violence to contain a potential threat and to repress the opposition.

The violence chiefly entailed state-led mass killings, targeted assassinations, disappearances, public beatings, and torture, mainly against ethnic Ndebele in the western and southwestern regions of the country.[131] The peak of the violence occurred during 1983 and 1984, and the primary perpetrators were a specialized paramilitary, a North Korean–trained unit called "Brigade 5," combined with other security forces and political party youth wing.[132] While standard genocide/mass killing databases put the figure of civilian deaths at 20,000 for the 1980–1988 period, an intensive study of the violence estimated between 3,750 and 6,000 deaths.[133]

Although the case is not formally a civil war—in which there is a clear insurgent organization seeking to overthrow a government or to secede—the

---

129. MacDonald 2009: 250.
130. MacDonald 2009: 235.
131. Catholic Commission for Justice and Peace in Zimbabwe 2008: 65.
132. Catholic Commission for Justice and Peace in Zimbabwe 2008.
133. Catholic Commission for Justice and Peace in Zimbabwe 2008: 285.

logic of violence conforms to the general pattern seen in this chapter: The state responded to the perception of an armed threat through the use of mass, group-selective violence to repress the threat. As noted, in the early 1980s, there were armed dissidents, some of whom were backed by South Africa. Those dissidents had access to arms caches, committed assassinations of white farmers and supporters of the ruling party, apparently abducted tourists, and at one point developed an operational military plan for several regions.[134] There were also a series of assassination attempts against the country's president, Robert Mugabe, in 1980, 1981, and 1982. In short, in the words of the report, Zimbabwe had "serious security problems" by early 1982, especially in the western half of the country.[135] The state response was to move into areas where the armed dissidents were active, which is also where political rivals had the greatest support, and to engage in group-selective violence against the Ndebele. At times the violence was indiscriminate, but it also became more selective as the campaign continued.[136]

Government officials threatened exterminatory violence. At a rally in March 1983, the Minister for State Security warned security forces would burn down "all the villages infested with the dissidents ... the campaign against dissidents can only succeed if the infrastructure that nurtures them is destroyed." He also referred to dissidents as "cockroaches" and to Brigade 5 as "DDT" and threatened to "cleanse" areas of dissidents and their supporters.[137] But in general the violence was primarily coercive. The purpose was to gain control over the dissidents and the political oppositions. Over time, the violence itself became more individually selective, and the state engaged in mass public beatings and mass public conversion meetings in which ZAPU supporters declared support for ZANU.[138] One military officer described the logic of violence as communicative, as being "cruel to be kind."[139]

Taken together, the brief case studies confirm that strategic security interests drive large-scale killing of civilians. In general, authorities in vulnerable states inflict mass violence against civilians to contain and counter armed threats. The turn to violence also follows some crystallizing event—some incursion, military advance, assassination attempt, or other surprisingly effective action on

---

134. Catholic Commission for Justice and Peace in Zimbabwe 2008: 59.
135. Catholic Commission for Justice and Peace in Zimbabwe 2008: 3.
136. Catholic Commission for Justice and Peace in Zimbabwe 2008: 87.
137. Catholic Commission for Justice and Peace in Zimbabwe 2009: 86–87.
138. Catholic Commission for Justice and Peace in Zimbabwe 2008: 87.
139. Catholic Commission for Justice and Peace in Zimbabwe 2008: 93

the part of the group posing the armed threat. This was the case in Nigeria, Uganda, Ethiopia, Somalia, Chad, Guinea, Equatorial Guinea, and Zimbabwe. States in turn respond with mass violence as a disproportionate response to such events—disproportionate in the sense that the violence targeted not only the armed and political elements but also those who were seen to support the threat or those who are likely to pose a threat in the future. Another clear finding is that war systematically elevates the extent of mass violence; in general, states facing a militarized opposition inflict more violence than states that do not, which further supports the general claim about the importance of threat.

Why kill civilians to contain threats? The most consistent logic is coercive. Vulnerable states, which fear their ability to contain or defeat threats conventionally and often have lost some territorial control, seek to impose heavy costs on their armed opponents. By imposing heavy costs, they seek to force armed opponents to abandon their fight or to communicate to civilians that they will suffer if they continue or start to support insurgents. Greater material threats and greater perceived vulnerability, combined with the capacity to inflict violence (through militaries and paramilitaries primarily), translate into larger-scale violence against civilians. All the cases unfold in this way.

In some cases, a preemptive logic is also in play. States in these cases target civilians not only to force the opposition to abandon the fight but also to preempt the ability to mount future opposition. In Equatorial Guinea and Guinea, for example, once the initial threat is contained, the repression turns to would-be future elite opponents. That logic is apparent in the Zanzibar Revolution as well, in which the Afro-Shirazis decimated the Arab elite population after a successful takeover of the state. As discussed in chapter 3, Burundi in 1972 conforms to this logic, as does the DRC in 1996 and 1997, when Rwandan military forces sought to destroy the Hutu refugee population after gaining the upper hand in the war. In general, a preemptive logic is most consistent with genocide.

Genocide takes place when the enemy is considered unwinnable and uncontainable. In most cases—coercive and preemptive—once states contain threats through violence, they deescalate. The Nigerian civil war, Sékou Touré's Guinea, Habré's Chad, and Zimbabwe provide illustrations—once the threat is contained, the repression subsides. But when states conclude that the enemy population is inherently unwinnable and uncontainable while retaining the capacity to inflict group-selective violence over time and space, then group destruction becomes the logic. Of the cases in this chapter, the DRC is the best illustration. Rwandan authorities chose a group-destructive strategy after concluding that repatriation measures and military operations had failed to contain the hard core of the Hutu threat and after concluding that those Hutus who fled westward were irretrievably hostile and even committed to genocide.

Why is violence group-selective? In case after case, states inflict violence against the social categories associated with the armed opposition. Several mechanisms are consistent with that choice. One is strategic: States that lack information and have little territorial control cannot identify who is an actual opponent and who is not, so they target the group as a whole. In these cases, identity categories may be an efficient cue from the perpetrators' point of view. The other is coercive: Through violence, states send a message to the armed opposition and their supporters that defection will be very expensive. The last is preemptive: States inflict violence on the group in order to prevent the group from regenerating the threat.

Each of these mechanisms rests on how state authorities define the battle. In each, authorities claim that the enemy is an identity group different from themselves—in Nigeria, the fight was against the Ibos; in Chad, against the southerners; in Ethiopia, against the Tigrayans; in the DRC and Burundi, against the Hutus. In these cases, authorities construct ethnic, religious, or regional groups as unitary categories that collectively support a rebellion and are hostile to those in power. In effect, state leaders construct an "us" as Tutsi, northerner, Amharic, or what have you, and they construct a "them" as some other categorical group.

That construct is not natural. It reflects, I submit, political ideas about who the primary political community is, whom the state is for, and how groups behave politically.

However, this chapter does not have the detail necessary to investigate founding narratives. The chapter also does not take up the question of the coalitions of national and local actors necessary to carry out genocide, at a minimum, and mass categorical violence more generally. I also have referred to "vulnerable" states that experience threat, but why they feel vulnerable also remains a little vague. More detailed case studies are needed, and that is what I hope to do in the chapters that follow, which are more intensive case studies.

In this chapter, I am guilty of doing what I criticize others for doing: comparing cases of large-scale violence to cases of large-scale violence. I have done so to establish common patterns. But a crucial question is why some cases where armed conflict is present, in particular armed conflict rooted in an identity population other than those in power, do not lead to mass categorical violence or genocide. If I am right, the answer should have to do with the degree of military threat, the political ideas that structure a regime, organizational capacity, or some other source of restraint. I shall make that case in the chapters that follow.

CHAPTER 5

Retreating from the Brink in Côte d'Ivoire

Côte d'Ivoire is a surprising "negative case" of genocide. For the first two and a half decades after independence, Côte d'Ivoire earned the sobriquet of "African miracle" for its consistent economic growth, political stability, professional bureaucracy, thriving bourgeoisie, and one of the most modern cities in Africa—Abidjan, the "Paris of West Africa." But beginning in the late 1980s, Côte d'Ivoire entered a severe crisis that lasted more than two decades, one that included economic decline, degradation of the country's infrastructure, and acute political instability. From the early 1990s, the latter entailed a nasty succession fight, the introduction of multipartyism, a coup, a failed election, a civil war, a stolen election, and a second civil war. Côte d'Ivoire thus experienced critical causal factors associated with the onset of genocide: serious political instability, armed conflict (one, as we shall see, in which the rebels represented an identity group), and economic decline.

In addition, compounding the crisis in the 1990s and thereafter, some political elites fomented an exclusionary nationalist ideology, "Ivoirité," that posited a hierarchy of citizenship along identity lines. Ivoirité initially was part of a tactic to insure the political dominance of the largest ethnic group in the country (the Akan) after the death of Côte d'Ivoire's founding president, Félix Houphouët-Boigny. But Ivoirité crystallized anti-foreigner, anti-northerner, and anti-Muslim sentiment in the southern and western parts of the country. The doctrine of Ivoirité also dovetailed with nativist claims to land, in particular in the fertile western and southwestern areas of the country where large numbers of Muslim migrants and immigrants had settled.

Several other factors increased the risk of genocide. In the 2000s, Côte d'Ivoire's fourth head of state, Laurent Gbagbo, came to power. Originally from the western part of the state and a lightning rod for autochthonous claims to land, Gbagbo and his political party fostered parallel militant institutions, notably student groups, youth wings, armed militias, and even death squads. A series of mass killing incidents, including group-selective ones that targeted northerners, Muslims, and non-Ivoirians, went unpunished. Moreover, throughout the crisis, party-backed media organizations published racist, inflammatory speech, what some outsiders called "hate media."

For these reasons, at two high points of the Ivoirian crisis—from 2002 to 2004 and from 2010 to 2011—Côte d'Ivoire featured many of the harbingers of genocide. Many credible observers warned as much, sometimes comparing Côte d'Ivoire to Rwanda. The first high point followed an armed mutiny on September 19, 2002, that developed into a civil war. The crisis triggered significant violence against civilians. Writing in October 2002, veteran journalist Stephen Smith warned of genocide, citing the specter of Rwanda[1]—as did other close and knowledgeable observers of Côte d'Ivoire. The organization Genocide Watch proclaimed in December 2002 that genocide was "imminent."[2] In November 2004, the United Nations Special Adviser on the Prevention of Genocide issued a warning on escalating violence and condemned hate speech and xenophobia in the country.[3]

The second high point followed a contested presidential election on November 28, 2010, in which Gbagbo lost but refused to cede power to his rival, Alassane Ouattara. In the crisis that ensued, pro-government security forces violently repressed protestors and targeted Muslims, northerners, and non-Ivoirians. In late March 2011, rebel forces advanced quickly, ultimately unseating Gbagbo on April 12. Although international forces ultimately aided the rebels, the presence of an acute political crisis, group-selective violence, and armed conflict—in this case, one in which the rebels won—again created a risk of mass categorical violence or genocide. The UN's Special Adviser on the Prevention of Genocide, as well as other UN agencies and

---

1. Smith 2002.
2. Genocide Watch 2002.
3. United Nations Office of the Special Advisor on the Prevention of Genocide 2004.

several conflict prevention nongovernmental organizations, warned again of the risk of mass atrocities and genocide.[4]

Yet in both cases, while group-selective political violence occurred, the Ivoirian political and military authorities refrained from the commission of mass, sustained, large-scale categorical violence. They retreated from the brink. While there is no precise count for either period, I estimate between 3,000 and 10,000 cumulative civilian deaths for the 2002–2006 period; the standard estimate for the second period is 3,000 deaths. Those sums indicate dynamics of violence that substantially differ from the major cases of categorical mass violence and genocide in independent Africa.

The Ivoirian patterns of violence thus present a puzzle: Given the presence of conditions that foster categorical mass violence and genocide, what explains why those outcomes did not occur? While the common answer to that question is the role of international actors[5]—and, indeed, they did play an important role—I shall argue that certain domestic factors served as significant restraints against the escalation of violence. I lay particular emphasis on the founding narrative that Houphouët-Boigny instilled and that served as a strong ideological counternarrative to Ivoirité. In addition, domestic military institutions, the country's economic structure, and some local factors created incentives for moderation and dynamics of deescalation.

Political Context and Background—The First Republic

From formal independence in 1960 to the late 1980s, Côte d'Ivoire was a remarkable story of African success. Central to the so-called Ivoirian miracle was its first president, Houphouët, who was born to an aristocratic Baoulé family in east-central Côte d'Ivoire. (The Baoulé is the largest and most politically significant Akan subgroup in the country.) The Ivoirian model was built on three main pillars: (1) economic growth through export-oriented agriculture; (2) political stability through the distribution of patrimonial largesse and ethnic balancing; and (3) close ties with France, which among other things guaranteed Ivoirian security through a large military base and whose tens of thousands of citizens were central to the economy and, at least initially, the public administration.

In neighboring Ghana, Kwame Nkrumah famously opined that the political kingdom came first; with it, all would follow. By contrast, Houphouët

---

4. ICG 2011a,b; UNNS 2011.
5. Akhavan 2009; Boyer 2006; Chirot 2005; Evans 2008.

instructed Ivoirians to grow "good cocoa and coffee" and to become rich.[6] That is a good summary of the developmental philosophy under the first president.[7] Agriculture was to be the main source of tax receipts and hard currency. The key products were cocoa and coffee but also cotton, rubber, sisal, nuts, and other agricultural products that could be grown in the country's fertile soil. The state would invest in human capital, infrastructure, and, eventually, industrial facilities.

In Houphouët's analysis, the three main factors of production for agricultural development were land, labor, and capital (including investments in seeds, fertilizer, transport, and farm equipment). At independence, Côte d'Ivoire had an abundance of land, in particular the forested areas of the west and southwest that remained largely uncultivated and were home to predominantly Krou populations. But if Côte d'Ivoire was abundant in land, it was not abundant in labor. The Krou populations were not historically vibrant agricultural producers (excelling, rather, in hunting). Moreover, the population density in the west and southwest was comparatively low.

To solve the labor problem, Houphouët intensified what had been a French policy of encouraging internal migration and immigration from West Africa, notably from the semi-arid and Sahelian countries to the north of Côte d'Ivoire, where fertile land was much scarcer and where there existed cultural and ethnic ties to Côte d'Ivoire—notably, Mali, Burkina Faso, and Guinea. Houphouët's famous phrase during this period is that the "land belongs to those who cultivate it," meaning that those who developed the land—cut down the forest and planted and harvested products, notably cocoa and coffee—could retain the property on which they resided.[8]

The net result was, on the one hand, substantial internal migration of Ivoirians, primarily from the center to west of Baoulé and from the north to west and southwest of Malinké/Dioula, Senufo, and other mostly Muslim northerners. On the other hand, there was substantial subregional immigration, principally of Muslims from Burkina Faso, Mali, and Guinea. Historical maps of the cocoa sector clearly reflect waves of settlement and development.[9] In 1975, some 47 percent of all residents in Côte d'Ivoire lived outside their department of birth.[10] So extensive was the migration that according to the 1998 census, in the southwestern and western regions—their nominal

6. Zolberg 1969: 151.
7. Akindès 2004; Fauré 1982.
8. Chauveau 2002; Fargues 1986.
9. Leonard and Oswald 1995: 126.
10. Fargues 1986: 205. A department is an administrative division of Côte d'Ivoire roughly comparable to a county.

autochthonous homelands—Krou populations constituted a substantial minority.[11] (Of the six regions in the west and southwest, Krou constituted greater than 25% of the population only in one: Dix-Huit Montagnes (20%); Haut Sassandra (18%); Moyen Cavally (28%); Fromager (22%); Sud-Bandama (22%), and Bas Sassandra (12%).[12]

Within Côte d'Ivoire, the dominant production model was and is small-holder, often family-run, agriculture. The majority of producers have plots less than five hectares in size; estimates in the 1950s and 1980s put the percentages of farms under five hectares at 70 percent and 60 percent, respectively.[13] A survey in the mid-2000s estimated that there were more than six hundred thousand cocoa-coffee producers in the country.[14] In short, cocoa and coffee production—as well as other export crops such as cotton, tree nuts, and rubber—is diffuse, rather than concentrated, with many small plots in the hands of hundreds of thousands of farmers.

As Ivoirian migrants and non-Ivoirian immigrants moved into the fertile forested areas of the west and southwest, they most commonly entered into "tutorat" informal patron-client relationships with the indigenous authorities and residents. These relationships allowed the "stranger" or "allogène" populations to cultivate tracts of land and to offer in exchange food crops, labor, and financial contributions to the "autochthon" populations.[15] In some cases, indigenous populations sold land to migrants as well or hired them primarily to provide the labor to work on their plantations.[16] There were in fact a variety of relationships, many of them informal. While initially successful and often an effective way to manage population mobility and migrant labor, the relationships often left formal ownership of the land in question, which became a flashpoint of conflict when Côte d'Ivoire entered the crisis years in the late 1980s and into the 2000s.[17]

The large volume of migrants and immigrants caused tension and resentment among at least some of the indigenous populations, giving way to sometimes violent conflict between Krou and migrant or immigrant populations.[18]

---

11. Institut National de la Statistique 2001b; see also Chauveau 2006; Dozon 1985; Fargues 1986; Hecht 1985; Ruf and Agkpo 2008: 7.

12. Figures calculated from disaggregated data provided to the author by Institut National de la Statistique.

13. Gbetibouo and Delgado 1984: 138; Zolberg 1969: 27.

14. Societe de Consulting et d'Application 2008.

15. Boone 1995; Chauveau 2006; Chauveau and Leonard 1996; Colin et al. 2007; Fargues 1986; Schwartz 2000.

16. Dozon 1985.

17. Mitchell 2012.

18. Dozon 1985; Hecht 1985.

Well before the crises of the late 1980s and 1990s, one close observer of western Côte d'Ivoire noted the rise of an "ideology of autochthony" among Bétés (the largest subgroup among the Krou) who viewed the large migration as a form of unwelcome colonization.[19]

That said, the net effect of open immigration and migration, state-led investment in inputs, and fertile land was a boom in agricultural production, in particular of cocoa and coffee. By the late 1970s, Côte d'Ivoire had become the largest producer of cocoa in the world, a position that the country continues to hold as of this writing. Around the same period, the country became the third-largest producer of coffee, a position it also still holds today.

As for politics, Houphouët's strategy combined authoritarianism, patrimonialism, the creation of a large civil service, and ethnic balancing—as well as close relations with France. Ideologically, Houphouët took pains to emphasize that in addition to growth and stability, Côte d'Ivoire should foster a culture of solidarity, peace, and dialogue.

Houphouët prized stability and order. "I prefer injustice to disorder," he once said.[20] An analysis of forty-seven of his presidential speeches reveals that stability is the leitmotif of his public addresses. Like most other post-independence leaders in Africa, Houphouët built and restricted political space to a single party, in his case the Parti démocratique de la Côte d'Ivoire (PDCI), which he founded in 1946. Until 1990, the PDCI was the only official political party in the country.

Though rhetorically committed to peace and dialogue, Houphouët brooked little opposition and dissent. Houphouët placated opposition through growth, patronage, and balancing, but when faced with open resistance his government did not hesitate to employ repression. One threat was a coup attempt in the early 1960s, which was met with arrests and purges of Bété politicians who were suspected of opposition and favoring socialism.[21] In 1970, following tensions over migration and immigration into the western forested area of Gagnoa—also a historically Bété area—there was an uprising that was brutally repressed, including the assassination of the protest leader Nragbé Kragbé, the arrest of hundreds, and the killing of Bétés in urban and rural areas.[22] A leading scholar of that region, Jean-Pierre Dozon, cites estimates ranging from "dozens" to "hundreds," even "thousands." Two hundred were

19. Dozon 1985: 74; Dozon 1997.
20. Médard 1982: 72.
21. Crook 1990: 653; Zolberg 1969: 345–68.
22. Dozon 1985: 81–82.

arrested.[23] However, these acts of killing and formal suppression of protest were uncommon.[24]

Houphouët's main tool for ensuring stability was elite accommodation.[25] One vehicle was the PDCI, which was an explicitly integrationist party.[26] Another was the creation of a large public sector, which included a techno-cratic civil service elite, a large education sector, and the development of a network of parastatal institutions.[27] The public sector was built on the basis of rents from agricultural exports, and it provided employment for upwardly mobile Ivoirian elites. By the mid-1980s, the public sector accounted for 40 percent of all modern employment jobs.[28] It is worth underlining Houphouët's deliberate strategy of investing in education. In 1975 education received 40 percent of the state's expenditure; 50 to 80 percent of the educa-tion budget was for higher education. A 1987 World Bank study concluded that "public support for education is unequaled by any other country in the world."[29]

An integral aspect of elite accommodation was what some scholars refer to as ethnic "balancing" under Houphouët.[30] In terms of appointments to ministries; employment in the civil service, education sector, and parastatals; and promotions within the PDCI, Houphouët made an effort to achieve proportional ethnic and religious representation. Aristide Zolberg refers to Houphouët's "mastery of ethnic calculus." The president said: "If unity had not been in our heart, we should have discovered it in our head."[31] Bakary refers to a "skillful system of ethnic 'quotas' that allows for a certain balance between the groups."[32] In other words, Houphouët understood that stability depended on multiethnic integration and balancing. Many elite Ivoirians in interviews spoke to me of how civil service administrators were deliberately sent to areas that were outside their traditional region of origin, in part to integrate the country.

Data on ethnic representation show that under Houphouët there was comparatively proportional representation for most ethnic groups in the country. Akan and Krou groups were typically overrepresented, and southern

23. Dozon 1985: 81–82.
24. Boone 1995.
25. Amondji 1986; Azam and Morrisson 1994; Médard 1982.
26. Zolberg 1969.
27. Akindès 2004; Azam and Morrison 1994; Crook 1990; Faure 1982.
28. Crook 1990.
29. Azam and Morrisson 1994: 26.
30. Akindès 2004.
31. Zolberg 1969: 74.
32. Bakary 1984: 35.

Mandé groups and Voltaic groups were typically underrepresented, but on the whole the governments were "well balanced."[33]

But Houphouët's system of ethnic management was not without its problems. First, while Houphouët promoted unity, he also intimated Baoulé superiority.[34] Second, Houphouët's vision was not a rejection of ethnic classifications but rather a recognition and informal institutionalization of them.[35] Thus, in contrast to a country such as Tanzania, where ethnic differences were downplayed, Houphouët followed a model of patrimonial management of ethnic diversity comparable to Nigeria (after the civil war) and Kenya. Third, in general terms, the northern, savannah areas of the country lagged in development indicators from the southern, eastern, and western areas.[36] There was, in short, regional inequality. All three of these issues would play out in the crisis years.

In sum, until the mid- to late 1980s Côte d'Ivoire was an exceptional African state. With a major expansion of export agriculture, the country achieved an average of 7 percent annual growth in GDP from 1960 to 1980. By 1980, the country had the second-highest per capita income in non-white-ruled Africa, after oil-producing Gabon. The country developed an effective commercial sector with what many referred to as a "planter bourgeoisie"; whether the term *bourgeoisie* is appropriate or not, wealth creation was significant. There was also the creation of a multiethnic technocratic civil service as well as a large and often admired education system. While the political system was not democratic, Houphouët achieved stability primarily through elite accommodation and patronage, with rare resort to violent repression.

At the same time, Ivoirian stability and growth masked major unresolved problems. One was a failure to manage political competition, dissent, and succession beyond Houphouët.[37] Another was that the patrimonial system depended on agricultural rents, which were vulnerable to price shocks. Yet another was citizenship. By the 1990s, at least a quarter of the residents were "non-Ivoirian," including those born outside the country and those who were born in Côte d'Ivoire but whose parents had not been. Non-Ivoirians remained without explicit political rights, and their upward mobility remained a source of resentment for at least some Ivoirians.[38] Finally is

33. Langer 2007: 172–73.
34. Akindès 2004; Memel-Fotê 1998.
35. Akindès 2009: 34.
36. Langer 2007: 170.
37. Akindès 2009.
38. For a long discussion of the history of the "foreigner" in Côte d'Ivoire, see Babo 2013.

the question of land and land rights. Even under French colonialism, but especially thereafter, there existed significant tensions between autochthonous populations and major influxes of Ivoirians from other regions and of non-Ivoirians into the forested areas in particular.[39] The coffee and cocoa boom was built on informal usufruct rights in which there remained significant lack of clarity about long-term ownership. Like the blind spots in Houphouët's political management of ethnic diversity, these problems became central in the crisis years.

Into the Crisis

In the 1980s and 1990s, the building blocks of the Houphouëtist system— export-led growth, state-led redistribution, paternalistic nondemocratic politics, stability, and open population movement—came undone. Economics was the leading edge. Starting in the late 1970s and extending into the 1980s, there was a steep decline in global commodity prices, including coffee and cocoa.[40] The decline in commodity prices meant a significant drop in state revenue, given that coffee and cocoa alone accounted for 60 percent of Côte d'Ivoire's export earnings.[41] The price drop also translated into less income for more than a million citizens involved in export crop production. The decline in state revenue coupled with high state expenditures in civil service employment, parastatals, and education drove Côte d'Ivoire into the hands of the IMF and the World Bank, which prescribed "structural adjustment." These programs in turn triggered cuts to public employment, higher fees in the education and health sectors, subsidy reductions, wage freezes, and then significant salary reductions, among other austerity measures. Eventually in the late 1980s, the state cut the price paid to producers of the main export commodities.[42] The common CFA currency was devalued in 1994. This unbundling of state largesse provoked protest mainly from its largely middle-class beneficiaries—students, teachers, health care professionals, and even soldiers—and the state responded with repression.[43]

Houphouët's political system was also upended. As in other African states at that time, Côte d'Ivoire came under domestic and international pressure to democratize the political system. Not ready for the change, Houphouët reluctantly agreed to allow non-PDCI parties to compete in the 1990

39. Zolberg 1969: 46.
40. Azam and Morrisson 1994: 20.
41. Azam and Morrisson 1994: 19.
42. Azam and Morrisson 1994; Crook 1990.
43. Akindès 2009: 37.

elections. The key opposition figure was Gbagbo, a longtime pro-democracy opponent, a university historian, a union activist, and a Bété from the southwest with an intellectual heritage to the earlier anti-PDCI, pro-Bété protest movement. Gbagbo had been arrested in the 1970s and then gone into exile in France in the early 1980s. Instrumental in the founding of the Front Populaire Ivoirien (FPI), which had a base of support among the Krou, students, and the urban intellectual left, Gbagbo returned to the country in 1988 and faced Houphouët in the 1990 elections, which the latter won with more than 80 percent of the vote.

But multipartyism was just the beginning. An even greater shock was the death of Houphouët himself in December 1993 and the nasty succession fight between two disciples that occurred after his passing. The first was Henri Konan Bédié, who was the president of the National Assembly and, like Houphouët, a Baoulé. The second was Ouattara, whom Houphouët had appointed prime minister in 1990 and who had implemented many of the most severe structural adjustment programs. Born in northern Côte d'Ivoire to a Malinké mother and a father from Burkina Faso, Ouattara represented to many Ivoirians northerners and even foreigners. Ouattara also had served in high-ranking positions in international financial institutions, notably the IMF and the Central Bank of West African States.

As speaker of the National Assembly, Bédié formally succeeded Houphouët, but the growing rivalry between him and Ouattara—as well as more generalized tensions between Baoulé and northerners in the PDCI—prompted Ouattara to help form the Rassemblement des Républicaines (RDR). That party's base of support came from those of northern origin, as well as from pro-market business elites and technocrats.

Thus, by the mid-1990s, Côte d'Ivoire was locked in a three-way political battle involving the FPI, with strong support from Krous, the left, and students; the PDCI, with strong support from the Akan and loyal Houphouëtists; and the RDR, with strong support from Muslims of northern origin, free market liberals, and technocrats. That basic tripartite political split was in play from the mid-1990s through the 2010 elections.

But the split between Bédié and Ouattara in particular shaped a key development in the runup to the 1995 elections and immediately thereafter. In late 1994, Bédié promulgated a law that restricted presidential candidates to those born to an Ivoirian mother and father—a naked attempt to exclude Ouattara from contesting the polls. In the same period, Bédié championed "Ivoirité," a notion that combines authenticity with being Ivoirian.[44] In effect, Ivoirité

---

44. Jolivet 2003.

was an attempt to draw a line between Ivoirian citizens and non-Ivoirian citizens—between an explicit "us" and "them," according to the group of intellectuals who elaborated the concept in 1996; the doctrine also explicitly classified Ivoirians into hierarchical categories.[45]

Ivoirité served a dual political and social function. On the one hand, Ivoirité was anti-foreign, even xenophobic, and nationalist.[46] It spoke to long-standing resentments against foreigners in Ivoirian society and, more subtly, to anti-Muslim bias among some southerners. Ivoirité also called into question the citizenship of northerners and Muslims, given that they often shared ethnic and religious heritage with non-Ivoirians from neighboring states.[47] In that sense, Ivoirité created a broad categorical "other" of Muslim northerners, who in turn were rendered as second-class citizens in this period.[48] In so doing, Ivoirité had an explicitly political calculation of weakening Ouattara and the RDR, whose base of support was among Muslims and Ivoirians originally from the north or neighboring states.

On the other hand, Ivoirité reflected a commitment to Akan superiority, at least initially.[49] Here Ivoirité played to fears among Akan, specifically Baoulés, that they would lose positions of leadership after Houphouët. Bédié's Ivoirité thus had a second political motive of weakening Gbagbo and the FPI. By speaking to the anti-immigrant sentiment in the country, Ivoirité was an attempt to steal the thunder of autochthony, which remained powerful among the FPI's base of support even though it was not yet explicitly championed by Gbagbo. In playing to inherent Akan superiority in the political realm, Ivoirité was also meant as a weapon against Gbagbo's claims to the presidency.[50]

Unresolved problems around land rights also came to a head in this period. The decline in commodity prices combined with the contraction of formal employment, especially in the public sector, put pressure on recently educated young Ivoirians. Facing grim employment prospects in urban areas, many returned home to their communities of origin. In the forested areas in particular, the younger generation called into question the informal land arrangements of their parents' generation, ones that often resulted in the leasing of large land tracts to migrants and immigrants. Indeed, many young Krous who had migrated to urban areas from their parents' rural lands in the

---

45. CURDIPHE 2000.
46. Akindès 2004; Dozon 2000; Jolivet 2003; Marshall-Fratani 2006.
47. Akindès 2004; Dozon 2000.
48. Dozon 1997, 2000.
49. Akindès 2004; Jolivet 2003.
50. Dozon 2000.

west and southwest now proved increasingly resentful, renewing claims to autochthonous rights.[51] The younger generation's call to reclaim traditional lands dovetailed with the Ivoirité focus on the rights of Ivoirian citizens over non-citizens.[52]

The growing tensions over access to land led to violence during the 1995 electoral campaign and to a new land law in 1998. Endorsing a version of Ivoirité, that law held that only Ivoirian citizens could be landowners. The law further stipulated that within ten years all landholders were required to obtain a certificate of ownership. In effect, the land law was a major risk to many Ivoirians who did not possess formal citizenship papers but who had farmed and developed land for a generation or longer. It was also an obvious risk to immigrants and their children, many of whom had cultivated and developed plots for decades.

In short, the late 1980s and 1990s constituted a period of intense political, social, and economic instability in which some of the foundations of the First Republic were called into question. The economic crisis meant that the patronage bargain was in crisis and households faced significant income contractions. In the wake of Houphouët's death, there was an explicit ideological resort to ethnic nationalism and to claims of indigenous rights. The 1994 electoral code, the doctrine of Ivoirité, and the 1998 land law all represent forms of institutionalized discrimination. They effectively created an inferior "them" category—the "foreigner"[53]—which referred in practice to non-Ivoirians and Ivoirians with cultural links to non-Ivoirians, notably Muslim northerners. The formal laws stipulated that this category did not have the same rights. Under Bédié, there was growing "Baoulization" of official positions.[54] Moreover, the brutal wars in neighboring Liberia led to a refugee influx, and weak economies in Mali and Burkina Faso generated greater migration into Côte d'Ivoire, creating further instability.

The Crisis Deepens: Coups, Violent Elections, Civil Wars

The crisis deepened with a military coup on Christmas Eve in 1999.[55] Led by mostly northern junior officers, the coup unseated Bédié and installed the former head of the Army, General Robert Guéï, as the head of a National

51. Dozon 1997.
52. Chauveau and Bobo 2008; Chauveau and Richards 2008.
53. Dembélé 2002; Dozon 1997.
54. Langer 2007.
55. Beugré 2011; Pape and Vidal 2002.

Salvation Council.[56] The coup leaders opposed, at least initially, the ethnic favoritism and nationalist exclusion under Bédié; they also endorsed Houphouëtism.

But those principles gave way to Guéï's quest for power, which included restricting Ouattara and implicitly endorsing aspects of Ivoirité. A key decision was made in January to issue new identity cards that would in turn be necessary to secure voting rights. The identity cards became a source of controversy, with FPI militants and officials, among others, complaining that false cards were being issued to non-Ivoirians. Guéï thereafter appointed a commission that eventually restricted presidential candidates to parents born to an Ivoirian mother *and* an Ivoirian father, to those who had never declared another nationality, and to those who had lived in Côte d'Ivoire over the previous five years. On that basis, a Supreme Court decision invalidated the presidential candidacies of Ouattara and Bédié in the October 2000 elections.

This period saw an intensification of discrimination against northerners—those whose names or dress might suggest they resembled non-Ivoirians from neighboring states. They often had their identity cards destroyed, which in turn made them vulnerable to more abuse.[57] In June, July, and September 2000 there were failed coups or assassination attempts against Guéï, the last of which led to the arrest, torture, and death of mostly northern soldiers, some of whom had been instrumental in installing Guéï.[58]

The October 22 presidential elections were also key. With Ouattara and Bédié excluded from the polls, the PDCI and the RDR called on their supporters to boycott, leaving principally Guéï and Gbagbo to contest. Early returns showed Gbagbo winning. Guéï in turn attempted to rig the results, prompting both FPI and RDR supporters to engage in large-scale street protests—but with different aims. RDR supporters wanted a new electoral process, while FPI partisans, supported by some gendarmes, wanted the true results of the election to be recognized. The differences turned to violence between supporters of the two parties. In the end, more than 150 were killed, and more were wounded. The principal victims were RDR supporters and northerners, many of whom were found in a mass grave in the urban district of Yopougon, which in turn became the symbol of the violence.[59]

---

56. Beugré 2011.
57. Balint-Kurti 2007; Human Rights Watch 2001; Pape and Vidal 2002.
58. Balint-Kurti 2007; Beugré 2011.
59. Bouquet 2005: 64.

On October 26, the Supreme Court announced that Gbagbo had indeed won the elections with nearly 60 percent of the vote, and he was sworn in as the country's fourth president. Gbagbo, in turn, announced a cabinet with no RDR ministers. In parliamentary elections held in December, Ouattara was again excluded from running (on the grounds he could not prove his nationality), prompting further clashes between security forces and RDR supporters. A December 2000 RDR rally in particular was violently repressed.[60] This period witnessed the continuation of racist, xenophobic tracts stipulating restrictions—such as intermarriage—on "foreigners."[61]

That said, in 2001 and 2002, Gbagbo took measures to regularize the crisis. Local elections were held in 2001 in which the RDR won a plurality, a reconciliation commission was established in the same year, and in August 2002 a new coalition government was put in place with significant representation from all political parties.

Events took another dramatic turn in the autumn of 2002. On September 19, disgruntled military officers led simultaneous attacks in Abidjan, Bouaké, and Korhogo. They were repulsed in Abidjan, but within days they effectively controlled the northern half of the country. General Guéï was killed on the first day, allegedly for being behind the mutiny; Bédié and Ouattara took refuge at embassies. Canceling a visit with the pope, Gbagbo flew back to Abidjan from Italy and declared that the "hour of patriotism" had arrived.[62]

The rebellion was led by the MPCI (Mouvement Patriotique de la Côte d'Ivoire), renamed the Forces Nouvelles in January 2003. The main rebel leaders were former officers who had fled Côte d'Ivoire under Guéï or Gbagbo because of discrimination and, in some cases, torture or arrest.[63] The main claims that the rebels made were to end discrimination against northerners and Muslims, that is, to counter the general politics of Ivoirité. Several officers received training in Burkina Faso prior to the 2002 attack.[64]

International forces responded quickly to the onset of armed conflict in Côte d'Ivoire. France, which maintained a military base in Abidjan, intervened on September 25, formally to protect French and American citizens. But their presence effectively became an interposition force, separating government from rebel forces and starting what would become later a fully elaborated

60. Bouquet 2005: 69–77 ; MIDH 2001.
61. Bouquet 2005: 75–76; see also Marshall-Fratani 2006.
62. Balint-Kurti 2007: 6; see also Kouassi 2010: 258–64.
63. Balint-Kurti 2007.
64. Balint-Kurti 2007.

buffer zone. The regional organization, the Economic Community of West African States (ECOWAS), similarly intervened diplomatically, negotiating a ceasefire on October 3—one that was promptly violated—and another one on October 17. By the end of November, two more rebel organizations appeared in western Côte d'Ivoire, one around Danané and Man and the other near Séguéla. Both had connections to Liberian fighters.[65] Meanwhile, government forces responded by arming and mobilizing militias in the west as well as encouraging their youth supporters to enlist in the army.[66]

The French brokered a more robust ceasefire in January 2003. The Linas-Marcoussis Agreement was a comprehensive agreement that included provisions aimed to meet the rebels' demands. These included a government of National Reconciliation, a technocratic prime minister, commitments to address citizenship and bias in the media, and other concessions. Even though fighting in the west would not end until May 2003 and there would be another outbreak in November 2004, the accord became the official template for political accommodation until 2007. An ECOWAS peacekeeping contingent was deployed in March 2003; it became a United Nations mission in April. The UN mission in turn had a comprehensive mandate, including to guide the country toward regularization of citizenship issues and elections. It also was central to establishing a buffer zone called the "zone of confidence" that effectively cut the country in two.

Violence continued in the western areas around the zone of confidence, but the equilibrium that characterized the country was what many Ivoirians and outside observers refer to as "neither peace nor war." That is, a new stasis was achieved from which both sides found reasons not to move—notably, the continued traffic in commercial products in the south and an elaborate taxation system in the north provided ongoing revenue to elites in both camps.

Throughout the 2002–2007 period, there was continued African-led mediation, which eventually led to a new peace agreement known as the Ouagadougou Accords, signed in March 2007. Among other things, the Accords called for naming the head of the Forces Nouvelles, Guillaume Soro, as prime minister; resolving the problem of identity and citizenship; preparing for elections through a registered list of voters; restructuring and integrating armies; and restoring public service to the north. After many delays, Côte d'Ivoire finally held presidential elections in 2010 in which the three major candidates—Gbagbo, Bédié, and Ouattara—contested.

---

65. Balint-Kurti 2007.
66. Bouquet 2005.

Gbagbo and Ouattara were the top vote-getters in the first round, and in the second round Bédié threw his support behind Ouattara, who in turn won the November 28 election.[67] However, Gbagbo refused to recognize the results, leading to a "constitutional coup" in which a constitutional court stacked with his supporters threw out large numbers of votes from the north and declared him the winner.[68] Therein set a new stalemate, one in which RDR supporters and northerners were again targeted, often violently. In this case, Gbagbo faced a phalanx of international and regional opposition. After four months of failed diplomacy, the Forces Nouvelles renamed themselves the Forces Républicaines de la Côte d'Ivoire (FRCI) and quickly advanced toward Abidjan. Eventually helped in Abidjan by United Nations and French military forces, the FRCI captured and arrested Gbagbo on April 12, 2011, paving the way for Ouattara to be named the country's fifth president.[69] Gbagbo was later arrested and transferred to the International Criminal Court, where as of this writing he faces charges of war crimes and crimes against humanity.

Patterns of Violence and the Risk of Genocide

The developments just described amount to a storm of the most important risk factors for genocide: acute political instability and armed conflict (succession battles, multipartyism, coup and coup attempts, the outbreak of two civil wars, and a nasty election fight); economic decline and increases in poverty; and the emergence of a nativist/ethnic nationalist discourse that built on historical resentments and created an identity category for discrimination. In addition, there was impunity for past violence—notably, for the mass grave at Yopougon but also for other killings that I shall describe in this section—and the rise of "hate media" that stoked xenophobia, violence, and resentment against foreigners, northerners, and Muslims.[70] Serious academic observers compared the Ivoirian pro-government media at its worst to Rwanda's RTLM.[71]

Also important was the creation of "parallel forces"—militant and militia institutions—that were closely tied to the security forces and the FPI under Gbagbo.[72] The former were a coalition of youth groups that went under

67. Bassett 2011.
68. Bassett 2011.
69. Bassett and Straus 2011.
70. Arnaut 2004; United Nations Office of the Special Advisor on the Prevention of Genocide 2002.
71. Bouquet 2005: 140.
72. United Nations High Commissioner for Human Rights 2004a.

the label "galaxie patriotique," which initially grew out of a student union organization.[73] A nationalist discourse that mixed autochthony, xenophobia, and independence from France was central to the political idiom of these militant groups.[74] "Côte d'Ivoire for Ivoirians" was a typical slogan.[75] These youth militant groups engaged in widespread intimidation and, occasionally, violent attacks on northerners, Muslims, and non-Ivoirians, especially in and around Abidjan.[76] In addition, several militia groups formed as self-defense organizations, chiefly in western Côte d'Ivoire near the war's buffer zone and front line. The armed militias in turn were supported and supplied by leading FPI figures.

What, then, were the main patterns of violence? The general pattern was sharp escalation in two critical periods followed by slow deescalation. The first period followed the onset of armed conflict in 2002; the second period followed the contested elections and eventual war in 2010–2011. The former period is represented in figure 5.1 with data from the Armed Conflict and

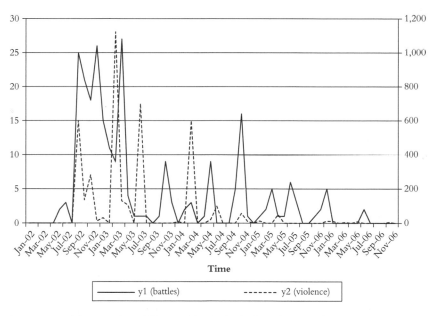

FIGURE 5.1   Violence against civilians and battle deaths (based on ACLED)

73. Banegas 2007; Human Rights Watch 2008a.

74. Arnaut 2004, 2005; Banegas 2006, 2007; Banegas and Marshall-Fratani 2007; Marshall-Fratani 2006.

75. Bouquet 2005: 72.

76. Human Rights Watch 2008a, 2011a, b.

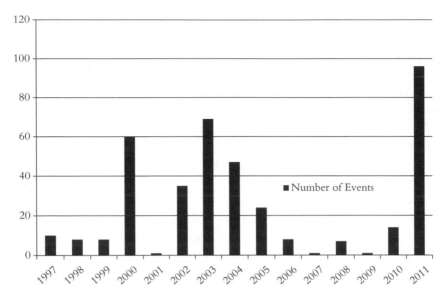

FIGURE 5.2   Number of violence against civilians events (based on ACLED). Courtesy of Tom Bassett.

Location Events Database, which records violent events from major media sources. The latter is represented in figure 5.2, also from ACLED. In both cases, the worst violence is often group-selective state repression or tit-for-tat intercommunal killing. In both cases, however, a pattern of sustained group-selective or group-destructive mass violence does not take hold.

The 2002–2006 Period

More specifically, I identify six sometimes overlapping patterns of violence in the earlier period. The first is what some call "la chasse aux Dioula"— the group-selective harassment of northerners, Muslims, and Muslim non-Ivoirians.[77] The collective and prejudicial label associated with that category is "Dioula," which refers to one ethnic group in northern Côte d'Ivoire but which became the marker of a category of foreigner-northerner-Muslim. Such harassment and persecution began in the 1990s when Bédié promulgated Ivoirité and Ouattara declared his political ambitions.[78] It continued under Guéï and after Gbagbo took power, in particular during the legislative and local elections of 2000 and 2001.[79] Once the war started, the harassment

---

77. Bouquet 2005: 108; Human Rights Watch 2001; UNHCHR 2003, 2004b.
78. Human Rights Watch 2001.
79. Bouquet 2005.

and persecution increased. Human rights organizations documented numerous cases whereby having a certain name, wearing certain clothes, or being identified as Muslim—thus indicating a northern orientation—became the pretext for street bribes, the ripping up of identity cards, cat-calling, and the like, generally at the hands of police, gendarmes, and the militant youth in the galaxie patriotique.[80] Just after the start of the war, security forces also razed neighborhoods in Abidjan that had a high concentration of northerners and non-Ivoirians.[81]

Closely related was a more general form of intimidation from the student and youth movements associated with the ruling party. The most important leader and instigator was self-described "General" Charles Blé Goudé, who headed Les Jeunes Patriotes (Young Patriots). During the war, militants in the galaxie patriotique attacked supporters of rival parties, set up roadblocks and harassed northerners, attacked French and ransacked French properties, and attacked UN personnel. When angered by the appointment of an opposition minister in the coalition government, they protested violently. When the French counterattacked and destroyed the Ivoirian Air Force in 2004, youth militants descended on the streets of Abidjan and began attacking French citizens across the city.[82] The youth movement operated most clearly in urban areas. As of this writing, Blé Goudé faces charges at the International Criminal Court.

A third pattern of violence during the war, especially in its early stages, was selective violence against specific political or military actors. Even though Ouattara and the RDR were not formally involved in the coup, pro-government politicians and militants blamed him and his party. Ouattara's house was burned, and attacks on RDR politicians and party offices followed in September and October.[83] Furthermore, in the immediate aftermath of the September attack, several attacks against politicians and prominent businessmen took place, in particular by pro-government forces but also by MPCI rebels.[84] A 2003 United Nations human rights report cites 150 assassinations, while a 2004 UN Commission of Inquiry cites a figure of 300.[85] There are numerous reports, all of which are difficult to verify, of pro-government "death squads" that had lists of people to assassinate.[86] They allegedly operated in Yamoussoukro and Abidjan.[87]

---

80. Bouquet 2005: 108; Human Rights Watch 2002; MIDH 2004b; UNHCHR 2003, 2004b.
81. Human Rights Watch 2002: 7–8.
82. MIDH 2004b.
83. Human Rights Watch 2002.
84. UNHCHR 2003.
85. UNHCHR 2003: 13; UNHCHR 2004b: 37.
86. Bouquet 2005: 120; UNHCHR 2003: 14; UNHCHR 2004b: 39.
87. UNHCHR 2004b: 44.

A fourth pattern is the violent suppression of political protest. Such violence took place in 2000 following the presidential elections and following the exclusion of Ouattara from running in the legislative elections. Another major event took place in March 2004 when opposition supporters from all major political parties protested against delays in implementing the Linas-Marcoussis peace accords and for "Ivoirianizing" the state.[88] Defying a warning from the interior minister, opposition protesters prepared to march—and were forcibly disbanded by security forces who in turn followed up with attacks on opposition-supporting neighborhoods, together with pro-government youth militants.[89] The repression by the security forces was well coordinated.[90] An Ivoirian rights organization out the death total at around 100;[91] a UN human rights inquiry put the figure of at least 120 dead;[92] Ivoirian opposition politicians, such as Bédié, put forth higher figures of 450 to 500 dead.[93] In the repression of the protests, it is clear that northerners and non-Ivoirians were targeted.[94]

A fifth pattern of violence relates to battlefield dynamics. The most frequent pattern occurred when military forces targeted civilians who had allegedly collaborated with the enemy after territory had changed hands. This occurred on several occasions in western Côte d'Ivoire before the buffer zone was established. One of the most notorious examples took place in December 2002, in Monoko-Zahi, where a mass grave of 120 mostly Muslim northerners and non-Ivoirians were found.[95] Mass graves and massacres in the 2002–2003 period were found in Daloa, Vavoua, Dah, Man, Bangolo, Toulepleu, Danané, Bouaké, Odienné, and Korhogo.[96] In some cases, pro-government mercenaries from Liberia killed civilians after capturing territory, again targeting northerners and non-Ivoirians.[97] The same was true in Daloa.[98] Human Rights Watch collected eyewitness statements that indicate a strong logic of punishing collaboration on a categorical basis. "You the Dioula, you support the rebels," a man was told before being killed in Man.[99]

---

88. Bouquet 2005: 139–40.
89. Bouquet 2005: 140; MIDH 2004a; UNHCHR 2004a.
90. UNHCHR 2004a.
91. MIDH 2004a.
92. UNHCHR 2004a.
93. Bouquet 2005: 141.
94. MIDH 2004a; UNHCHR 2004a.
95. UNHCHR 2004b: 37.
96. Human Rights Watch 2003; UNHCHR 2003, 2004b: 37.
97. UNCHR 2004b: 38; see also Human Rights Watch 2003: 39–40.
98. Human Rights Watch 2004: 16.
99. Human Rights Watch 2003: 19.

The MPCI also killed gendarmes and some of their family members in September 2002 after the government launched a failed offensive to recapture Bouaké in the center of the country.[100] In some cases, government helicopters attacked western towns, and sometimes civilians were targeted.[101] Such attacks declined after the middle of 2003, once the buffer zone was clearly established and patrolled by UN peacekeeping forces.

The final pattern was generally localized intercommunal violence, principally tied to rival claims to land access and ownership. During the course of the war, this form of violence was arguably the most extensive and the most common. In the most general pattern, these attacks pitted groups of indigenous populations in the west—generally Bété or Guéré—against non-indigenous or "allogène" groups—generally northerners, non-Ivoirians, and Baoulé migrants. Intercommunal clashes in which there would be attacks by autochthonous groups or counterattacks by allogène groups long predated the war. Tensions between indigenous populations in the west and southwest, on the one hand, and migrants and immigrants, on the other, date back to the colonial period and were clearly in evidence under Houphouët. Clashes over land clearly continued under Bédié and Gbagbo. The latter came from Gagnoa in the southwest, and his ascension to the presidency empowered indigenous groups to attack others.

In the context of the war, such clashes intensified, in particular in the western areas in or near the buffer zone.[102] The most common pattern documented was where "allogènes" were targeted or sometimes even completely removed from some villages; these, in turn, would be followed by counterattacks against indigenous groups by the initially targeted groups.[103] In some cases, state-supported militias would participate in the attacks. The best available resources on this form of violence are the quarterly human rights reports of the human rights office of the United Nations peacekeeping mission in Côte d'Ivoire, called UNOCI. The reports describe frequent sets of attacks and counterattacks in and around the buffer zone.[104] The worst violence happened around Douékoué, Guiglo, and Bangolo.[105]

---

100. Balint-Kurti 2007: 17; Human Rights Watch 2003: 25–26.

101. Human Rights Watch 2003: 22.

102. Some major incidents took place in and around Duékoué, Guiglo, Bangolo, Man, Fengolo, Gohouo Zagna, Baibli, Gonie Taouke, Oumé, Doekpe, Dieouzon, Douekpé, Tahoubly Gaé, Toulepleu, Sinfra, Gagnoa, Toazeo, Diahouin, and other locations. See Human Rights Watch 2003; MIDH 2004a, b; UNOCI Human Rights Reports 2005–2007.

103. MIDH 2004a.

104. UNOCI HR 2005–2007, e.g. 2006: 14–15.

105. Merrill 2005; UNOCI HR 2005–2007.

Cumulatively, the violence was worse than ever previously experienced in independent Côte d'Ivoire. However, the overall level was much less than many feared, and crucially for the thesis of this book it did not display the characteristics of mass categorical violence or genocide. For the 2002–2006 period, there is no standard estimate, but the toll almost certainly does not surpass 10,000 civilian deaths and is probably closer to 3,000 to 5,000 civilian deaths.[106] The 2003 UN human rights report estimated 1,000 to 2,000 killed.[107] That number unquestionably grew, given the violent urban repression in early 2004, the violence following Operation Dignity in November 2004, and the tit-for-tat violence that continued between 2003 and 2006 in the west and southwest. But with the exception of a few incidents, the numbers killed per event in the existing United Nations human rights documentation tend to hover between 5 and 20 deaths. Moreover, as figures 5.1 and 5.2 show, there is a clear pattern of declining violence after the first six months of warfare.

Much of the violence is group-selective. But the logic is principally repression coupled with negotiation—not group destruction or imposing maximal costs. The urban violence by security forces and militants against demonstrators and Dioula/foreigners was designed to intimidate, punish, and control potential opposition. The battle-related violence was designed to punish collaboration and to deter future collaboration. In these examples, the logic is within a communicative and coercive framework—to control a distrusted population—rather than to impose maximal costs on or destroy that population. The intercommunal violence in the west had the potential to escalate to something close to genocidal violence, in which the logic would have been to remove or eliminate "allogène" populations, but even there—for reasons elaborated below—the violence remained restrained and conformed more to a tit-for-tat logic of punishment and revenge, rather than group destruction. Moreover, many more rural locations with intermixed populations were peaceful than violent, even in the western and southwestern areas.

Top-level government policy also was ambiguous. At some times, national-level officials such as a Member of Parliament or military spokesman seemed to incite violence against civilian politicians and non-Ivoirians; some broadcast media did the same.[108] There were military calls—reminiscent of Rwanda—to search for "accomplices."[109] Gbagbo's call to patriotism speech

106. For a similar number, see McGovern 2011: xvii.
107. UNHCHR 2003.
108. Human Rights Watch 2002: 5; Human Rights Watch 2003: 13.
109. Human Rights Watch 2003: 13.

on September 20th was militant; he called the country to war, saying that when someone approached him with a sword he would draw his own sword. He called on the country to fight terrorism and those who oppose democracy and the Republic.[110] At the same time, some two weeks later on October 8, 2002, President Gbagbo addressed the nation, telling supporters: "Don't attack foreigners, don't attack your political opponents. Our struggle is not with them."[111] Interviews with military officers and government ministers indicate that there was a deliberate effort not to create an "enemy" category that could be reduced to a social identity. Gbagbo's official discourse, as cited in the October speech, was not to target foreigners or northerners even if he called on the state and the population to fight for the republic.

There are other important measures to note. Although the government is widely seen to have armed militias in the West, the government also appointed military prefects throughout the western areas where violence was the worst. Those military administrators consistently acted to quell the violence; several whom I interviewed were also originally northerner and Muslim. Overall, many more places in the country remained peaceful than were violent. Immigrants and migrants exist side by side throughout the forested areas of the west and southwest, yet in the majority of villages and throughout whole regions and departments there was little to no intercommunal violence reported. In other words, while the violence in Côte d'Ivoire was extra-local, the physical extent and scale of the violence was limited.

The 2010–2011 Patterns of Violence

The patterns of violence are similar during the 2010–2011 electoral crisis. In the urban areas, the main perpetrators resembled those in prior episodes of violence: gendarmes, specialized military units often with links to the presidency, and pro-government youth militants. As before, these actors violently suppressed demonstrations and protests; they ransacked opposition political party offices; they raided and attacked opposition-leaning neighborhoods. Throughout the period, there was consistent intimidation of northerners, Muslims, and non-Ivoirians, including at times inflammatory speech on the official, state-backed news programs.[112] Throughout the period, the logic of the urban violence was communicative and coercive: It was designed to

---

110. Gbagbo 2002a.
111. Human Rights Watch 2002: 5.
112. Human Rights Watch 2011a, b; Straus 2011b; UNHRC 2011a.

control Ouattara supporters through fear, intimidation, and selective killing; the violence did not exhibit a logic of group destruction.[113]

The second major theater of violence was the western area of the country. In these areas, there again was a pattern of tit-for-tat violence, a cycle of attack and counter-attack, between autochthonous and allogène communities in the region. Large-scale attacks took place around Douékoué and Guiglo, but there were also reports of intercommunal violence in Daloa, Gagno, Oumé, Sinfra, Bloléquin, and other locations.[114] The single worst incident took place in March 2011 in Douékoué as pro-Ouattara rebel forces captured the city from pro-Gbagbo forces and killed hundreds of Guérés (Krou).

All told, by the end of April, the United Nations estimated that about 3,000 civilians had been killed.[115] Some of the worst violence took place in the west and southwest, but a careful counting by the United Nations High Commissioner for Human Rights of the 1,012 killed suggests that roughly equal numbers of Krou and allogènes died, conforming to a tit-for-tat logic.[116] All told, the post-electoral violence represents terrible violations of human rights, but the strategy was to control the target population through limited violence, intimidation, and fear, rather than to destroy that population—despite the presence of all the most potent risk factors of genocide.

Sources of Non-Escalation and Factors of Restraint

The standard answer among diplomats, NGO workers, and many Ivoirians as to why the violence remained limited is external response. At the height of the civil war in 2002 and 2003, as well as at key points of escalation in 2004 and again during the 2010–2011 post-electoral crisis, a range of external actors reacted swiftly and decisively to contain the growing crisis in the country.

The initial military action came in 2002 from the French, which reacted within a week of the onset of the military confrontation to establish a buffer zone between rebel and government forces. Militarily, their action was followed with a deployment of ECOWAS troops, all of which morphed into one of the largest Chapter VII United Nations peacekeeping operations of the first decade of the twenty-first century. That mission was known as the United Nations Operation in Côte d'Ivoire (UNOCI). Diplomatically,

---

113. Straus 2011b.
114. Human Rights Watch 2011a; Straus 2011b; UNHRC 2011a, b.
115. UNHRC 2011c.
116. UNHRC 2011b.

from the beginning in September 2002 through the Ouagadougou Agreements in 2007, the Ivoirian crisis was the subject of intensive ceasefire and peace negotiations, resulting in eight different agreements (Accra I, II, III; Linas-Marcoussis; four Ouagadougou Accords).

Moreover, at key escalation points, international actors imposed sanctions and threatened judicial action against some of the instigators of violence.[117] During the post-electoral crisis, the United Nations Secretary General, UNOCI representatives, West African states, and ultimately the African Union consistently pressured Gbagbo to stand down.[118] French and UN forces later assisted the pro-Ouattara rebels to oust Gbagbo.

Several dimensions of these external actions are notable. First, the French intervention was swift, and the French military is a credible and formidable fighting force. Second, from the earliest stages right to the end in 2011, regional West African states were actively involved in mediation and diplomacy, often decisively. West African states had two principal interests: the fate of their nationals, of which there were more than five million in Côte d'Ivoire, and the economic stakes given that the Ivoirian ports are the main points of entry and exit for most goods. Third, the French and subsequent African and UN peacekeepers established an effective buffer zone. International peacekeepers also monitored ceasefires and provided information across enemy lines.[119]

In addition to raising the costs of violence on perpetrators, external action mitigated battlefield escalation, thereby reducing threat (at least in the first period). Specifically, external actors established a buffer zone that separated fighting forces, shared information between belligerents, and eventually created a joint military command.

But that is not the whole story; the success of international actions should be seen within the context that supported them. Based on my research, which included interviews with senior military officers and political actors, I conclude that at neither crisis highpoint did Gbagbo's forces develop a plan to systematically destroy, cleanse, or reduce the northern or Muslim population of Côte d'Ivoire. The pattern is one of escalation followed by deescalation—or pushing to the brink of violence but then retreating—and firmly within a repressive, communicative logic of violence. That dynamic cannot be explained by external actions alone. I emphasize five points.

---

117. Akhavan 2009.
118. Bassett and Straus 2011.
119. Fortna 2008.

Military Dynamics

Except at the very beginning in 2002 and at the end in 2011, the default military strategy on both sides was not to launch military offensives to defeat opponents and to retake territory. This diminished threat. Both sides were content with an equilibrium of "neither peace nor war," at least until 2011.[120] From the beginning, the political and military leaders on both sides quickly agreed to ceasefire and peace negotiations. To be sure, there were some exceptions when government forces, for no more than a day or two at a time, launched assaults on Bouaké to recapture the rebels' default headquarters there. But these offensives were quickly repulsed and then abandoned. Why?

One reason is clearly the international presence. Another, I contend, is the military dynamic between the two sides. On the rebel side, the leadership was composed of junior ranking officers who had little combat experience and who were apparently disgruntled over pay and promotions.[121] Their initial military strategy was primarily a mutiny, which in turn grew into a rebellion. But once established, the rebel military command did not seem to pursue a military strategy to capture Abidjan; after mid-2003, with the exception of the fight for Bouaké in 2004, the rebels very rarely engaged government military forces. Rather, the rebels' strategy was to hold territory, to develop a taxation system, and to collect rents. This was not inevitable, even with the international forces: The insurgents could have ignored the peacekeepers and pursued a military solution, especially as Gbagbo stalled between 2003 and 2007. Indeed, in 2011, the rebels did pursue a military solution.

On the government side, the army was structurally weak. Houphouët's vision was explicitly to have a weak and multiethnic army.[122] The country relied principally on France to guarantee security, and France maintained a large military base on the outskirts of Abidjan. During the crisis years of the 1990s, Bédié invested in the army to earn its loyalty, but its basis, size, and role still did not change significantly. Guéï was a military leader, but his tenure was short, and there is no evidence that he systematically sought to change the basic power of the military in the country.[123] An intellectual and democracy activist for many years, Gbagbo himself did not initially invest in the military. Once the war started, he appointed pro-FPI allies into positions of authority, expanded the army significantly, created a new security operations

---

120. This is stressed in McGovern 2011 as well.
121. Balint-Kurti 2007.
122. Ouattara 2011.
123. Ouattara 2011: 199.

command center, and recruited from among the galaxie patriotique.[124] But still, by the time that the war began, the Army as such was not hardwired for combat.

"We did not have a professional army," summarized a pro-FPI Army major in an interview. "The army was not constructed as a tool for war." He argued that the army was designed for maintaining order and stability; prior to the war, it conducted few military exercises, and officers were not extensively trained for combat. Another officer said: "I must tell you we were never an army for war. That's why we failed."

In a brief interview, Désiré Tagro, a key ally of Gbagbo and, at the time of the interview, the minister of the interior, simply replied that "the weakness of the army" was the reason why the government did not pursue a military solution or an offensive strategy in the war. An Ivoirian academic similarly characterizes the military as "syndicalized," meaning that soldiers and officers want to be treated as civil servants, with pensions, per diems, and housing allowances. Their interest is not combat.[125]

The weakness of the Ivoirian army could have produced a sense of military vulnerability, leading to elevated threat and the use of mass categorical violence or genocide to contain or destroy the threat. However, that was not the case here. The logic of genocide and categorical mass violence implies a military solution, a war, against an identity group to defeat or destroy an enemy. But the idea of a military solution was foreign to the military institutions in Côte d'Ivoire. The government strategy on balance never became to win a war, but to negotiate, and, as we shall see, to protect the economic structure of the country.

Also critical is that the Ivoirian military did not construct the war as a pernicious fight between identity groups. In interviews, high-level officers claimed that they never defined the enemy as an identity population. Nor in public statements did senior political or military officials routinely characterize the enemy as inherently pernicious or unwinnable. Nor was there, according to interviews with army officers and diplomats, a purging of northern or Muslim officers or soldiers. According to an Army major:

We called them "rebels," "assailants," and "soldiers of fortune," but there was no typology. *Not as northerners?* No, in the FANCI [the Ivoirian army], 30–40% come from the north. It was not easy to simplify the situation. In Côte d'Ivoire, there is a level of education, and we have 60 ethnic groups. We marry each other. There is intermarriage

124. Ouattara 2011: 200–202.
125. Ouattara 2011.

everywhere. You see a leader from the north married to a wife from the south, and vice versa an officer from the north who is married to someone from the south. At no point were families targeted. There was not a foundation of ethnic hatred in the war. In the heart of the nation, in the heart of people, that did not exist. People from the north were not suspected simply because they were from the north. . . . Ivoirité was a cultural idea used by politicians to win elections, to win over the people at the base. It was not in the minds of Ivoirians.

Similarly, an Army colonel said:

We could not at first define the enemy. Progressively we realized that they were our Ivoirian brothers who had external support. In the hearts of Ivoirians, we are *brassé* [intermixed]. We have 60 ethnic groups. We had no definition of the enemy. There was neither an ethnic nor a religious definition. They were our friends in front of us who identified with the north, who defined the situation in that way. *Why not?* It is part of the foundation of Côte d'Ivoire. The criteria in the army for entering or promotion are not ethnic. In our culture, one marries across groups.

Interviews with FPI government ministers produced very similar lines of argumentation.

One might have expected that in 2011, as the rebels advanced on government forces, that threat elevated, leading perhaps to a characterization of a total war between identity groups. Yet this did not happen. In fact, the army effectively stood down, and extensive interviews I conducted with officers suggested they had no appetite to fight to the death. None said they were deeply afraid of the rebels or northerners, even if they were critical of the rebels' decisions.

Founding Narratives

All of that begs the question of why state elites did not define the enemy as an identity category or as inherently dangerous. They could have. Ivoirité and the nativism within FPI circles lend themselves to defining the war in identity terms and to seeing the war as a final showdown between ethnic groups. My main answer is that Côte d'Ivoire has a strong counternarrative to framing the state as belonging to a particular identity group, which meant that framing the war as between two inherently oppositional groups was an alien way of interpreting and framing the conflict.

To understand why, it is critical to reexamine the founding narratives under Houphouët. For more than thirty years, Houphouët—a charismatic, sometimes revered figure given his initial accomplishments—preached the language of "dialogue" and "peace," often at length. In presidential speech after presidential speech, Houphouët emphasized the importance of tolerance, solidarity, prosperity, and discourse. An analysis of forty-seven public speeches on national holidays between 1961 and 1990 reveals that Houphouët's consistent message was that the country had to build national unity, to avoid violence, and to modernize. In about 50 percent of the speeches, he stressed values of solidarity or tolerance and peace (or both). He consistently referred to a "spirit of permanent dialogue" in the country. When he identified threats and challenges, the main ones were economic in nature, such as terms of trade, and the difficulty of developing a harmonious nation. He did not identify an identity category as a danger or threat. Nor did he identify Côte d'Ivoire as the rightful purview of any one ethnic or religious category. In short, unity, dialogue, economic growth, stability, peace, and multiethnicity represent core national values that Houphouët promoted. And, indeed, his political practices, as discussed above, reflected most of these principles. He sought multiethnic representation in his cabinets; he encouraged ethnic and religious mobility rather than exclusion and rigidity; and, under him, there was widespread ethnic intermixing or "brassage."

Consider representative excerpts from three Independence Day speeches, reprinted in the state-owned *Fraternité Matin*: On August 7, 1966, Houphouët said:

> Côte d'Ivoire, a land of frequent exchange, solemnly reaffirms its firm belief in the value of dialogue, in the necessity of confronting opposing points of view through peaceful solutions. . . . To think and act Ivoirian is to go beyond oneself and to have a constant fraternal dialogue with others, all others, no matter the tribe, professional category, or social class to which they belong. Stability is a priority as well . . . which results from a politics of peace, progress, justice, equality, solidarity, and fraternity. . . . Côte d'Ivoire cannot and does not want to be a dictatorship. Thanks to God and ourselves, it is a country where one does not kill, where brotherhood is truly accepted such that we pardon even the most serious faults, where one feels solidarity with everyone else.[126]

On August 9, 1967, he struck similar themes:

> The spirit of tolerance that animates us demands proof from us. That is why the permanent rule for our action is dialogue, loyal confrontation

---

126. Houphouët-Boigny 1966.

of points of view, even disagreements. . . . Committing to these rules of thought and action makes us in all circumstances determined to function in the interests of Ivoirians and in the interest of peace.[127]

And again on August 12, 1985:

For our modest part in Côte d'Ivoire, we try to sow and grow the seeds of peace, love, justice, liberty, tolerance, and solidarity everywhere. Ivoirians want peace; it is their second religion. . . . In Côte d'Ivoire, all the disagreements that persist are managed in a peaceful way through Dialogue and by excluding force.[128]

Figure 5.3 summarizes the first president's philosophy: "Dialogue: Peace is not a vain word." Even in his final days, as the country moved into multipartyism, he reiterated the same themes. On October 6, 1990, some three

FIGURE 5.3   Houphouët's themes of dialogue and peace. Courtesy of Tom Bassett.

127. Houphouët–Boigny 1967.
128. Houphouët–Boigny 1985.

weeks before multiparty elections, for example, he called "peace" his legacy, "the one I want to leave to you when I step down." He also called peace the country's most "precious treasury," urging his party supporters to stand by the principles of "unity, mutual trust, and solidarity."[129]

I do not know of survey research to gauge how widespread these values are among Ivoirians. But in interviews with political, academic, legal, and military elites across ethnic groups, some Ivoirians explicitly credited Houphouët with instilling a national culture of inclusion. Some, in particular those associated with Gbagbo and his party, were less inclined to give political credit to Houphouët (given the former president's opposition to Gbagbo and the FPI). Nonetheless, in interviews they cited values of dialogue as well as "métissage" and "brassage"—the intermixing of populations—as fundamental to the culture of the country. "Côte d'Ivoire is a product of métissage," said an Army colonel in an interview.

For example, in an interview, Sébastien Djédjé Dano, an FPI government minister, gave little credit to Houphouët. But he said that as soon as the war broke out, the FPI party leadership realized that interethnic conflict and inter-religious conflict should be avoided: "The risk was a war between Christian and Muslims or between the Bété and the Baoulé. We wanted to avoid all that. . . . Even on the military plan, we made that clear. . . . From the beginning, Ivoirians mobilized to have dialogue."[130] "The country is brassé," he continued, and it has a strong culture of peace.

In a separate interview, a law professor associated with the FPI claimed: "The country is totally mixed. This is a country of settlers. People are intermarried. Every southerner has a northerner in his family, and every northerner has a southerner in his family."

That Côte d'Ivoire is a multiethnic state built around values of openness, dialogue, and tolerance was the conclusion of a 2004 United Nations investigation by the Special Rapporteur on contemporary forms of racism, racial discrimination, xenophobia, and related intolerance. Visiting the country at the height of the war, he concluded that:

> Côte d'Ivoire has no tradition of xenophobia and Ivoirian society has developed a deep-rooted multi-ethnicity, a peaceful coexistence, based on intercultural values, mechanisms, and practices forged over many years by all the communities circumstance has thrown together, whether through migration, family, and cultural ties, or economics. The basic premise is borne out by the closeness of the inter-ethnic weave, as

129. Houphouët-Boigny 1990.
130. Interview, Abidjan, May 4 2009.

reflected in the large number of multi-ethnic families that have sprung from its mixed marriages, the rich fabric of its cultural and spiritual interaction, the mobility of the country's various ethnic groups and—an indisputable indicator of a culture of tolerance—the large number of foreigners in the country. All observers agree that mono-ethnic families constitute a minority of the Ivoirian population.[131]

Houphouët's speechmaking was not solely responsible for national values of tolerance or an image of the national community as "brassé." Côte d'Ivoire has many ethnic groups—there are sixty, often grouped into four or five large categories such as Akan, Krou, Malinké, and northern or southern Mandé. As discussed below, such groups have informal mechanisms of conflict mediation and solidarity that are common in West Africa. Those practices clearly predate Houphouët. Nonetheless, even if Houphouët did not create such ideas, he clearly emphasized them and elevated them to core national values for thirty years.

Houphouët's founding narrative constitutes, I claim, a strong counternarrative to group-selective violence among the political and military elites who would be essential to crafting and implementing such a policy of violence. Evidence is found in the interview data presented above. But consider some statements that Houphouët's successors made.

Bédié championed Ivoirité; he sought to exclude Ouattara from elections; he introduced the 1998 Land Law; and his administrations favored Baoulé.[132] An analysis of his public speeches reveals an emphasis on the economy, progress, and development rather than on social issues. But even Bédié did not completely abandon core values that Houphouët had instilled. In several official speeches, he emphasized aspects of peace, dialogue, and multiethnicity. For example, in a major speech on April 25, 1990, as president of the National Assembly, Bédié faced a restive state in the throes of democratic transition, economic decline, and structural adjustment. He emphasized the values of peace and stability, crediting Houphouët for "harmoniously integrating into his policies of peace and progress Côte d'Ivoire's natural principle of a pluralistic society based on ethics and tribes."[133] In a speech three years later to the National Assembly, on April 29, he emphasized the value of dialogue as indispensable.

As president, his speeches focused most commonly on the economy. But even on the eve of the 1999 coup, in an address to the National Assembly on December 22, he emphasized sovereignty, citizenship, and nationality.

131. UNHRC 2004: 12.
132. Langer 2007.
133. Bédié 2000.

He lauded the PDCI for fabricating a "unique melting pot" and fostering the values of dialogue and peace. Once ousted, he defended Ivoirité as non-exclusionary and an effort at cultural integration.[134] Whether one takes Bédié's claims at face value, that he defended his record in such terms is indicative.

General Guéï's first address on December 24, 1999, claimed that Bédié was ousted because he refused "dialogue." In a radio interview the following day, in defending his decision to allow Bédié to flee, he asserted that "Côte d'Ivoire is a country of forgiveness and tolerance." On January 21, he condemned Ivoirité and emphasized "brotherhood and solidarity." To be sure, Guéï ultimately embraced a politics of exclusion toward Ouattara. But nonetheless he sought to defend the legitimacy of his actions, including the coup, under the cloak of the core values Houphouët had promoted. That is a further indicator that such values had normative currency and legitimacy.

The greatest risk of mass categorical violence took place under Gbagbo, given the onset of war, his party's use of parallel paramilitary forces, and the rise of nativism. But Gbagbo himself had an ambivalent relationship to Ivoirité, which he claimed was a creation of Bédié's and was a Pandora's box that it would be "irresponsible" to open.[135] While many core FPI supporters among westerners interpreted Gbagbo's rise to the presidency as an opportunity to act on nativist claims to the land, Gbagbo himself was more elusive.

His main ideological presentation over the course of his long career was to fight for democracy, to achieve a second or "true" independence for the country, and to "refound" Côte d'Ivoire, notably with greater autonomy from France.[136] In interviews from the 1990s and 2000s and in official FPI programs, Gbagbo's leitmotifs are liberty, democracy, modernization, autonomy, and above all "refounding" the nation.[137] As a socialist, labor organizer, political detainee, and long-time opponent to Houphouët, many of his supporters admired Gbagbo as a leftist, pro-democracy militant, his own man, and a "symbol of the anti-colonial struggle," as one pro-Gbagbo author wrote.[138]

Nothing explicit in his various writings speaks to refounding the nation along identity lines. In his 2000 statement laying out his presidential vision, he wrote explicitly of the importance of unity, solidarity, reconciliation, and peace. While sharply critical of Houphouët as a dictator, Gbagbo nonetheless referred to a political program "based on openness, tolerance, and dialogue."[139]

---

134. Bédié 2000.
135. Soudan 2010.
136. Memel-Fotê 1998; Soudan 2010.
137. Front Populaire Ivoirien 2000; Gbagbo 1995, 2000.
138. Gnakalé 2006: 191.
139. Gbagbo 2000: 13.

To be sure, these are propagandistic statements, and throughout his career Gbagbo resorted to street protest and intimidation, usually through youth groups. But there is little evidence of identity-based exclusion or hierarchy as central to his "refounding" narrative. The same is true of the many written statements that key elites from his party or government have published.[140] In an interview, the head of the party, Pascal Affi N'Guessan, categorically denied that his party championed Ivoirité or exclusion; that was the work of the PDCI. "There is no interethnic problem" in Côte d'Ivoire, he insisted, arguing that Ivoirians refuse to see the conflict as between groups. Again, such claims serve the party and himself, but the framing itself is important and consistently against the idea of seeing a primary and exclusive political community or as seeing the state as the property of one identity group.

Though firmly committed to staying in power, Gbagbo's political strategy was to combine repression and intimidation with nominal accommodation and inclusion. He often played on both themes, sometimes in quick succession. For example, at a rally shortly after the massacre at Yopougon in 2000, he championed reconciliation, but he also warned ominously of conspirators plotting against him and his supporters chanted slurs of "Mossis get out."[141] Within weeks of establishing his presidency, he spoke of the value of reconciliation and national unity. In mid-2001, he established a National Reconciliation Forum, to which he appointed a northerner as the head, and which concluded among other recommendations that Ouattara should be granted citizenship. But at the same time Gbagbo resisted implementing real reforms that would regularize politics in the country. In short, Gbagbo tended to tack back and forth between populism and militancy, on the one hand, and the ideals of unity and inclusion, on the other.

Consider the extremely heated period following the onset of war in 2002. Upon returning from Italy, he called for patriotism from his supporters in a militant speech, as noted above. But in a key speech on October 8, 2002—the second since the war started—he explicitly warned against xenophobia. He defended his right to rule, lambasted the "armed attackers," and told them to lay down their weapons. "I am for dialogue," he said. "I am for dialogue. I

---

140. For example, Séry Bailly (2005), a minister and academic, wrote a book entitled *Ne Pas Perdre le Nord* (Don't lose the North), in which he argued against identity-based division and against northernist ideology that saw history through the lens of discrimination. Moïse Lida Kouassi (2010), also a minister under Gbagbo, frames the FPI's struggle as one for democracy. He also presents himself and Gbagbo as being committed to identity-based and democratic diversity for Côte d'Ivoire (e.g. 170, 197, 249). Even Blé Goudé (2006) makes France his principal target and resists the term *xenophobic*. These are, to be sure, interested self-representations, but they are nonetheless revealing and stand in contrast to equivalents in places such as Rwanda.

141. *New York Times* 2000.

am not for war. This war, we fight it because it was imposed on us. I am for peace." He expressed his commitment to mediation. He went on:

> Foreigners are not our problem today. Foreigners are not our problem. Our fight is a fight to liberate our country. And not to attack foreigners. We have laws. Foreigners who live with us as long as they respect our laws, we have no problems with them. Do not attack foreigners. Do not misunderstand this fight. Do not misunderstand the target. Our enemies today are the attackers, those who remain armed. If as I hope they lay down their arms in the days that come, then we will have discussions with them, as they will no longer be enemies or adversaries. Do not attack foreigners. Do not disperse them. We do not do that.[142]

Starting in October, he entered into political negotiations that led to a reconciliation government being established in early 2003; he also created a Ministry of National Reconciliation. In this period, the central ideological theme was that Côte d'Ivoire should achieve a "second independence," which largely meant freedom from France's neocolonial interests and influence.[143] But the 2003–2010 period was also marked by Gbagbo playing political games, announcing election dates and then canceling them, and generally pursuing a strategy of maintaining a "neither peace nor war" equilibrium.

When the electoral campaign heated up in the late 2000s, Gbagbo again did not embrace exclusionary politics. The director of Gbagbo's reelection campaign was a northerner, as was one of his most influential advisers.[144] When asked in a lengthy *Jeune Afrique* interview about the fact that the majority of northerners support Ouattara, his response was: "It is my responsibility to convince them it is in their interest to vote for me."[145] His response was not to dismiss, demean, or intimidate northerners. He did not consider northerners unwinnable. And—though this is hard to interpret politically—in his personal life, Gbagbo's second wife, Nadiana Bamba, was a northerner.[146]

This depiction of Gbagbo is not meant to absolve him, the leaders of his party, or his supporters from egregious human rights violations. The International Criminal Court indicted the former president in 2011. Rather, the depiction

---

142. Gbagbo 2002b.

143. Banegas 2007; Piccolino 2012; Smith 2011. In a memoir, Blé Goudé (2006: 102, 117) defines his objective as the "total liberation of our country." Though no fan of Ouattara and other non-FPI elites, his main vitriol is directed at France, for instance the chapter called "Ma Vision de la Politique."

144. Airault 2010.

145. Soudan 2010.

146. Mieu 2009.

suggests a more nuanced portrait than is often presented, one that indicates a tension between militancy and populism, on the one hand, and some of the core national values that run through Côte d'Ivoire's political space, on the other.

One final, more anecdotal piece of evidence: In 2011, President Ouattara announced the formation of a truth commission. It was modeled on the example of South Africa's Truth and Reconciliation Commission, and Desmond Tutu even came to Côte d'Ivoire to offer his blessings. But the official title in Côte d'Ivoire differed from the one used in South Africa. In Côte d'Ivoire, the body was titled the "*Dialogue*, Truth, and Reconciliation Commission" (emphasis added). Its inaugural meeting, on September 28, was held in the "Hall of Peace" of the Félix Houphouët-Boigny Foundation in the first president's hometown of Yamoussoukro. The symbolism suggests that the themes of Houphouët's founding narratives remain current.

As my interviews with military officers above suggest, these narratives interacted with how the enemy was defined during the war. Consider this interview with a junior officer. I asked him about defining the enemy as an ethnic group:

> We are a regular army; we have universal rules that we follow. One cannot kill an unarmed civilian. That would be irresponsible. *But in other places armies kill civilians when fighting wars.* You see your enemy and you cannot do anything against them so you kill civilians, ah no, no, no, we don't do that. That's impossible. . . . At a certain moment, people said it was the Dioula who are destroying the country, the people of the north. They were civilians. We did not say that in the army. In the army, we had everyone, north, south, this and that. Gbagbo succeeded in calming people down. He said, "We have an enemy. It is the MPCI. It is the rebels. Not the others." It was during the crisis. People wanted to attack the Dioula. He calmed things down. No, we don't do that. To define the enemy as an ethnic group? That could never work. In Côte d'Ivoire, we marry each other by love not by ethnic group not by region. A Bété has a Dioula wife. For example, me, I had a child with a Burkinabé woman. We could not define the enemy as an ethnic group.

Or consider this interview with an officer in the special forces:

> *What was your objective in the war?* It was to protect the people and the goods of the country. *What about attacking civilians?* "Ah, never!" I am a professional. I went to MPT (a military academy). In 10 years we never touched a single civilian, honestly. I spent my time protecting civilians. We don't just do whatever. We went to school. When one of my men

touched a civilian, that was wrong. That was death! *How did you define the enemy?* Even if you have an enemy, you don't touch them. Never! *How about defining the enemy as an ethnic group?* Ah no! We have 60 ethnic groups here. Someone who is here is from the north; someone there is from the south; the mother here is from the north, and the mother there is from the south. It is not possible to have a fight between ethnic groups. I often make a comparison with the U.S. How many states do you have? 52? You never fight each other. That's bullshit. That's a lie to say that there could be ethnic fighting or massacres! We are all related [*parenté*]! My sister is burkinabé! [from Burkina Faso originally]

What we see in these excerpts—and what recurred and recurred in elite interviews on five separate research trips to Côte d'Ivoire—was a theme of "brassage." Over and over again, unprompted, elites claimed that Côte d'Ivoire is fundamentally a multiethnic national community, where intermixing of populations is the norm. Such a narrative cuts against the idea of defining Côte d'Ivoire as serving one identity category and in turn makes defining "enemy" as an identity category unthinkable—or at least very hard to think.

Institutional Resonance of the Founding Narrative

A narrative of brassage dovetails with Houphouët's founding principles, but there are other, more material sources of such a notion. One is migration, which is extensive, such that by the 1990s there was little territory that was ethnically or religiously majoritarian.

According to the 1998 census, only five of the country's twenty regions are majority Christian.[147] Based on disaggregated census data, I calculate that only nine of twenty regions have one ethnic group greater than 50 percent of the population. A similar ratio (54%) holds for the country's fifty-nine departments. Non-majoritarian demography is especially pronounced in the most tense areas in the war (the west and southwest). For example, Fromager is Gbagbo's home area, but the census shows the population to be 23 percent Akan, 22 percent Krou, and 30 percent non-Ivoirian.

In Haut Sassandra, Sud Bandama, and Bas-Sassandra—all in the west and southwest and potential FPI strongholds—the ratios are similar. The first is 22 percent Akan, 11 percent Krou, 35 percent southern Mandé, and 18 percent non-Ivoirian; the second is 26 percent Akan, 22 percent Krou, and 36 percent

---

147. Bassett 2011; Bouquet 2005: 177–86.

non-Ivoirian, and the third is 31 percent Akan, 12 percent Krou, and 42 percent non-Ivoirian. Consider Moyen Cavally, where some of the worst violence took place: It is 16 percent Akan, 28 percent Krou, and 36 percent non-Ivoirian. These population ratios suggest from where an ethnic nationalist or nativist impulse might arise, but they also indicate a geographic space literally crisscrossed by many identity groups.

Another source of "brassage" is intermarriage. Ivoirians in interviews frequently cite the extent of interethnic and inter-religious intermarriage in the country as evidence of how fundamentally multiethnic and multireligious the country is. There are not, to my knowledge or the knowledge of statistical officials I interviewed, reliable data on cross-identity intermarriage. Ivoirian intellectuals and governmental officials insist that intermarriage is more common than not, especially among upwardly mobile and urban populations. Marriages are also international. One 2005 government study of marriages in Abidjan measured whether Ivoirians married other Ivoirians. That study found that one in five marriages were between Ivoirians and non-Ivoirians, a statistic that speaks to the frequency of cross-identity marriages.[148]

Coupled with the Houphouëtist political narrative on dialogue, tolerance, unity, multiethnicity, peace, solidarity, and modernization was a political practice of open migration and ethnic balancing. At the social level, the country is marked by intense ethnic and religious physical mobility, as well as interethnic and interreligous marriage. Taken together, these narrative emphases and actual practices contribute to a sense that the country is fundamentally intermixed. That shared perception, I believe, constitutes a powerful restraint on any effort to redefine the Ivoirian political community or national space in terms of one ethnic or religious bloc and to foment violence along those lives.

Another area to examine is the history of political coalitions. The fear of genocide holds that a southern Christian bloc would destroy northern Muslims. A Christian/southern coalition would require a political alliance between the two principal southern language groups, the Akan and the Krou. But such a coalition is unlikely. The two main parties representing the groups, the PDCI and the FPI, respectively, have consistently been political opponents in Ivoirian history. The FPI was formed in opposition to the PDCI. At least as of this writing, the two parties have never entered into a political coalition. By contrast, the RDR (representing mainly northerners) has been in coalition with the FPI (against Bédié in the 1990s) and with the PDCI (against Gbagbo in the 2000s).[149] Many leading RDR cadres,

148. Institut National de la Statistique 2007: 18.
149. Bassett 2011.

including Ouattara, were politically trained and disciplined within the PDCI under one-party rule.

The history of political coalitions is rooted in shared agricultural interests between the core supporters of each party. In the country in general, the three main farming migrant populations are Baoulé/Akan, Muslim/northern, and immigrant groups. As the census data demonstrate, these three groupings are each numerically as large in western and southwestern areas as are Krou populations. As economic data (below) also show, the Krou are much less represented in agriculture than the other main groups in the country. In effect, this means that the economic interests of the Akan are generally more aligned with northerners and non-Ivoirians. The politics of autochthony hurt the Akan as much as the non-Ivoirian/northerners. Prior to the onset of armed conflict, the dominant pattern of violence between "allogènes" and autochthons in the west was between Baoulé and Krous. For example, in the runup to and aftermath of the 1995 elections, in places such as Fengolo and Gagnoa, the primary targets of Krou populations were Baoulé.

The history of political coalitions also resonates with Houphouëtism. The Akan represent about 40 percent of the country, and the dominant sub-group of the Akan, the Baoulé, represent about 20 percent of the population. Houphouët calculated that neither the Akan nor the Baoulé could exclude other groups. He developed an explicit, multiethnic strategy for ruling and for building the PDCI party.[150] The idea of non-exclusionary domination of any one group and the practice of multiethnic coalitions were built into the political development of the party and the country under Houphouët. To be sure, the PDCI under Bédié in the 1990s championed the exclusion of Ouattara. But the trajectory of coalition-making in the country, which is underpinned by shared agricultural and migration interests, favors an alliance between the Akan and northerners. Moreover, the practice of politics under Houphouët was to build multiethnic coalitions in part because the Akan and Baoulé were not an outright majority. In short, the political dynamics of coalition-making in the country cut against the formation of a majoritarian southern/Christian bloc, and they reinforce and interact with an ideological emphasis on unity and multiethnicity.

Finally, there is a history in the country of formal and informal intergroup alliances at the local level. These range from inter-clan and inter-familial to interethnic processes of conflict management and prevention. The alliances include everything from refusing to spill blood with an intercommunal ally, providing shelter and food, mediation, and so forth. The alliances permeate

---

150. Zolberg 1969.

the country. A map produced by the Ivoirian League of Human Rights shows that pacts of non-aggression, solidarity, peace, and cousinage (more on which in the next chapter) are widespread in every region. While such alliances can undoubtedly be broken in periods of intense escalation, in the context of other powerful factors of restraint they create an additional domestic source of deescalation and non-escalation at the meso level.

Economic Incentives for Restraint

There are also economic sources of moderation. Most important are the structure and scale of the Ivoirian economy. Ivoirian elites are aware of the central importance of agricultural production, trade, and commercial activity; they appreciate the wealth generation in the country, and during the war they were wary of jeopardizing it.

The Ivoirian economy is built around the production and export of primary products, most importantly cocoa and coffee, but also rubber, palm oil, timber, cotton, and nuts. The Ivoirian ports are regional hubs for import and export; the Port of Abidjan is the second-largest port in Africa and the largest container terminal on the continent. Over time, the country has developed thriving commercial and transportation sectors. Moreover, Côte d'Ivoire has comparatively large trade associations as well as middle-class actors who have domestic clout and inherent economic incentives to protect the sources of their wealth and therefore to preserve stability.

Côte d'Ivoire's agriculture sector is vast, and the export of primary products is the largest source of state revenue. Throughout the 1970s, 1980s, and 1990s and even through the 2000s, cocoa and coffee dominated the country's Gross Domestic Product. Even as late as the mid-2000s, cocoa and coffee accounted for about 50 percent of GDP and nearly 60 percent of export revenue.[151] This is the case even as Côte d'Ivoire began in the 2000s to drill and export petroleum products. According to government statistics, 3.2 million people in Côte d'Ivoire work in agriculture (representing more than 50% of all work in the country); of those, 1.2 million were involved in cocoa and coffee production.[152] In short, agricultural production is a giant in the Ivoirian economy and a leading source of state revenue.

These sources of wealth and revenue—as well as commercial traffic and trade—are violence-sensitive. Agricultural activity is widespread across the country, rather than enclaved, so any large-scale disruption caused by mass

---

151. Economist Intelligence Unit 2008.
152. Institut National de la Statistique 2001b: 82.

violence would interrupt the labor, harvest, maintenance, and transportation of commodities. Were sustained, large-scale violence to take place, it would have major negative repercussions on agricultural production. Furthermore, the main labor supply for primary products in the fertile west and southwest are Ivoirian migrants and non-Ivoirians. Those laborers are precisely the would-be targets of any state-led categorical mass violence campaign. According to the 1998 census figures, of the total 3.2 million involved in agriculture, 25.6 percent were non-Ivoirian, 31.2 percent were Akan, and 27.3 percent were northerner (Voltaic or northern Mandé); these three categories represent the allogène communities in the west and southwest. Only 7.5 percent were Krou.[153] In short, any campaign of mass violence against foreigners and migrants would negatively impact the main labor supply for the state's key source of revenue. Awareness among the military and political elite of these structural dimensions of Côte d'Ivoire's political economy created incentives to deescalate or moderate the use of violence over time.

One piece of supporting evidence comes from trade statistics. According to the Economist Intelligence Unit and the International Cocoa Organization, cocoa production did not fall but expanded during the course of the conflict. In the six years prior to the 2002 conflict, the average annual export tonnage of cocoa was 1.2 million tons. In the six years after 2002, the annual average was 1.35 million tons of export.[154] Similarly, if one compares the volume of tonnage being imported and exported from the country's two main ports of Abidjan and San Pedro, the volume of freight increased during the course of the crisis from 16 million tons in 2002 to 18 million tons in 2006.[155] Government statistics further show that the overall total volume of all exports dipped in 2003, but the volume started to increase again by 2004 and grew thereafter.[156] That said, it should be noted that coffee production declined during the war crisis period, extending a pre-2002 trend, from an average of 202,000 tons to an average of 119,000 tons comparing the six years before 2002 and the six years afterward.[157]

The consistent and even growing agricultural commodity production and exports across most sectors, even in light of armed conflict, demonstrate a state interest in maintaining those economic sectors. After an initial dip due to the war, military and political elites consciously sought to protect and

153. Institut National de la Statistique 2001b: 83.
154. International Cocoa Organization Annual Reports, available at www.icco.org/about-us/icco-annual-report.html, accessed June 20, 2014.
155. Economist Intelligence Unit 2008: 60.
156. Institut National de la Statistique 2008a: 32.
157. UNCTAD Reports.

reignite the agricultural sectors. I do not have direct evidence from Gbagbo or his closest advisors; however, the idea of protecting core economic activities came through in interviews with high-ranking military and government officials. Consider this quotation from an Army colonel interviewed in 2009:

> When the crisis broke out, we said to ourselves that this was an internal crisis. What was necessary from the government side is that we had to preserve the essential structure [*tissue*] of the economy and to avoid destroying the infrastructure. We could not destroy the infrastructure and we had to avoid harming the country's patrimony. That was the essential strategy—to avoid destroying the economic tissue of the country and its patrimony. *What was the economic tissue?* There were the agricultural products, minerals like diamonds, gold and petrol, the roads and the road system, and the two ports. We had this sentiment in the military; it was shared among the politicians and later the international community had the same position. One had to preserve the essential, and we were inspired by the experience of Liberia.

Other interviews yield much the same awareness—namely, to limit the extent of damage and to protect the economic foundation of the country. "There were economic stakes" of the conflict, said an Army major with close ties to the head to Army's top general in an interview. "We could not destroy infrastructure."

Another colonel, in a 2012 interview after the post-electoral crisis, explained why they did not put up more of a fight:

> In our mind we did not want to destroy our country, and that is why we avoiding using dangerous munitions. In Yamoussoukro, we did not want to have fighting in the political capital. And in Abidjan again, we did not want to destroy the country. Many of us had the opportunity to see what had happened in Liberia, the DRC, and elsewhere, and we saw the disaster. We did not want to see that kind of disaster in our country.

A related dimension is that Cote d'Ivoire has, by African standards, a comparatively large middle class, a social stratum that includes government employees in the public administration and education sectors as well as small business owners throughout the country. According to government statistics, there were more than 120,000 public administration and education employees who received, on average, nearly $13,000 per year in the year 2005.[158] The 1998 census showed 196,000 total public sector employees.[159] Despite the war, throughout the entire

---

158. Institut National de la Statistique 2008b: 24.
159. Institut National de la Statistique 2001b: 63.

crisis, all public employees received their salaries. Even in 2011 after the severe political disruption in Abidjan, when Ouattara was the newly installed president, he promised to backpay salaries of public employees who missed their salaries in the previous month due to economic sanctions imposed externally. Moreover, there is a large number of private businesses in the country. Statistics from 2000 compiled by the Chamber of Commerce show 20,117 total businesses, typically with more than six employees, in the formal sector as well as another 25,342 "micro-businesses" with five or fewer employees.

There are other measures. According to the 1998 census, there were 407,000 Ivoirians who had received a professional diploma, 906,000 involved in commerce, and 157,000 involved in high-level intellectual or scientific work.[160] Data from 2006 show that there were more than one million plane passengers in the country in that year.[161] Using a different method, the African Development Bank in 2010 measured 3.9 million citizens in the Ivoirian lower and upper middle classes, representing nearly 19 percent of the population.[162] In sub-Saharan Africa—even after eight years of armed conflict and more than a decade of crisis, given that these data were measured in 2010— Côte d'Ivoire had the fifth-largest middle class in sub-Saharan Africa, topped only by Botswana, Gabon, South Africa, and Ghana.[163] (This is a measure of per capita consumption at between $4 and $20 per day, which excludes the vulnerable or "floating" middle class but includes the lower and middle class categories in the African Development Bank report.)[164]

The social and political milieu of President Gbagbo, including many ministers and many high-level actors in the FPI—that is, those who would be responsible for any escalation on the political side—is the Ivoirian middle class. Prior to becoming a politician, Gbagbo was a university lecturer, as were many people in his cabinet and in high positions in the government. Their social networks and their own professional rise were through the country's middle class. In short, the Ivoirian middle class stood to lose a great deal were the country to explode, and awareness of that by political and military elites served as a source of restraint on the escalation of violence.

A third dimension concerns the presence of organized economic interest groups. From the beginning of the crisis, the Chamber of Commerce, associations of large businesses and medium and small businesses, and transport unions, among other organized associations, put private and public pressure

160. Institut National de la Statistique 2001b: 49, 59.
161. Institut National de la Statistique 2008a.
162. African Development Bank 2011.
163. African Development Bank 2011: 5.
164. African Development Bank 2011: 2.

on the government to tone down the conflict. Moreover, judging from interviews in the cocoa sector, large commercial enterprises also made clear to the
authorities the risk of escalating violence. For example, in 2006, a leading
business group, the Confederation Generale des Entreprises de Côte d'Ivoire,
held a forum on the negative effects of the conflict on the economy. In
attendance was the Ivoirian prime minister, Charles Konan Banny, himself
the former governor of the Central Bank of West African States. Such is
one example of the high-level attention to the risks that conflict posed to the
economy and to the organized response on the part of formal business or trade
associations in the country.

Putting several of these themes together, an influential major said in an
interview:

> Côte d'Ivoire is a land of encounter and exchange [*rencontre*]. I compare
> Côte d'Ivoire with the United States. Everyone marries everyone. You
> have Christians and Muslims in the same family. The identity ques-
> tion has really not been that important. In neighborhoods, you have
> everyone next to everyone. I have a Lebanese member of my family.
> You have intermarriage, between Ivoirians, between north and south,
> between west and east. We are so imbricated that it is hard to divide
> the population along those lines . . . in the sociology of the country it
> is just not possible. There is a culture of respect for the other and toler-
> ance. *What is the role of Houphouët in this?* Ninety percent of Ivoirians
> recognize what he did for the country even if they fought against him.
> He had the security to anticipate. He was proactive. He did not wait
> for the crisis to beak. He had social heft. And he had methods, good
> or bad, that preserved tranquility. *And what about during the war?* No
> actor wanted the situation to degenerate. Cocoa has an importance
> not only for the Ivoirian economy but also for the French, Belgian,
> and Swiss economies. It had a role of toning things down, of needing
> a semblance of peace. *Was this felt inside the army?* Our training officers
> don't do politics, but we understand the mechanisms in any case. There
> are interests. Look, half of this country did not pay for electricity or
> water. The government tolerated that. The company agreed to do it.
> Why? Because you had to preserve a minimum of infrastructure. There
> are economic interests to do so. All the subregion had people here.
> They sent money back. There are regional interests. *Did the soldiers
> understand this?* For the average soldier you were attacked and the rebels
> who attacked were ADO's soldiers [ADO refers to Ouattara's initials.]
> In the minds of soldiers, it was ADO's war. Others perceived them-
> selves as victims. After the crisis stared, Gbagbo gave the army a lot of

means. There was a certain connection between the individual and the institution. *Why not attack civilians to defend him?* The constitution is the soldier's Bible, especially in a crisis. Between disorder and justice, I choose justice. There are rules. The Army attaches itself to those rules.

These were the consistent themes of my interviews with a range of military officers over time in Côte d'Ivoire. The nation is multiethnic and mixed; the economic infrastructure was important to preserve; and the Army was rule-bound. While one cannot credit Houphouët alone with these ideas, they are in fact the central messages on which he sought to found the Ivoirian state.

Local Dynamics

The factors isolated so far operated primarily at the national level. But it is conceivable that local actors would be a source of escalation, given the nativist claims to land and territory and the formation of militia groups in the west. But again the Côte d'Ivoire case points to local sources of restraint.

One is what interviewees describe as "an equilibrium of force." This was present in particular in the western parts of the country where the fighting was most intense. The idea is that, given settlement patterns, no one ethnic community could dominate any other. As a result, attacks by one side resulted in equally harmful attacks by another side. This was true especially in those areas where nativism was strongest, that is, in the west and southwest, where Krou populations were minorities. Over time, according to interviews in the area, the non-domination of any one group led to an equilibrium of non-escalation. Each side knew that actions would be met with a counter-reaction.

There were also local costs to escalation. In particular, the main farmers in the west and southwest are allogènes. They had the skills and experience in planting, growing, and harvesting cocoa and coffee plantations and also had experience in planting, growing, and harvesting food crops. When allogène farming communities were attacked, interviewees in the western areas pointed to the food shortages that resulted, in addition to the harm to the coffee and cocoa production. The local costs in turn created a grudging acceptance by autochthonous communities of allogène communities, according to interviewees, a process that over time favored an equilibrium of non-escalation.[165]

---

165. McGovern 2011: 82–83 also has evidence along these lines.

Lastly, during the crisis, local governments as well as local and international nongovernmental organizations helped to establish interethnic peace committees throughout the western and southwest regions most affected by the violence. These committees created channels of communication between representatives of different ethnic groups. When disagreements or incidents of violence occurred, the leaders on the committee would meet to try to sort out the problems. Again, in the context of high-level pressure to commit violence, such mechanisms would likely be weak bulwarks against the violence, but in the context of non-escalation at the national level they created mechanisms of violence diffusion at the local level that local actors say mattered.

Despite a theoretical expectation that genocide was likely in Côte d'Ivoire, that outcome did not occur. I acknowledge international actions, which have received the lion's share of existing credit, but my emphasis is on domestic factors—military, ideological, political, economic, and local—that cut against escalation. Of those, I especially emphasize Houphouët's ideological legacy.

I recognize that the variables that I have identified in this chapter are interactive and potentially endogenous. Did Houphouët's economic model favor a founding narrative of dialogue and multiethnicity, or vice versa? Was external attention and military intervention successful because of Côte d'Ivoire's economic structure and importance, or did the dynamics not escalate because of the economic structure? Was external action successful because the belligerents did not want to fight to the end, or did they not want to fight to the end because of the external military action? Was the absence of a definition of the enemy as an identity category a function of the military dynamics or the prevailing ideological constructs in the country?

My research design for Côte d'Ivoire cannot answer these and related questions. However, the factor that stands out in comparative perspective is the founding ideals of the state. As we shall see in the next two chapters, in both Mali and Senegal—the book's next negative cases—key elites created a founding narrative of the state that emphasized pluralism, multiethnicity, and dialogue. These are narratives that deemphasized particularistic definitions of the primary political community. In contrast, the opposite was true in Sudan and Rwanda. While in each case there are specific factors that favor escalation or deescalation, it is how leaders define the national political community and the purpose of the state that separates the cases.

CHAPTER 6

The Politics of Dialogue in Mali

Mali in the early 1990s possessed conditions that favor genocide. Militarily, Mali faced an armed conflict that grafted onto a perceived racial cleavage between "white," nomadic Tuareg and Arab groups, on the one hand, and "black," sedentary, mostly southern groups that dominated the state, on the other. As in Rwanda, the 1990s conflict harkened back to one in the 1960s that had been violently crushed and for which the perpetrators of violence against civilians went unpunished. By 1994, the existing peace agreements were crumbling, and a nativist militia with an explicit cleansing agenda, the Ganda Koy, had formed. Politically, after three decades of dictatorship, Mali was in the midst of a turbulent transition to democracy. In 1991, there was a military coup that ultimately led to a national conference, a new constitution, and a new election. A new, democratically elected president came to power, but elite challengers and street protestors regularly contested his authority. In 1994, as in Côte d'Ivoire, the currency was devalued by 50 percent, and the president appointed his third prime minister in less than two years. Violence was in the air. Tuareg civilians had been killed on the basis of their identity.[1] Tuareg victim groups claimed a risk of genocide; Amnesty International warned of a dangerous spiral of ethnic violence.[2]

---

1. Amnesty International 1994; Baqué 1995; BBC 1994a; Claudot-Hawad 1995; French 2005; Lecocq 2002.
2. Amnesty International 1994; Claudot-Hawad 1994; Lecocq 2002: 275.

But Mali did not go the way of Rwanda, Sudan, Burundi, Nigeria, or other situations in which fragile states respond to armed conflict and political upheaval with mass categorical violence against civilians. Rather, the political leaders in Mali doubled down on what the president at the time, Alpha Oumar Konaré, called the "masterword" of his political approach: dialogue. The state initiated a series of regional and local community meetings in which locals aired differences; the prime minister toured the northern region of Mali, where the violence was concentrated, to encourage peace; the army incorporated former rebels into the armed forces; political and military leaders took a hard line against the militia; and President Konaré took every public opportunity to insist that national unity, the peace agreement, inclusivity, and tolerance were his terms of reference. The problem was a "national Malian problem," not a Tuareg one, President Konaré said in a radio interview at the height of the crisis in November 1994.[3] "The sacred duty of the president of the Republic is to protect the equality of all before the law," he said in a major address to the nation in June of the same year.[4] By 1995, the violence in the north was effectively over. In 1996, the deal was sealed when former combatants burned some three thousand guns in a "Flame of Peace" ceremony.[5]

That peace lasted for about a decade, but when new insurgencies broke out in 2006 and 2012, the political leadership's response was similar. In 2006, Mali's new president, Amadou Toumani Touré, told Malians in a national address to embrace each other and not to confuse Tuareg civilians with those who fight.[6] In 2012, after a new rebellion sparked anti-Tuareg attacks in the capital, President Touré went on national television and radio to appeal for national unity, to encourage Malians to "maintain a sense of brotherhood that has always characterized us," and to avoid confusing civilians with insurgents.[7]

Touré lost power in a military coup not long after that speech. In March 2012, capitalizing on dissatisfaction within the military and within the political class—largely over issues of corruption and the inability to quell the rebels—Captain Amadou Sanogo seized control of the state. Touré went into exile. However, the coup did not stop the advance of the insurgents, who represented a mixture of Islamist fighters and Tuareg separatists. Fearing a takeover of the Malian state by Islamist forces, France intervened militarily in early 2013, drove back the insurgents, and helped to shore up Mali's territorial integrity. Later that year, Mali held national elections, and after two

---

3. BBC 1994b.
4. Konaré 1994c.
5. Poulton and ag Youssouf 1998.
6. Présidence Mali 2006.
7. Présidence Mali 2012.

rounds of voting, Malians overwhelmingly elected Ibrahim Boubacar Keïta as president. Though a political opponent of Touré, Keïta was in fact the prime minister who, under Konaré, had toured the north to encourage peace. In his first public statement after being elected president, Keïta promised to be the "president of national reconciliation" whose "first duty . . . will be uniting all Malians—without exception—around the ideals of peace and tolerance."[8]

As in the 1990s, the 2012–13 crisis presented a serious risk of genocide and mass categorical violence. Resentment in the south against Tuaregs and Arabs was widespread. Actors within the Army had committed violence against Tuaregs and Arabs after retaking parts of the north. As in the early 1990s, local militias had formed to fight the Tuaregs and Arabs. In February 2013, the United Nations Special Adviser on the Prevention of Genocide issued a warning about identity-based violence in the north.[9] Forecasting models in that period placed Mali at great risk of mass atrocities.[10] Yet, despite such fears, just like in the 1990s, a policy of mass categorical violence against Tuaregs or Arabs never materialized. To the contrary, Malians elected a leader with a track record of emphasizing dialogue; once elected, he strongly advocated reconciliation.

What explains this trajectory—both in the 1990s and the 2010s? My central argument is that Mali's political leadership in the 1990s explicitly fashioned and championed an ideological vision around the values of democracy, dialogue, and a multiethnic national community. The political elite expressly grounded their vision in informal and formal institutions of alliance, mediation, consensus, and dialogue that, for them, dated back to the great days of the Mali Empire from the thirteenth to the fifteenth centuries. This ideological vision shaped a political and military approach that favored deescalation, incorporation, and eventually peace. While other factors of restraint were present, I contend that the founding narrative of democracy and dialogue, one that was fashioned at a critical juncture in Malian political history and that drew inspiration and legitimacy from everyday practices and a vision of the past, pushed the political dynamic in Mali toward inclusion and away from massacres.

To be sure, other factors mattered. Mali is a large, weak state, and the concentration of would-be targets of mass categorical violence lived in the north,

---

8. "Mali's Keita Vows to Be 'President of Reconciliation,'" Fox News, August 21, 2013, available at www.foxnews.com/world/2013/08/21/mali-keita-vows-to-be-president-reconciliation/, accessed June 21, 2014. Keita made similar public statements in the following months as well.

9. "Statement of the Special Adviser of the Secretary-General on the Prevention of Genocide on the situation in Mali," press release, United Nations, available at www.un.org/en/preventgenocide/adviser/pdf/SA PG%20Statement%20on%20Mali%20-%201%20February%202013%20-%20FINAL.pdf, accessed June 21, 2014.

10. Private communication with author.

where the state's presence was light. In addition, in the 1990s, the rebels' aims were to gain more autonomy or, at the limit, independence in the north, and the rebels were divided. In short, the threat that they posed to the south and to the capital, Bamako, was weak. But we know from the counterexample of Darfur (see chapter 8) that a divided rebellion in a remote region of a large, spread-out state, a rebellion, moreover, that posed a distant threat to the capital, could elicit mass categorical violence against civilians. As in Darfur, Mali had a willing and able local militia whose views resonated with the Janjaweed militia in Darfur—in Mali, the Ganda Koy wanted to remove the "slave-owning," "white" Tuaregs. In Sudan, the state entered into a quasi-military alliance of violence with the local armed groups, which together ultimately led to hundreds of thousands of deaths. In other words, in certain states even remote threats will produce a politics of mass violence. Not so in Mali. The key difference is the set of legitimating founding narratives that animated the political leadership in both places. In Sudan, it was a vision of ethnic (Arab) domination and control. In Mali, it was a vision of pluralism, dialogue, inclusion, respect for the other, and democracy.

Moreover, in 2012, the insurgents were stronger, and many among them wanted to capture the entire Malian state. Without French military intervention, the insurgents might well have captured Bamako. Yet even when confronted with real military vulnerability, political and military elites refrained from putting into practice a campaign of mass categorical violence. In fact, the key leaders—both Touré and Sanogo—explicitly promoted policies of inclusion and framed the fight as one to preserve pluralism and unity over separatism.[11] My answer to why this happened concerns the political grammar of the state, a founding narrative that favored incorporation and dialogue over violence—even in the face of repeated rebellions and military vulnerability. I do not mean to suggest that all is well in Mali. The situation remains fragile and tense as of this writing; violence and devastation have been real. Many Malians have become skeptical of political leaders and disgusted with corruption. But the founding narratives make genocide and large-scale, sustained, group-selective violence an unlikely choice at the national level.

The Mali case also speaks to some potential alternative hypotheses, in particular ones that surfaced in relation to Côte d'Ivoire. One potential counterclaim to the book's argument is that in Côte d'Ivoire the would-be target group, Muslim northerners, were roughly equal in size to the would-be perpetrators, Christian southerners. Yet in Mali the would-be target groups, Tuaregs and Arabs, were less than 10 percent of the population, comparable demographically to the Tutsis in Rwanda. In Côte d'Ivoire, many observers point to the critical

---

11. On the language of the military junta under Sanogo, see Bleck and Michelitch 2014.

role that external intervention played. Yet, in Mali—at least during the 1990s and 2006 military crises—no external military forces intervened. Finally, Mali also serves to counter the claim that the recipe for genocide and mass categorical violence is an insurgency rooted in uncontrolled territory and in a distrusted population in a weak, low-income state. In the 1990s, 2000s, and 2010s, Mali had all of those conditions—yet the political and military trajectory tacked away from escalation and mass killing.

Political Background and Context

Formerly French Sudan, Mali is a large country in the Sahelian band of West Africa. The country is one of the poorest in the world; in the 1990s, Mali was one of the five least developed nations in the world, according to the Human Development Index.[12] The main foreign exchange earners are and were cotton and gold, both of which are concentrated in the southern regions of the state. The country is divided into eight regions and the district of Bamako. The rebellion and the main events of concern in this chapter took place in the arid northern desert, an area comprised of the three regions of Gao, Kidal, and Timbuktu. The north constitutes about 66 percent of the physical territory but only about 9 percent of the population.[13]

Like many African states, Mali is a multiethnic, multilinguistic, and, to a lesser extent, multireligious state. The largest ethno-linguistic grouping is Mandé speakers, which includes the Bambara and Malinké groups. Together, they constitute about half the population, and each of Mali's six heads of state has been a Mandé speaker. Concentrated in the north but living throughout the country, Tuaregs constitute about 7.5 percent of the Malian population. "Arab" Moors, also concentrated in the north and active in the rebellions, are slightly more than 2 percent of the national population. In the northern three regions, the two other most significant ethnic populations are the Songhay and the Peul, respectively 6 percent and 17 percent of the Malian population. The main leaders and recruits in the Ganda Koy militia were Songhay, but Peul also formed an armed militia in the 1990s. To the extent that a risk of genocide existed in the 1990s, the principal targets would have been Tuaregs and perhaps Arab Moors, and the principal perpetrators would have been an alliance between Mandé speakers, who led the state, and Songhay speakers, who led the militia. The same alliance could have materialized again in the 2010s.

---

12. Docking 1997: 199.
13. INS 2011. These population figures come from the 2009 census, but the ratios are similar for the 1990s.

As a nomadic and semi-nomadic cross-border population in the African desert, Tuaregs have long been a source of fascination to outsiders. Much is written about Tuareg society, culture, and practice—a rich, complex, and long scholarship that goes well beyond the scope of this study. But a few points are worth underlining. "Tuareg" is best thought of as a cultural identity marker that refers to a people that share a Berber language and alphabet (Tamasheq) and, to a degree, a cultural history. But "the Tuareg" do not exist as a single actor. Tuaregs reside in multiple states in northwest and north-central Africa, principally in Mali, Niger, Algeria, Libya, and Burkina Faso. In each, they are minorities. The Tuareg are thus divided across states, each with a different history. Tuaregs are also subdivided by region and lineage within states—the Tuareg of Kidal, for example, are different from the Tuareg of Timbuktu in Mali. Tuareg communities are also hierarchical; internal status cleavages within Tuareg society are critical, and indeed an important dynamic within Tuareg communities and in relation to southern Malian communities is the existence of slaves, or *Bellah*. The main terrain where Tuaregs historically reside is arid and desert, and the main economic activities that they historically practice are nomadic pastoralism, pastoralism combined with agriculture, and caravan trade across the desert spaces. In modern times, Tuareg of course do much more; they are teachers, politicians, doctors, musicians, and so forth.[14]

Although internally divided, the Tuareg maintain and are perceived to maintain a distinct racialized identity vis-à-vis the populations of southern Mali. In a major study of the Tuareg rebellions, historian Baz Lecocq concludes that Tuaregs and southern Malians actively maintained mutual stereotypes of each other. In post-independence Mali, he argues, the political and military leaders considered Tamasheq-speakers "white, feudal, racist, pro-slavery, bellicose and lazy savage nomads."[15] By contrast, the Tamasheq-speaking communities considered southerners to be "an overwhelming mass of religiously ignorant and uncivilized blacks with whom they had nothing in common."[16] While encouraged under French colonialism, these images, Lecocq argues, animated the First and Second Republics. He concludes that these differences drove the various rebellions. Behind the stereotypes, the economies of north and south were not integrated, and the northern regions were in general marginalized in terms of development assistance and in terms of political representation in the state prior to the 1990s.

---

14. Bernus 1992; Boilley 1999; Bourgeot 1994; Hall 2011; Keita 2005; Krings 1995; Lecocq 2002.

15. Lecocq 2002: 44.

16. Lecocq 2002: 44–45.

The 1990s rebellions were not the first in Mali's north. Tuareg insurgents famously resisted French colonial rule and authority in the 1910s, an insurgency that was brutally repressed.[17] More importantly for thinking about the risk of genocide in 1990s Mali, Tuaregs also rebelled in 1963—three years after Mali's independence from France. The roots of that rebellion are complex. On the one hand, Mali's first president, a colorful socialist and anticolonial leader named Modibo Keïta, promoted a vision of Malian nationalism based on Mandé culture. He chose "Mali" as the country's name, in part to harken back to the great Malian Empire of the thirteenth to fifteenth centuries. He in turn actively promoted Malian national culture—with griots telling tales every night on Radio Mali—and draping parliament in expressions that came from the former emperor Sunjata (Sundiata) Keïta.[18] In textbooks, Mali's great glorious past was celebrated, often in a static and unrealistic way—one that was in part a response to the evisceration of Mali's past under French colonialism.[19] In so doing, Keïta built on and cultivated an everyday, pronounced sense of Malian history, to which I shall return.

But Keïta's nationalist vision was built around southern, sedentary Mandé (and Songhay) traditions. In Lecocq's analysis, the vision excluded and alienated the Tuaregs and Moors of the north; Malian officials conceptualized Tuaregs as "savage others" who generated a "nomad problem" for the state.[20] The regime also actively and rigidly sought to remake how life and the economy were practiced in rural areas.[21] In the north, the Keïta administration sought to change Tuareg culture by trying to eliminate the chiefs system, by endeavoring to liberate subservient *Bellahs*, by promoting sedentarization, and by imposing a tax on cattle.[22] Northern Mali, with its dependence on nomadic pastoralism, was referred to as "useless."[23] Such actions frustrated and angered some Tuareg, ultimately engendering resistance. That was coupled with strong revulsion to southern authority, at least among some Tuareg.[24] One captured rebel in 1963 said simply: "We, nomads of the white race, can neither conceive nor accept to be commanded by blacks whom we always had as servants and slaves."[25]

17. Boilley 1999; Bourgeot 1994.
18. Diarrah 1986: 86–89; Lecocq 2002; Konaté 2006.
19. Ba Konaré 2000b.
20. Lecocq 2002: 96, 74.
21. Amselle 1978; Diarrah 1986.
22. Lecocq 2002: 81–95.
23. Benjaminsen 2008: 829.
24. Lecocq 2002.
25. Lecocq 2002: 134.

In 1963, Tuareg insurgents attacked. The state's response to the rebellion is consistent with other counterinsurgency campaigns in remote areas in which the rebels belong to an ethnic category not well represented in the central state. In particular, Malian military forces collectively targeted civilians and rebels alike, exacting significant damage on the civilian population. The number of rebel fighters was comparatively small, a total of not more than 250.[26] The Malian military had far superior numbers of soldiers and equipment. But the rebels had tactical advantages in the desert, where they were mobile and where they used camels to attack and then retreat, sometimes to Algeria. By contrast, the motorized equipment of the government armed forces was fairly ineffective on the terrain.[27]

Unable to defeat the rebels, the army turned on Tuareg civilians, whom they "viewed as accomplices and potential rebels."[28] The repression was severe. At first declaring a region forbidden for everyone, the Army then created regroupment zones. The Army poisoned wells, machine-gunned herds and killed herdsmen, forced marriages, and executed key personalities as well as those being accused of disloyalty.[29] The rebels officially laid down their weapons in August 1964.

Though not a genocide, given the comparatively limited scale, the violence had the characteristics of mass categorical violence: large-scale, group-selective violence that conforms to a logic of coercion and repression. Once the authorities established effective control over the battlefield dynamics, the violence against civilians subsided.

The 1960s repression had many important legacies. One is the memory of atrocities and repression, in particular within the Tuareg communities, which in turn further drove those communities away from the south.[30] For example, writing in the 1990s, one important Tuareg political leader labeled the 1960s repression an "extermination."[31] Herds were also significantly depleted, which created vulnerability when drought hit in the 1970s. Many Tuareg also fled the country, seeking work in Libya, Algeria, Niger, and other countries, which in turn helped shape the 1990s rebellion. In addition, once the rebellion ended, the north was further marginalized.[32] One French scholar speaks of a "systematic marginalization" of the north for two decades after the rebellion.[33] Another

---

26. Lecocq 2002: 137.
27. Lecocq 2002: 137–44.
28. Lecocq 2002: 151.
29. Lecocq 2002: 152–63.
30. Keita 2005.
31. Ag Baye 1993: 247.
32. Ag Mohamed et al 1995; Lecocq 2002; Lode 1997a, 1997b; Poulton and ag Youssouf 1998.
33. Bourgeot 1994: 13.

describes how Tuaregs were asked to give up their nomadic ways of life and how southern rule meant the "negation of the Tuareg community" and "renunciation of the very idea of a nation or of a Tuareg people."[34]

In sum, when looked at in historical perspective, Mali had key background ingredients of genocide when the political and military crisis hit in the 1990s and the 2010s: a racialized and marginalized minority relegated to second-class status, a nationalist vision built on an image of a primary political community that does not explicitly include and arguably excludes the minority in question, and finally a past rebellion in which the state deployed significant violence against civilians and for which perpetrators were never punished. In other locations, such conditions drove mass categorical violence when severe military and political crises occurred. But something different happened in Mali.

Into the Crisis (The Second Republic)

Modibo Keïta was overthrown in a military coup in 1968. Keïta's successor, Moussa Traoré, governed the country until 1991—a period known in Mali as the "Second Republic." Hostile to independent political activity and suspicious of rivals, Traoré ruled Mali as a corrupt authoritarian state, abandoning some of Keïta's socialist policies and pursuing a pragmatic foreign policy.[35]

With regard to the north, Traoré's policies were consistent with those of his predecessor. While Tuaregs held a few token seats in the government and in Traoré's party, Tuaregs in general lacked significant political representation and influence in the national government, in the national civil service, and throughout the education sector.[36] By the early 1990s, there were only two secondary schools in the north.[37] Civil servants from the south resented being posted to the north and interacted little with the population.[38] No Tuareg was allowed to enter the national army.[39] If the regime overall was authoritarian, the experience of the north, which had been under military rule since the rebellion, was the most authoritarian.[40] Moreover, like the Keïta regime, the Traoré regime favored sedentarization and agriculture over the nomadic pastoralism that the Tuaregs and northern Arabs practiced.[41] The

34. Claudot-Hawad 1992: 145.
35. Poulton and ag Youssouf 1998: 27.
36. Humphreys and Ag Mohamed 2005; Keita 2005; Krings 1995; Poulton and ag Youssouf 1998.
37. Lode 1997a: 13.
38. Poulton and ag Youssouf 1998: 29.
39. Lode 1997a: 12.
40. Keita 1998: 11; Lode 1997a: 13.
41. Abdalla 2009; Humphreys and Ag Mohamed 2005; Krings 1995.

northern regions were in "exceptionally poor condition" relative to other regions before the 1990s.[42] In addition to these institutional factors, there remained the persistent question of an identity cleavage between north and south, especially between Tuaregs and Arabs on the one hand and sedentary populations, which dominated the south, on the other. Before 1990, many Tuaregs expressed a feeling of identity-based discrimination. Many felt like "second class citizens" in Mali.[43]

The absence of representation, the regional marginalization, the perception of discrimination, and the legacy of the 1960s repression all were essential long-term background conditions for the 1990s rebellion. But there were also more situational, shorter-term factors that increased stress in the north and that precipitated the insurgency. Central among these were sustained droughts in the 1970s and 1980s, which created stress on the northern populations and which also led to the migration of Tuaregs from northern Mali into Algeria and Libya. The difficulty of coping with droughts should be seen in the context of the policy environment, both the general pro-sedentarization policies toward the north as well as the legacies of the repression of the 1960s, both of which left pastoralists in a weaker position to cope with diminished rainfall.[44] In addition, political elites were accused of embezzling aid.[45]

External events also mattered. In particular in Libya, from the 1960s forward, General Muammar Qaddafi incorporated Tuaregs into his Islamic Legion and into the regular army, and Tuaregs in turn were deployed to wars in Chad, Lebanon, and Palestine, where they gained military experience. However, in Libya, the contraction of oil prices in the 1980s as well as Libya's battlefield losses in Chad led to a decommissioning of Tuaregs from the armed forces. Civilian Tuaregs also were retrenched from key economic sectors, namely the petroleum sector. All of these created reasons for Tuaregs to leave Libya and to assert demands within Mali.[46] Both within Mali and in the neighboring states, there were many young Tuaregs who lacked employment and employment prospects. They were nicknamed the "Ishumars," a Tamasheq word that derived from the French word for unemployed, "chômeurs." The rebellion was sometimes called the "war of Ishumars."[47]

In addition, the early 1990s was a period of democratic awakening on the continent after the end of the Cold War and the opening of previously closed

---

42. Humphreys and ag Mohamed 2005: 274.
43. Ag Baye 1993: 248.
44. Benjaminsen 2008.
45. Benjaminsen 2008; Keita 1998; Lecocq 2002: 176.
46. Humphreys and ag Mohamed 2005; Keita 1998; Lecocq 2002.
47. Lecocq 2002.

authoritarian regimes. Within Mali, a vibrant pro-democracy movement had already formed and was putting pressure on the then unpopular Traoré regime, which—as in Rwanda—created a new window of opportunity to act.

On June 28 and 29, 1990, about fifty rebels attacked Tidermene in northeast Mali, which was followed by an attack on Menaka. Initially led by Iyad ag Ghali, the rebel organization called itself the People's Movement of Azawad (MPA). (Azawad is the Tamasheq name for a large part of the northern region.) The insurgents, whose initial formal demands were to end marginalization, initially had just six Kalashnikov rifles but stole weapons and vehicles during their attacks.[48] A major boon to their ranks was the state response. Malian military forces responded initially with mass violence, which prompted more rebel recruits.[49] Even though the rebel group never exceeded several thousand people, the insurgents were effective against government forces, as one Malian Army colonel attested.[50]

In this period a second rebel organization formed, the Islamic Arabic Front of Azawad (FIAA). Initially considered a potential rival to the MPA, state military forces killed both Tuareg and Arab civilians alike. In a decisive misstep, following a rebel attack, the commanding officer of the Malian army in the north sent for thirty-one leading nomadic leaders. They were all executed in the town of Léré, and some of those who were killed were Arabs. From then on, the FIAA and the MPA fought with common interests.[51]

Following the initial successes of the rebels, Traoré realized that a military solution would be difficult.[52] The northern region is massive. Moreover, Traoré faced a major pro-democracy challenge to his government in the form of student and street protests; politically, his priority was the democratic opposition in the capital, not the rebellion in the north.[53] The presidency at first turned to Tuareg traditional authorities, some of whom he had integrated into the party and the government, but it became clear that there was an internal split between traditional authorities and younger, angrier Tuaregs.[54] But from that point forward he pursued a ceasefire and peace settlement, which culminated in the January 1991 Tamanrasset Accord, named after the Algerian city where they were signed.

The Tamanrasset Accord called for a series of security, decentralization, and special development provisions for the north, including a promise of

---

48. Ag Mohamed et al. 1995: 11–12; Lode 1997a: 21; Poulton and ag Youssouf 1998: 56.
49. Benjaminsen 2008: 829; Lode 1997a; Poulton and ag Youssouf 1998: 56.
50. Keita 1998: 15.
51. Lode 1997a: 22.
52. Keita 1998.
53. Lode 1997a: 23.
54. ag Mohamed et al. 1995: 10; Poulton and ag Youssouf 1998: 57.

47.3 percent of development funds for the north.[55] However, the Accord faced obstacles. Having been conducted in secret and with the text of the agreement remaining secret, the state appeared to have offered significant concessions. The Accord was met with disapproval from public opinion, especially in the south. Sedentarists in the north, who had been left out of the negotiating process, worried about their fate, and soldiers on both sides found reason to fault the agreement.[56] This dynamic was similar to what happened in Rwanda around the Arusha Accords, as discussed in chapter 9. Moreover, in this period, the rebels split up into four organizations. Three splinter groups disavowed the Accords, including two Tuareg groups who now claimed to fight for independence and the FIAA. The continued fighting precipitated new cycles of violence, including rebel banditry and attacks on Tuareg civilians by army soldiers.[57]

Separately from the rebellion, but crucially for understanding the course of events, Mali experienced a violent political transition in 1991. Starting in 1990, the regime faced increasingly strong domestic pressure to end the one-party system. This came in the form of an ad-hoc coalition of civil society organizations, nascent opposition political movements, lawyers, and trade unionists.[58] By January and February 1991, there were regular street demonstrations, which were crushed by security forces. The culmination came in March 1991 with a series of mass demonstrations in which the security forces killed as many as 200 civilians in Bamako. Facing a potential domestic uprising, military forces staged a coup on March 26, arresting Traoré and creating a National Reconciliation Council that soon shared power with civilians in an entity called the Transition Committee for the Safety of the People. The coup leader, who in turn was elected the head of that Committee (and effectively the head of state), was Colonel Amadou Toumani Touré, the same Touré who was elected president in 2002 and overthrown in 2012.[59]

From the beginning of the transition, the new authorities and pro-democracy activists made an effort to recognize the legitimate demands of the northerners. For the democracy advocates, the rebels' grievances were part and parcel of the movement to overthrow Traoré's dictatorship. For example, the new governing committee was composed of fifteen civilians and ten military officers. Among those civilians were two representatives

55. Ag Mohamed et al. 1995: 13.
56. Ag Mohamed et al. 1995: 13; Keita 1998; Lode 1997b: 413; Poulton and ag Youssouf 1998: 60.
57. Lode 1997b.
58. Centre Djoliba 2002; Wing 2008.
59. Centre Djoliba 2002; Docking 1997; Wing 2008.

from the rebel movements.[60] The committee also created a participatory National Conference, which hammered out the details of a new democratic constitution for the country.[61] One of the topics for explicit discussion was the situation in the north, which included a special session in Timbuktu in late November 1991. In short, the Malian democrats sought to include, rather than exclude, the northerners in the transition.

This initial position is arguably most visible in a key national address that Touré made just prior to the November meeting in Timbuktu. In the speech, he outlined his vision of a unified multiethnic country; he recognized the grievances of northerners and called for a "national pact," a term that would come to define a new peace agreement signed in April 1992:

> A military solution is costly and not desirable. It should be envisaged only in the final instance if there is no other way to protect national unity. That is why Mali has chosen another path, that of dialogue and reconciliation. . . . We have to commit ourselves to respect our unity and to take into consideration our differences. Only this recognition can make all Malians, whatever their origins, traditions, or modes of life, feel at ease in his country, not having to choose between being Malian or whatever his particular identity, whether Bambara or Tamasheq, Songhay or Dogon, Peul or Arab. In this way, unity is reinforced because quarrels and misunderstanding are avoided. . . . Our mission is that each Malian, sedentary or nomad, urban or rural, from the river or the desert, completely feels like a citizen, responsible and respected, loyal to the laws and protected by them, solidarity with all citizens. . . . That is how we define democracy. . . . We have to stop all violence.[62]

This speech is an example of how Mali's political elites promulgated a new founding narrative around an inclusive vision of the national political community—a vision that I argue restrained the escalation of violence.

Following the speech and the November meeting, the government, insurgent, and Algerian leaders set up a series of discussion meetings to resolve the civil war, which ultimately led to the National Pact.[63] The Pact called for the cantonment, disarmament, and integration of insurgents into the national armed forces and police; incorporation of former rebels into the

---

60. Poulton and ag Youssouf 1998: 61.
61. Wing 2008.
62. Touré 1991e, p. 2.
63. Ag Mohamed et al. 1995; Diarrah 1996; Lode 1997b.

civil administration; a special development fund for the north; repatriation of refugees; and elimination of certain northern military posts, among other provisions.[64] It was, as Touré promised, premised on a vision of inclusion and unity.

On the national political stage, the National Conference gave way to a new democratic constitution and to national elections in June 1992.[65] A trained historian and an opposition publisher, Konaré won the election as the head of the ADEMA party. Touré peacefully relinquished power, and Konaré vowed again and again, as we shall see, to respect the terms of the National Pact—even when it looked as if the agreement would crumble.

The Crisis Deepens and then Subsides: 1992–1996

Despite the Malian government's commitment to peace and despite the same among the majority of the rebel leadership, the conditions on the ground did not improve materially in 1992 and 1993. In 1994, the situation seriously degraded, with a rise in civilian violence and the appearance of militia forces with explicitly racialist and nativist demands. Politically, the country remained fragile.[66] Konaré faced steep opposition from students and other political parties.[67] In his first twenty months in office, Konaré was forced to appoint three different prime ministers. In January 1994, the West African currency, the CFA, was devalued by 50 percent, creating significant hardship within Mali's already quite poor population. One close observer of Malian politics called the situation in 1994 "a seemingly impossible set of circumstances in which to govern."[68] But with a strong commitment to dialogue and regional and local "concertations," the conflict turned around in late 1994 and 1995. By 1996, the war was officially ended.

In the immediate aftermath of signing the National Pact, problems arose. First, implementation was slow, in part because of the political changes in Bamako and the absence of international funding. Second, the leaders of the various armed groups did not exercise sufficient control over their organizations. On the rebel side, two new splinter groups formed; both insisted that they would not abide by the Pact. Rebel actors or armed actors claiming to be rebels engaged in banditry in the north. On the government side, discipline was weak after the military coup. Third, the integration of the rebels

---

64. Ag Mohamed et al. 1995; Lode 1997b; Poulton and Youssouf 1998.
65. Clark 2000; Docking 1997; Wing 2008.
66. Lecocq 2002: 254.
67. Couloubaly 2004.
68. Docking 1997: 195.

into the Army was done too hastily and created resentment among regular soldiers. Finally, sedentary farming groups in the north, especially the Song-hay, were not a central part of the negotiation and peace process. After the agreement was signed, some worried about their own livelihoods in the midst of conflict and about Tuareg domination in any postwar arrangement. All of these issues created major challenges. While the Malian government and the mainstream rebel leaders remained committed to the Pact, there was a loss of faith in the process and a loss of support among the public.[69]

In the north itself, during the first four months after the agreement was signed, there were between 50 and 120 attacks.[70] These were followed by "blind reprisals" against Tuareg and Arab Moor civilians, especially in urban areas.[71] The news stories were "full of violent attacks on the nomads."[72] Even in Bamako, there were fears of a pogrom, which led Tuareg and Arab civilians to seek shelter at embassies.[73]

Nonetheless, the government sought to abide by the Pact. The government also established mobile units to support the peace process that crisscrossed the north.[74] There were efforts to integrate rebel soldiers into the Army.[75]

But in 1994 the situation deteriorated further. In the context of the CFA devaluation, the rebels made more demands that further alienated the public. These included high quotas for northern soldiers in the army and representa-tion of northerners in Malian embassies.[76] There were further disagreements between the rebels.[77] In May, two violent incidents took place, one in which integrated rebel soldiers killed two Malian soldiers and another in which integrated rebel soldiers opened fire on a crowd in front of a hospital.[78]

Another key change took place when the Ganda Koy ("Masters of the Land" in Sonrai) formed, also in May. Led by a former Army captain, the Ganda Koy explicitly sought to protect sedentarists against pastoralists. The organization was rooted in Songhay northern communities, but it enjoyed popular appeal beyond the Songhay, given the worsening attitudes toward Tuaregs and Arabs among southerners.[79] For its part, the rebels accused the government of

---

69. Ag Baye 1993; Ag Mohamed et al. 1995; Lode 1997a,b; Poulton and ag Youssouf 1998.
70. Amnesty International 1994: 4; Lode 1997a: 29.
71. Lode 1997a: 28.
72. Lode 1997a: 29.
73. Ag Mohamed et al 1995: 28.
74. Lode 1997a: 28.
75. Ag Mohamed et al. 1995: 28–29.
76. Ag Mohamed et al 1995: 30.
77. Poulton and Youssouf 1998: 70.
78. Poulton and Youssouf 1998: 70.
79. Poulton and Youssouf 1998: 71.

supporting the militia. In one incident, Ganda Koy militia attacked Tuaregs and Arabs. When the rebels counterattacked, Malian soldiers ambushed them, giving rise to fears of collusion between the state's armed forces and the militia. Indeed, one former Army colonel later claimed that the Ganda Koy were given arms by government security forces.[80] In this key period, other violent incidents took place, including Army attacks on civilians, violence between Ganda Koy and rebels, and intra-rebel violence.[81]

The general deterioration prompted the government and rebel leaders to negotiate. The government also initiated regional concertations, not only for the north but also for the rest of the country.[82] In late 1994, government reshuffled the armed forces, removed units with bad discipline and appointed a new defense minister who, among other things, contacted newspaper editors to implore them not to publish articles that could incite ethnic hatred.[83] The Army also tried to change internal attitudes toward Tuaregs by initiating community meetings and delivering aid.[84] Those who had family ties to Tuaregs and Arabs were also promoted into positions of leadership.[85] In 1994 and 1995, local community-based actors initiated dialogue among themselves (in particular, between pastoralists and farmers in the northern region) to resolve differences and to end the fighting.[86]

Throughout this period, the political leadership in the form of the president and the prime minister consistently and unequivocally voiced support for a peaceful solution. They also consistently disavowed attacks against civilians and the use of militias.[87] By 1995, the fighting had effectively ended. In 1996, the "flame of peace" ceremony was held in which weapons were burned; the ceremony marked the end of the conflict.

The Risk of Genocide and Patterns of Violence

The risk of genocide in Mali in the early 1990s, especially 1994, was real. There was extreme political instability in the form of a new regime, street protests, a coup, and significant turnover within the first administration.

---

80. Keita 1998: 20.

81. Poulton and Youssouf 1998: 73–74.

82. Ag Mohamed et al 1995: 35; Couloubaly 2004: 79; Lode 1997a: 31–32; Poulton and Youssouf 1998; Wing 2008.

83. Lode 1997a: 31.

84. Keita 1998: 21.

85. Keita 1998: 23.

86. Benjaminsen 2008; Lecocq 2002; Lode 1997a; Poulton and Youssouf 1998.

87. Ag Mohamed et al 1995: 35; Diarrah 1996: 42; Lode 1997a: 30–31; Poulton and Youssouf 1998: 74.

There was a financial crisis, which, in combination with the devaluation of the currency, created considerable hardship on the population. This followed fourteen years of negative cumulative per capita growth.[88] Most importantly, there was an armed conflict, one that grafted onto an ethnic cleavage within the society. As part of that armed conflict, government forces and militias killed civilians on the basis of their ethnic identity, collectively categorizing civilians and rebels alike. No punishment for these crimes took place; there was impunity. Moreover, there formed, as we shall see, a racist, nativist language of "national belonging" among some armed actors. As in Rwanda, the 1990s conflict was the successor to an earlier one in which the state too used mass killings of civilians to suppress a rebellion. Yet in the 1990s, rather than turning to a "final solution," the Malian state leaders clearly articulated a politics of inclusion, dialogue, pluralism, and compromise, and they clamped down on militias who wanted otherwise.

Before turning to that policy of dialogue, I want to examine the escalatory language and the patterns of violence. At least initially, the state associated Tuareg and Arab Moor civilians with the rebels claiming to represent them.[89] Lecocq estimates that from June 1990 to October 1995, between 2,500 and 3,500 civilians were killed, the majority of whom were Tuareg civilians.[90] He refers to "pogroms" against Tuaregs.[91] Even in Bamako, Tuareg homes were attacked from the beginning of the conflict.[92] One journalistic account from the period details how even in 1991 and 1992 government forces raided Tuareg villages, attacks that "regularly turned into full-scale massacres, with soldiers shooting the entire male population of the village."[93] "The troops hunt us like animals," said one refugee quoted in the story. "Whenever they see a Tuareg, they kill him. It makes no difference whether it is a man, a woman, or a baby."[94]

A 1990 report described how for two months, in the areas around Gao and Timbuktu, troops killed men, raped women, pillaged and burned homes, and whipped and tortured others. A commander of paratroopers is quoted as saying at a public meeting: "The solution concerning the Tuareg is their extermination. I have come here to take care of that, and I will not waste my bullets, because one litre of gasoline is enough to burn 10 Tuaregs."[95]

---

88. Docking 1997: 199.
89. Amnesty International 1994.
90. Lecocq 2002: 257.
91. Lecocq 2002: 269.
92. Lecocq 2002: 268.
93. Rowland 1992: 44.
94. Rowland 1992: 44.
95. Lode 1997a: 24.

In another town, a commanding officer is said to have told Tuareg women: "We shall kill your husbands over there and we shall marry you in order to get children with you who will love us."[96] "The army made no distinction between Tuaregs," wrote two close observers.[97] A 1994 Amnesty International report describes how government forces, militia groups, and rebels were killing civilians in reprisal attacks. The report details massacres in which as many as fifty civilians were killed. The report details other cases in which dozens of Tuareg or Arab civilians were killed in response to rebel attacks.[98]

Perhaps the greatest danger was from the Ganda Koy and the political currents that the movement represented. The Ganda Koy was responsible for some of the worst massacres against civilians in late 1994, including ones in which hundreds were killed.[99] The leaders of the Ganda Koy and the documents it produced, in particular one called the "Voice of the North," were explicitly racist. One pamphlet declared: "Fellow citizens of the North, let us sweep away all nomads from our villages and cities, even from our barren land! Tomorrow the nomads will install themselves there as dominators. Black sedentary people, from Nioro to Ménaka, let us organise, let us take up arms for the great battle that awaits."[100] In a massacre in October 1994, Ganda Koy militants attacked a Tuareg camp, killing between 60 and 300 civilians. Justifying the action, a Ganda Koy spokesman was quoted as saying that "the Tuareg and Moor populations are more or less accomplices of the rebellion. We give ourselves the right to judge and punish them."[101] Some Malian press outlets published interviews in which they referred to a "hunt for red ears" or "white skin," references to racial stereotypes about Tuareg.[102]

Another report, this one by an anthropologist, refers to the way in which the Ganda Koy openly preached the extermination of "white" Tuaregs and Arab Moors. The militia's documents refer to a "wayward, stateless people without a homeland who came to the desert in miniscule tribes." The same document refers to Tuaregs and Arab Moors as racists and slaveowners. "Banditry is normal" for them. Most ominously: "They are a foreign body in the fabric of the society." These sentiments were echoed in the Malian press, according to the author.[103] Other self-defense groups also appeared in this period.[104] A *New York*

---

96. Lode 1997a: 24.
97. Poulton and Youssouf 1998: 56.
98. Amnesty International 1994; see also Lecocq 2002: 274–76.
99. Claudot-Hawad 1994; Lecocq 2002.
100. Lecocq 2002: 272.
101. Baqué 1995: 30.
102. Baqué 1995: 30; Claudot-Hawad 1994.
103. Claudot-Hawad 1995: 30; see also Bourgeot 1996; Lecocq 2002: 280.
104. Amnesty International 1994; Bourgeot 1996.

Times report from the period quotes a youth in Timbuktu who said, referring to Tuaregs, "The day may soon come when you can't find any of those people in these parts."[105] The same story shows how even government authorities were quick to suspect Tuaregs of harboring pro-slavery intentions.

In short, in addition to the structural conditions favoring genocide, there was categorical violence against a specific social identity group and public, exterminatory rhetoric. Local actors wanted, it seems, to initiate group-destructive violence against the Tuaregs and Moors. However, in the end, Mali's trajectory was clearly not genocide: The violence deescalated. Though the final numbers of dead are not precisely known, the various estimates reflect an outcome more like Côte d'Ivoire and Casamance than like Rwanda, Sudan, Biafra, the DRC, or Burundi. As noted above, one estimate claims that between 2,500 and 3,500 civilians were killed in the five-year period.[106] Another places the number between 6,000 and 8,000 total deaths.[107] While a tragedy for those who suffered these losses, the outcome was far short of the scale of violence that characterizes genocide.

Sources of Deescalation and Restraint

My central argument for explaining the outcome is that an explicit political ideology that emphasized democracy, multiethnic inclusive citizenship, and nonviolent dialogue acted as a significant restraint on the escalation of state violence. Mali was in the throes of a major political and military crisis, but the political leadership that made the key decisions viewed themselves as the midwives of democracy. Rather than positing the military threat as an alien enemy, the pro-democracy leaders endeavored to incorporate the insurgents, seeing the armed struggle as consistent with the aims of the new democratic era. In taking power but then establishing a National Conference and handing over power, Touré set the tone in 1991, and his specific articulations about the problem in the north were consistent with the democratic ideology. President Konaré endorsed, deepened, and intellectually grounded these values and took actions in the tense years of the mid-1990s; the leadership and vision that he espoused served to deescalate the crisis.

From where did this ideology spring? I credit the political elite for crystallizing a specifically democratic and inclusive ideology. This choice was not inevitable. In many states at that time, leaders resisted democracy, often claiming that democracy was a Western imposition. Even opposition figures, while

105. French 2005.
106. Lecocq 2002: 258.
107. Humphreys and ag Mohamed 2005: 248.

lauding democracy, infrequently embedded their opposition in an inclusion-ary, multiethnic vision of the state. Many parties instead argued it was their chance to have a piece of the national cake. Yet in Mali that was not the case. An inclusionary vision was not also necessary for an electoral majority. Indeed, Malian leaders *could* have scapegoated the Tuareg and sought to build a southern, sedentarist majority on the basis of exclusion.

To understand the choice, a critical element is the cultural milieu in which the political elites worked.[108] In Mali, there exist norms, practices, and institu-tions on which the elite drew to craft political values of mediation, inclusivity, and dialogue. Again, this was not an inevitable choice, and indeed prior Malian leaders were not democratic and, as we have seen, many Malians expressed violent views. But the political elite—many of whom were intellectuals and democratic true believers—attached their vision of democracy to a strong Malian culture. To be sure, "culture" is a broad category, one that incorporates many elements and is adaptable. For example, Mali's first president also cel-ebrated Mali's culture, but his vision was more exclusionary and was consistent with socialism. Yet the informal institutions in Mali's culture and the history of the Malian empire provided other raw material, one that the political elites spun into a narrative of dialogue, integration, and democracy.

Existing Literature

The existing literature consistently recognizes that the political leadership in Mali after the fall of Traoré took key steps that led to peace.[109] "The Malian political authorities since the transition constantly sought a negotiated solu-tion to the conflict in the North," write the authors of a major analysis of the period.[110] Political scientist Susanna Wing argues that the Konaré government used "dialogue as the foundation for policy-making" and was committed to political inclusion and the incorporation of previously marginalized groups.[111] In a memoir and analysis of the period, one of Konaré's ministers wrote that the former president "consistently chose dialogue and concertation as the only way to solve problems" even in the face of the rebellion and harsh criticism from political opponents and civil society critics.[112] Konaré's mode was to privilege consensus and human relations over coercion.[113] Other authors, as described

---

108. De Jorio 2003; Docking 1997.
109. Poulton and ag Youssouf 1998.
110. Ag Mohamed et al 1995: 28–29.
111. Wing 2008: 62, 155–57.
112. Couloubaly 2004: 54.
113. Boilley 1994: 121.

below, explicitly link the emphasis on dialogue and democracy to the Konaré administration's interpretation of Malian political culture and history.[114] This emphasis on top-down leadership is not to dismiss local peacemaking initiatives and community meetings that, starting in late 1994, were critical for building and cementing peace.[115] However, the ability for the local initiatives to succeed occurred within a political environment that both encouraged such dialogue and stressed a pluralist, pro-negotiation policy.

Speeches under Touré

Explicit commitments to democracy and dialogue are evident in the catalog of speeches that Touré gave and were published in the Malian press during the sixteen months he was in power in 1991 and 1992. For example, in his statement that opened the National Conference in July 1991, he laid out the objectives of the Conference as a "space of dialogue, concertation, to reinforce national unity and reconciliation, social peace, and dialogue so that democracy triumphs."[116] In a speech a month later in which he described the work of the governing Transitional Committee, he claimed, "Our wish is to resolve all the problems in our country with concertation."[117] In an address to the nation on Mali's Independence Day (September 22), Touré emphasized "values that are true to democracy," including respect for the other, pluralism, nonviolence, and multipartyism. Making reference to the rebellion and encouraging Tuaregs and all other ethnic groups to take part in the process of building a democratic country, he added: "Dialogue and nonviolence remain the only possible path to resolve the real problems concerning economic development and the political and socio-cultural fulfillment of all Malians."[118] Indeed, in every head-of-state speech (N = 10) retrievable in the Malian state newspaper, *L'Essor*, Touré consistently emphasized democracy, social justice, freedom, dialogue, national reconciliation, and openness. This was the case in the May Day speech 1991 in which he talked about a "spirit of dialogue and openness."[119] Even in the face of a reported attempted coup, Touré reemphasized the importance of the path of democracy.[120] There is also the crucial speech in November on the situation in the north, quoted at

---

114. De Jorio 2003, 2006; Docking 1997; Konaté 2006; Pringle 2006.
115. Ag Mohamed et al. 1995; Lecocq 2002; Lode 1997a; Poulton and Youssouf 1998.
116. Touré 1991b, p. 2.
117. Centre Djoliba 2002: 449.
118. Touré 1991d, p. 2.
119. Touré 1991a, p. 6.
120. Touré 1991c, p. 2.

length above, in which he lays out the importance of dialogue and a pluralist vision of the national community.

In short, at a critical juncture in Malian history—in the aftermath of a coup, in the middle of an armed conflict, and in the throes of a fragile political transition—the country's military leader and head of state explicitly emphasized dialogue, democracy, national unity, and a multiethnic inclusive vision of the nation. Touré's vision was one of mutual understanding, integration, and negotiation, rather than one of exclusion. Even at the height of the crisis in August 1994—more than two years after he had stepped down—he gave a prominent full-page interview in *L'Essor*. In the interview, Touré reaffirmed his commitment to national unity, peace, and the terms of the National Pact. He also clearly articulated a multiethnic vision of the country: "We need to quickly and very quickly identify the problem and find urgent solutions in order to avoid a terrible rupture to our unity. For that, we need every single patriot, nomad and sedentary, white or black, because our country belongs to all."[121] Such is a good summary of the inclusive aspect of the political ideology that Touré (and later, Konaré) advocated: "Our country belongs to all."

Speeches under Konaré

The values of dialogue and mediation were even more pronounced under the presidency of Touré's successor. Konaré explicitly grounded the values of democracy, tolerance, and discussion in Malian culture, history, and traditions. One of the most important words of his political approach, which at his inauguration he labeled the "masterword" of his policy, was *concertation*—a word also used under Touré. *Concertation* formally translates from French as "dialogue," but it has the added valence of a respectful discussion of views. Konaré, Touré, other Malian political elites, and Malians in general use the word in addition to *dialogue,* so in translation I retain the original French.

An analysis of presidential speeches by and interviews with Konaré in the crisis years of 1993 and 1994 (N = 20) show an unwavering commitment to democracy, dialogue, respect for difference, and nonviolence. Some speeches took place on national holidays, such as New Year's or Independence Day; others were more impromptu. These speeches were usually featured prominently in the local press, often filling several pages. My intention is not to assess their audience effects but rather to use the public pronouncements to characterize the content of the president's political vision.

---

121. Touré 1994.

For example, in his New Year's speech in January 1993, Konaré emphasized the values of democracy, social peace, dialogue, tolerance, and discipline.[122] In a speech later that month, celebrating the Malian national army,
Konaré closed by lauding the army "in the service of a democratic Mali" that
was being built with a sense of "solidarity and justice" and "a strict moral
respect for dialogue and tolerance."[123] In an April speech, following violent
street demonstrations in the capital, Konaré offered a full-throated defense
of democracy and nonviolence. "We knew that to leave behind the tragedy
of March 1991," he said, making reference to the crackdown on democratic
activists under Traoré, "the road toward democracy would be long and difficult. We had to show to Malians another way besides recourse to violence."[124]
In that year's Independence Day speech, he lauded various actors, including
the Malian Armed Forces for their efforts to integrate ex-rebels. He called
these Malians "descendants of an ancient culture."[125]

In his New Year's speech in 1994, Konaré again defended democracy,
decentralization, and the principles of dialogue. The speech is worth quoting
at length to give a sense of the president's language:

> Mali is for many in Africa an historic example, a reason to hope. That cre-
> ates in each of us a responsibility in relation to the process of consolidating
> our democratic institutions. . . . My dear compatriots, after a year and a
> half as head of state, there has not been one message to the nation where
> I have not reaffirmed that for all the problems our country faces there is
> no better weapon than democracy. . . . It is this virtue of dialogue and of
> concertation, this virtue of respect for the other while recognizing differ-
> ence that has allowed us to obtain some remarkable results in the treatment
> of the question of the North. Even if I know that we need greater efforts,
> given the resurgence of banditry in the regions in question. But the gaps
> in the application of the National Pact to date are due to complex logisti-
> cal problems and occasionally—we cannot hide this—to administrative
> weaknesses and to internal problems within a fluid society and not due to
> a rupture of trust between interlocutors. That is the key.[126]

As regards the rebellion and insecurity, the New Year's speech is critical. On
the one hand, Konaré explicitly affirms his commitment to democracy as the
"best weapon" for all problems. But—at a moment when the situation in the

---

122. Konaré 1993a, p. 2.
123. Konaré 1993s, p. 1.
124. Konaré 1993c, p. 2.
125. Konaré 1993d, p. 2.
126. Konaré 1994a, p. 2.

north was gravely devolving—he connected the commitment to democracy to the need for dialogue in the north. And, rather than abandoning the focal point of the National Pact in a difficult moment, he reiterated his support for it.

The speeches that followed in that same crisis year show a doubling down on the same ideas. For example, in a speech commemorating the March 26 coup, Konaré said, "I reiterate to everyone my constant wish always to resolve the problems of the nation, no matter how serious, with dialogue and concertation."[127]

In perhaps one of the most important speeches—at the height of the crisis in the north, after the formation of the Ganda Koy and a strong resurgence of violence in the north—Konaré marked the second anniversary of his presidency in the following way:

> On June 8, 1992, I said that concertation would be the "masterword of our policies." Despite numerous disturbances, including physical and oral violence that characterized the two years that just passed, I could act in no other way than by dialogue and concertation. . . . I am proud to be at the head of a People who know how to make tolerance and dialogue their cardinal virtues. A modern state, Mali had to add to its ancestral foundation an institutional infrastructure that could consecrate a real democracy. . . . The sacred duty of the President of the Republic is to protect the equality of all before the law and before the future. On June 8, 1992, I said that the "National Pact did not constitute the victory for one group over another." At the moment when Mali benefitted in the sub-region from excellent expertise in the treatment of minorities, one could not let the demons of passion force us into another age. . . . Today like yesterday, I call on men and women of our country, old and young, yes to the youth, to always defend the ideals of March 1991, and among those ideals are effort, work, respect for the other, respect for elders and for parents.[128]

Though I have truncated a long speech—one that spanned three pages in *L'Essor*—the excerpts show the poles of his political vision: dialogue, concertation, democracy, respect for the other, and tolerance. In that context, he affirms his commitment to the National Pact. And he grounds these values in Mali's "ancestral foundation," to which I will return.

On Independence Day in 1994—again near the height of the crisis and tension in the north—Konaré again used his presidential platform to champion dialogue, peace, reconciliation, unity, and the terms of the National Pact. But he also encouraged the population to see the northern problem as one of

---

127. Konaré 1994b, p. 2.
128. Konaré 1994c, pp. 1, 3.

"misunderstanding," rather than one of enemies, and he praised the recently initiated regional meetings and discussions in which, he claimed, citizens were embracing what brought them together, rather than what drove them apart. Here again the vision of the state is one that fights against "exclusion" and one that celebrates unity:

> The nation is a unitary body. Each year on September 22, Independence Day reminds us what a unified nation can accomplish. Today it is our democratic ideal, to fight against exclusion. . . . [lauding the regional concertation, he added] These concertations extend the politics of dialogue that we have always emphasized. I hope that they are the beginning of a new era of exchange in the context of reconciliation and dialogue in the context of responsibility. . . . In this, we will exclude no one and no one should be excluded. In the past, there were misunderstandings among citizens of our country between the components of the nation. The problem of the North comes from those misunderstandings. For a month, the sons of Mali have been debating this, in tolerance and in serenity. Everyone has been remembering the ties that unified all the communities of the North before.

Taken together, as I have argued, these speeches display and signal a coherent ideological approach. That approach valorizes democracy and dialogue above all, and it seeks to ground support for democracy and dialogue in a vision of Mali's past. The national community is imagined as inclusive; rather than demonizing northerners, the president invites his audience to understand them. With these speeches, Konaré established a policy of dialogue and deescalation, rather than escalation, in particular at critical moments when the escalation of violence was real and possible.

Interviews with Konaré

Beyond his national platform, Konaré was also consistent in all the interviews and statements retrievable through a Nexis-Lexis Academic search. For example, in an hour-long feature radio interview with Africa No 1 (based in Gabon but carried through the BBC), again at the height of the crisis, he championed freedom, openness, and the right to strike. When asked about how he planned to "to solve this problem of the Tuareg rebellion once and for all," Konaré gently corrected the journalists. The problem is not a "Tuareg problem," he insisted, but a "national Malian problem." He went on:

> The problem of the north is a tragedy. . . . [A]ll democrats understood that there was a time when the fight of our brothers from the north was a

fight for social justice and solidarity. . . . The National Pact that we signed with the Unified Movements of the Fronts of Azaouad [sic] is founded on the key principles of the unity of Mali and the territorial integrity of Mali, but also a Mali of diversities. I insist on this: Mali is a country of diversities. For us, our honor as democrats depends on the good management of a Mali of differences. . . . We made a certain number of mistakes in the implementation of the pact because the sedentary communities were not involved enough. The sedentary and nomad dignitaries were not sufficiently involved either but what I can tell you is that there is no genocide in Mali. Those who are at the helm of affairs in Mali today are just incapable of doing this. We were forced to stop, I repeat stop, the development of self-defense groups. . . . We clearly said that the armed forces and the security forces must intervene in favor of all the communities within the framework of a law-abiding state by respecting human rights. There is no military solution to the problem of the north.[129]

One can see similar positions in a series of interviews that Konaré conducted with a French journalist after the Malian political leader stepped down in 2002. In these, Konaré again defended a Mali that was "plural and unified, of all colors and all regions! In a democratic debate, you cannot take the path of violence."[130] In these interviews, Konaré again vibrantly defends the idea of a multiethnic community: "Mali is a country of diversities" and "plural and unified." The good management of democracy meant the good management of pluralism. In the radio broadcast, he redefined the problem in the north as a "national" one, not a Tuareg one.

In short, Konaré's democratic ideological conviction prompted him to label the situation in non-inflammatory terms, in terms that favored deescalation, rather than escalation. In these interviews—as in others—he endorsed the terms of the National Pact, he recognized the grievances of the rebels—calling them "brothers" and connecting their fight to the fight for democracy—and he clearly disavowed the use of armed militia groups. These are the top-level, macro positions that helped push Mali away from mass violence.

Elite Interviews

Interviews with high-level officials (prime ministers, defense ministers, the commission of the north, political party leaders) published in *L'Essor* in the 1991–1994 period conformed to the vision that Konaré championed. Malian

---

129. BBC 1994b.
130. Cattanéo 2004: 115.

political and military elites consistently advocated democracy, dialogue, and unity, and they disavowed the use of violence, including that of Ganda Koy. This was the case even if some claimed they understood the reasons why Ganda Koy had formed.[131]

To supplement these written statements from the period in question, I conducted a limited set of elite interviews with former Malian political and military officials. Even though the interviews took place fifteen years after the crisis, the former officials unequivocally endorsed the idea of dialogue, a multiethnic community, and democracy—all rooted in Mali's past.

Consider this interview with the former prime minister and president in 2013, Ibrahim Boubacar Keïta, who prominently toured the north in 1994 to calm tensions. Keïta said that the way to make peace was through internal dialogue and by implicating civil society. "In the Third Republic," he said, referring to his time as prime minister, "we tried to manage differently, to respect and to integrate them and to accept them in the new system we were building. We wanted to build a nation and with respect." In other words, the policy was inclusion. Reflecting on his time, he continued:

> In 1994, I went to the North. I took risks. I was surrounded by soldiers. But I had to show that we were capable of managing the country. I said, "You are Malians. You have rights. You will be respected, but be in the Republic. Put down your weapons." I repeated this again and again for 20 days in the North. My mission was very clear. . . . I worked with a man who had a very clear vision, President Konaré. . . . He was a historian, and that allowed him to have a very clear path. You need armed force to maintain order in a Republic but not for repression. You need to maintain order and have dialogue—in secure conditions. When you show a man that you respect him, that you consider his value, you allow him to be at ease. . . . We wanted a multiracial, internally cohesive country, one with integration. We are white and black. We are *métis* [mixed]. We would do everything to comfort the other in recognizing his difference. We were tolerant of every person on his own terms. We wanted to affirm an old solidarity.

Asked about the roots of this approach, he—like others—emphasized Malian traditions, culture, and history. Mali is an old country, he explained, adding:

> Malian culture—Malianism—is respect for the other. The regard for the other is singular in Mali. We remain singular in our identity. We are bearers of a great history that is rooted in trade and commerce between

---

131. For instance, interview with Diagouraga 1994, p. 3.

people. The relation to the other is sublimated to a rare degree. We have in this country joking relationships. We use it for conflict resolution.

I shall return below to the points about Malian history and culture, but the ideological position is—unprompted in the interview—very close to what Konaré and Keïta himself espoused at the time: a multiethnic community complete with an emphasis on tolerance, dialogue, and democracy.

These themes resurfaced in other elite interviews. For example, in an interview with Soumeylou Boubèye Maïga, defense minister under Konaré, he explained the approach to the rebellion in the following way: "In the 1990s, the idea was to have the rule of law and to have a unitary state with greater integration of all citizens. We had to resolve conflicts and to create more space for discussion, mutual understanding, and consensus. The idea was that the Third Republic had to guarantee this." The terms here are precisely those of the period when the crucial decisions were being made: a broad national consensus, mediation, building a democratic nation over the long term.

An interview with an another collaborator within the administration, Ousmane Sy, who served as the head of a decentralization commission in 1993 and then as a minister in Konaré's second term, argued that the Malian political leadership was quite conscious of the need to promote dialogue and consensus and to promote a vision of the nation, and its past, that rested on the idea of multiethnic inclusivity and understanding.

> We have a culture in which we look to have consensus and dialogue. We used that. We opened dialogue, and we had community concerta-
> tions . . . *Were you conscious of this at the time?* I can assure we were totally conscious. We were aware that the solution was not only a military one but also a political one. We understood the need for dialogue, for consensus, and for inclusivity. . . . We are a Sahelian culture, open, part of a space of encounter with diverse respect for people. The fundamentals of Malian culture and social capital are that we accept we are different but that we have a common patrimony. There is not a single Tamasheq that does not have a relation with a Peul or a Sonrai [Songhay] family. We have a culture based on centuries of cohabitation—based in part on conflicts but also on pacts. Each community has its particularism, but we have a common identity. In 1990s that is how we had the intercommunity meetings. People found their common identities.

Another interview was with Cheibane Coulibaly, an author, sociologist, and university official who also served as an informal mediator during the crisis years. He emphasized the local actors and the ways in which, after a certain point, they took steps that induced peace. The key from a political point of view, he said, was that the political leadership encouraged community dialogue, adding: "We have this culture here. In houses. In villages. Everywhere. We do reconciliation before conflict. Even small kids. They are implicated in *cousinage de plaisanterie* [joking alliances, as discussed below]. . . . That is the advantage of the great empires—in the Charter of Kurukun Fuga [the ruling code of Sunjata Keïta], after conquest, they shared power. It is codified in our culture." The conclusion from these interviews and others is that there existed in the 1990s an explicit, self-conscious political ideology grounded in a construction of Malian culture and history that valued dialogue, mediation, and pluralism. That ideological vision, in my view, was central in the government policies of deescalation, inclusion, and peace.

The Origins of the Politics of Dialogue and Inclusivity

In explaining the origins of the political ideology, one could argue that the ideology was derivative of an instrumental strategy. Ruling a poor country with a demoralized army not well positioned to fight in the northern arid and desert space, the leadership chose dialogue. Pluralism was the outcome of the absence of military capability, rather than pluralism shaping a policy of deescalation. The argument is plausible but faces three major problems. First, the strategy of inclusion and peace was both costly and, at the time, unpopular in parts of the country. The north was promised a suite of development funds that were desperately needed throughout the country, and judging from the existing literature the tide of Malian popular opinion was hostile to compromise in the north.[132] Second, violence *could* have been the strategy. To distract Malians from the economic and other problems of the day and to quell a restive opposition, the Touré and Konaré administrations could have ratcheted up the violence, demonized the Tuareg, and pursued some type of maximalist violence. That is what the Rwandan authorities did in the midst of their crisis in the 1990s. Third, there is no a priori reason why a military solution could not have been possible. The Army could have continued bombing the north; it could have allied with local militias. Through that combination—as in Darfur in the 2000s, Mali in the 1960s, or many of the cases described in chapter 4—the state could have sought a military solution.

To develop my claim, I take my cue from the elite interviews that, together with the existing literature, suggest that Malian culture and history matter. Mali's leaders espouse a self-consciously proud history, one of grand empires

---

132. For instance, Ag Mohamed et al. 1995; Boilley 1994.

and epic heroes, in particular Emperor Sunjata Keïta. Contemporary Mali is replete with everyday practices and informal institutions of integrative social interaction, in particular through the practice of joking relationships and, even deeper, through joking alliances between clans and ethnic groups.[133]

This past and this cultural space did not inevitably produce an ideology of democracy. Rather, in Mali there is a constructed past for which the agency of Mali's political and intellectual establishment should be recognized. Under Keïta, the great Mali Empire and Emperor Sunjata were celebrated daily and narrated by griots and in song. They were constructed as a foundation for Mali's postcolonial identity. Under Traoré, there is less evidence of a celebration of Mali's past but also no repudiation of it. But under Konaré, the president instrumentalized the past to develop a cultural politics of citizenship and democracy. Culture was explicitly central to Konaré. Rosa de Jorio writes of how Konaré drew on Malian culture to consolidate democratic national citizenship. The cultural practices included creating public monuments, such as an obelisk to celebrate the coexistence of various ethnicities of the country.[134] As another acute observer of Mali notes, this emphasis on political culture was an explicit way to build solidarity in the midst of a very tense situation that "seriously threatened national cohesion."[135]

In short, in Mali there was an ideological fashioning both at independence and in the 1990s. That fashioning was rooted in and resonated with everyday cultural practice, but the vision of Malian nationalism that emerged was not inevitable. It was the work of imagination, as Ben Anderson, the scholar of nationalism, reminds us. In other words, some credit must be given to the agency of the political leaders of the time, in particular to Konaré.

Connecting Mali's practice of politics to the country's culture and traditions is a mainstay of existing scholarship. In explaining Mali's surprising success as a democratic state, Timothy Docking argues that a major factor is "the nature of political culture that has pervaded society in this part of the Western Sahel for centuries. Indeed, for generations the ancestors of present day Malians practiced certain political norms and institutions" that support democracy, including accountability, pluralism, responsiveness, human rights, and participation.[136] Wing similarly roots Malian participatory constitutionalism in historical, cultural, and local practices of dialogue and governance.[137] In the same vein, former U.S. Ambassador Robert Pringle

---

133. Camara 1976.
134. De Jorio 2003, 2006.
135. Konaté 2006: 72.
136. Docking 1997: 201.
137. Wing 2008 8, 173.

writes that the Mali Empire of the past "holds center stage in the county's present-day national imagination, which is inspiring and reinforcing the process of democratization."[138]

Lecocq, who sees Bambaran nationalism as not necessarily inclusive of Tuareg societies, writes, "In Malian societies, history forms the basis of social and cultural life."[139] The legacy and epic of Sunjata, which was promoted in schoolbooks, on the radio with griots, and through artistic bands as well as championed by political leaders, is very influential in social and political organization in Mali, he claims.[140] Shaka Bagayoko writes that there are "strong cultural connections between pre-colonial past and post-colonial states."[141] The spirit of the past imbues the present in Mali.[142] Doulaye Konaté writes of a whole set of cultural mechanisms, to which I shall return, that promote peace.[143]

The connection between the past and the present—or more specifically the legitimization of a democratic politics of dialogue using a specific conception of the past—is especially clear in some of the statements and writings of Konaré and his wife, Adame ba Konaré, who is also a historian. In his key June 1994 speech, for example, Konaré referred to Mali's "ancestral foundation," which supports democracy. In a 1999 speech, he rooted traditions of peace, tolerance, consensus, negotiation, and mixing of culture in the ancient empires. These aspects Africans should promote as part of their heritage.[144] Referencing his decision to create a Ministry of Culture, he said, "Culture is the foundation of development."[145] As he argued, "The past has to be part of the present."[146] "The need for dialogue is a democratic requirement for our fragile countries. This need is found in many of the cultural traits of our country. . . . This quest for consensus [is] one of the great values in our country, one of our great contributions."[147]

These ideas are extremely clear in the writings of Konaré's wife, to whom the president was close.[148] In a series of essays and in a book, Ba Konaré extols Mali's past, arguing that a culture was forged long ago and that "Malians

138. Pringle 2006: 11.
139. Lecocq 2002: 69.
140. Lecocq 2002: 69–73.
141. Bagayogo 1978: 106.
142. Bagayogo 1989: 445; see also Amselle 1998: 57.
143. Konaté 1999.
144. Ba Konaré 1999.
145. Cattanéo 2004: 98.
146. Cattanéo 2004: 134.
147. Cattanéo 2004: 121.
148. Couloubaly 2004: 84–85.

derive their values from their ancestors." She praises the values of diversity and the legacy of the hero Sunjata and argues that Mali's history allows Malians to "hold their heads high." She further cites the specific values of humility, tolerance, patience, justice, sharing, and solidarity, which she argues derive from Mali's ancient culture and collective memory but were also explicitly cultivated under Konaré.[149]

Perhaps her vision is best articulated in her book *Os de la Parole*, an explicit meditation on the use of political power that she argues embraces Malian and Bambaran nationalism. Here again she expresses a strong conviction in the importance of democracy, consensus, moderation, tolerance, solidarity, and humility. She also expresses a vision of a multiethnic national community, all rooted in Bambaran culture: "Mali is a country that succeeded in ethnic integration. For the large majority, Malians are completely *métis*, the product of a mixing of several ethnic groups. Interethnic marriages, with roots in our history, are sociologically normal in Mali. Our different kings and emperors adopted the same strategy to conquer rebel cities, realizing that force could not alone force them to stand down."[150] In another statement, she connects her political vision to the work of a historian, and she explicitly talks of unearthing the past to ground the present:

> I think, for us, for us historians, we have to dig up the past to exhume elements that favor a moralized democracy, a democracy founded on values of humility, patience, solidarity, sharing, social justice, peace, security, liberty. . . . I am speaking of a mentality that belonged to another age; Africans had the potential for a democracy founded on these values. There I can also be a witness: during the decade when my husband led Mali, I observed, listened, and analyzed. I could see how much the Malian people valued social justice, peace, tolerance, patience, humility, a spirit of dialogue, negotiation, and consensus. Tolerance and patience, here are two cardinal virtues that make a leader. . . . Historians can unearth these values . . . to govern is to have a mission for a collectivity and not for one clan or whatever group. To celebrate our ancestors as war heroes is not what we need; today, they are the heroes of peace, heroes by their actions to reassure people, who have fought for liberty and justice, in a spirit of total abnegation, heroes who place humans at the center of their fight.[151]

---

149. Ba Konaré 2000a: 15, 22.
150. Ba Konaré 2000a: 40.
151. Ba Konaré 2004: 25–26.

In the First Lady's writings, we see explicitly how the political leadership and intellectuals sought to ground democratic politics in a constructed vision of the past. To be sure, Ba Konaré's views are not identical to those of her husband. But as an influential member of the Malian political elite and as a prominent intellectual, she is articulating an ideological vision that is rooted in a specific conception of the past, one that favors dialogue, mediation, and inclusivity. Those seem precisely to be the ideas that shaped the policies and approaches of the Konaré administration, even during the most intense periods of violence.

Alongside this vision of the past and of Malian culture sit everyday cultural practices to which Malian elites and the presidential couple have referenced in interviews and in their writings. Principally, they include "joking relationships" and "joking alliances" (in French, "cousinage" or "rapports de parenté"; in Bambara, "sanankuna"). Especially important for mediation, joking alliances occur between clans and ethnic groups. They date back to the Mali Empire of the thirteenth century in which the alliances were formed between family lineages as a way of solidifying peace.[152] In contemporary Mali, joking alliances are still in force; they are learned at a young age and are a feature of everyday interaction.[153] Groups that are in joking alliances "play" at conflict through teasing, but they do not engage in conflict and are in fact bound not to commit harm against each other. Some scholars see joking alliances as playing an integrative and mediating role in a multiethnic society.[154] In an experimental study, Thad Dunning and Lauren Harrison found that joking relationships contributed to cross-cutting political support—subjects evaluated political candidates from other ethnic groups more favorably if they were in a joking relationship with them.[155]

But the cultural practices in Bambaran culture extend beyond joking alliances and relationships. The idea of mediation is central in Mali; the key figures of mediation are griots or *jeli* whose role is to recount stories but also to mediate disputes.[156] Griots are "people of words" who promote dialogue, and the role of mediation and dialogue are both fundamental to the social relations in Bambara/Malinké societies.[157] Griots have played a central role in the construction of Malian national identity. Political leaders, including and especially Modibo Keïta, called on them to recount the Epic of Sunjata on

---

152. Camara 1976.
153. Dunning and Harrison 2010.
154. Camara 1976; Konaté 1999.
155. Dunning and Harrison 2010.
156. Camara 1976.
157. Camara 1976: 215–35; see also Bagayoko 1989.

national radio, and their stories were played to music and broadcast regularly on national radio.[158]

Even beyond joking alliances, griots, dialogue, and mediation, some Malian scholars point to a whole host of values and practices that lend themselves to deescalation. These include values of moderation (*sabali*), agreement (*bèn*), and respect for the other (*niongo gasi sigui*); moderation is a cardinal virtue in Bambaran culture.[159] There are other ancient practices and institutions, such as agents of diplomacy and peace (*niamakala*).[160] In effect, concludes Malian historian Konaté, "there is not a break between tradition and modernity in the daily life in Malian societies" with respect to these social practices that lend themselves to mediation, and he sees their impact in the peaceful settlement of the north in the mid-1990s.[161]

I do not mean to suggest that the political ideology that Touré and especially Konaré fashioned in the 1990s was a natural expression of Bambaran culture and everyday practice. Rather, these and other political elites crafted a national narrative and an ideological orientation from the society in which they lived—an ideology that clearly emphasized consensus, mediation, dialogue, tolerance, and respect for the other. On the one hand, the ideology had popular resonance and legitimacy. As observers attest, the past is very present in modern Mali. On the other hand, the vision of the past was constructed, fashioned, and promoted—it was in effect the championing of a certain kind of democratic, inclusive nationalism, one that served as a source of restraint on a conflict that could have easily escalated to much greater violence than was the case.

The ideological innovation of Mali's pro-democratic leaders is visible in relation to the official pronouncements of their predecessors. President Keïta, the country's first leader, embraced the legacy of the Mali Empire to legitimize African rule; he was even rumored to be a descendant of Sunjata Keïta.[162] He called on and celebrated griots, promoting them through the modern national media. But Keïta's official speeches—at least the twelve retrievable ones on New Year's and Independence Day—bespeak an official endorsement of the values of socialism as well as a stated commitment to solidarity, unity, and dignity, among other values. Traoré was in power longer, but an analysis of forty-two available speeches on New Year's, May Day, and Independence Day reveals a workaday tendency toward elaborating details about

158. Diawara 1999: 118–19; Konaté 2006: 54–55.
159. Konaté 1999: 28, 43.
160. Konaté 1999: 32.
161. Konaté 1999: 38–39.
162. Diawara 1999.

the economy, development, and various accomplishments and challenges. No cogent or lofty vision comes through in his pronouncements. That said, he did not repudiate Malian culture as backward or consistently invoke any deep threat to Mali, beyond at times drought. Like Keïta, he stressed solidarity (which appeared as a promoted value in 55% of the speeches), dignity (appearing in 52%), and patriotism (24%). Traoré also stressed reconciliation (19%), dialogue (14%), and tolerance (7%).

Mali's political and military crisis could have turned out much differently than it did. In the 1990s, Mali had the ingredients Rwanda possessed and that are, in fact, determinants of mass categorical violence: deep political instability complete with intense political rivalry, an armed conflict, an economic contraction, and a legacy of unpunished violence against civilians. Mali possessed a nationalism that was in effect Bambaran and that had the potential to exclude groups constructed as non-Bambaran, in particular the Tuareg and Arab Moors.[163] On the ground, local actors organized into a militia and developed a nativist ideology. The Malian state was weak, possessing limited infrastructural and military capacity, but with enough weapons and political support local actors would have seemed willing to carry out mass violence against the "white" populations associated with the rebellion. The political strategy could have been demonization and violence as a way to impose a "final solution" and to build a political coalition and popular support.

But that is not what happened. The strategy was dialogue, community meetings, inclusion, and a doubling down on the terms of a crumbling peace agreement. In the end, that policy prevailed. While to be sure, there was significant violence against civilians, the numbers were quite low compared to the genocide and mass categorical violence cases in this book and in other studies, and the trajectory of violence was deescalation that ultimately led to peace.

My argument is that leadership from the top was essential for shaping this path. The leadership's ideological terms of reference were democracy, dialogue, and pluralism. Those terms in turn shaped how they interpreted threats and how they chose to respond to them. This was not an inevitable outcome, but in crafting a coherent vision the Malian political elite pulled from a cultural stock that they also in turn shaped and manipulated. In particular, they drew on an imagined past and a cultivated present, one that gave pride of place to values that underpin democracy and compromise: dialogue, mediation, tolerance, respect for the other, and alliance. That constellation of

---

163. Amselle 1998; Lecocq 2002.

values, in my view, was the key mechanism of restraint that allowed Mali not to go down the path that engulfed Rwanda, Sudan, Burundi, and other countries at key points of political and military crisis. It is also a political vision that is consistent with what Houphouët espoused in Côte d'Ivoire and with what, as we shall see, the political leadership in Senegal championed as well.

My empirical focus in the chapter was the crisis in the 1990s. But as noted in the introduction, a major military crisis flared in late 2011 and especially 2012. Tuareg separatists teamed up with Al-Qaeda Islamists, gained territory, and threatened the capital. The material military conditions were thus more dangerous in the 2010s than the 1990s. Yet, despite renewed fears of genocide, President Touré stuck to a vision of democratic inclusivity. Even after he was deposed, the leaders of the military junta countered the language of the rebels with entreaties to Malian territorial unity and inclusivity. The result was relatively limited violence against Tuareg and Arab citizens, despite what appeared to be popular resentment against them. The 2013 elections brought Ibrahim Boubacar Keïta back to power, and he too vowed to restore unity and promote dialogue and inclusion.

While these events occurred as I was finishing this book, which limited my ability to research them in depth, the trajectory of events is consistent with my argument. In Mali, starting in the 1990s, political elites established a founding narrative of the state that shaped how elites then and later interpreted and responded to threat. That narrative created a political grammar that made sustained, group-selective mass violence against citizens an unlikely strategy. A counternarrative was possible, especially after the junta took power, but the founding narrative of dialogue and inclusion had staying power and continued to influence elite decisions. The situation in Mali remains fragile, and the future is unknowable, but there is reason to believe that the narrative of inclusion, democracy, and dialogue will continue to limit the likelihood of genocide occurring in that country.

CHAPTER 7

Pluralism and Accommodation in Senegal

Like Mali and Côte d'Ivoire, Senegal possesses conditions that favor genocide and mass categorical violence. In particular, for more than twenty-five years, the Senegalese state has faced an insurgency in its southern region of Casamance. The insurgency's leadership and core support base are associated with a minority group, Christian Joolas, in a state where Muslims and Wolof-speakers dominate. Moreover, the war has been long; multiple formal and informal negotiations have failed; insurgents keep fighting; and the physical terrain makes control and information-gathering difficult, which some theory suggests fosters mass killing. The state could have been tempted to choose a "final" solution to end a long war against insurgents who refuse to relent, or the state could have orchestrated mass killings because they lacked information about who was a rebel and who was a civilian.

At times, state security forces did commit significant human rights violations in Casamance, including group-selective violence against Joolas. However, the overall strategy did not veer toward mass categorical violence or genocide. Rather, the main approach was military containment and political incorporation. The tactics also included some creative responses, such as cultural initiatives to demonstrate the national unity of the country and public commitments to pluralism, democracy, and the rule of law as a rhetorical counter to a separatist insurgency. The estimates of the total number of individuals (combatants and civilians) killed reflect these strategies and tactics. During more than twenty-five years of armed conflict, the high-end estimate is 5,000 killed.[1] At least to date—the armed conflict continues as of this writing—the Casamance case is clearly not one of genocide.

In interviews with political and military elites, many recoiled at the idea that genocide could take place in Senegal. "That would never happen here" is the typical response I heard. But given the conditions I have spelled out, genocide should have been thinkable. That it was not is precisely why the case is valuable to study.

Before proceeding, I want to note that the ethnic dimension of the Casamance rebellion is complex. On the one hand, rebel leaders claim that they are fighting for Casamance independence, not for an ethnic homeland. They assert a distinct regional identity, history, and culture for Casamance; they also claim discrimination at the hands of a Dakar-centered state.[2] The separatist movement is thus formally not an ethnic one. Moreover, Casamance is one of Senegal's most ethnically and religiously diverse regions outside Dakar, the capital, and Joolas are neither religiously nor politically homogeneous.[3]

On the other hand, in practice, many Senegalese elites and citizens associate the rebels with a specific identity category.[4] The insurgents' core supporters and most rebel leaders are non-Muslim Joolas.[5] As in Mali, there are cultural, institutional, and religious differences between the Joola and other main groups in Senegal.[6] And as a finger of land south of the Gambia, Casamance is physically isolated from the rest of Senegal.

In short, while the rebellion is not simply ethnic in nature, the ingredients for characterizing it as such are present—that characterization was an available choice to ruling authorities. After all, the Rwandan Patriotic Front in Rwanda had some Hutu leaders, it was committed to presenting itself not as an ethnic movement, many Tutsis did not support armed resistance, and Tutsis did not have homogeneous preferences before the genocide. Yet the Rwanda state and many Rwandans equated the RPF with Tutsis. The same principle applies to Darfur.

Why Senegal did not orchestrate mass violence is consistent with the theory developed in the book. The material military threat was limited; the state's vulnerability was low. Senegal was not in a deep crisis during the rebellion. While the economy contracted in the 1980s and early 1990s and while opposition to

---

1. Humphreys and ag Mohamed 2008: 248; Marut 2010: 26.
2. Diédhiou 2011; Marut 2010; Thomas-Lake 2010.
3. Darbon 1988, Lambert 1998; Marut 2010.
4. Marut 2010: 63.
5. Marut 2010: 63.
6. Beck 2008; Darbon 1988; Diouf 1994; Foucher 2007; Hall 1999; Roche 1985.

the ruling party was strong, the country's institutions were stable. The rebels also are internally divided; they have controlled little territory and never threatened to capture major towns in Casamance, let alone anywhere in the Senegalese mainland.

Senegal had also incentives to moderate violence—restraints were strong. Casamance is agriculturally rich, often described as the country's "bread basket," and a source of significant tourism dollars. Small-holder agriculture and tourism are violence-sensitive economies—mass killing in Casamance would have ruptured two key sources of wealth and revenue in the state. Moreover, the political leaders of Senegal pride themselves on being a showcase for liberal democracy on the continent, and they instrumentalize and depend on their international reputation to earn aid dollars in the international system. Senegal's army is professional and disciplined, a leader in many regional and international peacekeeping missions. A bout of mass violence would thus have jeopardized Senegal's reputation, which in turn would have material consequences. In short, mass categorical violence made little strategic sense—the rebellion posed a limited threat, which meant escalation would have little benefit, while the costs of such a strategy would have been significant.

But rationality does not explain everything in the realm of genocide, and the Senegalese authorities could have overreacted to the military challenge. They could have armed local militias, who would have had their own interests in escalating violence against Joolas. To explain why not, I emphasize Senegal's founding narrative. Senegal's political leaders across some fifty years of independence have cultivated an image of pluralism as core to Senegal's national identity. From the first to the most recent president, the political leadership has emphasized that Senegal is a diverse but unified nation. The values they promote are African brotherhood, humanism, democracy, dialogue, and the rule of law. At the level of political practice, accommodation and integration are the hallmarks of Senegalese statecraft. In short, Senegal's founding narrative and its main forms of political praxis run squarely counter to the dynamics of genocide and mass categorical violence.

Conflict Background and Political Context

The Casamance lies south of the Gambia, a finger of territory between that country and Guinea-Bissau. Geographically separate from the rest of Senegal, Casamance has a distinct topographical identity; in general, the region is lusher, more forested, and more riverine than the areas to the north.[7] A

---

7. Roche 1985: 15.

seventh of all of Senegalese territory, Casamance is nonetheless an important producer of agricultural products in the country; it is often called Senegal's "bread basket," even if that term overstates the case.[8] The main export products are groundnuts, rice, cotton, cashews, fish, fruit, wood, and marijuana, the latter especially since the 1970s.[9] Before the outbreak of war, the region accounted for about 7 percent of total production in the country.[10] Tourism is also a major source of revenue in the region, as it is for the country as a whole. Despite the conflict in the area, Casamance was a destination for about 8 percent of all tourist visitors to the country in the late 1990s, but the region's capacity is much greater—the region has about 20 percent of all tourist beds in the country.[11]

Demographically, Casamance is about 12 percent of the Senegalese population.[12] Home to more than twenty ethnic groups, Casamance is ethnically diverse; of the groups, three dominate: the Joola (31% of Casamance population), the Peul (26%), and the Manding (15%).[13] The Joola are concentrated in the Ziguinchor subregion, where they constitute 61 percent of the population.[14] They are about 5.5 percent of the entire Senegalese population, making them the country's fourth-largest group, after the Wolof (44%), the Halpulaar (including Peul, Tukelëër, and Lobe groupings—23%), and the Serer (15%).[15] The Joola are not uniform, in part because of their decentralized political and social structures.[16]

Senegal is overwhelmingly (94%) Muslim.[17] The same is true for Casamance, which is 86 percent Muslim.[18] But within Senegal, Casamance has the largest concentrations of Christians and animists. In particular in Ziguinchor, the population is about 17 percent Christian and nearly 8 percent animist, compared to the national percentages of 5 percent and 1 percent, respectively.[19]

Casamance's political history is also distinctive. It was the site of Portuguese outposts dating as far back as the seventeenth century, and it was not until 1886

---

8. Marut 2010: 49.
9. Darbon 1988: 200; Marut 2010: 50.
10. Darbon 1988: 56.
11. Crompton and Christie 2003: 63–65.
12. RDS 2008.
13. Darbon 1988: 28.
14. Diouf 1994: 39–40.
15. All figures from Diouf 1994: 23, based on the 1988 census.
16. Darbon 1988: 31.
17. Diouf 1994: 43.
18. Marut 2010: 28.
19. Diouf 1994: 91; Marut 2010: 61.

that the Portuguese ceded the area to the French. But, the resistance to French rule, especially among the Joola, who fought the longest until 1920, made it difficult for the French to consolidate the Casamance as such, which didn't happen until the 1930s.[20] By contrast, the French had established colonial territories in northern Senegal dating from the mid-eighteenth century, and even as early as the late nineteenth century four communes had voting rights to elect representatives to the French National Assembly.[21] In part because of this late resistance and colonization, as well as its geographic position, the region remained administratively separate from the rest of Senegal until the end of World War II.[22]

After World War II, the French extended the right to vote to all Senegalese beyond the first four communes.[23] That period saw the rise of Senegal's most instrumental late colonial and early independence leader, the young poet, intellectual, and eventual first president, Léopold Sédar Senghor. In 1948, Senghor formed the Bloc démocratique sénégalais. His main rival at the time was his former mentor, Lamine Guèye, who had formed the Parti socialiste sénégalaise in 1935. Guèye's center of gravity was the first four communes. By contrast, Senghor's strategy was to win over elites in more rural or peripheral areas, including the heads of Muslim brotherhoods and of ethnic political and social organizations.[24]

In that context, the first political formations in Casamance came into existence, in particular the Mouvement des Forces Démocratiques de la Casamance (MFDC).[25] The MFDC existed to promote Casamance interests. Contrary to the claims of the separatist rebel leaders who started the insurgency in the 1980s and used the same name for their organization, the original MFDC was one of several regionally or ethnically oriented political organizations operating in Senegal. And those were the organizations, including the MFDC, that Senghor targeted for support and from which he eventually received it.[26] In exchange, Senghor included Casamance leaders in his party and, later, his administration; he always insisted, after the MFDC folded in 1954 and after Senegal won independence in 1960, that the *Casamançais* were "entirely Senegalese."[27]

A humanist committed to the universal value of African cultural life and an eventual member of the French Academy, Senghor was in many ways

20. Darbon 1988: 60; Marut 2010: 56; Roche 1985.
21. Zuccarelli 1987.
22. Darbon 1988: 62.
23. Zuccarelli 1987.
24. Zuccarelli 1987: 45.
25. Marut 2010: 70.
26. Marut 2010: 70.
27. Marut 2010: 74–75.

a remarkable independence-era politician. As the drift of African politics moved toward one-party, authoritarian rule, Senghor took steps toward democratization in Senegal in the late 1960s, and he legalized multiparty politics in the mid-1970s.[28] Senghor also voluntarily stepped down—to the surprise, it seems, of many Senegalese—on New Year's Eve of 1980, twenty-one years after becoming the country's first president. He was, as many argue, a "democratic humanist," even if he tended to centralize and personally control his party and the state.[29] In addition, as I shall describe below, his modes of coalition building, his vision of the national community and national values, and his personal biography inscribed a tradition of pluralistic and incorporative politics that in turn played out in several different areas, including how the state responded to an armed challenge.

The Origins and Dynamics of the Rebellion

The origins of the rebellion include a mixture of grievance, opportunity, and responses to state violence. The key leaders of the separatist movement were Father Augustin Diamacoune Senghor and Mamadou Sané (known as "Nkrumah").[30] Diamacoune was a well-known figure due to his religious and cultural broadcasts on Senegalese national radio. Sané had earned a scholarship to pursue secondary education in Morocco but ended up in France. Together they formed a new political entity with the same name as the original MFDC. Their vision was for Casamance to become an independent state. The MFDC leaders then and later claimed that the French originally intended Casamance to be administered as a separate colony and that Senghor had promised the original MFDC leaders in the 1940s the chance to revisit the issue after twenty years in exchange for their support at the time of independence.[31] Both claims have never been validated, and a French court that reviewed the former found no juridical basis for an independent Casamance. The new MFDC leaders also claimed consistent discrimination at the hands of northern Senegalese.[32]

The political context in the early 1980s, when the rebellion took off, also mattered. The 1970s were a period of political opening. In 1974, Abdoulaye Wade formed the first main opposition party, the Parti democratique sénégalais (PDS), and in 1978 he performed surprisingly well in presidential elections. The party registered important gains, particularly in Casamance, where the party picked

---

28. Zuccarelli 1987: 180.
29. Zuccarelli 1987: 102.
30. Foucher 2007; Marut 2010.
31. Marut 2010; Thomas-Lake 2010.
32. Marut 2010; Thomas-Lake 2010; also interviews with the author in Dakar.

up its first mayorship.[33] In 1980, Senghor relinquished the presidency to his protégé, Abdou Diouf. These openings sparked expressions of political grievances, including regional ones. The period also demonstrated to Casamance intellectuals the limits of their regional-specific concerns, which tended to have little play within political parties centered in the north, such as the PDS.[34]

Another key issue was migration from other parts of Senegal, as well as from other countries in the region, combined with the implementation of a national land law. On the one hand, Casamance, especially the Ziguinchor subregion, was a magnet for internal migration. Data from the 1980s show that Casamance attracted the second-highest number of migrants from other regions, second only to Dakar.[35] Casamance was attractive because of its potential in the agricultural and tourism sectors. The late 1970s also saw the application of a national land law, which awarded untitled land to the state. In Casamance in particular, where land was often not registered, the application of the law led to expropriations, including land owned by Father Diamacoune. Both the migration to the region and the application of the land law gave rise to nasty disputes over land.[36] *Casamançais* in turn defended their rights in terms of their autochthony against "invaders."[37]

Finally, the state was in mild retreat starting in the late 1970s. The Senghor regime was built around a clientelist model that distributed resources through an extensive and hierarchical network in return for loyalty.[38] In the late 1960s, in response to growing restiveness, the Senegalese state expanded its vehicles for patronage by investing in state-run enterprises and institutions. But by the 1970s, given the extent of borrowing and other problems, the foundations began to decay.[39] In 1979, Senegal entered into its first structural adjustment program, which reduced state resources and eventually diminished the resources the state had at its disposal to placate a budding opposition. This was particularly acute in Casamance, where families had invested heavily in education (especially in Ziguinchor) but where the newly educated youth found few opportunities for employment.[40]

Taken together, these were some of the central (and overlapping) conditions in which the independence movement began.

---

33. Marut 2010: 92.
34. Foucher 2007: 176; Marut 2010: 93.
35. Marut 2010: 86.
36. Foucher 2007: 176; Marut 2010: 83–85, 96; Thomas-Lake 2010.
37. Foucher 2007: 176.
38. Boone 1990.
39. Boone 1990.
40. Foucher 2007: 176.

It is worth noting that, despite the MFDC's claims, Casamance was not doing especially poorly compared to other regions. For example, Ziguinchor had the highest levels of elementary education.[41] Indeed, on a host of other measures of social and economic development, the region is comparable to others outside of Dakar, reflecting a development pattern of privileging the center (Dakar and its environs) at the expense of the peripheries. This is not to say that there is not poverty in the region—there is and was, but not exceptionally so.[42] In a World Bank study, Macartan Humphreys and Habaye ag Mohamed disaggregate regional indicators, finding that Casamance was not the most badly treated region. Moreover, they find that of the two administrative regions in Casamance, Ziguinchor fared particularly well, while Kolda did not. Yet the former is the heart of the conflict, both where the fighting is concentrated and from where the rebels recruit.[43] They find that Casamance is not exceptional in terms of the number of doctors per capita, the number of phone lines per capita, household income, and other poverty measures— even if the region was anomalous in terms of surfaced roads and access to drinking water.[44] Nor is the case of political exclusion convincing. Senghor and later Diouf nominated leading Casamance elites to be government ministers, including, most notably, Émile Badiane, who was a founder of the original MFDC and became minister of education in 1964.

Nonetheless, for the reasons articulated above, a rebellion took hold in the 1980s. The key first political action was planned for December 26, 1982, in which Diamacoune and Sané planned a march in Ziguinchor in which they would lower the Senegalese flag and hoist a white one to express, peacefully, a desire for independence. The two leaders were arrested before the march, but the demonstration proceeded. Some of the protestors were armed with traditional weapons, and, despite a generally peaceful procession, the event took a turn for the worse when the protestors lowered the Senegalese flag. Senegalese gendarmes fired on the crowd.[45]

Following the violent breakup of the crowd and the arrest of the nationalist leaders, the Senegalese state targeted Joola civilians. The state repression in turn pushed Joola toward the separatists and appeared to legitimize the separatist discourse of anti–Casamance, anti-Joola discrimination.[46] Moreover, following the arrest of the initial two leaders, more militant actors filled the political

---

41. Foucher 2007: 174; Marut 2010: 89.
42. Marut 2010: 29.
43. Humphreys and ag Mohamed 2005: 269.
44. Humphreys and ag Mohamed 2005: 270–71.
45. Marut 2010: 100–101.
46. Foucher 2007: 176; Marut 2010: 103.

vacuum. Three leaders in particular—Sidy Badji, Léopold Sagna, and Alioune Badji—were all military veterans of the French or Senegalese armies. During 1983, they developed an agenda that lent itself more toward armed struggle rather than peaceful demands. On December 18—less than two weeks after three gendarmes had been killed and mutilated when they went to a meeting of separatists—the three led a march on Ziguinchor in which several hundred men were armed with traditional weapons. There they encountered the fire-power of the state. The resulting death toll, which included the latter Badji, was likely higher than the official toll of twenty-four.[47]

Following the attacks and subsequent new rounds of state repression, Sidy Badji formed the armed wing of the MFDC called "Atika," which trans-lates as "fighter" in Joola. He would go on to lead the rebellion until the first ceasefire agreement was signed in 1991. From that period forward, the rebellion divided and then divided again. The first split was between a more radical southern and a more moderate northern front.[48] The splits continued. Writing in 2003, Vincent Foucher identified three main armed factions—the Front Nord, which was active around the northwest and loyal to Sidy Badji; the "moderate" Front Sud, which was in the southwest of the region and loyal to Father Diamacoune; and the more "hardline" Front Sud, which was south and southeast of Ziguinchor and under the leadership of Salif Sadio.[49] After a 2004 peace agreement was signed, the rebellion split again; various factions are still fighting state forces.

The internal divisions and the duration of the armed conflict speak to some of the central characteristics of the Casamance rebels. They are, to use Foucher's apt words, simultaneously "resilient" and "weak."[50] While various factions suc-ceeded in attacking government or military targets, coercing Casamance citi-zens, kidnapping tourists, and placing land mines, the rebels never came close to defeating the Senegalese military in pitched battles or to capturing key towns.[51]

Yet the rebels proved resilient; as of this writing, they constitute the lon-gest insurgency in sub-Saharan Africa. Why? To be sure, the guerillas have enjoyed some popular support, in particular at the start of the rebellion.[52] But the geography of the area—forested and riverine (an "aquatic labyrinth," in the words of one of the key French authors on the rebellion, Jean-Claude Marut)—is paramount. The terrain gave the rebels many locations to hide;

47. Foucher 2007: 177; Marut 2010: 106.
48. Thomas-Lake 2010.
49. Foucher 2003.
50. Foucher 2007.
51. Marut 2010: 163.
52. Marut 2010: 114; Thomas-Lake 2010.

government ground assaults were difficult to mount, given the often hard-to-access areas and the absence of roads through the forests and canals.[53] The forest access also allowed the rebels to develop, over time, a war economy, based in no small part on marijuana.[54]

In addition, various rebel factions have benefited from relatively porous borders with Guinea-Bissau to the south and Gambia to the north.[55] Even if those states did not always provide direct control to the rebels—though there is good reason to believe that the Gambia did at various points in the conflict—the ability of the insurgents to seek shelter, find weapons, or sell their contraband in those states have been critical to the ability of the rebels to survive.[56]

State Strategies and Patterns of Violence

From the beginning to the end, Senegalese political authorities have insisted on the country's territorial integrity. They would not grant independence. From there, however, tactics varied. At times, the state arrested and tortured presumed supporters or engaged in violent village sweeps. But the main military strategy was to establish a coercive presence in strategic, well-protected locations in Casamance in order to maintain territorial control. Politically, Diouf sought to divide the rebel leadership and to encourage a moderate side to negotiate a political solution. He typically operated through intermediaries. More populist and voluntaristic, Wade sought to deal directly with the rebel leaders. Both presidents delivered and promised resources to woo leaders and the region. They also deployed, as I shall discuss, a rhetorical salvo that valorized democratic pluralism over separatist insurgency. Elected in 2012, Macky Sall has to date focused on negotiations and other peaceful mechanisms to resolve the conflict.

The patterns of violence reflect these strategies. While human rights organizations rightfully decried abuses at different points in the armed conflict, the annual death tolls almost never exceeded one hundred civilian deaths. Interviews with senior military and political officials consistently attest to approaches that fall quite short of mass violence. For example, General Amadou Abdoulaye Dieng, a former zone commander and military governor in Casmance under Diouf, said in an interview: "The main principle was to have a show of force but not to use it. One is there for peace—to maintain order and discipline." He said that a military solution was not possible in the Casamance conflict.

---

53. Marut 2010.
54. Evans 2003.
55. Evans 2000; Foucher 2003; Marut 2010.
56. Foucher 2007: 178.

Interviewed in 2010, his claims are subject to retrospective bias. But quotations from newspaper interviews he gave in June 1990 when he was appointed military governor suggest the same. He declared himself "open but firm" and noted that the "laws of the country have to be respected to protected the national integrity of the country." At the same time, he said that concertation was necessary: "I believe that Senegal is a land of dialogue."[57] In another interview, he said, "Republican Law must be respected. . . . Those who do not want peace know that the army has the means to impose it no matter the price."[58]

Interviews with other key officials under Diouf strike similar themes. General Mamadou Mansour Seck, head of the armed forces under Diouf, said in an interview: "The choice was not all military. The choice was diplomacy and negotiations and after that force. . . . The role of the army was to be a deterrent. It was not to kill but to be present."

High-ranking officials under Wade voice the same. For example, a spokesperson for the Senegalese Army under Wade, Colonel Antoine Wardini, claimed that destroying the rebellion "was never the objective that the state assigned; it was more to neutralize the MFDC and to permit the state to move towards negotiations."[59]

Latif Aidara, a close adviser to President Wade and considered one of the most influential in his administration with regard to Casamance policy, said in an interview: "The strategy was to favor [the MFDC's] divisions and to discuss with those who were ready to discuss. [Wade] said independence was not an option." With regard to the military, he said, "The choice was to have a dynamic of peace without making war. The army was present in Casamance. The army's mission was to secure the population."

Similarly, Youba Sambou, minister of armed forces under Wade, said in an interview: "For the state, it was officially not a war but a position of securing people and goods. . . . The President gave me a mandate to secure and pacify the entire region."

While at different points in the history of the crisis, the political and military tactics changed—from more and less violence against civilians and the MFDC, from a variety of methods to weakening the MFDC, to different initiatives to negotiate—these military and political officials speak consistently to a policy of force to secure the region but with an eye toward a nonviolent settlement of the crisis. The strategy was to combine coercion with persuasion and, at various points, negotiation—a "carrot and stick" approach to wear down the

---

57. Keita 1990a, pp. 1, 7.
58. Keita 1990b, p. 13.
59. Marut 2010: 161.

enemy rather than to crush it.[60] This is evident even as one looks more closely at how the Diouf and Wade administrations managed the conflict.

Casamance Policies under Diouf

In the beginning, Diouf seemed angered at the outbreak of the violence and determined to restore order. In his traditional New Year's speech at the end of 1983, he labeled the violence in Casamance the work of "subversives." "The authors of such acts are trying to tear up national unity so dearly and so irreversibly obtained, to sap the foundations of our young pluralist democracy, and to question the sum of the effort that the entire Senegalese people," he said, vowing to "never pull back, never hesitate, not when it concerned repressing all forms of sedition" and the question of national unity.[61] A *Washington Post* report from mid-1983 similarly found that the rise of the MFDC had "deeply distressed" the Diouf government.[62]

The tactics that the Diouf government pursued in the 1980s reflect these principles. On the one hand, the government pursued a law-and-order approach. In 1982, the state arrested political leaders in the MFDC, sentencing them to five years. Throughout the 1980s, according to Amnesty International, government forces arrested "several hundred" people, allegedly torturing and killing some of them.[63] Most were arrested for being MFDC members, for expressing political support for the MFDC or Casamance independence, or for aiding armed rebel combatants. Even if such acts reflect policies that betray Senegal's stated commitment to human rights—reaffirmed in a meeting between Diouf and Amnesty International officials in 1989—the level of violence here must be considered restrained in comparison to how other states respond to armed challenges, as discussed in chapter 4.

On the other hand, the state pursued nonviolent measures to weaken the rebellion. In 1983, Diouf named four *Casamançais* to his cabinet of twenty-nine ministers.[64] In 1988, he introduced an Amnesty Law to pardon MFDC leaders. Explaining that decision, he said that the MFDC leaders had followed a "wrong path" but that they should "not be penalized for it all their lives. I want to give them a new chance so that they can become reintegrated . . . and once again contribute toward the construction of Senegal."[65]

---

60. Marut 2010: 35.
61. Diouf 1984, p. 6.
62. Dash 1983.
63. Amnesty International 1990.
64. Dash 1983.
65. Diouf 1988c.

Diouf's speeches from this period also present democracy, the rule of law, national unity, and dialogue as a foil to the actions of the MFDC. Consider, for example, his traditional New Year's speech from the same year. In that address, he asserted that the virtues of the Senegalese people are tolerance, unity, patriotism, and sacrifice. He lauded Senegal's long history of democracy, adding, "Democracy does not support excesses. Nor does it support weakness. It demands support from each and everyone to a group of principles including submission to rules. If excess can kill liberty, democracy is forged by the use of arms to defend it. I hope that these virtues can prevail over intolerance, egoism, and division."[66]

A similar theme was struck in his Independence Day speech in which he positioned democracy, independence, and the integrity of the state against "all forms of aggression":

> Each among you has a responsibility in consolidating and perfecting our democracy so as to construct a strong and respected state. If pluralism is reduced to constant confrontation, to a screen behind which one only fights, it will only destroy our political life. As I said in 1982, pluralism is a sign of political vitality that must not become for our country a source of quarrels, division, and weakness. True pluralism must be a complement of positive efforts to build the country, with uninterrupted dialogue, concertation, and peace, a strong and prosperous nation. Senegalese, I am the president of all Senegalese and my government will be the government of all Senegalese.[67]

The military dynamics shifted in the 1990s. With various bursts and declines of violence, the decade was the most intense militarily. In April 1990, the MFDC launched a military offensive, triggering the appointment of a military governor and a new cycle of attack and counterattack. More than a year later, a first ceasefire was announced on May 31, 1991. That peace was short-lived, giving way to another ceasefire announced on July 8, 1993. The two parties agreed that a French expert would determine whether Casamance had a historical right to claim independence. The subsequent report released that year found that Casamance was indeed an integral part of Senegal, a conclusion subsequently rejected by MFDC leader Father Diamacoune. Violence reprised in 1995 with new MFDC attacks and the kidnapping of four French tourists in 1995, leading to another ceasefire, another reprise in violence—one of the worst in the entire conflict—and then eventually a new round of peace

---

66. Diouf 1988a, p. 10.
67. Diouf 1988b, p. 5.

initiatives in 1998 and 1999, including a meeting between President Diouf and Father Diamacoune. There followed a series of meetings in Banjul in which the MFDC met to try to harmonize their demands.[68]

In the 1990s, the Senegalese state pursued a similar strategy of coercion and nonviolent persuasion, but with greater intensity than in the 1980s. On the one hand, the state again arrested political leaders and suspected MFDC cadres; several were tortured, according to Amnesty International.[69] A long report by that organization details the ways in which state security forces principally used communicative violence—arrests, torture, public violence, and attacks on villages—to "create terror in the hearts of the people to dissuade them, once and for all, from supporting the MFDC's independence movement."[70] Arrests were sometimes made on the basis of denunciations but also on the basis of ethnic categorization.[71]

Other sources describe the period in similar terms. In a 1995 essay, Marut describes how "the hunt for rebels is raging in Casamance."[72] He claims that in this period the military was seeking to eradicate the rebellion coercively, which betrayed the official political narrative that a military solution was not possible.[73] Like some human rights advocates, Marut employs the word "ratisser" (or sweeping) of villages, as well as aerial bombing, in which civilians were arrested or killed.[74] Visiting Casamance in the early 1990s, anthropologist Michael Lambert found hardly a village untouched and considerable fear among the Joola that they would be collectively targeted.[75] U.S. Department of State Human Rights Practices Reports quote local press and human rights organizations as alleging that the Senegalese army used indiscriminate bombing of civilian areas in response to MFDC attacks on civilians in 1993; it estimated more than 250 civilians killed that year.[76] Two years later, after the 1995 reprise in violence, an estimated fifty civilians were killed. In 1997, estimates were in the "tens" of deaths at government hands.[77] Marut calls the 1990s a "dirty war" in which soldiers killed, raped, and blindly repressed with impunity.[78]

68. Based on Amnesty International 1998b; Marut 1995, 2010; Thomas-Lake 2010; United States Department of State Human Rights Practices 1994–1999.
69. Amnesty International 1998b.
70. Amnesty International 1998b: 1.
71. Amnesty International 1998b: 6.
72. Marut 1995: 163.
73. Marut 1995: 163.
74. Marut 1995: 165.
75. Lambert 1998: 585.
76. United States Department of State Human Rights Practices 1994.
77. United States Department of State Human Rights Practices 1998.
78. Marut 2010: 116–17.

In sum, in the worst periods of the war in the 1990s, the army engaged in offensive, sometimes retaliatory attacks. At times, these devolved into violence against civilians, even ethnic targeting. But the state eventually deescalated violence.

Interviews with high-ranking military officers suggest some deliberate restraint in how the state used violence. Asked how the enemy was defined in this period, General Seck responded: "I will admit errors were made, but the most important principle was that if someone holds a weapon, if they are a combatant, then they should be arrested. There was an effort to distinguish rebels from civilians. There were errors, incidents, but 'ratissage' is never a word that we used." General Dieng offered a more detailed response:

> It was always organized bands, combatants. Atika, Sidi Badji and politi-
> cal leaders such as Father Diamacoune. My sense is most were former
> soldiers but there were practically no officers; they were a band of rebels
> that had no organized structure, no occupation of territory. My strategy
> was to occupy the terrain, to allow for no space to maneuver, but then
> they would go across the border to Guinea Bissau and Gambia. We
> defined the hard core of the rebellion as Joola and especially the Catho-
> lic, animist Joola but there was no real unity on the ethnic and religious
> front. The Father had people with him who were Muslim, such as Sidi
> Badji. There was not ethnic or religious unity. . . . *Did you see the Joola
> population as the enemy?* Never. I think most people were not interested
> by this movement. I am convinced that if we did a referendum people
> would vote to belong to Senegal.

In other words, these military elites—at least as they presented themselves to me—did not see the ethnic category as a unified, unwinnable population, and it did not perceive them or the armed rebels as especially threatening.

Coupled with the military strategy, the state also pursued a series of measures to resolve the conflict through persuasion and negotiation. As early as 1991, President Diouf established an Office of the Coordinator for Casamance Peace Initiatives and later the National Committee for the Management of Peace in Casamance.[79] Diouf typically operated then and afterward through Casamance "cadres," elites who were close to his political party but who were from Casamance originally.[80] He supported ceasefires in 1991 and 1993 as well as an inquiry into the territorial status of Casamance. Diouf also sought to split off the hardliners and militarists within the MFDC so as

---

79. Thomas-Lake 2010.
80. Foucher 2009: 149.

to negotiate with the moderates.[81] Later in 1999, through the Banjul meetings, he encouraged the MFDC to unify so as to present a more coherent negotiating position.[82] Marut doubts whether Senegal was committed to true negotiation, preferring instead to dissolve the organization.[83] Still, it is clear that diplomacy and other forms of nonviolent persuasion were as pronounced as, if not more pronounced than, the military effort.

Even more interesting are what Etienne Smith calls the "cultural politics to combat separatism."[84] This entailed seeking to delegitimize the MFDC as an ethnic movement and rhetorically opposing such a movement to the territorial nationalism and pluralism at the heart of Senegal.[85] It also included a state-supported project, initially called the "Festival of Origins," in which officials actively invoked and staged *cousinage* relationships between Joola and Serer as a way of emphasizing the deep, peaceful ties between those communities.[86]

The project began in 1993 and 1994 under the leadership of an influential party member from Casamance, Saliou Sambou; it led to the formation of an organization that operated from 1994 to 2000, which in turn organized meetings and delegations that were sanctioned by Diouf.[87] In other words, even at the height of the military crisis, the Senegalese state drew on a narrative of nonviolence and pluralism to counter the militancy and separatism of the MFDC.[88]

Smith contends that the contribution to peace was modest.[89] But the initiative speaks to how the Senegalese state crafted a response to the armed conflict. Interviews with officials, such as Sambou, reveal that the objective was to "convince Senegalese that they form a single people, a single nation despite the diversity of race and multiple ethnic-cultural heritages."[90] The purpose was to show that the "Senegalese people existed before the Senegalese nation."[91] It was, in the words of Ferdinand de Jong, "a way of incorporating the Joola into the nation."[92] The goal was to invoke and underline an inclusive national narrative.[93]

---

81. Foucher 2003: 110; Thomas-Lake 2010.
82. Thomas-Lake 2010.
83. Marut 2010: 350.
84. Smith 2011: 556.
85. Lambert 1998.
86. Smith 2010a: 557.
87. Smith 2010a: 562–63.
88. Based on De Jong 2005; Smith 2010a: 555–618.
89. Smith 2010a: 563.
90. Smith 2010a: 558.
91. De Jong 2005: 404.
92. De Jong 2005: 404.
93. Smith 2010a: 617.

Diouf's speeches reflect the approach. For example, in his New Year's 1996 speech, he said, "To know how to figure out the essential through dialogue and a permanent search for consensus . . . is the Senegalese exception."[94]

Perhaps one of the most interesting moments came at a conference on "cultural convergences at the heart of the Senegalese nation" that Diouf ordered in 1994.[95] The idea of the conference was to bring together Senegalese intellectuals, experts, academics, and traditionalists to define the nation in opposition to ethnic particularism.[96] In his opening address—a theme echoed in presentations on citizenship, nationhood, and identity—Diouf lauded the diversity and "brassage" at the heart of the Senegalese nation.

> Let us not forget that our country is only truly itself, that is loyal to its history and spirit, when it is based on its culture, both plural and one, both old and still young. . . . And to bring us toward the next millennium, our very own culture, made from a long tradition of *brassage*, *métissage*, and respect for pluralism in all its dimensions—ethnic, linguistic, or religious—will remain our most reliable source of vitality. . . . I want to insist on this lesson, one I would call ethical, that belongs to our history made of deep currents of cultural *brassage*, despite conflicts we have seen, and that is transmitted by *cousinage à plaisanterie* or other social mechanisms that constantly remind us that we have to live together in harmony and in peace. This lesson, that we have to keep present in our minds and our hearts, in this period where the world offers the distressing spectacle of micro-nationalisms and tribalisms of another age that . . . take humanity back to barbarity.[97]

In short, the president presented plurality and intermixing as an ethical and historical foundation for the nation and in opposition to "micro-nationalisms." The multiethnic, ethical nation against barbarous tribalism—the argument is the very opposite of genocide. Faced with an armed challenge, the Senegalese state's response was to deploy the concept of democratic, moral, plural, big tent politics, not the exclusionary claim that the state belongs to such and such a group whose authority a minority group has no right to challenge.

---

94. Diouf 1996, p. 4.
95. De Jong 2005: 404.
96. Tambadou 1996.
97. Tambadou 1996: 8–10.

Casamance under Wade

In 2000 Abdoulaye Wade was elected. In his electoral campaign, Wade vowed to solve the Casamance conflict in one hundred days. In contrast to the heady, aloof, manager-from-above style of his predecessor, Wade presented himself as a populist, street-smart, get-things-done sort of man. According to Latif Aidara and other observers, Wade premised his Casamance strategy on dealing directly with the MFDC, rather than through intermediaries, and on increasing pressure on the bordering states of Guinea-Bissau and the Gambia.[98] Wade also appointed Youba Sambou, a Casamance Joola, as minister of the armed forces; met with Father Diamacoune in Dakar and then in Casamance; punished soldiers who committed abuses; appointed a former NGO leader and historian, Nouha Cissé, as head of a new Casamance peace commission; and initiated cultural weekends and peacebuilding workshops. He also sizably increased the military budget, making it clear that securing the area remained a priority.[99]

Wade's strategy did and did not find success. On the one hand, after his election, violence in Casamance resumed.[100] But by March 2001, a provisional peace agreement had been signed, a process that culminated in December 2004 with the signing of a formal peace accord.[101] During the period, the state's human rights abuses declined.[102] Nonetheless, the accord broke down in 2006.[103] Thereafter low-intensity violence ebbed and flowed; it continues as of this writing.

Aidara, Wade's advisor, dismissed the idea of pursuing a strategy of total war against the Joola. He offered two sets of explanations. First, he said:

> In Casamance those who make war are the Joola, but not all of Casamance is one ethnic group. The Joola are about 800,000 in all of Senegal, and the Joola are not all separatists. Since independence, the Joola have always participated in elections, always had ministers, always had prefects, always had people in the army. The majority is not for independence. They are frustrated like other groups on the periphery. It is similar to other areas in Senegal. . . . In short, the majority are not separatists and realpolitik did not support total war given that the separatists were a minority.

98. Evans 2000; Foucher 2003.
99. Foucher 2003; Thomas-Lake 2010.
100. Evans 2000.
101. Thomas-Lake 2010.
102. Foucher 2003: 104.
103. Thomas-Lake 2010.

In other words, he did not see the Joola as either unified or as the enemy.

Second, he went on to describe the challenges of isolating rebels from civilians and rooting out the rebels. In other contexts, such claims provide a justification for violence against civilians, but Aidara said that Senegalese culture would not permit such violence. The international community also mattered:

> The [MFDC] movement is diffuse in the population. The rebels are among the population. When the army goes in, people put their weapons under their beds. Then they go out and dance, make music. After two months, they regroup and communicate. That form of conflict is hard to deal with unless you eradicate the entire population. *Well, why not eradicate the entire population?* Realism. Local culture will not allow Senegalese to kill them. There is the world environment. The Joola are also not only in Senegal.

An examination of Wade's official speeches from the period reflects these positions. In his first New Year's speech, Wade invoked his commitment to direct dialogue; he also recognized the "injustices and exclusions" that were at the base of the conflict.[104] In his speech a year later, he invoked his commitment to "permanent contact" with MFDC leaders to have a definitive peace.[105]

His Independence Day speeches affirm a commitment to pluralism and unity-in-diversity, reminiscent of Diouf. In his April 2003 speech, for example, Wade lauded the "republican values of liberty, equality, peace and solidarity" as integral parts of the Senegalese national identity and as reference points for Senegalese. Later in the speech, he argued:

> A lucid reading of contemporary conflicts comforts us fully in the wisdom of our choice, that of tolerance, respect for others, love of neighbor and social harmony, whatever our beliefs also individual. This is the spirit in which the Senegalese nation, united in its diversity, will be found again tomorrow . . . [In regard to the MFDC] despite everything, I consider them my children and just Senegalese who are entitled to benefits that the state has a duty to provide all Senegalese without discrimination.[106]

---

104. Wade 2001, p. 2.
105. Wade 2002, p. 3.
106. Wade 2003.

In a speech a year later, Wade similarly claimed that Senegal's traditional values included the respect of differences, diversity, and tolerance.[107] Again in 2005, he stressed:

> Our people developed long ago by finding, through its ancestral virtues of peace, tolerance and respect for others, the foundations of a peaceful coexistence in which difference is experienced and accepted as a source of richness and complementarity. Engaged in this great adventure that is building a free and prosperous nation, rooted in its values and open to the outside . . . we are trustees, beneficiaries, and debtors of this rich heritage that makes us experience our differences today in social harmony and national cohesion.[108]

Unlike Diouf, Wade recognized and endorsed the grievances of the *Casamançais*, a position equally recognized in interviews with key officials under him, such as Aidara and General Sambou. But like Diouf, in his fashioning of Senegalese national values, Wade invoked diversity, pluralism, and tolerance. These positions shaped and legitimized a policy of incorporation of the MFDC—"my children," in Wade's words—in a spirit of pluralism.

Sources of Restraint

The interviews provide some insight into why the Senegalese state used limited coercion and incorporation as a strategy to defeat a quasi-ethnic armed challenge. On the military front, the state had effectively contained weak, internally divided insurgents. In addition, many *Casamançais* rejected the rebellion. From a strategic perspective, then, the costs of using mass violence would have outweighed the expected gains. Targeting the Joola as an ethnic category would have alienated a population that was already "winnable" from the state's perspective and would have exposed the state to international condemnation. Casamance is an important supplier of agricultural products to the rest of the country as well as an important source of tourism revenue. Both are violence-sensitive industries, such that mass violence would have disrupted the revenue and agricultural supply. By contrast, with limited coercion, the state could defend its territory.

But that Senegalese authorities reasoned in this way—the threat was limited, the Joola were not all rebel supporters—should not be taken for granted. The authorities could have feared that the Casamance rebellion

---

107. Wade 2004.
108. Wade 2005.

would inspire similar actions in other peripheral regions, as per the Sudanese authorities. The Senegalese could have lumped the Joola into a single hostile category, treating them as would-be enemies. They could have considered them unwinnable, given the long history of rebellion. The Joola were considered, after all, to be different. In interviews, Senegalese military officers made it clear that they perceive cultural differences between the Joola and other Senegalese. The same is true in the academic literature. In his study of ethnicity, Makhtar Diouf finds that, with the exception of the Joola, the Senegalese form a cultural identity bloc.[109] The region is physically peripheral from the center and navigationally impenetrable; those conditions could have translated into low information about who was a rebel supporter and who was not, giving rise to a strategy of collective punishment. By the same token, to compensate for low information or low physical penetration, the Senegalese army could have armed local ethnic militias, given ethnic and religious heterogeneity in Casamance. Again, they did not.

The reasons why Senegal did not go down that path have to do with what I have called the political grammar of the state. The state's founding narrative is about pluralism. The idea takes different forms under different leaders and at different times. Under Senghor, who presented himself as a product of *métissage*, one finds an extended discourse on African ethical humanism. Under Diouf, there is an emphasis on democracy, the rule of law, and the value of dialogue. Under Wade, national unity in diversity is key. And even under Senegal's latest political leader, Macky Sall, who was elected in 2012, one finds the same. For example, in an interview the day after his electoral victory, he traced his various cultural and family influences, identifying himself as a "Senegalese of synthesis," a theme he had also struck in his campaign.[110]

Senegal's dominant modes of political practice are consistent with pluralism. The keywords that scholars have developed to characterize Senegal's politics are about inclusion: clientelism, brokerage, alliances, cooption, and syncretism. Even the terms "Wolofization" and the "Islamo-Wolof model," both of which are regularly used to describe social and political developments in the country, are seen as inclusive rather than destructive processes.

Defining the nation as plural and practicing a politics of absorption run squarely against a politics of exclusion that inevitably lies at the heart of genocide. Faced with an armed threat, rather than define the right to rule or the body politic as the provenance of a primary social category, the state responded in the opposite way—to define the state as a multiethnic, plural space in order to

109. Diouf 1994: 52.
110. Radio France International, March 26, 2012.

delegitimize the "provincial" claims of the rebels. Rather than seek to eliminate or to destroy the source of the resistance, political leaders sought ways to incorporate it—through mediators, negotiations, and payoffs. Even if one doubts the sincerity of the extent to which the central state was willing to concede in that process, and even if at moments the state used excessive coercion, the consistent practice was to retreat from violence and seek forms of political inclusion.

A Nation of Métissage

What evidence is there for claiming pluralism is at the core of Senegalese founding narrative? One indirect piece of evidence is that scholars of the country regularly note the absence of ethnic politics.[111] Etienne Smith calls Senegal "pluriethnic for good."[112] In a landmark study of ethnicity in Senegal, Makhtar Diouf describes Senegal as marked by ethnic harmony.[113] He notes that ethnicity features neither in how political support is built nor in how political opposition is articulated; he finds ethnicity to be a part of the lived everyday reality of many Senegalese, but Senegalese do not experience their particular identities as being in opposition to national unity.[114] Even in the sphere of religion, Leonardo Villalón finds that despite the dominance of Islam, political cleavages based on faith are "virtually non-existent" in the country.[115] These various observations are synthesized in an apt phrase from Ferdinand De Jong, who refers to a "nationalist narrative of métissage" in Senegal.[116] The nationalist discourse "imagines the Senegalese nation as comprising distinct ethnic groups involved in constant cultural convergence."[117]

The idea of Senegal as an ethnically plural nation is evident in much of the formal discourse. A Senghor quotation sums up the position well: "We are in reality a country of movements and encounters, of métissages and exchanges."[118] Senegal is a "land of openness and dialogue . . . of cultural crossings," said Abdou Diouf.[119] For Wade, "unity in diversity" was a central theme in his formal presidential speeches; his 2005 Independence Day speech, quoted above, in which he lauds differences in the context of national cohesion, is a good example. Or consider this quotation from a former minister

111. O'Brien 2002: 144; Smith 2010a: 19.
112. Smith 2010b: 291.
113. Diouf 1994: 15.
114. Diouf 1994: 43–49.
115. Villalón 1995: 2.
116. De Jong 2005: 408.
117. De Jong 2005: 408.
118. Quoted in Diouf 1994: 7.
119. Diouf 1990a, p. 4.

of culture: "The nation is the kaleidoscope of our differences."[120] To be sure, these are cherry-picked quotations, but my review of Senghor's prolific writings and speeches as well as all of Diouf's and Wade's speeches on New Year's and Independence Day finds no exception to this characterization of the national component of the nation. The Senegalese nation is ethnically plural.

The origins of this vision are hard to pinpoint. But, as in the other cases, I afford credit to the political leaders who were active during critical, foundational moments in the country's political history. Each in turn fashioned a political narrative that was rooted in widespread cultural ideas and practices.

The country's first president was particularly instrumental in stewarding the first twenty years after independence and taking steps toward establishing Senegal as a democratically plural country. Both Diouf, whose authority was challenged by the MFDC, and Wade, who was the first president after Senghor's and Diouf's party was electorally defeated, were also important.

Senghor had a grand vision of African civilization and its role in the world. Steeped in a racist world that largely devalued black contributions, Senghor turned that vision around. He did not deny race as a category of analysis; he insisted on "négritude" and "Africanité," but his vision was strongly of African unity. As a writer with an advanced degree and as a poet, he developed at length his thesis of négritude as forming a coherent cultural and ethical space that would contribute to universal civilization. His worldview—one that he preached consistently—was that of a "dialogue of cultures" in which Africans would be open to other influences but also retain their foundations and contribute to global civilization.[121]

Senghor's vision of négritude, as the above quotation suggests, is that of a space of pluralism, convergence, and intermixing as well as of dialogue and humanism. He defined the four essential values of black civilization as intuitive reason, plural dialogue, belief in the other world, and humanism.[122]

To arrive at the idea of a unified black civilization, the idea of métissage clearly emerges. For Senghor, there was an Africa of superficial differences that masked an underlying racial and cultural unity—a unity in diversity. Africans have an "outer inter-racial mixture . . . superimposed on [an] inner intra-racial mixture."[123]

Senghor's personal and political biography radiated métissage. Educated in France and a member of the French National Assembly before Senegalese

---

120. Smith 2010b: 271.
121. Senghor 1964, 1971, 1977, 1983, 1993.
122. Senghor 1988: 108–11.
123. Senghor 1971: 35.

independence, he married a French woman. He was a "double minority" in his own country, Serer by ethnicity and Christian by religion. Though his first language was Serer, he addressed the nation, typically, in French or in Wolof. In his recounting of his past, he often stressed that he was a product of intercultural mixing.[124] One biographer, Christian Roche, claims that Senghor often referred to himself as a "cultural métis."[125] Similarly, De Jong finds an emphasis on métissage and cultural convergence in Senghor.[126] De Jong, too, affords significant credit to Senghor and to Cheikh Anta Diop for contributing to a "widespread Senegalese discourse on cultural identity" that recognizes ethnic diversity but strongly values unity.[127] In sum, Senghor established a founding narrative of Senegal as a plural nation, as open and diverse but unified.

The theme is especially clear in his second address to the nation on December 31, 1960. In that speech, he picked up a theme that all other Senegalese presidents also articulated:

> Before the historic night of August 19–20 [when Senegal broke away from the Mali Federation to become Senegal], we were already a nation, I mean a people animated by a common wish for a common life despite differences of race, religion, and social group. . . . A collectivity, to be a nation, does not demand that all its members agree; they are not a series of robots. It demands, despite differences of opinion and differences between its members, their life in common be preferable to all other life.[128]

As president, Diouf did not renounce Senghor's ideas. The main leitmotif across Diouf's official speeches was the value of democracy. He defended Senegal as a democratic leader in Africa and beyond. In that context, Diouf often celebrated pluralism and dialogue. But he also returned to the theme of unity in diversity, often in the context of democracy. For example, in a 1986 speech on secularism, he argued as follows:

> Secularism is one of the fundamental assets of our people, inscribed in its history, its practices, and its way of living. Secularism is an irreversible option in our democracy. It is inscribed in our Constitution. . . . The State is in the service of no religion. . . . Do we need to recall that

124. For instance, Senghor 1988: 10.
125. Roche 2006: 168.
126. De Jong 2005: 403–4.
127. De Jong 2005: 402.
128. Senghor 1983: 38–39.

this option conforms completely to the virtues of tolerance, dialogue, and conviviality? . . . Our secularism must support, thanks to the work of all, the peace of our cohabitation and fraternal humanity.[129]

Across his speeches, these are the themes: dialogue, peace, tolerance, democracy, and national unity in the midst of diversity.

Even though Wade was a historical opponent of both Senghor and Diouf, his definition of the nation and its values is very close to his predecessors, as seen above.

Practices of Incorporation

The ideological, nationalist vision of democratic pluralism carries over and reinforces social and practices in the country. Formally, the Senegalese Constitution is non-exclusionary. The law forbids parties based on religion or ethnicity. The Constitution further recognizes French as the official language, but it also—in an inclusionary gesture—recognizes six other "national languages," including Joola.[130] But within the scholarship on Senegal, the informal practices receive even greater attention, and those practices speak to deeper forms of everyday politics and social interaction that favor incorporation over exclusion.

The analytical watchwords that scholars use to describe Senegal all bespeak practices of inclusion. One of the most consistent terms that characterize Senegalese practices of politics is *clientelism*.[131] Clientelism is not often a normatively positive term—clientelism rewards loyalty over merit and can favor all sorts of inefficient outcomes.[132] Under Senghor, the system of clientelism was a pyramid that reached up to the president, meaning that power was centralized and personalized.[133] But clientelism, as Beck insightfully describes, is fundamentally about a process of brokerage in which local elites exchange political support for patronage. In that sense, the politics is one of incorporation.

Other scholars employ different terms. Vincent Foucher labels both Senghor's and Diouf's policies as promoting "coercion and cooption."[134] He also refers to a "great Senegalese political tradition of reciprocal assimilation of elites."[135] Momar Diop and Mamadou Diouf argue that the political system is based on the integrative mechanisms of "negotiation and buying

---

129. Diouf 1987, p. 2.
130. Diouf 1994: 109–10.
131. Beck 2008; Boone 1990; O'Brien 1992; Diop and Diouf 1990; Diouf 2002; Smith 2010a.
132. Diouf 2002.
133. Diouf 2002; Zuccarelli 1987: 102.
134. Foucher 2003: 119.
135. Foucher 2007: 188.

alliances."[136] Robert Fatton references a "politics of alliance and cooption."[137] Such political practices are not cause for celebration—they are not always democratic and they are often stifling.[138] But they also speak to modes of incorporation—cooption and assimilation.

In a major study, Smith insightfully and exhaustively analyzes how joking relationships have been one of the major "arts to make society," as he claims. He shows how all of Senegal's first three presidents used cousinage relationships. Cousinage captures some of the ideas present in the discourse on pluralism—a recognition of particular identities, but ones that are integrationist. They favor inclusion. Senegalese politicians draw on this. He calls Senghor a "master of inter-ethnicity" who "played ethnic politics not to foster indigeneity or exclusion but to win political support and build a coalition."[139]

Still other scholarship points to fundamentally inclusive political and social practices. In his major study, Dennis Galvan points to "syncretism" as one of the defining features of how Senegalese manage competing practices.[140] Donal Cruise O'Brien refers to an "accommodationist tradition" within Senegal's dominant Sufi brotherhoods.[141] In his study of Republican Islam in Senegal, Jean-François Bayart refers to a "politics of accommodation" in Senegal.[142]

Another central theme in the spread of Islam as the dominant religion and Wolof as the lingua franca in Senegal. The term *Wolofization*[143] conveys the latter, while the notion of an "Islamo-Wolof model"[144] in Senegal synthesizes the two. The processes are seen in the literature as integrating, as contributing to the formation of a nation.[145] To be sure, the spread of Wolof has had the effect of marginalizing non-Wolof-speaking, non-Muslim groups, such as the Joola.[146] But even here, studies of Wolofization suggest a largely informal, accommodationist expansion, rather than one of conquering through elimination. O'Brien refers to "linguistic hybridization" and notes that Wolofization engendered little social conflict.[147] Key for him is that Wolofization occurred separately from state policy; for state elites French remains the language of

136. Diop and Diouf 1990: 10.
137. Fatton 1987: 3.
138. Diop and Diouf 1990.
139. Smith 2010a: 421.
140. Galvan 2004.
141. O'Brien 1998: 26.
142. Bayart 2010: 405.
143. O'Brien 1998.
144. Diop and Diouf 1990: 46; Diouf 2001.
145. O'Brien 1998: 26.
146. O'Brien 1998; Diédhiou 2011: 250–51; Diop and Diouf 1990: 47.
147. O'Brien 1998: 46.

policy and policy-making. Wolofization is about constructing a nation "from below."[148] For Smith, too, Wolofization is assimilationist.[149] Wolofization exists without destroying other languages.[150]

In short, despite a process of linguistic, cultural, and religious expansion, the dominance is consistent with the terms that characterize political and social practice in Senegal: syncretic, plural, and accommodationist.

Like the Mali example, Senegal's trajectories of violence provide some evidence to counter some leading explanations of genocide. An insurgency on the periphery rooted in a population with a distinct identity and a long history of resistance did not trigger sustained, mass violence. Here the state practiced counterinsurgency with restraint. Moreover, the would-be target population was a minority. Unlike in Côte d'Ivoire, where Muslims and Christians had some parity, here the state forces represented the overwhelming demographic majority. Finally, unlike in Côte d'Ivoire, the international community did not intervene to protect the Joola.

The book's theory provides an explanation for why genocide was never in the cards. The Casamance rebellion was weak; the state was stable. Moreover, pluralism is core to the state's founding narrative. Senegal would have paid significant reputational and some material costs if it had pursued genocide. In short—in terms of the material military threat, the founding narrative, and economic sources of restraint—Senegal had a very low probability of genocide, and indeed of all the cases in the book the levels of state violence in Senegal emerge as the lowest on an annualized basis. In the end, to combat rebels, the state pursued coercion and inclusion. Leaders did not say that Christian Joolas have no right to challenge the authority of the rightful Muslim leaders of the country. Such a response would have been contrary to the ideals cultivated for more than forty years in Senegal. Rather, political elites doubled down on Senegal's core values of diversity and dialogue.

---

148. O'Brien 1998: 30.
149. Smith 2010b.
150. O'Brien 2002: 150.

CHAPTER 8

Endangered Arab-Islamic Nationalism in Sudan

Independent Sudan has been one of the most violent states in Africa. From the eve of independence until the first decade of the 2000s, Sudan experienced multiple civil wars, multiple waves of violence against civilians within those civil wars, and long periods of military dictatorship in which open dissent was dangerous. The episodes of violence with the highest magnitude took place within three distinct, if linked, armed conflicts: the North-South civil war between 1955 and 1972, the North-South civil war between 1983 and 2005, and the Darfur civil war from 2003 to 2006. In each of these armed conflicts, but especially the latter two, the state orchestrated campaigns of mass categorical violence against civilian populations associated with the insurgents. While I discuss each episode, my focus in this chapter is the Darfur crisis, for which the best documentation exists.

A central feature of the violence is coordination between the government's armed forces and the irregular armed groups that the state supported and armed. The coalitions of violence, however, were different from those in Rwanda where national actors created coordination through vertical integration of the civilian administration, the army, and civilians. In Sudan, where the country is physically very large—the largest in Africa before South Sudan split off in 2010—national actors entered into decentralized alliances with armed groups, alliances generally shaped by mutual security interests, shared ideological frames, and opportunism on the part of local actors. Like Mali but unlike Rwanda, the Sudanese state is far-flung and weakly consolidated in the peripheral regions where the insurgencies were concentrated. Yet, in contrast to Mali, where in the 1990s national actors stepped in to control emerging militias, in Sudan the state encouraged, fomented, supplied, and coordinated local armed groups.

The violence in Sudan was devastating. In the peak periods of war, the combined military and irregular forces engaged in sustained, widespread violence against civilians. On the ground, the attacks typically included murder, rape, village destruction, well poisoning, and sometimes capture of civilians for eventual sale into slave networks. From the air, the government dropped explosives or deployed attack helicopters on villages and fleeing civilians. By and large, the attackers selected targets on the basis of the victims' categorical identity. In the North-South civil war, the targets were "blacks," "slaves," and "infidels"—in other words, non-Muslim, non-Arab civilians. In Darfur, the identification was along a non-religious identity axis—against non-Arabs. Even if imprecise, the mortality estimates give a sense of the scale of violence. The standard figure for twenty-three years of violence in the second North-South civil war is at least two million civilian deaths, an estimate that includes both direct and indirect mortality (death from disease and malnutrition, which was a result of the war). In Darfur, the estimate range is effectively between 100,000 and 400,000 civilian deaths, with a concentration of violence in 2003 and 2004.

In short, the violence in Sudan was mass categorical violence—sustained, widespread, organized, group-selective violence that resulted in a large proportion of deaths of the target population. The scale of violence was significantly higher than anything witnessed in the prior three chapters. In contrast to the negative cases in which national-level political and military elites consistently scaled back short periods of mass killing in favor of negotiation, dialogue, or more modest applications of coercion, the most common strategy in Sudan was sustained mass killing and displacement of civilians.

What distinguishes the wars in Sudan from those in the other countries? As in Mali and Senegal, the wars in the south and in Darfur took place on the periphery of the state. While the Sudanese rebellions challenged the state in various ways, including dismemberment through secession, the armed resistance movements never seriously threatened the capital, Khartoum. As in Mali, Senegal, and for a while Côte d'Ivoire, they were regionally concentrated insurgencies. Sudan is not a clearly stronger, wealthier, or more capable state than the others—especially not in the peripheries. Across the periods of violence, the Sudanese economy experienced periods of significant contraction (in the 1980s) as well as an oil boom during the height of the Darfur crisis. Arguments about state strength or economic deprivation seem not to account for the between-country variation. Unlike Senegal and Côte d'Ivoire but like Mali, Sudan had long periods of military rule, but in Sudan democratic periods were also highly violent. Indeed, the practice of arming Arab militias expanded significantly under a democratic regime in the mid-1980s, which does not lend merit to arguments about regime type as the key variable. As in Mali and Côte d'Ivoire and to a lesser extent Senegal, all the cases had periods of state-orchestrated violence that went unpunished. In short, the prominent alternative hypotheses do not seem to explain the variation.

Like the other cases, Sudan's atrocities occurred during wartime. Sudanese officials readily claimed that the violence was part of a war effort; they framed the violence as counterinsurgency and justified it in the name of state protection and security. Empirically, unexpected battlefield gains by insurgents seem to trigger high-magnitude, state-orchestrated violence. But as the previous chapters show, armed conflict and territorial gains by enemy opponents do not automatically trigger mass categorical violence. In Mali, Côte d'Ivoire, and Senegal, states faced insurgencies that at times made territorial gains but the military and political elites making the key decisions chose different strategies to counter and contain armed threats to their regimes.

Why was Sudan different? Part of the answer to why state leaders perceived high-level threats from insurgencies on the peripheries could be the internal fractionalization within the northern political class in Khartoum, which as we shall see was indeed highly factionalized, primarily by Sufi orders. But a comparative glance does not support that hypothesis: in Mali and Côte d'Ivoire, there was a great deal of elite-level contestation and fractionalization during the military crises. Moreover, even though they were internally divided, the Sudanese northern elite had a consistent position on the insurgencies in the south: Crush them. Nonetheless, in Sudan the northern elites that control Khartoum are a small group in a massive state that has faced or could have faced insurgencies in multiple peripheries. Each insurgency that appeared was difficult to contain, and judging from their public discourse the northern elites perceived the broader region to be full of enemies, notably in Ethiopia, Uganda, and Chad (at different times). In short, even though the Darfur and southern insurgencies never really threatened the capital, northern elites perceived vulnerability.

But other factors mattered, especially Sudan's founding narrative. Sudan is a state with many social cleavages. Two of the most important are between communities who claim an Arab lineage and those who do not and between those who are Muslim and those who are not. In the other states examined in the book, political leaders at critical junctures sought to create a foundation for national identity that did not inherently privilege one segment of their population. In Sudan, the political choice was different. At the critical period just before independence and into the independence period, Sudanese political elites based in the north defined and fashioned the state as belonging principally to Arabs and Muslims. Sudan subsequently experienced multiple periods of political turbulence and regime change—from military coup to democratic transition and back to coup. In a few of these periods, northern political elites—the ones who consistently retained control of the state—articulated a different vision of the state. But those visions had little staying power, and Sudanese political elites consistently tacked back toward the founding narrative of Arab-Islamic nationalism, one that created a hierarchy between a superior Muslim and Arab core group and an inferior, non-Muslim and non-Arab marginal group. In other words, unlike in Côte d'Ivoire but like in Rwanda, there was no strong counternarrative to ethnic nationalism in Sudan. Arab-Islamic nationalism was an equilibrium point among the northern power-holding class in Sudan.

The political choice to defend an Islamic and Arab character to the nation despite Sudan's multiethnic and multireligious diversity is not my focus. But I observe two points. First, the northern political and commercial elite that has controlled the state has been, since and before independence, highly fractured between Sufi orders. In the face of this elite division, political elites have selected religion and ethnic identity as a source of unity and consensus among the potential power-holding class, and they have sought to define and remake the core political community on that basis. Second, the choice of Islam and Arabness follows patterns of hierarchy, governance, and slave exploitation that preceded and extended into the imperial periods prior to independence. In particular, as northern elites crafted their vision for the Sudanese state at independence—a critical juncture—they turned their gaze toward the pre-colonial past as a source of reclaimed pride in the face of the humiliation suffered at the hands of external overlords. That past was one of Arab and Muslim domination over the southern slavelands. That vision was furthermore consistent with the patterns of colonial rule that governed the north as an administratively and culturally separate space from the south. In short, the founding narratives crafted at political junctures were inscribed in a long-range history.

Whatever the origins of the choice, Arab-Islamic nationalism in Sudan shaped the strategies of violence in war. When confronted with an armed challenge from non-Arabs or, depending on the war, non-Muslims, the state's response was to crush the insurgency with maximum violence. From the point of view of the state leaders, non-Arabs and non-Muslims did not belong at the heart of the state, and the moves to incorporate, placate, and assimilate the armed opposition evident in Mali, Senegal, and Côte d'Ivoire were largely absent in Sudan. The northern elite's founding narrative figured a national community in which the armed claimants to power had no proper place at the ship of state and were not for whom the state acted. Much more important to the northern elite was shoring up a habitually weak alliance of the nation's core power-holders of Muslim Arabs. In these ways, Sudanese founding narratives created a framework in which maximum violence was thinkable and in which there was no perceived obligation to protect, negotiate with, and incorporate the identity group associated with the insurgency. The enemy and their supporters were, in the eyes of the political and military elite, external to the primary national community, so there was little restraint in unleashing mass violence to contain or eliminate the threat.

But that is not all. In Sudan's large, far-flung state, local actors have a degree of autonomy from national actors. They also have their own incentives for violence. In both the second North-South civil war and in Darfur, the state entered into alliances primarily with local Arab groups who pursued their own largely material interests in exacting violence against the non-Arab civilian communities who were deemed enemies of the state. Often poor and vulnerable themselves, local Arab militias had short-term material interests in capturing property or slaves, but they also had long-term interests in securing access to fertile pastureland and water, both of which are scarce resources in much of Sudan. With a green light and often weaponry from the central state, the local armed actors independently contributed to the escalation of violence; in effect, they capitalized on the armed conflict and state support to solve fundamental livelihood problems. This was a key factor of escalation.

Finally, Sudan's political economy enjoys few sources of structural restraint against the execution of mass categorical violence. The areas where the violence and wars took place typically were marginal to the core areas of agricultural production in the Nile-fed, north-central parts of the country. In later periods, after oil production came online and became a principal source of state rents, the violence on the Darfur periphery had little to no impact on oil production. Petroleum is not a violence-sensitive source of state rents—Darfur was in flames, but the state's oil flow was largely unaffected. Taken together, the dynamics of war, a hierarchical founding narrative, and local actors interacted to create powerful sources of escalation and few sources of restraint. That was the deadly mix that shaped the patterns of mass categorical violence in Sudan.

Background and Political Context

The politics and practices of independent Sudan cannot be understood apart from the (largely) imperial century and a half that preceded it.[1] That is true for all the cases in the book, but I focus here on a slightly longer *durée* than I did in Côte d'Ivoire, Mali, and Senegal in order to capture some of the long-running dynamics between northern and southern Sudan, between Arabs and non-Arabs, and between Muslims and Christians.

Three distinct historical periods stand out. The first was the Turkish-Egyptian conquest, often called "the Turkiyya," from the 1820s to the 1880s. In this period, the representatives of the Ottoman Empire in Egypt sought to increase their power in part by controlling and exploiting the area to the south of Egypt, namely what we now call Sudan. After punishing raids, the Ottomans established control over the Sudanese territory and came to impose an administrative system on northern Sudan, with Khartoum as its capital, and a new taxation system to support it. The new rulers also used their superior military power to penetrate into the southern areas, where they organized large slave-gathering missions. The two factors played out together: The new taxation system forced northerners to seek new revenue or to abandon their lands, both of which pushed recruits into slaving.[2] The period also saw the emergence of certain categories of domestic Arabized elites, in particular "jal-laba" traders and some Sufi orders; these became the imperial state's favored collaborators.[3] The Turkiyya thus contributed to, even created, a territory with a structured, racialized inequality at its core. The north, anchored in the riverine Arabized areas in and around Khartoum, was the seat of power and that of commercial, administrative, and educational development. By contrast was the infidel "African" south where slaves could be captured.[4]

When they resisted Turkish-Egyptian rule, Sudanese elites did so in the name of religion. It was "an indigenous Muslim protest movement against foreign domination," one that became central to the nationalist imagination in the mid-twentieth century and thus to understanding the patterns of violence in Sudan.[5] A former shipbuilder who called himself the "Mahdi," a charismatic Islamic prophet, began an ultimately successful uprising in 1881. But the Mahdist state that followed from 1885 to 1898 further entrenched patterns

---

1. Daly 1993, 2007; De Waal 2007; Johnson 2003; Sikainga 1993; Warburg 2003; Woodward 1990.
2. Daly 2003: 3; Johnson 2003: 5; Warburg 2003: 13.
3. Warburg 2003: 6–13.
4. Johnson 2003: 6.
5. Warburg 2003: 23.

of governance in the Turkiyya. The Mahdist state was an Islamic, prophetic one; there was no separation of church and state;[6] it was a "jihad state."[7] The Mahdist state had little regard for the non-Muslim areas of the south, where it failed to consolidate control, "ruled by raid," and reinforced the "master-slave dichotomy" established under the Turkiyya.[8] Within the Muslim north, the Mahdist state divided the population into believers who followed the Mahdi (Umma) and non-believers who did not. The division sharpened rivalries between Sufi orders, in particular engendering resistance from the Umma's largest rival, the Khatmiyya.[9] The rivalry between the Umma and the Khatmiyya much later became one of the salient features of independent Sudan and a source of fragmentation among the northern Arab elite.

The third period, often called the Reconquest, saw the British take control of Sudan with assistance from both Egypt and northern Sudanese elites whom the Mahdist state had alienated. The British-Egyptian Condominium period lasted from 1899 until independence in 1956. British rule—the British dominated the partnership—had many far-reaching consequences, from hardening the borders of modern Sudan to establishing a civil administration, an army, and export agricultural schemes. But the conclusion of most historians is that British rule widened development disparities between north and south and entrenched social and cultural differences between the regions. The Mahdist state had not controlled the south, and resistance to imperial domination lasted longer there than in the north. The south was indeed not fully under colonial control until the 1920s.[10] The British in turn opted to rule the south separately from the north, along explicitly "African" rather than "Arab" lines. In contrast to the north's more modern administration, the south was to be governed by "traditional authorities."[11] In practice, northern groups, in particular elites from the central Nile Valley, gained power and prominence under British rule. The north also gained from significant investments in education, commercial agriculture, and civil administration. By contrast, the south languished in human and infrastructural development terms—at least until the terminal colonial period—further entrenching regional and racialized inequalities that existed prior to the onset of the Condominium. In the terminal colonial period, the British tried to make up for the developmental disparities, but that push was counteracted

6. Warburg 2003: 41.
7. Johnson 2003: 7.
8. Daly 1993: 4.
9. Johnson 2003: 6, 9; Warburg 2003: 25.
10. Johnson 2003: 10–11.
11. Johnson 2003: 11.

by demands among northern nationalists for an increasingly quick timetable for independence.

Three paragraphs on nearly 140 years of pre-independence history cannot do justice to the actual empirical complexity of the period. But as in Nigeria, Rwanda-Burundi, Chad, and other locations—territories where colonial authorities explicitly grounded their developmental priorities on the basis of a racial-religious interpretation, thereby creating hierarchies and inequality across identity categories—the course of events that followed independence cannot be understood without recourse to the preceding period. In Sudan, the imperial experience structured differences and inequalities between a Muslim, Arabized north—one anchored in the riverine areas of north-central Sudan but deeply internally divided between Sufi orders—and a non-Muslim, "African" south.

Independence and the First North-South Civil War

In 1956 Sudan became the first sub-Saharan African state to achieve independence. In the period leading up to that critical juncture and just after, northern political elites articulated a vision of an independent state whose center of gravity was the north, in effect continuing patterns of administrative and economic inequality under the imperial state. Northern independence leaders also promulgated a vision of the national community as Arab and Islamic in character. In their vision, an Arab-Islamic identity would furnish Sudan with a basis for national pride and, ultimately, unity. The experience of foreign domination had been humiliating in their minds, so the elites looked to imagined glories of Islam and the Arab world to ground their future. For this, both the Mahdist precedent and other independence movements in the Arab world served as inspiration.[12] The most influential political parties that emerged were structured around the northern Sufi networks, and those networks did not penetrate into the non-Muslim south.[13] In short, the vision of who could partake in independence and whom the state served were northern Arab Muslims; they were the primary political community.

This was not an inevitable choice. Sudan is a country of great ethnic and religious diversity with more than 110 languages spoken.[14] According to the first (and, to my knowledge, only) ethnic census conducted in the country in 1956, Arabs constituted 39 percent of the total population; Arabic was

---

12. Al-Rahim 1973: 38; Johnson 2003: 35.
13. Woodward 1990.
14. Abdelhay 2007.

spoken among 51 percent of the population.[15] While the Arabic language provided a slim foundation for a national majority, Arab identity as such did not. That said, about 52 percent of the northern regions identified as Arab.[16] Islam, by contrast, was the dominant faith, with more than 70 percent of the country identifying their religion as Islam. Thus, for politicians who oriented themselves to the north—who saw the north as the center of gravity for the state—Arab-Islamic nationalism offered a basis for a reliable majority. However, that the northern elite oriented themselves to the north, in a way that excludes the south from the primary political community, requires explanation. Moreover, as we saw from the previous three chapters, where founding narratives did not single out majorities as the primary political community, the choice to emphasize an Arab-Islamic character of the state did not happen inevitably. In Sudan, as in the other cases, I place emphasis on the leaders who made choices about how to craft their vision of the state.

In any case, two processes followed from the emerging nationalist vision. First, northern Muslim Arabs created little space for southern elites in the formal processes that led to independence. This was true both for the formal negotiations as well as for the domestication of the administration. A Sudanization commission in the 1950s established Sudanese as responsible authorities throughout the civil administration. But "Sudanization" meant placing northerners in all key positions in the army, police, business, education, and other sectors, including in the south.[17]

Second, northerners sought to remake the south in their own image. Though divided between themselves, the main northern political parties considered rapid Arabization and Islamization of the south as "one of its most significant missions" to unite the country.[18] In this vision, the southerners were considered "orphans"[19] or "lost brothers"[20] in the sense that colonial interference had interrupted what would have been an inevitable process of Islamization and Arabization, a process that independence would resuscitate. For many northerners, southerners had no inherent religion or culture of their own and therefore would accept Islamization and Arabization.[21] Such views reflected an inherent belief in the racial and cultural superiority among

---

15. HRW 2004: 63. The 2010 CIA Factbook, the last on Sudan before South Sudan seceded, also listed the Arab population as 39%.

16. That was the case by 1993, according to Abdelhay 2007: 32.

17. Al-Rahim 1969, 1971; Daly 1993; Deng 1995; Johnson 2003; Lesch 1998; Sikainga 1993; Woodward 1990: 89.

18. Warburg 2003: 144.

19. Deng 1995: 4.

20. Lesch 1998: 23.

21. Malwal 1981: 37.

northern political elites toward southerners.[22] Islamization and Arabization of the south was akin to a Sudanese Manifest Destiny.[23]

Unsurprisingly, from the perspective of non-Muslim, non-Arab southern elites, these developments were alarming. For them independence risked creating a new form of colonization, one led by northerners, many of whom held pejorative views of the south and southerners. The political counterargument among southern elites was to advocate for federalism in which the south would retain regional autonomy. But northern elites rejected that idea.[24] This was the context in which the first civil war broke out in 1955, a year before independence was formally granted. The initial form was a mutiny in the southern town of Torit, where a southern unit refused a transfer to the north. The mutiny spread to a dozen other towns, and the mutineers killed northern officers and administrators as well as their families.[25]

At the dawn of independence, therefore, Sudan was a fundamentally divided state. The northern elites articulated a vision that held no place for southerners, as they were in effect continuing structural inequality between the two populations. An outbreak of civil war around that cleavage reinforced that division, as did policies after independence. Sectarian divisions within the northern elite (generally divisions on the basis of Sufi orders) were prominent in the first two years of parliamentary rule, but there was nonetheless consensus around the centrality of Islam and Arabic for national unity. The National Constitutional Committee, formed in September 1956, for example, had only three southerners among the forty-six positions on the committee. The committee not only rejected federalism but also adopted a centralized political system in which Shari'a would be the source of law and Arabic the official national language.[26]

In 1958, the civilian government was overthrown in military coup. The new head of state, General Ibrahim Abbud, in turn aggressively pursued Islamization and Arabization. In that way, he extended the founding narrative of Arab-Islamic nationalism rather than providing a counter to it. In quick order, the new government made Friday the national holiday; Christian missionary schools were nationalized; Arabic became the language of instruction in schools; conversion to Islam was encouraged; and Christian missionaries were increasingly harassed before being completely expelled in 1964.[27] The policies reflected the northern consensus that Arabization and Islamization were to be

---

22. Deng 1995: 3–5; Sikainga 1993: 79.
23. Daly 2007: 254.
24. Alier 1971: 19; Deng 1995: 93, 135; Johnson 2003: 22; Malwal 1981: 1.
25. Johnson 2003: 28; Lesch 1998: 36.
26. Lesch 1998: 37.
27. Deng 1995: 138–39; Johnson 2003: 30.

the sources of unity for Sudan. But the effect in the south, in particular, was to alienate the non-Muslim and non-Arabic speaking population even further.[28]

The military government gave way to a popular protest movement in October 1964, a movement in part inspired by desultory policies toward the south in the war. A caretaker government took measures to rethink policies toward the south, a process that was most clearly expressed in the formation of a Round Table Conference in which southern politicians and ideas that devolved power to the south were given some prominence. But the alternative vision was quickly undercut by a return to the consensus themes of northern rule, which revolved around northern centralized control, Islam, and Arabization. Parliamentary elections in 1965 and 1968 resulted in coalition governments led by the traditional sectarian political parties and gains for an Islamist organization, the Islamic Charter Front.[29] Reflecting the traditional foundations of governance, the new prime minister, Sadiq al-Mahdi, the great-grandson of the Mahdi and the leader of the Umma party, wrote in 1966: "The dominant feature of our nation is an Islamic one and its overpowering expression is Arab, and this nation will not have its entity identified and its prestige and pride preserved except under an Islamic revival."[30] A year before, in Somalia, he similarly affirmed, "Islam has a holy mission in Africa, and southern Sudan is the beginning of that mission."[31] A 1968 draft constitution similarly recognized Islam as the official religion, reiterated that Arabic was the official language, and posited Shari'a as the source of law; atheist parties would be banned.[32]

In the first decade of self-government—a critical period—we thus see consistent ideological pivoting among the northern elite toward Arab-Islamic nationalism. Whether military or civilian leaders, the northern elite envisioned a Sudan in the image of Islam and Arabism, a vision that encouraged an initial mutiny that in turn gave way to a low-grade armed rebellion. As the military responded with violence, prominent southern leaders and students left for exile, adding to the momentum of the rebellion. The movement gained further ground in 1964 when it intercepted a ship of arms destined for Congolese rebels, but the rebels soon fractured into different movements and internal divisions.[33]

The patterns of state violence against civilians in the first war are not extensively documented, but every indication suggests the beginnings of the collective

28. Deng 1995: 139.
29. Lesch 1998; Sikainga 1993: 82–83.
30. Sikainga 1993: 83.
31. Malwal 1981: 41.
32. Lesch 1998: 42.
33. Deng 1995: 140–41; Johnson 2003: 31–32.

targeting that would become entrenched in the second war and beyond. Govern-ment military forces burned villages and arrested southern elites in the first years of the war during the 1950s.[34] The level of violence increased after 1965, after parliamentary democracy was restored. In the 1965 to 1969 period, several major massacres took place.[35] In 1967, Prime Minister Sadiq al-Mahdi visited the south and visibly wept at a grave of fallen northern soldiers. After his visit, southern detainees were pulled out of prison and massacred.[36] During the period, all south-erners in areas where guerillas were present were considered rebel supporters.[37] Tribal leaders were killed.[38] Overall, according to one southern politician, south-erners felt that northerners had employed maximum repression while refusing to address southern grievances.[39]

In sum, in the first decade and a half of independent Sudan, the dominant political patterns of governance were in evidence. Power was concentrated at the center in particular among a merchant, land-holding, and clerical elite. Deeply divided by sectarian and power rivalries—Alex de Waal following Peter Woodward aptly calls Sudan a "turbulent state"[40]—the northern elite found ideological unity in crafting a state in an Islamic and Arab image. "The basic mechanism of strength in a weak, divided, unstable state was religious affiliation," wrote one author.[41] That approach in turn largely mini-mized the place of southern, non-Arab, non-Muslim Sudanese who already were in positions of structural inequality prior to independence.

The state's response to the armed challenge, in particular after the rebellion gained strength—at least based on the limited data that exist—was to respond cal-lously to southern grievances with extensive coercive violence. While one should be cautious about the precision of such estimates, the standard estimate of civilian deaths during first war period (1955–1972) is 400,000 to 600,000 deaths.

The Second North-South Civil War

The unstable coalition governments of the late 1960s gave way to a second military coup in 1969, this time led by General Ja'far Muhammad Numayri. Sudan's new military leader initially positioned himself against Sudan's three

---

34. Johnson 2003: 31; Malwal 1981: 62.
35. Deng 1995: 142; Malwal 1981: 63–64.
36. Malwal 1981: 42.
37. Deng 1995: 142.
38. Deng 1995: 143.
39. Malwal 1982: 63–64.
40. De Waal 2007.
41. Woodward 1990: 133.

most dominant political parties of the moment, in particular the parties led respectively by the Khatmiyya (the Democratic Unionist Party), the Umma, and the Islamists (the Islamic Charter Front). Instead, he oriented himself, at least initially, toward the weaker Sudanese Communist Party, whose base was urban, professional, and affiliated with the trade unions. Given this comparatively weak support base, Numayri sought to broaden his ruling base through political overtures to the south. He did so through negotiations that culminated in the Addis Ababa Agreement of 1972, which mark the end of the first North-South civil war. Indeed, it was under Numayri (at least the first six or seven years of his rule)—a repressive military dictator—that Sudan experienced its first sustained counternarrative. The Agreement granted regional autonomy, envisioned a regional assembly to the south, and permitted English as a language of instruction. The Agreement also articulated a vision of a multi-ethnic, plural Sudan, one that combined its Arab and African heritages. Indeed, judging from a review of more than twenty of Numayri's political speeches, he embraced, at least initially and publicly, the idea of a culturally plural Sudan.[42]

However, the alternative approach was neither deep nor lasting. The Agreement afforded limited power to the south to set taxation, economic, and legislative policy.[43] Political support for peace or the Agreement's terms was weak in the north and south, respectively.[44] The discovery of oil in southern territory during the 1970s further undermined the Agreement. Northerners wanted control over the resources, continuing a pattern of the center's resource exploitation of the periphery, while southerners wanted to benefit directly from the revenue. A proposed major water scheme, known as the Jonglei Canal project, threatened to flood southern lands, further alienating southerners.[45] But a critical factor in the Accords' ultimate demise was Numayri's politics. His initial peace overtures reflected less a deep personal and political commitment to a new Sudan than a tactical move by an opportunistic dictator to stay in power, and once his calculations for political survival shifted, so did his policies.[46] In particular, in the face of growing opposition and coup threats from northern elites, Numayri pivoted back to the anchor of Sudanese politics: a founding narrative of Arab-Islamic nationalism and an alliance of riverine, northern Arab elites. In 1977, Numayri announced a National Reconciliation government. He brought Sadiq back

42. Deng 1995: 157; Johnson 2003: 39–41; Lesch 1998: 45–47; Malwal 1981: 246.
43. Johnson 2003: 40–41.
44. Johnson 2003: 55.
45. Daly 1993: 21; Johnson 2003: 48.
46. Daly 1993: 20–21; Deng 1995: 160; Johnson 2003: 56; Lesch 1998: 47.

from exile and freed Hassan al-Turabi, the leader of the Islamic Charter Front, later appointing him attorney general. Numayri and his new government turned to Shari'a, culminating in the so-called September Laws of 1983, which declared a restrictive form of Islamic law as national code for Sudan, including punishments such as stoning, flogging, and amputation.[47]

The September Laws were both a nail in the coffin of the Addis Ababa Accords and a return to the main themes of Sudan's founding narrative. Earlier that same year, Numayri had unilaterally dissolved the Southern Region, violating the Agreement's terms; together with the center of gravity that the Reconciliation Government represented and the Sudanese leader's growing Islamization, a new southern rebellion took root in 1983. The rebel organization that came to lead the new rebellion was the Sudan People's Liberation Army/Movement (SPLA/M). Led by John Garang, a colonel and head of Staff College in Omdurman, and supported by Ethiopia, the SPLA/M chose a political platform of national unity rather than separatism, criticizing unequal development in the country.[48] Overcoming initial leadership and ideological divisions, the SPLA/M would go on to become the torchbearer for armed southern resistance, initially staging guerilla attacks and then coming to hold some territory by the mid-1980s.[49]

Together with a weak economy, the resumption of war contributed to declining political fortunes for Numayri. In 1985, a popular uprising prompted the Army to remove Numayri from power while he was visiting the United States, then a critical Cold War ally. The military established a transitional council, which gave way to national elections in 1986 and then the return to power of the Umma and the Democratic Unionist Party in a new national coalition. Sadiq emerged again as prime minister, but he refused to repeal the September Laws, as the leader of the interim military council had.[50] Indeed, Sadiq was explicit in his commitment to Islam as defining Sudanese law, as were the other two largest electoral winners of the 1986 elections. "We wish to establish Islam as the source of law in Sudan because Sudan has a Muslim majority," Sadiq said in 1986.[51] Under Sadiq too, the methods for fighting the southern insurgency changed. Although the practice of arming militias that bordered the SPLA/M-supportive communities began under Numayri, the tactic expanded in the democratic period.[52]

---

47. Africa Watch 1990: 21–23; Daly 1993: 24; Lesch 1998: 87–92.
48. Johnson 2003: 60–63.
49. Johnson 2003: 68.
50. Johnson 2003: 71–73.
51. Johnson 2003: 79.
52. Johnson 2003: 81.

As in the 1960s, Sudan's democratic period was short-lived. In 1989, a coalition of military officers and politicians staged a coup. The nominal leader was General Omar al-Bashir, who became president, but the political force behind the coup was Hassan al-Turabi, the leader of the Islamists, now renamed the National Islamic Front (NIF). Bashir and Turabi committed themselves to establishing an Islamic state in Sudan.[53] Bashir called Islamic law a principle to die for, and Turabi referred to Sudan as an "Islamic Republic."[54] A 1991 penal code made apostasy illegal,[55] and a 1992 fatwa declared Muslim rebel supporters apostates and non-Muslims heathen for which Islam provided a duty to kill.[56] Support for militias to fight counterinsurgency wars increased, in particular through the creation of the Popular Defense Force, which formalized existing militias, created institutional mechanisms to support them, and led to the recruitment of tens of thousands. In addition, the Islamist leaders ushered in widespread and repressive changes in the polity and banking sector, including banning parties, trade unions, and newspapers; purging the civil service and army; replacing key cadre with Islamists; and arresting professionals in a variety of sectors.[57]

The formal promulgation of an Islamist state with an Arab foundation under the NIF represents a repressive and extreme return to the nationalist tendencies that predate 1989. From the early days of independence to the NIF's rise to power, northern political elites have returned to religion as a source of unity and definition among the fractious power-holding northern elite. In other words, the NIF's Islamization of state and nation are not an aberration. They are versions along a nationalist continuum that have consistently shaped northern Sudanese politics. The same is true for the practices of civilian targeting. While the NIF encouraged, expanded, and Islamized militia support, the practice was already present during the democratic period of the 1980s and even before. The policies reflect continuity with, rather than a departure from, the dominant political tendencies and practices in the country since independence.

The Darfur Crisis

My focus is the western Sudanese region of Darfur, whose history overlaps with but differs from other peripheral areas. Because local actors and local conditions independently shaped the violence in Darfur (given the decentralized, far-flung nature of the state), it is crucial to take stock of the region.

---

53. Lesch 1998: 113–14.
54. Lesch 1998: 129–30.
55. Johnson 2003: 128.
56. Lesch 1998: 130.
57. Africa Watch 1990; Burr and Collins 2006: 245; Daly 2007: 249.

In contrast to southern Sudan, Darfur is primarily Muslim and, rather than external influence from neighboring Ethiopia, Libya and Chad more sharply shaped the trajectory of conflict in Darfur. Whereas there is a small population that self-identifies as Arab in the south, in Darfur there are several groups that claim Arab descent.

Roughly the size of Texas, Darfur was home to some 6.5 million people prior to the onset of war and violence in 2003. Then split into three administrative regions (North, South, and West), the term *Dar Fur* refers to the "land of the Fur," named after the largest (non-Arab) ethnic group in the region and its associated Sultanate. The Fur Sultanate was one of the last areas to come under colonial control in the British era, remaining autonomous until 1916. Integration into the colonial state yielded limited development gains, but it came laced with British beliefs in Arab superiority; even after independence, Darfur received limited resources to develop its infrastructure, education, and civil administration. Its history is one of marginalization and limited state control.[58]

Largely composed of semi-arid and arid spaces, Darfur's history is also one of environmental vulnerability and competition over access to the region's precious livelihood resources of water, fertile soil, and pastureland. This competition, which in turn is linked to ethnic identity, constitutes one of the long-term lineages of violence in Darfur. Identity is complex in Darfur. The region is home to more than three dozen ethnic and sub-ethnic groupings.[59] Within those groupings, there are two main cleavages. The first is between sedentary farming communities and pastoral herding communities. The second is between groups claiming Arab descent, such as the Baggara and Rizeigat tribes, and non-Arab groups, such as the Fur, the Masalit, and the Zaghawa. These cleavages often, but not uniformly, overlap—that is, those who identify as Arab historically are semi-nomadic herders while non-Arabs typically are sedentary farmers. That said, many Arab families grow crops, and many non-Arabs raise livestock. Both groups also participate in non-farming and non-husbandry professions.[60]

Across time, the livelihood practices and identity differences between the various groups in Darfur animated mutual suspicions, and at times confrontation, but they were not in the aggregate a deadly cocktail. By most accounts, there existed usually local informal and formal mechanisms for managing disputes over access to resources. But starting in the 1970s and 1980s the foundations of local cooperation for a variety of reasons began to come undone. One is the onset of a particularly severe drought, and associated famine and

58. Cockett 2010: 31–33; Daly 2007; Flint and de Waal 2008: 11–12.
59. Tubiana 2005.
60. Flint and de Waal 2008: 1–15.

desertification, which increased competition for the region's increasingly scarce resources. In response, some herders encroached or threatened to encroach on farmers' lands, which prompted farmers to find ways to protect their lands. The rainfall patterns also prompted new migrations, with attendant claims and counter-claims over who had access to land rights. Over time, and for political reasons, the process escalated. Some nomadic herders began purchasing weapons to protect their livestock and to increase the roaming range of their animals, while some farmers bought arms to protect their land.[61]

Two more political factors were instrumental in the process of local escalation. The first is political manipulation from the center. Numayri had abolished the Native Administration, which despite its flaws had developed institutional mechanisms for mediating local conflicts. As tensions increased in the region, local Darfuri Arabs appealed to Khartoum for support. Northern politicians, in particular under Sadiq and later Bashir, responded by promoting Arabs in local government positions, thereby increasing Arab power and leverage in the region and marginalizing non-Arabs.[62]

The second critical factor concerns a regional dynamic with Chad and Libya. In order to unseat a government in Chad, Libyan leader Muammar Qaddafi with support from post-Numayri governments funded Chadian rebels based in Darfur. The presence of Chadian rebels in Darfur in the 1970s and 1980s had two principal effects. The first was that it led to the availability of cheap weapons, which facilitated the mutual arming between local Arabs and non-Arabs.[63] The second was the growth of Arab supremacist ideology in Darfur, cultivated chiefly by Libya but with support from Sudanese leaders. Libya is the apparent source of an Arab supremacist organization called the "Arab Gathering" or "Arab Alliance." The Arab Gathering distributed writings in the 1980s claiming that the "zurga" (pejorative for non-Arabs) had ruled long enough. Later tracts expressed similar forms of Arab resentment and presented plans for Arab claims to local power. These developments made racialized identities more salient and sharpened differences between Arabs and non-Arabs in Darfur.[64]

The first major outbreak of violence took place in the late 1980s in what is called the "War of Tribes."[65] The main attackers were migrant and resident

---

61. Burr and Collins 2006: 237–38; Daly 2008: 215–17, 230–32, 243–44; Flint and de Waal 2008: 44–45; Johnson 2003: 139.

62. Burr and Collins 2006: 237–38, 287; Prunier 2005.

63. Flint and de Waal 2008: 46.

64. Burr and Collins 2006: 281–83; Daly 2008: 243–46, 265–67; Flint and de Waal 2008: 45–52; Johnson 2003: 140; Prunier: 2005: 45; Tubiana 2005.

65. Daly 2007: 244.

pastoralists who attacked Fur in an effort to secure more permanent grazing lands. The fighting began in fall 1998 and lasted until spring 1989. One estimate puts the toll at 5,000 Fur civilians killed and 40,000 Fur homes destroyed, compared to 400 Arabs killed and 400 Arab tents destroyed.[66] Anther estimate is 2,500 Fur dead and 400 villages burned, compared to 700 tents and homes destroyed.[67] Each side accused the other of seeking to create an "Arab" or "African" belt.[68] The short-term drivers of the violence remain unclear, but the violence followed a particularly severe drought between 1983 and 1985, mutual militia arming, the influx of automatic weapons (including from the Sudanese government under Sadiq), and the new racialized ideals promoted by the Arab Gathering.

A peace conference and local reconciliation agreement between mediators and heads of communities brought a short-term peace in the region, but the peace was precarious.[69] One key development took place in 1991 when an SPLA/M commander, Daud Bolad, led a march into Darfur. His forces were quickly crushed, but the tactics were important: The state relied on local Arab militias to fight the war.[70]

A second key development was building political support for the NIF in Darfur, which historically supported the Umma party because the Umma's Sufi network extended to non-Arab groups into Darfur. The NIF's strategy dovetailed with its Islamist, pro-Arab orientation: It sought to capitalize on local Arab grievances and recent political mobilization to weaken the non-Arab groups, in particular the Fur, Masalit, and Zaghawa, each of which had local conflicts over land with different Arab groups. In 1994, the state divided Darfur into three states, making the Fur a minority in each. Local Arabs in turn were appointed to key local government positions.[71] In Dar Masalit, new policies sought to undermine the authority of the Masalit Sultan there. The governor of Western Darfur decreed the fragmentation of the Dar into different "emirates," handing the majority to Arabs; these "emirs" in turn could, it was later decided, elect a new Sultan, thereby signaling the eventual replacement of the local Masalit Sultan.[72]

In the same period—the third key development—intercommunal relations deteriorated. Local Arabs were seeking to win the upper hand; the

---

66. Johnson 2003: 140.
67. Flint and de Waal 2008: 55.
68. Burr and Collins 238; Daly 2007: 246; Johnson 2003: 140.
69. Africa Watch 1990: 86.
70. Burr and Collins 2006: 281; Flint and de Waal 2008: 56.
71. Daly 2007: 262; Flint and de Waal 2008: 56–57.
72. Daly 2007: 262–63; Flint and de Waal 2008: 58–59.

Masalit feared that they were being ousted. Resource raids on cattle or lands expanded, and the Masalit and local Arab groups mutually armed and fought. In 1997, the state declared a state of emergency in Darfur, later naming a Sudanese general as a military governor who in turn trained local Arabs as militias. Local disputes quickly escalated, and the balance of force favored the Arabs. As many as several thousand Masalit were killed.[73] Similar confrontations between Baqqara Ruzayqat (an Arab group) and Zaghawa took place in southern Darfur in the second half of the 1990s.[74]

In sum, the runup to the big war in the 2000s witnessed a confluence of factors. There was environmental stress on a vulnerable landscape, which forced some to defend their land and others to migrate or find new lands. Those changes put pressure on weak land rights, ones that were open to political manipulation. Enter the regional influences—the influx of weapons, the promotion of racial supremacist ideologies—and the domestic political ones—an Arab-Islamist state committed to changing the politics of the past in Darfur and to using militias to fight proxy wars. Local Arabs saw a political opportunity to upset the power imbalances and solve problems over access to resources; national political leaders saw an opportunity to secure a political base.

Two further developments are important to how the violence in Darfur ultimately unfolded. The first is that a split between Bashir and Turabi, one that reflected tensions within the NIF, became public in 2000 when the latter was removed from the NIF. Turabi turned to support from the provinces, in particular from Darfur, and Bashir feared that Turabi would lead an armed movement against him, perhaps from Darfur. That led the NIF to turn again to local Arabs.[75] The other key development concerns the gradual ending of the North-South civil war. Beginning in 2001, the government and the SPLA/M entered into comprehensive peace negotiations. After numerous rounds of talks, the two sides reached an agreement; in January 2005, government and rebel delegations officially ended the war, to much international acclaim. However, Darfur was not represented in the negotiations. The non-Arabs of Darfur, who had experienced a slow process of increased marginalization and violence, worried about their future in a postwar Sudan that did not explicitly recognize their concerns.

Taking their lead from past uprisings, the non-Arab groups turned to rebellion. The two main movements were the Sudan Liberation Front/Army (SLF/A) and the Justice and Equality Movement (JEM). The former emerged from ethnic militias, in particular Fur and Zaghawa ones but

---

73. Daly 2007: 263; Flint and de Waal 2008: 58–63.
74. Daly 2007: 264; Flint and de Waal 2008: 64–66.
75. Daly 2007: 271; Flint and de Waal 2008: 68–69.

eventually Masalit as well. Their chief concerns were Arab predations combined with an Arab supremacist ideology in the region and the resulting loss
of power, land, and resources among non-Arabs. The rebellion started as early
as 2001, although the SLF/A as a manifestoed, formal political organization
with evident SPLA/M influence did not appear until 2003.[76]

The central government's first response was to arrest its leaders and prominent Fur, as well as some Arab militants.[77] But the rebel attacks continued.
The national government in turn reached out to local Arab leaders to fight
on their behalf, and local Arab groups and leaders associated with the Arab
Gathering found common positions. As the SLF/A gained ground and after
it announced itself in 2003, the government responded by deploying troops
to the region.[78] But the SLF/A continued to attack, prompting the government to start to attack whole villages where the rebels operated.[79] The SLF/A
was stronger militarily than the JEM, which included Islamists and whose
core leadership was the Kobe subgroup of Zaghawa.[80] The state also feared
that JEM would team up with Turabi, given his Islamist commitments, and
perhaps other former NIF insiders.[81]

At first, the central government misjudged the extent of the danger and
considered the unrest a local affair. The governor of North Darfur, where
the rebellion was then concentrated, sought to negotiate and calm tensions.[82]
But by early 2003, hardliners within the NIF began to call for a more robust
military response, and in April Bashir vowed to "crush" the rebellion.[83]
Increasingly hurt by aerial bombardments, the SLF/A commanders decided
to attack planes on the ground, which led them to an intense April 25 attack
on El Fasher Airport, in which the rebels destroyed seven planes and captured the overall commander of the Sudanese Air Force. It was one of the
most successful insurgent acts against the Sudanese state at any point in any
war—including the years of violence in the south.[84]

The successful attack, and the rebels' continuing success immediately
thereafter, changed the course of the war. The central state replaced the more
conciliatory governor, released one of the key Arab militia leaders (Musa
Hilal, who had briefly been detained as part of the initial effort to negotiate

---

76. Burr and Collins 2006: 289; Daly 2007: 280; Flint and de Waal 2008: 82, 90–91.
77. Flint and de Waal 2008: 84.
78. Flint and de Waal 2008: 85–87, 97.
79. Flint and de Waal 2008: 98.
80. Flint and de Waal 2008: 110.
81. Flint and de Waal 2008: 100–101.
82. Flint and de Waal 2008: 116.
83. Flint and de Waal 2008: 118–19.
84. Daly 2007: 282; Flint and de Waal 2008: 121.

and calm tensions) and began a campaign of destruction. The violence was coordinated from the center, and the essential vision was to link the Sudanese armed forces and military intelligence with Arab recruits and militias on the ground. The main tactic was to attack civilians in order to defeat the rebels.[85] The violence quickly escalated, and in the second half of 2003 and 2004 the joint military-militia attacks were particularly devastating. Tens of thousands of non-Arab civilians were killed, hundreds of villages were destroyed, and more than two million fled their homes, many of whom perished for lack of access to sufficient food, water, and medical care. The violence was sustained—for more than a year the attacks, which targeted a categorical identity population, were relentless—against non-Arabs in general, but especially Fur, Zaghawa, and Masalit, and the violence was on a massive scale. While estimates vary, as discussed below, some 200,000 civilians died in two years.

We see here a two-level, intersecting process of escalation. At the local level, from the 1980s forward there was growing tension and violent confrontation. At the national level, state leaders bolstered local Arab groups, ultimately leading to the decision by non-Arabs to revolt. Once begun, the insurgency did not generate mass categorical violence. The national actors allowed a local governor to mediate and contain the dispute, backed by military power. But those efforts failed, while the insurgency developed and then scored a major battlefield victory. The national-level actors perceived a much greater threat, one that could perhaps ally with domestic opposition in Khartoum and with the southern movements. The state strategy then shifted toward an escalation of violence, with the state supplying, recruiting, and encouraging local Arab armed groups to fight. The local actors in turn responded with their own interests, which had an independent effect on escalation. In terms of explaining the process of escalation, then, we have a growing insurgency and the inability of the state to contain it, which led to greater threat perception, and local actors who saw an opportunity to solve serious livelihood matters and who joined national actors in an opportunistic military and ideological alliance. Once the national state entered directly into the violence, the scale increased dramatically, as the propositions from chapter 1 would suggest.

Patterns of Violence

Coming a decade after the genocide in Rwanda, the mass violence in Darfur quickly catapulted the crisis there to the top of international attention. A grassroots campaign emerged to label the violence genocide in order to

---

85. Daly 2007: 282–83; Flint and de Waal 2008: 123.

trigger a stronger international response.[86] The United States endorsed that view. Secretary of State Colin Powell and President George W. Bush called the violence in Darfur genocide, even if such a designation did not translate into new foreign policy.[87] Others contested the label, including the authors of a United Nations Commission of Inquiry in early 2005. Both positions have merit, as discussed below, but for the analytic purposes of the book the case was clearly one of mass categorical violence—sustained, widespread, coordinated, large-scale lethal violence targeted at civilians who were selected for attack on the basis of their identities.

In many ways, the most appropriate empirical comparison is less Rwanda and more previous episodes of violence within Sudan. In particular during the second North-South civil war, as in Darfur, the state empowered local armed groups to attack the civilian communities that were supporting the insurgences. The state gave its authority and its resources to the militias, and the two sets of actors teamed up in an opportunistic alliance—strengthened by converging interests and an ideological commitment to Arab supremacy—to wreak devastation on non-Arab communities. As in Darfur, the target population was typically defined in categorical terms, as "blacks," "infidels" (non-Muslims), or "Dinkas." As in Darfur, the typical attacks combined Air Force bombings with army and militia raids that singled out men for murder and women for rape or capture. Whole villages were bombed and burned, and the means of survival—food reserves, livestock, and wells—were often looted or deliberately destroyed, such as by poison or arson. Even if the government at times entered into political negotiations, the practice of violence was wholesale destruction with little restraint. Many civilians died from the direct violence, but many more died indirectly, because they were vulnerable to disease and dehydration once displaced or to famine when no rainfall was forthcoming.

North-South Civil War

There exists little in the way of systematic documentation of variation in the temporal and spatial patterns and levels of violence in the long war in the south. J. Millard Burr makes rough annual estimates, concluding that as many as two million civilians died between 1983 and 1998.[88] That estimate (or an extended one through the war's termination in 2005) is standard in

---

86. Hamilton 2011.
87. Straus 2005.
88. Burr 1998.

cross-national genocide studies.[89] Yet, as Douglas Johnson argues, there are problems with the baseline data and with the extrapolations on which the summary estimates are made.[90] In short, there is little in the way of a precise, reliable estimate of the total number killed in the twenty-two-year North-South civil war. There are also few detailed data on when or where the violence intensified and deescalated. Nonetheless, within existing scholarly and human rights accounts there is little doubt that the war strategy involved massive, group-selective targeting of civilians.[91]

By several accounts, the practice of supporting militias began under Numayri after the outbreak of war in 1983.[92] As the southern rebels gained ground, Numayri initially floated the idea of mass conscription, but facing opposition he instead turned to the practice of arming and supporting local militia forces, a practice dating to at least the Turkiyya.[93] For their part, local armed groups had formed in response to confrontations around access to local resources; local pastoralists also had been displaced from mechanized farming schemes supported by the central state. In choosing to support local militias and in forging a wartime alliance, the state capitalized on this economic frustration at the local level.[94] Empowering Muslims who claimed Arab descent was also consistent with Numayri's Islamist turn in the waning years of his tenure.

But waging war through local armed groups outside the military hierarchy was not the unique province of military dictatorship. The practice expanded significantly after Sadiq al-Mahdi assumed the premiership in 1986. Continuing to face a growing SPLA/M, one with regional support, as well as an officer corps loyal primarily to his political rivals, Sadiq looked for alternative means to prosecute the war. Sadiq then exploited his networks within the Umma party, in particular by leaning on Misiriya, Rizeigat, and Rufaa Arabs in several regions.[95] The government also supported anti-SPLA/M southern armed groups as part of a divide and rule strategy, one that has been a consistent feature in how the north seeks to weaken opposition on the peripheries.[96] Human rights reports indicate that the state's armed forces fought a "dirty" war—killing and torturing civilians while seeking to control garrison towns

---

89. For instance, Harff 2003; Ulfelder and Valentino 2008.

90. Johnson 2003: 143.

91. Africa Watch 1990; Amnesty International 1990; Burr 1998; Burr and Collins 2006; Daly 1993; de Waal 1993; Johnson 2003.

92. Africa Watch 1990; de Waal 1993; Johnson 2003.

93. Africa Watch 1990: 65; Johnson 2003.

94. Africa Watch 1990: 67; De Waal 1993: 143–48; Johnson 2003: 82.

95. Africa Watch 1990; De Waal 1993: 142; Johnson 2003: 81–82.

96. Africa Watch 1990; De Waal 1993: 142.

and supply routes. The military also limited food trade and relief supplies.[97] But the worst documented violence was at the hands of the militia, who responded to SPLA/M attacks or even to local disputes with massive violence against non-Arab civilian populations. A good example is the March 1987 massacre in Ed Da'ien, when Rizeigat Arab militiamen massacred more than 1,000 Dinka civilians in two days after an SPLA/M attack.[98]

The use of militias faced some opposition from within the military hierarchy. As a measure to regularize the militias and to respond to opposition from within the officer corps—as well as to military advances on the part of the SPLA/M—Sadiq's government proposed in 1989 to institutionalize the armed groups as "Popular Defense Committees." The measure ultimately failed, and Sadiq was deposed as head of state that year. However, his successor, Omar al-Bashir, was one of the military officers who had supported the use of the militias. Once the NIF took power in 1989, the state further expanded their use. Increasing the power of parallel forces was part of the NIF's general strategy of Islamizing and appropriating institutions. The NIF created the Popular Defense Forces, which served to create new institutional avenues to support the militias. The NIF also declared a Holy War in the south.[99]

The militias did not act alone. Detailed human rights reporting shows a pattern of attacks in which the irregulars worked "very closely" with the armed forces of the state.[100] Under Sadiq, the chief institution was the Army. But once the NIF came to power, a new practice became institutionalized—the use of aerial bombing of wide swaths of territory where insurgents operated.[101] Burr finds that aerial bombing increased into the 1990s.[102]

All told, the net result between the militia violence, the Army attacks, and the Air Force bombing was massive civilian suffering. Many died from murder. But many also died from forced displacement and wholesale village destruction. The government-militia alliance forced people from their homes, burned villages, interrupted trading and supply routes, destroyed the means to survive—food, shelter, water, livestock—and, at times, blocked relief aid. All this created enormous privation on the civilian population and caused it to be especially vulnerable to external shock, such as drought. For example, as many as 250,000 alone died in the famine between 1986 and

97. Africa Watch 1990: 67–78.
98. Africa Watch 1990: 84.
99. Africa Watch 1990: 94–95; De Waal 1993: 155; Johnson 2003: 83, 152.
100. Africa Watch 1990: 90.
101. Burr 1998.
102. Burr 1998.

1989, according to Africa Watch,[103] and those years were among the worst in terms of overall civilian death tolls, according to Burr's estimates.

Nuba Mountains

One of the theaters of war for which detailed reporting from the early 1990s exists is the Nuba Mountains, an area of South Kordofan. The Nuba are a collection of more than fifty mostly non-Muslim, non-Arab ethnic groups who, as in Darfur, are technically situated in the north. The Nuba cohabit Kordofan with Arab groups, principally pastoralists. Like other non-Arabs in Sudan, discrimination against the non-Arab Nuba dates to well before independence, but marginalization after independence increased. So did disputes with local Arabs over access to livelihood resources. Baggara Arabs, themselves poor and displaced by mechanized farming schemes, nonetheless benefited from government support during local disputes. These various factors—pro-Muslim bias within the state combined with backing local Arabs in resource disputes—led some youths and elites to turn to the SPLA/M after the second war began.

Violence in the area began formally in 1985 when the SPLA/M attacked a Baggara cattle camp, killing some sixty civilians and wounding more. The attack created a further incentive for the Baggara to turn to the state, and as it had elsewhere the state turned to the Baggara to contain the SPLA/M in the area. The 1980s violence was devastating. The militias killed civilians, burned villages, and destroyed livestock, while the army attacked civilians where the SPLA/M made territorial gains. But, as with the rest of the war, the violence intensified after the NIF came to power. In 1989, the SPLA/M announced a new Nuba fighting unit, the New Kush Division. The army and militia responded with more intense violence, which in turn created conditions for a large-scale famine in the early 1990s. The 1992 declaration of a Holy War further escalated the situation. The government created population centers or "peace camps" to which it encouraged the population to flee, but once they reached there, women were raped and children were educated to be Islamists. The state's aim, concludes African Rights, was to depopulate areas of Nuba, a practice that the organization called genocide.[104]

Even these brief sketches show that the patterns of violence experienced in Darfur were not unique. In the North-South civil war, and in the Nuba Mountains—where, as in Darfur, Arab and non-Arab groups live in greater

---

103. Africa Watch 1990.
104. African Rights 1995.

proximity than in the south, all told—the dynamics of armed conflict strongly shaped the patterns of violence against civilians. The rise to the power of the NIF, which was ideologically more committed to Islamism, Arabism, and militancy, further escalated the violence. Their use of aerial bombing, combined with an expanded counterinsurgency alliance with local Arab groups, provided the capacity to find, sort, and destroy large numbers of non-Arab civilians.

Darfur

All this sets the stage for examining the origins of the violence in Darfur in the 2000s. As in Kordofan, prior to the outbreak of sustained mass violence Darfur experienced growing, sometimes racialized tension over access to resources. A new phase of violence began after two insurgent groups formed and, as in Kordofan, after they made significant battlefield gains, notably the spectacular attack on El Fasher Airport. Shaken by these advances at a time when the north was in negotiations to end the war in the south and coming on the heels of an important split within the heart of the Islamist regime, the state chose to respond with overwhelming force to crush the rebellion, one led by non-Arabs. The state chose local armed groups as the main agents of violence on the ground, thereby exploiting micro-level and community-level grievances over access to vital resources. For their part, local actors worried not only about their own survival—the arrival of newly powerful non-Arab groups was also interpreted as a new phase in the escalation of the local conflict resources. Furthermore, local actors perceived an opportunity to secure longer-term access to the lands that they needed for their own survival.[105]

The state coordinated the attacks on non-Arabs. On the one hand, the state provided weapons, training, intelligence, and authority to local actors who in turn recruited from the Arab population. On the other hand, the state also deployed its military to engage in joint attacks, in particular using the Air Force but also the Army. As in other cases, ideology strengthened what was in this case a tactical alliance between national-level and local-level actors. In Khartoum, the Islamist, Arab-centric regime chose local Arabs as their collaborators, who in turn were animated both by Arab supremacist ideas stemming from the Arab Gathering and local interests articulated in categorical terms—in their minds, Arab groups were fighting non-Arab groups for control of vital territory and even survival. In the end, the strategic objectives of the two key actors in the tactical alliance diverged. The state's main interest was to crush the rebellion, while the local actors sought permanent access to land and resources.

---

105. Haggar 2007; Tubiana 2005, 2007.

In other words, local actors had some autonomy in pursuing their own agenda while conducting the state's counterinsurgency business.[106]

According to an account of a local senior militia commander, the state encouraged local actors to recruit militias to depopulate the area. When visiting Darfur after the El Fasher attack, Vice President Ali Osman Taha reportedly told local leaders, "Just bring your people, Arab people, from there, and I give you the weapons, the money, the horses, the camels, the uniforms, everything. Like that. . . . He said to us, we need only land. We don't need people here. We need only land. That is what he said to us."[107] The central pattern was—as in the other wars—to engage in widespread violence against the population seen to support the insurgents. That population was defined in categorical terms and in opposition to the defenders of the nation and territory. That meant attacks against non-Arab groups. Data from Darfuri non-Arab refugees suggest that perpetrators consistently used racialized, often derogatory references to non-Arabs as they attacked.[108] The attackers labeled their targets "blacks," "slaves," and "Nuba."[109]

The patterns of violence strongly support the conclusion that perpetrators defined their targets on the basis of a categorical identity. A central tactic in the war was to destroy villages and depopulate large areas of land of non-Arabs. One of the most common patterns was for the Air Force to bomb an area, which would be followed by ground attacks from militia or Army forces or both in combination. There is considerable evidence that the militia, army, and air force acted in a coordinated fashion during attacks. After studying the matter in some depth, officials at the U.S. State Department concluded that there was close coordination between Sudanese armed forces and the militias.[110] After the attacks, the perpetrators also set fire to homes, destroyed or looted food stocks, including livestock, and poisoned wells. Rape was also widespread, and men who were found during the ground raids were often singled out and killed.[111]

The result was, as in the other wars, massive civilian displacement. And that displacement was the primary source of mortality in Darfur. Lacking access to food, clean water, shelter, and medical care, many displaced Darfuris

106. Flint and de Waal 2008; Haggar 2007; Tubiana 2005, 2007.

107. Cockett 2010: 188.

108. Hagan and Rymond-Richmond 2008.

109. Cockett 2010: 187–89; Daly 2008: 283; Hagan and Rymond-Richmond 2009: 109, 127–34; UN Commission of Inquiry 2005; U.S. State Department 2004.

110. U.S. State Department 2004.

111. Amnesty International 2004; Flint and de Waal 2008: 145; Hamilton 2011; Human Rights Watch 2004; United Nations Commission of Inquiry 2005.

died because of disease and malnutrition. According to one detailed report, direct killing accounted for about a third of all deaths.[112]

The most intense violence was between mid-2003 and mid-2004, dropping off again in early 2005 after the state had achieved many of its military objectives.[113] The total number killed through early 2005 is contested. The range is between roughly 50,000 and 400,000 deaths directly or indirectly related to the violence.[114] Assembling a team of experts, a U.S. government review found that the most reliable estimates were on the conservative end of the range, at less than 150,000 deaths.[115] Publishing in *Science*, John Hagan and Alberto Palloni estimate about 200,000 deaths in the first thirty-one months of the crisis.[116]

Whatever the final number of deaths, the violence was clearly mass categorical violence. There was group-selective violence against non-Arab civilians. The violence was repeated in a similar pattern across thousands of villages. The violence was sustained at a high level for nearly two years. There was direct coordination, and there was a joint alliance between national and local actors. The violence was also large in scale, targeting a substantial portion (most) of the non-Arab population of Darfur.

Was the violence genocide? The main existing objections to such claims is that (a) the intent to destroy a group at the state level has not been proven, and (b) that the main objective was counterinsurgency.[117] The former may be true, but that is partly a function of existing gaps in evidence (which could be overcome as more information becomes available); it is also possible that the incentive to destroy non-Arab groups was less national and more local. Not enough data exist to know yet. But the latter objection is a red herring: that the state's interest was to defeat an insurgency is not inconsistent with the fact that the method chosen may be genocide.

As argued in chapter 1, genocide is measurable in part by whether perpetrators seek to destroy the reproductive and survival capacity of target groups. Genocide is also measurable by a dynamic of continued physical destruction once the military threat is contained or the war is already lost. On these scores, there is mixed evidence from Darfur. Perpetrators clearly sought to destroy the ability for the group to survive and reproduce. They

---

112. Coalition for International Justice 2005.

113. Flint and de Waal 2008: 150–51.

114. Coalition for International Justice 2005; GAO 2006; Hagan and Rymond-Richmond 2009: 96.

115. GAO 2006.

116. Hagan and Palloni 2006.

117. De Waal 2007; UN Commission of Inquiry 2005.

targeted all gender and age categories of non-Arabs; they burned homes, destroyed livestock, and poisoned wells. All of these measures destroyed the non-Arab groups' capacity to survive and regenerate in the affected regions. Yet the violence also diminished over time and well before an eventual international peacekeeping intervention in 2007. The declining violence seems largely a function of battlefield gains—the insurgency was contained; the rebels had retreated to several mountainous spaces, and the state-militia forces controlled the overwhelming bulk of territory. That suggests a coercive logic to the violence: The objective was to contain the rebellion, at least among national actors, rather than to destroy the group as such.

Two interpretations are possible: One is that both logics of violence were present in this case, but at different times, as in Nigeria. Genocide took place when the state and local groups did not know if the insurgents and their supporters were containable. Mass categorical violence took place once the military gained the upper hand. The other interpretation is that national actors always pursued a coercive strategy while local actors pursued a genocidal one. National actors condoned the locally initiated genocide as long as the military outcome was uncertain, yet national actors in turn reined in local actors as the tide shifted. Over time, more data should help analysts sort through these different interpretations.

Sources of Escalation and Restraint

Why mass categorical violence (or genocide) was the main strategy to fight peripheral insurgencies remains the key question. One hypothesis might be that the state's repressive character established patterns of coercive responses that in turn were translated into attacks on civilians in wartime. But while the Islamist regime escalated violence, the wartime patterns of violence were present in periods of democratic rule in Sudan in both the 1960s and 1980s. Moreover, the two main peace overtures in the south occurred under non-democratic regimes, first under Numayri and later under Bashir.

Another hypothesis is that the state lacked information either because of its capacity or because of its lack of territorial control. Without the professionalism, hardware, or intelligence to distinguish rebel from civilian, the state targeted both as a response to armed threat.[118] Another variant is that, lacking territorial control, the state was unable to generate sufficient specific information to know who was a rebel supporter and who was not. The cheaper choice was indiscriminate violence.[119]

---

118. Ulfelder and Valentino 2008; Valentino et al. 2004.
119. Kalyvas 2006.

These arguments are plausible. Indeed, descriptive accounts of why the state chose to arm militias suggest a choice dictated in part by political economy: The state's military resources were stretched across multiple locations in a huge state. Arming militias was financially cheaper and more popular than large-scale conscription.[120] Alex de Waal called the Darfur violence "counter-insurgency on the cheap."[121]

But in terms of information, the militias were local; they had, or could have, information about who was who and where the insurgents operated.[122] There seems to be no effort on the part of the local actors (or state) to obtain information to distinguish civilian from combatant or to concentrate on villages where insurgents operated. These were campaigns of violence against categorically defined enemies.

Looking comparatively, however, there is little evidence that Sudan had less capacity, in military or military intelligence terms, than Mali or Côte d'Ivoire. In fact, the Sudanese army was arguably stronger and more experienced than in Côte d'Ivoire and in Mali. Moreover, an argument about low-cost insurgency downplays how costly the violence was: There was a massive international outcry, which ultimately prompted sanctions and a string of international indictments, including against Bashir himself.

Another hypothesis is that Sudan turned to mass violence in periods of extraordinarily difficult times—in periods of economic stress or of particularly turbulent politics. But while politics are to a degree always turbulent in Sudan, there is little evidence to suggest that violence peaked in particularly politically and economically unstable periods. The violence in Darfur occurred, to the contrary, as oil revenue was coming online and as the state was ending international isolation through a peace agreement with the south.[123] The long periods of mass violence across the two North-South civil wars also run contrary to the idea that spikes in stress produce spikes in violence. Manus Midlarsky argues that the prospect of territorial loss through peace with the south prompted an overreaction in Darfur.[124] But the idea that territorial loss prompts a turn to extreme violence is undercut, at least in part, by the continuity in patterns of violence between the North-South civil war and that in Darfur.

Instead, as I have argued, the wartime threat was critical. As elsewhere, the context of armed conflict changed the menu of options that became thinkable.

---

120. Tubiana 2005.
121. De Waal 2004.
122. Cockett 2010: 191.
123. Cockett 2010: 8.
124. Midlarsky 2005.

From the perspective of the state, the application of violence became both legitimate and necessary as a response to armed threats to state sovereignty. Deployment of various agents of violence infliction—the army, the air force, and local armed groups—is also more thinkable in war. Moreover, the escalation of violence correlates closely to the onset and dynamics of threat perception in war—as the rebels gained, violence against civilians increased. In the south, in the Nuba Mountains, and in Darfur, the practice of arming militias and targeting non-Arabs occurred after insurgents gained strength and territory. While there are cases of significant violence occurring outside formal war—for example, the land-related killings in Darfur in the late 1980s—these occurred on a smaller, local scale and without the state's blessing.

In interviews, Sudanese political and military elites readily defend their application of violence as a legitimate response to armed threats. According to senior U.S. officials who interviewed Bashir and Taha at the height of the crisis, the leaders framed the Darfur operations as counterinsurgency.[125] In an interview with Reuters in 2004 (again at the height of the violence), the Sudanese military chief similarly articulated a logic of counterinsurgency in response to questions about violence in Darfur. "The [rebel] militia are attacking the government from the villages," he said. "What is the government going to do? It will bomb those villages. It will attack those villages because the villages were attacking them."[126] Here we see the logic of violent collective categorization that underpinned the operations: "villages" (in other words civilians from particular groups) had attacked the government, so the government's response was to attack villages. In Sudan, as elsewhere, one cannot separate the logic of mass categorical violence from the logic of waging war—at least from the perspective of the perpetrators.

But, as we have seen, war is not a sufficient explanation for strategies of mass violence. To explain the decision to target an identity population as the enemy, I emphasize the character of nationalism in Sudan—the country's founding narrative, which holds that the state belongs primarily to and is in the service of Islam and Arabs. In contrast to the negative cases studied in the book, nationalist elites at independence and virtually every other regime change thereafter fashioned a superior identity category to whom the state belonged and to which they attached a myth of descent. In Sudan, the northern elites imagined a lineage to the Arab world and to the spread of Islam, and they embraced a vision of Arab-Islamic glory as a reaction to the predations of colonialism. In so doing, they created an identity hierarchy within

---

125. Cockett 2010: 225.
126. McDoom 2004.

Sudan. Arabs and Muslims were, in Sudanese nationalism, more sophisticated and more fit to rule than non-Muslims and non-Arabs. On this, the literature is consistent: Non-Arabs and non-Muslims are viewed within the north as inferior beings, as afterthoughts, as lost brothers whose resources should be controlled and who should submit to Arab, northern, central rule.

Putting these mechanisms together, when non-Arab or non-Muslim citizens rebelled on the periphery, the state was not inclined to compromise or to accommodate them because Sudanese nationalism did not imagine the insurgents and their supporters to deserve an equal place at the center. The political reflex was thus not to incorporate but to ignore and, as the threat grew, to crush. The strategy became to employ whatever means necessary to force the peripheral populations to submit to northern rule. If large numbers of non-Arabs or non-Muslims died as a result, the ideological foundations of the state did not train northern leaders to value such suffering because they were not the primary political community that the state served. Violence was also consistent with past practices toward the south—slavery and resource raids, in particular—and with how the south was a marginal territory, an area that had been manipulated by outsiders, notably Christians and the British. There was, in other words, no strong counternarrative to the founding one that held Muslim and Arabs to be the core citizens.

The third dimension concerns territorial domination. As I have argued, mass categorical violence requires the capacity to identify, sort, and inflict violence against a specific identity population across space and time. In this case, that was partly achieved through aerial military power. But crucial to the organizational capacity of violence was the entry into alliances with local armed actors; they were the ones who identified targets, who did house-to-house searches, and who inflicted much of the violence. This was a decentralized coalition of violence, not the vertical administratively heavy model of Rwanda and Nazi Germany. As we have seen, the state turned to local actors to fight the wars in the south and in Darfur. The state armed, authorized, trained, and generally assisted the local actors. Their interests converged. But their interests were not the same. Among the local actors, one finds a depopulating incentive that dovetailed with the national interest in crushing the rebellion.

The local actors were situated in ecologically fragile areas where there existed significant pressure on the region's precious resources, notably land, grazing pasture, and water. In Darfur but also in parts of the south, local actors who had been engaged in prior confrontations over access to these resources took advantage of the state's license to violence to carve out swaths of land in order to secure, or even expand, their livelihoods. Such concerns about deprivation animated the local actors, as did security—they feared that resurgent, armed non-Arab groups would pose a threat to their long-term access and survival in the region. For the local actors, then, there were strategic incentives to extirpate communities that were consistent with, but different from, the strategic objectives of the national state. But overall we find in this case a national-local alliance that created the capacity to select and destroy an identity category in a particular region.

Sudan's founding narrative reinforced the national-local alliance. The North-South and Darfur alliances were coalitions of Arab groups fighting non-Arab groups. So did folk racism—many Arabs imagined themselves as belonging to a superior civilization when compared to non-Arabs. In other words, the national-level ideology had resonance with and reinforced common beliefs at the local level. All told, these ideas shaped the alliance and, during the war, created few incentives to restrain the violence against a category of citizens defined as inferior and distinct from the core national identity.

Finally, beyond weak counternarratives to Arab-Islamic nationalism, Sudan had little in the way of restraint on violence. This was true for the domestic economy. In contrast to Côte d'Ivoire but like Mali, the theaters of war were peripheral to the main zones of economic production—with one exception. Half the country's income and assets are in the capital, according to one estimate.[127] Prior to the discovery of oil, which then generated more than 90 percent of the country's foreign exchange, the southern economy was not only very weak, it also contributed little to the overall national output. Northern elites thus faced few economic and revenue costs to employing mass violence in the south. Once oil was discovered in the south and in the borderlands between north and south but production was not yet online, the north had an incentive to depopulate the oil zones and to claim territorial control of them. The mass violence had a destabilizing effect on the population, but that largely occurred before oil began pumping from the south, and moreover, the oil rents required little in the way of southern labor once the wells became operational.

That begs the question of why northern elites entered into serious peace negotiations in the early 2000s that ultimately ended the North-South civil war in 2005. By the logic of my argument, the northern elites must have calculated that peace and stability in the south would facilitate the exploitation of petroleum, which until then had been limited in part because of the war-related risks. The international firms who would dig for and transport the oil were wary of investing heavy equipment while war was still active. Thus, even though the 2005 Comprehensive Peace Agreement ultimately paved the way for southern secession, and with that secession the loss of the majority of

---

127. Cockett 2010: 30.

oil fields, the agreement enabled the north to obtain significant revenue from the piping of the oil through its border. In short, once oil was discovered, the north, which wanted that revenue, had the choice to depopulate and defeat the insurgency to gain territorial control or to make peace to find a way to generate revenue. They seem to have concluded that the latter was preferable after their inability to extirpate the population and the insurgency and enough sustained mediation from the international community. But these are hypotheses that require greater analysis as more data become available.

Turning to Darfur, the key point is that the violence and disruption in the region had no effect on oil production, which was concentrated in the south. Even if Sudan's international reputation was sullied, oil remained a commodity in high demand, and the state had little trouble selling the product on international markets. Thus, unlike in Côte d'Ivoire, where the agricultural industry created a powerful source of restraint, few such economic incentives in Sudan existed.

The Character of Nationalism

Of these factors, I focus on Sudan's founding narrative, given its essential role in shaping patterns of violence. The simple conclusion is that, with the exception of a period under Numayri, Sudanese northern political elites consistently sought to forge national unity around the twin poles of Islam and Arabism. In Islam and Arabism, Sudan's first generation of political elites found a source of pride in response to external colonial interference. That a Mahdi—an Islamist figure—led the first successful anticolonial movement added to this image of Islam as a source for independence and nationalism. In short, Islam and Arabism was a point of consensus among the riverine northern powerholders, one that provided a political pole around which they sought to forge unity in the face of marked internal divisions. A form of latent prejudice prevalent in northern Sudan reinforced that embrace of Islam and Arabism, which excluded non-Arabs and non-Muslims in the state.

On these points, the scholarly literature is consistent. One scholar of Sudanese nationalism in the independence era found that a dominant feature is the glorification of Islamic and Arabic culture.[128] Northern political parties saw Arabization and Islamization as the solutions to cultural diversity and specifically to the "problem" of the south. For them, the British had reversed a long process of Arabization and Islamization, a process that independence

---

128. Al-Rahim 1973.

would rekindle.[129] Those "fully participating in the state increasingly identified themselves with Arab lineages," while they identified "those outside the state not only as unbelievers, but as slaves. or as enslavable."[130] Despite their divisions, Sudan's main political parties had a vision of Islam as the religion of the state and Arabic as the official language; they were united in their decision to keep hegemony in hands of the Muslim, Arabic-speaking, riverine elite to the exclusion of other regions.[131] Even Alex de Waal, who insightfully labors for inserting complexity into any political analysis of Sudan, argues that northern political elite adopt Islamic and Arab identities "reflexively."[132]

Two major studies of Sudanese political history make similar points. Francis Deng concludes that northern elites championed an Arabic-Islamic identity as the umbrella concept that unites a diverse community and ultimately the state. That vision is fundamentally hierarchical, he argues: Northern elites portrayed their culture, religion, and race as superior to that of black Africans. The former are considered free, superior, and proud in contrast to the latter, who are inferior, heathen, slaves, and the legitimate target of slavery. Arabism and Islamism are at some level assimiliationist—Islam in particular will absorb non-Muslims—but at base there lies a deeply pejorative view toward non-Arabs as of a lower status.[133] That too is the conclusion of the African Rights analysis of the war in the Nuba mountains, which concludes that non-Arab Nubians were considered second-class primitives and were victims of a "racism that pervades northern life."[134]

Ann Mosely Lesch similarly concludes that northern ethnic nationalism is at the core of conflict in Sudan. Consistent with other studies, she finds that Muslim Arabs from the Nile Valley have dominated Sudanese political economic and cultural life since independence. Those elites have consistently sought to "to shape the identity of the country in their own image" as culturally Arab and religiously Muslim.[135] Groups that did not fit that image were to assimilate or remain separate.[136] For Lesch, this vision of Sudan as an Arab and Islamic state has been consistent across the main political parties in the north. Jok Madut Jok concludes the same: The state has been controlled by groups that identify as Arab and have sought to forge national identity as "Arab" and "Islamic."[137]

---

129. Johnson 2003: 35; Sikainga 1993.
130. Johnson 2003: 75.
131. Warburg 2003: 144; see also Hamilton 2011.
132. De Waal 2007: 25.
133. Deng 1995: 3–6, 15, 26, 35.
134. African Rights 1995: 5.
135. Lesch 1998: 15, 213.
136. Lesch 1998: 21.
137. Jok 1997: 2.

In short, within the scholarship, there is a consensus that Arab-Islamic nationalism is central to northern Sudanese politics. At independence and since, the main political actors have consistently and actively sought to fashion an image of the state and the core national community as Muslim and Arab. That vision is hierarchical—non-Arabs and non-Muslims are inferior.

Head-of-State Speeches

An analysis of fifty head-of-state speeches from independence supports this conclusion. The analysis also reveals consistent reference to threats. More so than in the Côte d'Ivoire, Mali, and Senegal, the Sudanese head-of-state speeches routinely invoked perils within and outside the country—"plots," "saboteurs," and various forms of "enemies." There was also a consistent emphasis on the active remaking of state and society—from Abbud to Numayri to Bashir, heads of state claimed to be leading a "revolution" to save Sudan. In short, Sudan head-of-state speeches consistently emphasized three themes—an exclusive identity character to the state, a state besieged from within and from the outside, and a committed militancy to overcome the country's problems. To the extent that head-of-state speeches made reference to those who fall outside the image of the Muslim majority, some leaders discussed national citizenship as a basis for rights. But the implication was that non-Muslim citizens are secondary.

The twin poles of threat and militancy are found across the heads of state, in particular the military leaders who have led Sudan for all but ten years of independence. For example, Abbud delivered a speech on November 17, 1959, in which he lauded the Army for "rescuing" the country and warned against internal "saboteurs" who would not deter the revolution.[138] General Numayri on the first anniversary warned of plots against the revolution and implored the domestic population to "recognize," "crush," "hunt," and "strike" at reactionary forces.[139] In other speeches, he liberally referred to "dangers," "agents" of reaction, "infiltration," "conspiracies," and "enemies."[140] Even Sadiq al-Mahdi, whose speeches were less militant, labeled rebels tools of foreign "aggression."[141] But the most extreme militancy is clearly

---

138. Abbud 1959.
139. Numayri 1970a.
140. For instance, Numayri 1970b, 1974, 1979.
141. Al-Mahdi 1986b.

under Bashir, who saw the Revolution as clearing out "blood suckers,"[142] "enemies,"[143] "infiltrators,"[144] and "traitors,"[145] among other references. Consider this 1989 speech:

> I vow here before you to purge from our ranks the renegades, the hirelings—enemies of this people and enemies of this nation. . . . Our Armed Forces are determined to liberate every inch of our country sullied by the traitors and renegades. . . . Purging is a national duty. We shall, as we have promised you, purge our ranks of all the corrupt, the treacherous, the betrayers, the enemies of the people. . . . Anyone who betrays this nation does not deserve the honor of living. We as a government and a revolution shall continue with the purges. We ask you, you decent people, to purge your ranks of outlaws and renegades. There will be no fifth column. . . . The responsibility is a collective one.[146]

Bashir's speeches mellowed as time went on, but the sense of a persistent threat against which the masses must guard remained a recurring theme.

In terms of the character of the national community, there were consistent references to a Muslim majority and to "our Arab people" across the heads of state. Under Numayri, there was often an explicit recognition of Sudan's African character as well, in particular in his first seven or eight years in power. For example, in one speech he discussed how the state's constitution affiliates Sudan with the Arab nation, but he added that "affiliation which does not contradict or exceed our African commitment."[147]

But starting in the late 1970s and into the 1980s, Numayri's speeches had more explicit Islamic content—for example, by opening or concluding his addresses with Koranic verses or making frequent references to God, praising God, and God's will.[148] This became especially explicit after the 1983 promulgation of the September Shari'a Laws, as in this Eid speech from 1984:

> Let this occasion of the blessed festival be an opportunity to renew our pledge of faith through adherence to the course of piety, as individuals and groups, and affirm what we pledged to God, namely to adopt the Islamic course as a way of reconstructing the Sudanese nation. . . . This

---

142. Al-Bashir 1989a.
143. Al-Bashir 1989b.
144. Al-Bashir 1989d.
145. Al-Bashir 1995b.
146. Al-Bashir 1989d.
147. Numayri1975.
148. For instance, Numayri 1979, 1980, 1981, 1982, 1983, 1984.

is a choice the nation agreed to unanimously and adopted as a way of progress and achievement. We are following no other path but the path of Islam.[149]

Numayri's explicit embrace of Islam was matched with similarly explicit references to Sudan as an "Arab nation." For example, in a wide-ranging foreign policy speech, he referred to "the voice of the Sudan" as "the first and loudest in the search for a formula for unified Arab action and for a commitment to an Arab strategy by which all will abide."[150]

Though more moderate in his manner of expression, Sadiq al-Mahdi's speeches as prime minister leave little doubt as to his commitment to Sudan as an Islamic state. His approach in that regard represents continuity with Numayri—and with those of Abbud before Numayri. For example, in a national address in 1986 after becoming prime minister, he declared, "The watchword of the free Sudanese people has always been Islam."[151] He also stated, "We wish to establish Islam as the source of law in Sudan because Sudan has a Muslim majority."[152] In reference to non-Muslims, he typically struck a condescending tone: "Even non-Muslim Sudanese hold religious beliefs"[153] and "Non-Muslims can ask us to protect their rights."[154] A year later, in a speech that sought to account for southern grievances, Sadiq claimed that the state was "trying to balance Islamic expression" with the rights of others. Thus, even when recognizing the "rights of others," which he explicitly pledged to protect, it was still in the guise of a state that is Muslim first and foremost.[155]

Under Bashir, the appeal to Sudan as an Islamic state intensified. The NIF was formally committed to an Islamic state, and that idea translated into his speeches. In one of his first speeches after the coup of June 30, 1989, he claimed to have "no enmity toward southerners" but also made it clear that Sudan was an "Arab state" and that "all Arab states" supported the revolution.[156] But Bashir quickly shifted to more belligerent language. The Army was composed of "soldiers of God"[157] who were determined "to liberate

149. Numayri 1984.
150. Numayri 1981.
151. Al-Mahdi 1986a.
152. Johnson 2003: 79.
153. Al-Mahdi 1986a.
154. Johnson 2003: 79.
155. Al-Mahdi 1987.
156. Al-Bashir 1989a.
157. Al-Bashir 1989c.

every inch of our country."[158] "If the rebellion wants peace," he said two months later, "we are ready for peace and prepared for peace, but if they do not want peace, we, God willing, are prepared for war. . . . God is great, and glory to Sudan!"[159] In an address to the national assembly in 1992, he called the war in the south a "strike against Islam" and a "threat to national existence in its entirety." He went on to discuss Sudan as a country of diversity where tolerance was key, but nonetheless "a country in which a majority of the population are Muslims [and] Sudan has chosen Islam as a source of its political system and a guide for its public life."[160] Later that year, Bashir again declared the rebellion an existential threat to Sudan's national identity. Referring to peace overtures under Sadiq and to the decision to launch a coup, he commemorated the revolution's third anniversary as follows:

> On the morning of 30 June, three years ago, we were on the brink of signing a document of surrender, which would have placed our affairs in the hands of our enemy who would have caused Sudan, as we know it today, to disintegrate and have erased its Islamic-Arab identity. Today our enemies are scattered, retreating, and divided, while our country has asserted its identity and maintained the spirit of the land. . . .[161]

Nearly every recorded speech consulted from the 1990s made explicit reference to the Islamic character of the state.[162] Consider the following example on the coup's sixth anniversary: "We, the sons of the Sudanese people, have decided to defend our state and our Shari'ah. We will defend our territory. We will not relinquish an inch of our territory to an agent, enemy, or traitor. We will provide arms. We will provide arms to everyone able to bear arms. We will train the youth. We will train everyone who is able to bear arms and to use arms. We will be fully prepared."[163] Out of sample head-of-state speeches (from other sources) suggest the same themes. For example, in a May 1993 speech, he declared: "Our existence is originally linked to the implementation of this Shari'a. Therefore, it is a matter of principle for us. . . . It is better for us to die in the cause of that principle and we are ready for that."[164]

---

158. Al-Bashir 1989d.
159. Al-Bashir 1990.
160. Al-Bashir 1992a.
161. Al-Bashir 1992b.
162. Al-Bashir 1993, 1995a.
163. Al-Bashir 1995b.
164. Lesch 1998: 129.

Even in the 2000s, Bashir talked about policy choices as being in the service of the "restoration of Arab and Islamic solidarity."[165] That changed, at least publicly, as Sudan entered more serious political negotiations with the SPLA/M. In a 2003 speech, for example, Bashir had kind words to offer SPLA/M leader John Garang. Bashir in turn talked of "nationalistic pluralism" that "brings together all people of Sudan in all their cultures and in all their religious creeds."[166]

In sum, the head-of-state speeches support the conclusions in the existing literature about the nature of Sudanese nationalism, which places Islam and Arabism at the center and other religions and identities on the periphery. But the analysis also reveals two other dimensions. The first is the persistent underlying presence of threat and vulnerability, and the second is recourse to militancy. Both dimensions are consistent with arguments in the book, namely that threat is a driver of violence. The greatest threat occurs in wartime. That is true for Sudan, but in Sudan we also find ubiquitous insecurity, which seems to augment the perception of threat in wartime—a sense of endangerment that requires diligence and aggression to destroy.

In Sudan, the founding nationalist narrative posited an Arab-Islamic core identity population, one that provided a source of unity for a fractious north, a sense of history, lineage and pride, and an antidote to the humiliations of colonialism. Across fifty years of independence, there was variation in how much that narrative was emphasized. As in other states, there existed hardline positions in which stressing an Arabic-Islamic identity was the central mission of the government and more moderate positions in which the Islam and Arabism was more of a background influence, a guiding principle. Nonetheless, for all northern governments, hierarchical nationalism was a magnet around which each administration eventually gravitated and in which it sought the foundations for unity. With the exception of a brief period under Numayri, there was not a sustained counternarrative that elites forged at different critical junctures.

But it was also an endangered nationalism. Internally, Sudan's elite was highly fragmented, and as soon as independence had been established Sudan faced dismemberment in the form of a civil war. Sudan was in a hostile neighborhood, as well, facing at different points active opposition from Ethiopia, Libya, Chad, and Uganda. Egypt was a dominant neighbor to the north and one with intense interests in protecting its access to the Nile. A

---

165. Al-Bashir 2000.
166. Al-Bashir 2003.

reading of head-of-state speeches gives flavor to the country's endangered nationalism: specters of plots, sabotage, enemies, and infiltrators are present in the majority of speeches, across all administrations. The rhetorical response was to insist on militancy and to double down on the identity foundation of the state.

These factors played into how the state responded to insurgencies on the peripheries. Formally threatened, the state acted to protect its core and to destroy threats outside of that core. As leaders of an endangered state, Sudanese elites found little space to compromise. The Arab-Islamic nationalism reinforced that position. Those who challenged state sovereignty were not within the primary political community, and at most times the idea of accommodation thus was alien. By contrast, when other Arab Islamic elites challenged a ruling coalition, state leaders either acted to accommodate them (as under Abbud, Numayri, and the various coalition governments) or to contain (but not destroy) them, as under the NIF.

The logic of mass violence in Sudan's wars was not so much that of utopia and purification, and it was also not that non-core groups lacked citizenship rights entirely. In Sudan, as in Habyarimana's Rwanda, there are explicit recognitions of non-core identities as being citizens, but those rights are secondary, granted by the majority as an act of tolerance. In that sense, the rights are fragile; they are not constitutive of the primary political community. When the state felt threatened, it withheld those rights. As the danger persisted, state elites felt justified in going to whatever lengths needed to destroy the threat, to protect the primary political community, and to shore up essential alliances. Whereas in other countries, factors of restraint—ideological, economic, or political—might push elites away from escalation, where those restraint mechanisms are weak—as in Sudan—the strategy persisted as mass violence.

CHAPTER 9

Fighting for the Hutu Revolution in Rwanda

In the early 1990s, Rwanda faced a political and military crisis that was not unlike those experienced in Côte d'Ivoire and Mali. An armed rebellion representing the interests of an excluded minority defined in group-identity terms invaded the country and challenged the state militarily. At the same time, a newly born political opposition movement upended the domestic political arena. These developments followed a period of economic contraction and stagnation in the late 1980s. In other words, as in Côte d'Ivoire and Mali, the early 1990s in Rwanda was a period of intense political turbulence and armed conflict as well as economic hardship. In 1993, the main parties to the military conflict signed a peace accord that was favorable to the insurgents and that eroded the power of the ruling party. The development—a formal peace accord, one subsequently opposed by government loyalists—was similar to the process in Mali in the early 1990s and Côte d'Ivoire in the 2000s. As in Côte d'Ivoire and Sudan, the ruling authorities in Rwanda invested in parallel institutions, in particular militias and a civilian defense program, to guarantee their security and to protect their power. In Mali, local actors formed militias.

Yet the trajectory of violence differed dramatically in Rwanda. In Mali, the authorities sought to contain parallel institutions, to control the violence, and to sign a more comprehensive peace deal. In Côte d'Ivoire, the terrain remained deeply contested up until and through the 2010 elections, but the strategies of violence remained limited and expressed a logic of repression and score-settling. By contrast, in Rwanda the violence escalated sharply. Rather than serving to tame passions and establish the architecture for a nonviolent transition, the peace agreement radicalized key elites in the ruling party and governmental military establishment and led them to seek ways to circumvent the terms of the peace deal, both politically and militarily. The rebels also prepared for a military showdown rather than a negotiated settlement or electoral process.

The climax came on April 6, 1994, when Rwandan President Juvénal Habyarimana was assassinated. Habyarimana's supporters viewed the assassination as the work of the minority Tutsi rebels and the largely Hutu political opposition. Within twenty-four hours, the hardliners within the presidential camp had moved to eliminate the leadership of the political opposition, and within seventy-two hours they had outmaneuvered moderates within their own establishment to install a new government of hardliners.[1] In the capital and in other areas of fervent political support for the deceased president, loyalists immediately blamed Tutsi civilians for the supposed machinations of their rebel co-ethnics and massacred many civilians. Meanwhile, the rebels advanced from their positions and reignited the military battle for control of the country. In that context, the now-radicalized hardliners within the presidential camp, including key supporters within the army, the civilian administration, and the militias, sought to extend the collective lethal targeting to the entire Tutsi civilian population, a position that the interim government supported. Controlling the balance of force within government-held territory, they were successful. Even as the rebel army advanced and eventually took control of the country, the Hutu hardline forces engendered the civilian administration and the civilian population to identify, sort, and destroy Tutsi civilians across the small nation of some seven million inhabitants. Three months later, at least 500,000 Tutsi civilians had been killed, representing about 75 percent of the residential Tutsi population.[2]

What differentiated Rwanda from the negative cases? What do Rwanda and Sudan share? No two cases are identical, of course. In Rwanda, the event that sharply escalated the violence was a presidential assassination, which was a radicalizing strike that crystallized fears and hardline positions; in no other case examined here did such a cataclysmic assault on a legitimate peace process take place. In Rwanda, the international interposition force was weak and ill prepared to intercede or shape the military dynamics. Yet, as important as these elements were, they have analogs. In Mali and Senegal, where no mass

---

1. Des Forges 1999; Guichaoua 2010.
2. Des Forges 1999.

violence campaign occurred, there was no international interposition force. In Sudan, there was no politically equivalent shock like a presidential assassination. In the North–South civil wars, the mass violence took shape gradually through collective targeting from the air and on the ground through militias. In Darfur, the April 2003 rebel assault on El Fasher Airport was shocking, and the strike rapidly escalated the violence in the region. But an insurgent attack on a military outpost has a different valence than assassinating a president in a nominal period of peace.

The intensity of war in Rwanda was exceptionally high, and that contributed to a sense of acute threat. In the period in which the genocide took place, the president had just been assassinated, and rebels were rapidly advancing. The threats were real, present, and clear. By contrast in Mali in the 1990s and in Senegal, the insurgents were not nearly as strong as those in Rwanda, and in neither case were they strong enough to capture the central state's governing apparatus. However, the same is largely true for Sudan, whose outcomes were similar to that in Rwanda. In Sudan, both the Darfur rebels and the southern rebels were effectively contained to their regions of operation throughout the long wars. Rwanda and Sudan both had highly divided governments, and they were weak in that sense, but the same is true for Mali. Finally, in Côte d'Ivoire, the rebels were powerful, arguably stronger than the government side. Indeed, in 2011, following the contested elections, the rebels, with international support, succeeding in rapidly overrunning government forces. And in Mali in early 2012 the rebels also posed a real material threat. Yet in both Côte d'Ivoire and Mali, the decision-making elite did not orchestrate or support a campaign of mass categorical violence. In short, material military threat matters for how elites construct threats, and hence for their willingness to use mass violence against civilians, but military intensity alone cannot explain variation.

I conclude that the strongest commonality among the mass categorical violence cases, and the factor that the negative cases lack, is the ideological dominance among the political and military elite of a hierarchical, nationalist founding narrative. When combined with a military confrontation that posed real risks to the ruling establishment and to their core political project in the presence of weak restraints, the founding narrative pushed decision-making elites to frame the conflict as one between a core, threatened "us" defined in identity terms and an undeserving "them," also defined in identity terms. The founding narrative in turn influenced decision-making elites to orchestrate and sustain a strategy of violence that, in the presence of weak restraints, escalated to mass categorical violence in Sudan and genocide in Rwanda.

In Rwanda's case, the founding narrative was the Hutu social revolution. The narrative held that as the overwhelming numeric and once-persecuted majority, Hutus should rule and should organize themselves to prevent a return of Tutsi power and oppression of Hutus. That orientation became a center of gravity among military and political elites across more than thirty years of postcolonial rule. In the context of military threat in the 1990s (and in the 1960s), the narrative shaped the state response, prompting elites to apply violence to protect Hutu power, to conceptualize the enemy as an unwinnable collective identity category, and in the end to unleash a campaign of total violence against their historical enemies. Rwanda has unique features—the violence was extraordinarily swift and participatory—but the case reinforces the theory that the deadly cocktail of acute threats in war and a founding narrative emphasizing an identity group as the core of the state combined with the capacity to carry out violence and weak restraints is the scenario most likely to produce genocide and its variants.

Political Context and Background

Rwanda is a small, landlocked country in Central Africa. Prior to the 1994 genocide, the country had a little more than seven million inhabitants with more than 90 percent living in rural areas and dependent on smallholder agriculture and animal husbandry. Demographically, the country is divided into three principal ethnic categories, Hutus, who comprised between 85 and 90 percent of the population; Tutsis, who comprised between 10 and 14 percent; and Twa, who comprised about 1 percent of the population. The history of the ethnic categories is complex. Current scholarship indicates that the distinction between Hutu and Tutsi was an internal one that gradually took on significance within the Rwandan monarchy. And it was within the later stages of the Rwandan monarchy, in particular in the nineteenth century as the monarchy expanded and became increasingly hierarchical, that the categories Hutu and Tutsi became the source of a critical social cleavage in which Hutus were considered lower-status farmers while Tutsi were higher-status herders.[3] Outside the kingdom, clans and lineages were the most significant markers of status and differentiation, and as the kingdom expanded the significance of the terms *Hutu* and *Tutsi* sharpened.[4] That said, even within the nineteenth-century kingdom, there was a great deal of regional diversity and identification, and the categories were fluid. With enough wealth, status, and animals, a Hutu could become a Tutsi.[5]

---

3. Vansina 2001.
4. Newbury 1978.
5. Des Forges and Newbury 2011; Newbury 2001.

Whatever the exact origin of the terms, the European encounter with the region had a definitive impact on how the categories *Hutu* and *Tutsi* became understood. Impressed with the hierarchical organization of the Rwandan kingdom and under the influence of local Rwandan informants, the first Europeans imposed a racial interpretation on the social cleavage that they found. In particular, they defined the Hutu/Tutsi distinction as a racial one, hypothesizing that the Tutsis were a superior race of "Caucasoid" (white-like) cattle herders who had descended from north Africa and the Middle East to dominate over the lowly Bantu "negroid" farmers.[6] That racial interpretation then became the cornerstone for building a colonial architecture in the country. First German and then Belgian colonial authorities sought to rule through what was (in their minds, anyway) a preexisting Tutsi power structure. But through their interventions—selecting Tutsis for European education and training, rationalizing, bureaucratizing, monetarizing the previously complex domestic authority structure, and systematically elevating Tutsis to positions of power within the colonial administration— the European experience widened the Hutu and Tutsi social cleavage in Rwandan society.[7] The European interlude also racialized and institutionalized the differences between the groups, both through the introduction of quasi-scientific racial measurements and the introduction, in the 1930s, of personal identity cards that marked ethnicity. These interventions had the effect of stabilizing and essentializing previously more fluid identities that had been context-specific—that is, they had been associated with the hierarchical and status system within the Rwandan royal court toward the end of the nineteenth century.[8] Given the introduction of new inequities in the colonial system as well as new, often coercive taxation powers to Tutsi chiefs, the European intervention also had the effect of increasing the resentment attached to the categories, in particular on the part of Hutus toward Tutsis.[9]

The Hutu Social Revolution

The initial arrangements practiced by the European authorities changed after World War II. Belgium faced pressure from the United Nations to prepare its trust territory for self-rule. Beginning in the mid-1950s, Belgium introduced reforms that allowed for greater Hutu participation in the local

---

6. Chrétien 2003.
7. Lemarchand 1970; Newbury 1988; Rumiya 1991.
8. Newbury 2001.
9. Newbury 1988.

administration and that allowed for greater Hutu elite education. In this period, new missionaries in the Catholic Church also developed sympathy for the heretofore oppressed Hutu majority, and the Europeans encouraged aspiring Hutus to articulate their grievances to a wider audience, in particular in Belgium.[10] The process was dynamic. Hutus were encouraged to assert themselves politically, and as they did, privileged Tutsis within the monarchy and the civil administration acted to preserve the status quo hierarchy that benefited them. The terminal colonial period thus had three principal players: (1) an increasingly educated and aspiring Hutu counter-elite who sought to change the racially codified distribution of power and privilege; (2) an entrenched Tutsi elite who sought to contain the threats to the existing system; and (3) the Belgian authorities, as well as the clergy, who, while they initially enacted gradual reforms that allowed for greater Hutu representation and power, eventually came to back the Hutu counter-elite.

For understanding the resulting founding narrative that took hold in this period, it is critical to understand this dynamic process and how actions by the first and third group often came in response to the second group, and vice versa. The events that led to the Hutu social revolution were thus not inevitable, and the resulting political and ideological developments were historical products, ones that would in turn have lasting influence in Rwandan politics and society.

Facing an increasingly aspirant Hutu counter-elite and a Belgian administration evidently sympathetic to such concerns, the response of elite Tutsis was to downplay the importance of domestic ethnic differences and to encourage a swift transfer of power from Belgium to Rwanda, thereby allowing the domestic governing elite to continue to hold power. In response, the Hutu counter-elite came to insist on the importance of ethnic categories and to infuse the language of freedom and justice into the ethnic terms. The clearest manifestation of this dynamic was a document called the "Bahutu Manifesto," which was drafted and signed by a group of nine Hutu intellectuals in 1957. The Manifesto was written in anticipation of a visiting United Nations mission and in response to an earlier "Statement of Views" from elite Tutsis in the country's High Council. The latter defined the political problem as one between domestic elites and the Belgians. In so doing, the High Council statement effectively denied the relevance of the internal cleavage between Hutu and Tutsi.[11]

---

10. Lemarchand 1970: 107; Longman 2010: 70.
11. UNVM 1958: 42–46.

As a response to the Statement of Views, the Bahutu Manifesto defines the problem facing Rwanda before independence as an "indigenous racial" one. In particular, the Manifesto decries the "political monopoly held by one race, the Mututsi" as well as the economic, social, and cultural "monopolies" held by Tutsis. The Manifesto calls for advances for Hutus in the governing, education, and other sectors as well as other reforms that would end the "permanent subordination of the Muhutu to the Hamite." Of particular concern is that independence not be framed in "white-black" terms:

> While we agree that the current Mututsi administration should participate more and more in the Government of the State, we feel that such a warning should be issued against a method which, while tending to eliminate white-black colonialism, would leave a worse Hamitic colonialism over the Muhutu. The difficulties which might arise from the Hamitic monopoly over the other more numerous races which have lived in the State for a longer time, must be eliminated. . . .
>
> [I]n order to keep a close check on this racial monopoly, we strongly oppose, for the time being at least, the discontinuance of the practice of entering Muhutu, Mututsi, or Mutwa on official or personal identity cards . . . [Muhutu object to] the privileged position of a favoured monopoly which threatens to reduce the majority of the population to a position of systematic inferiority and to an undeserved sub-existence.[12]

The Manifesto thus recognizes race as the marker of oppression and therefore of liberation. The authors insist on keeping racial markers on official documents so as not to disguise how power is distributed in the country. The Manifesto also refers to Tutsi power as a form of minority "Hamitic colonialism" against a majority who "have lived in the State for a longer time," that is for people who were more original than the Tutsis. The Manifesto thus takes the racial classifications imposed by the Europeans and embraced by at least some of the Tutsi elites and upends them. Rather than being a source for continued domination, the Hutu counter-elite used the categories to express a desire for democratic emancipation. None of this was predetermined—rather, the specific articulation of a nationalist vision emerged from decisions made by a variety of actors at the time and in response to the history of political ethnicity under colonialism.

The language of the political parties would go on to reflect these priorities. The signatories of the Manifesto formed the "Mouvement Social Muhutu"

---

12. UNVM 1958: 39–42.

in 1957, which later became the "Parti du mouvement pour l'émancipation des Hutus," or PARMEHUTU. In the period between 1957 and independence in 1962, the pro-Hutu political movements continued to articulate an analysis of the situation in domestic racial and ethnic terms. That is, they labeled Rwanda's political problem one not only of European colonialism but also of Hamitic or "feudal" colonialism, which had to be abolished before independence from Belgium was declared. A good statement about the language of dual colonialisms is the "Passionate Appeal" (Appel Pathétique) that Parmehutu issued in 1960 to anticolonialists the world over:

> The populations of Ruanda-Urundi want . . . an independence that lifts the two colonialisms that history has superimposed on the populations: the colonialism of Tutsis and the European supervision.
>
> The first colonialism in Ruanda is feudalism of a colonialist character: the Hutu population, 85% of the country, have been submitted to an inhuman feudal-colonial regime by Tutsis; the Tutsi colonials, of Ethiopid race, barely represent 14% of the population.[13]

In this statement, we have a more complete expression of the nationalism that characterized the public vision of many of the Hutu independence leaders in Rwanda. Independence meant a racial reversal of power. In this vision, there are at least three salient dimensions: (1) the Hutus were the majority and the original people; (2) the Hutus were later repressed by an invading minority of "Hamites" who ruled over the majority in a cruel feudal system; and (3) true democracy meant rule by the original people and the rural masses, that is, rule by Hutus. This is a racial nationalist vision—one that held the Hutus to be the core political community, Hutu freedom and development to be the core political project, and Tutsi power to be a threat to the core community and the political project. This is the vision that anchored the Revolution, that constituted Rwanda's founding narrative, and that was maintained as such through the first and second Republics.

The events that led ultimately to a formal reversal of power in the terminal colonial period were complex. They took place in a tense and polarized period from 1957 to 1962, and they involved critical actions from the three central actors described above (the Hutu aspirant political class, the Tutsi old guard, and the Belgians). Excellent detailed accounts exist in which there are clear nuances and multiple voices within each bloc.[14] But to summarize some key events: in July 1959 the Tutsi king died unexpectedly after receiving

13. Nkundabagenzi 1961.
14. Lemarchand 1970; Reyntjens 1985; Newbury 1988.

an antibiotic shot from a Belgian doctor. His death crystallized the fears of many Tutsis, hardened their political positions, and ultimately increased Tutsi elite alienation from the Belgians. In November of the same year, Tutsi party youth attacked a leading Hutu politician, in turn leading to a counterattack against Tutsi elites by Hutu crowds, further counterattacks by Tutsis against Hutu political figures, and yet more violence against Tutsi families. Ultimately, the Belgians intervened to stop the violence and, in its aftermath, radically restructured the administration. Whereas before the November 1959 events, every chief was Tutsi and all but ten subchiefs were Tutsi, afterward the Belgians allotted half the chiefdoms and more than half of the sub-chiefdoms to Hutus.[15]

The Belgians clearly interpreted events through a racial prism. Writing years later, the Belgian colonel who led the military operation to stop the violence referred to a revolution in which Hutus—a "population oppressed, pushed to the end of their patience and silence"—revolted against their "Tutsi masters."[16] The resident governor, Jean-Paul Harroy, subtitled his subsequent book on the period "from feudalism to democracy."[17]

In 1960, communal elections were held. The main Tutsi-led party boycotted, and the main Hutu-led party, PARMEHUTU, won an overwhelming majority of 74 percent. The leader of the party, Grégoire Kayibanda, a former journalist who was one of the authors of the Bahutu Manifesto, became president in 1961, the same year that the Belgians and leading Hutu political figures announced the formation of a republic and the end of the monarchy. In July 1962, Rwanda achieved formal independence.

The First Republic: 1962–1973

Kayibanda launched economic, social, cultural, and institutional initiatives.[18] He emphasized tolerance, discipline, work, and austerity.[19] But the new president did not like political opposition. On the first anniversary of independence, in an address to the nation, he recounted how political opposition could "distract" the population and how he wanted a "crushing majority" in the country.[20] Indeed, at independence, the MDR-Parmehutu was the dominant party, but there were two other principal opposition parties—APROSOMA,

---

15. Reyntjens 1985: 269.
16. Logiest 1988: 7.
17. Harroy 1984.
18. Kayibanda 1964; Paternostre de la Mairieu 1994: 175–219.
19. Kayibanda 1964.
20. Kayibanda 1964: 84.

a largely Hutu party, and UNAR, which represented the interests of the for-merly elite Tutsis. However, the leaders of MDR-Parmehutu quickly moved to destroy political challengers, and by 1965 Rwanda had become a single-party state, with the MDR-Parmehutu as the only party allowed to exist.[21] The single-party system did not, of course, eliminate internal divisions. One clear aspect of Kayibanda's tenure was regional favoritism, and his home area of Gitarama was the regime's center of gravity from where key powerholders in the government came.[22] There were also numerous personalized rivalries and divisions.[23] The regime is thus accurately described as authoritarian but also regionalist and fractious.

Ideologically, Kayibanda positioned himself as the champion of a demo-cratic revolution that had overthrown feudalism. This orientation is observ-able in Kayibanda's speeches. In them, Kayibanda consistently referred to how "democracy defeated feudalism" in the Revolution.[24] The main interest of the regime, he repeatedly claimed, was to rule on behalf of "the Rwandan popular masses."[25] To mark independence, the president remarked how the "Rwandan Revolution of 1959 had overturned the feudal regime," which was antithetical to "liberty, peace, loyalty, cooperation, [and] the common good."[26] On a May Day speech in 1963, he emphasized how his party had achieved an "authentic freedom" for the "popular masses" and how feudal-ism and neocolonialism had been vanquished.[27] The Revolution was pre-sented as a victory for the democratic masses against feudalists. There was often an implicit equation between Hutus as the formerly downtrodden popular masses and Tutsis as feudal overlords. One of the most astute Rwan-dan observers—a human rights activist who was critical of Kayibanda—recalls how many Rwandans saw the former president as having "freed the Hutu masses from Tutsi domination":

> At the time of the social revolution, the Hutu portrayal of their own history was based on a model inspired by European history. They com-pared themselves to the serfs of the Middle Ages and the Tutsi as feudal lords. This made them feel that they were struggling for freedom from the domination of a caste of nobles. . . . But this was not only a social revolution; it was also a national revolution. The Hutu were motivated

21. Reyntjens 1985: 449.
22. Lugan 1997: 419; Reyntjens 1985: 498.
23. Lemarchand 1970: 262; Reyntjens 1985: 479–98.
24. Kayibanda 1964: 7.
25. Kayibanda 1964: 12.
26. Kayibanda 1964: 22, 27.
27. Kayibanda 1964: 49–50.

in their actions by the belief that they represented the original people who had inalienable and eternal rights on Rwandan soil. Suddenly they viewed the Tutsi not only as a race, but as a foreign race, a race of conquerors who had imposed their domination over the Hutu and had to be driven out of the country.[28]

The treatment of domestic Tutsis was both violent and accommodating. On the one hand, President Kayibanda promoted tolerance and promised to respect minority rights.[29] Even in angry speeches directed to Tutsis (more on this below), he made it clear that Tutsis were "citizens" and that "peace is for all Rwandans for any and all citizens whoever they are."[30] According to a hagiographic biography, Kayibanda allowed Tutsis to represent as much as 20 percent of the administration, schools, and universities—"double" their demographic presence.[31] On the other hand, Tutsi civilians were subject to significant violence. One historian claims that the sum of experience for Tutsis under the First Republic was persecution and treatment as second-class citizens and scapegoats.[32]

Indeed, during the violent events of 1959, many Tutsis were brutally chased from their homes or killed; others fled on their own. In 1962, some exiled Tutsis began armed incursions on Rwanda, which in turn triggered reprisals against Tutsis inside the country. By 1963, more than 100,000 refugees were living abroad. A decisive moment came after an armed incursion in December 1963 by exiled Tutsis. In that operation, Tutsi exiles entered Rwanda from Burundi, rallied Tutsis living in Rwanda, and then marched toward Kigali before they were stopped by Rwandan troops with Belgian assistance. In the aftermath, the regime assassinated political elites, and with official encouragement in one region there were mass killings of as many 14,000 Tutsi civilians.[33] Thereafter Tutsis were subject to capricious violence at times.[34]

The official reaction to the armed incursions was virulent. In his speeches, Kayibanda referred to the attackers as "feudalists who became terrorists" who endangered national development[35] and as "*Inyenzi* terrorists" who were led

---

28. Sibomana 1999: 94–95.
29. Kayibanda 1964: 83.
30. Shimamungu 2006: 41, 43.
31. Paternostre de la Mairieu 1994: 180.
32. Lugan 1997: 433.
33. Reyntjens 1985; Straus 2006b: 184–88.
34. Lemarchand 1970: 256.
35. Kayibanda 1964: 121.

by "feudal ex-chiefs" that wanted to harm the "democratic government."[36] On May 1, 1964, he stated, "We remain loyal to the idea of democracy and liberty that guided the Hutu movement during the 1959 revolution." In a New Year's Day speech in 1965, he called diplomats and high-level civil servants to his residence, where he saluted the defeat of a "snake" that used "neocolonial subversion" and "threatened the very existence of the state."[37]

In one now-infamous speech directed toward Tutsis outside the country, he effectively offered to welcome Tutsis back to Rwanda but threatened them if they did not. Many years later, the speech became symbolically important in the runup to the genocide, and Colonel Théoneste Bagosora—one of the masterminds of the genocide—invoked it as evidence that Tutsis in the 1990s provoked violence against themselves. The speech thus deserves careful consideration.

Kayibanda began by both chastising and offering a "fraternal" hand, but his language was riddled with aggression:

> My dear compatriots, Rwandan refugees both men and women:
>
> Beyond the worries which the folly of some of you caused me when, through terrorist campaigns organized abroad, they troubled their brothers to live in peace in our democratic and independent Rwanda, aside from the affliction that the dishonesty of some of you has caused in accusing us of genocide, leaving aside the suffering which we have endured when perhaps well-intentioned people have made available the most modern instruments of information accessible to your slanderous maneuvers, notwithstanding all that, we believe it useful to extend to you a fraternal handshake, with the hope that many among you will accept it.

He continued by saying that many refugees had left without any intention of harming Rwanda. But some "fanatics" refused to accept the Revolution. Through their terrorist actions, they in turn were putting the lives of Tutsis inside the country at risk. Here Kayibanda angrily turned the tables:

> Who is guilty of genocide? Ask yourself honestly the question and respond from the depths of your conscience. The Tutsis who remained in the country who are afraid of a popular uproar which would be born of your incursions, are they happy with your conduct? Who is a genocider? Those who rely and finance your terrorist campaigns and fratricides, do they also mention that the Bahutu will never allow themselves

---

36. Kayibanda 1964: 162–63.
37. Kayibanda 1965: 1.

to be defeated and that in response to your blows they have no intention of opposing a dubious heroism? Who is the genocider? . . . Now let us discuss your future and your children. We urge you to think of these innocent beings, whom yet be saved from the suffering where you are directing your ethnic group. We repeat this particularly to you Tutsis. . . . Do you believe that you have fulfilled your civic obligations by allowing your wives and children of the age of 15 into your terrorist ranks? Once again, who is genocidal? If we presume the impossible, that you manage to take Kigali by attack, how shall you measure the chaos engendered of which you will be the first victims? I will not insist on this point: you can imagine it, and if not, you are acting as henchmen and desperados! You say it among yourselves: "This will be the complete and precipitous end of the Tutsi race." Who is genocidal then?

Kayibanda encouraged refugees to lay down arms and for those who wish to return to Rwanda. He continued:

The Revolution occurred and became violent due to your leaders at the time, in November 1959: your group was defeated . . . while my Government exercised tolerance with respect to the opposing wing which remained in the country, you have conspired to engage in armed resistance. Time and again you have been defeated and time and again you have caused great loss of human lives. . . . Since the first of July 1962, the Republic of Rwanda has been independent. Its democracy and institutions which were democratically created through the will of the people shall remain devoted to all its citizens without exception or discrimination.[38]

His fawning biographer remarkably calls the message "realist" and the work of a "sincere man."[39] However, we have elements here of the Rwandan founding narrative with a preview of the logic of genocide in the 1990s. The narrative holds that the core political project, as represented by the Revolution, is that the popular masses revolted against an oppressive feudal order. That change equals democracy. Implicit here is the equation between "popular masses" and Hutus, on the one hand, and feudalists and Tutsis, on the other hand. The narrative thus places Hutus as central to the core political project and as the rightful powerholders. Tutsis have a place in post-Revolution Rwanda. For Kayibanda, at least rhetorically, Rwanda observed human rights and was "devoted to all citizens without exception." However, once out of power, Tutsis had no right to challenge the core political project, the Revolutionary order, and if they were

---

38. Shimamungu 2006: 39–42.
39. Paternostre de la Mairieu 1994: 195.

to threaten it—as they did in the 1960s—then they would face the consequences. In this speech, Kayibanda thus evoked a coercive logic: In challenging
the Revolution, the Tutsis provoked violence against themselves. He called them
the "genociders." He invited them to desist, lest they face more violence and
even worse, and if they desisted they were notionally able to be incorporated
into Rwanda. If not—if they proved to be unwinnable—they would face "the
precipitous end of the Tutsi race." In the genocide period, high-level elites presented much the same logic to explain the violence that occurred.

The founding narrative of the Revolution shaped this response: It pushed
Kayibanda (and other Hutu leaders at the time) to frame the political struggle
as between a primary ethnic community in whose interests the state served
and a non-core ethnic community whose interests threatened the majority.

As it turned out, the Rwandan state won the upper hand against the armed
exiles. Refugee attacks continued through 1967.[40] But the intensity of the
attacks diminished, the government's security capacity increased, and the violence against Tutsi civilians decreased.[41] Even so, Kayibanda reminded his country that the threat persisted, as for example in an Independence Day speech
on July 1, 1966, in which he warned that "external forces, taking advantage
of the vulnerability of some services that are still young and insufficiently
equipped [seek] to establish their antennas of neocolonial exploitation."[42] In
other words, the Tutsi threat to the Hutu revolution persisted. He struck a
similar note a year later when he hailed the "emancipation" of the "popular
masses" from "the servitudes of feudalism that collapsed." In short, the founding narrative of the state remained a fixture throughout the First Republic.

The Kayibanda government eventually fell in 1973. Internally divided
between north and south, between landholders and peasants, and between
personalities, the regime persisted largely through authoritarian control and
centralization.[43] But in 1973, several issues converged to bring Kayibanda's rule
to an end. One key issue was that, according to the constitution, Kayibanda
could not seek another term. Another issue was the genocide against Hutus in
Burundi in 1972. In Rwanda, Hutu students and some professionals in early
1973 purged Tutsis from schools, universities, businesses, and public administration. That violence prompted a military coup on July 5, out of which
Habyarimana, then the head of the military, emerged as the new strongman in
the country and from which Rwanda's Second Republic was born.[44]

---

40. Guichaoua 2010: 34; Reyntjens 1985: 471.
41. Reyntjens 1985: 471.
42. Kayibanda 1966.
43. Lemarchand 1970: 228–40; Reyntjens 1985: 479–95.
44. For a summary, see Straus 2006b: 188–91.

The Second Republic: 1973–1994

Habyarimana ruled Rwanda from 1973 until the start of the genocide in 1994. For reasons that I detail below, Habyarimana's record is not clear-cut. On the one hand, he promoted a vision of Rwanda on the basis of unity, reconciliation, peace, and even Tutsi integration. He explicitly wanted to move Rwanda away from the divisions that he claimed characterized the Kayibanda state. Rwandan and outside observers attest to the ways in which anti-Tutsi sentiment decreased, at least until 1990. Habyarimana called his efforts a "moral" revolution, one that grounded the Second Republic. On the other hand, Habyarimana clearly endorsed the Social Revolution. He framed his presidency as an extension of the democratic and masses-based political change that occurred at independence. In these ways, Habyarimana embraced and perpetuated Rwanda's founding narrative of a Hutu democratic majority who had overcome the oppressive feudalist Tutsi monarchy. Habyarimana was torn between these two positions—one in which he fashioned himself an expansive, inclusive, for-the-good-of-the-country president and one in which he tenaciously held to the fundamental principles of the Revolution, which is that Hutus should rule in the name of the majority.

However one interprets the ethnic politics of the regime, other dimensions of Habyarimana's rule are clear. First, Habyarimana shifted the center of gravity from south-central to northwest Rwanda, from where the new president came. Second, Habyarimana continued to restrict the political arena and to rule with limited executive constraint, at least until the 1990s. After Kayibanda, Rwanda remained a one-party state, albeit with a new party—the Mouvement révolutionnaire nationale pour le développement (MRND), which Habyarimana created in 1975. Every Rwandan belonged to the MRND. Some describe a virtual merging between the party, state, and society. James Gasana, an opposition figure and former minister of defense, calls Rwanda a "party-state" under Habyarimana.[45] For his part, Kayibanda was confined to his home, where he subsequently died in 1976, and some fifty key leaders from his government and mostly from the south were executed.[46] Though that violence represented a rupture with the founding Republic, Habyarimana remained committed to the founding principles of the Revolution. Third, at least through the mid-1980s, Rwanda's economic and infrastructural development improved.[47] Habyarimana's focus was rural

45. Gasana 2002.
46. Gasana 2002: 29; Reyntjens 1994: 30.
47. Erny 1994: 76.

development.[48] (Every year he announced a theme, and most themes focused on rural life, such as the "Year of Agriculture." Rwanda's per capita income increased quite favorably compared to other countries in the region.)[49] The regime was well liked by donors, opened itself to the outside, and enjoyed a favorable international reputation.[50] Habyarimana adopted an avuncular, paternalistic approach to the population, particularly in rural areas.

André Guichaoua, a leading scholar of Rwanda and the Habyarimana period, aptly describes the Habyarimana regime as "educational totalitarianism."[51] Habyarimana was no democrat; party control remained tight. There was no real space for political dialogue and debate. The vision was top-down, hierarchical control. In these ways, the regime was authoritarian. But Habyarimana fashioned himself a peacemaker, a father to the nation, someone who strove to be above the fray and omniscient. He also was an advocate of mobilization and participation, embodied by the *umuganda* (communal work) program. Taking personal responsibility for development was an important theme of his.

Habyarimana's speeches in his first decade in power demonstrate these tendencies. When he spoke on Independence Day and New Year's Day and to commemorate the date of his seizure of power, Habyarimana typically lauded the 1959 Revolution and lambasted the Kayibanda government for sullying revolutionary ideals. Consider, for example, one of his first addresses to the nation after taking power in 1973, a key speech that he himself in later years referred to as the one that articulated his fundamental principles: "If our 1959 social revolution was a decisive step for the emancipation of the Rwandan masses, the noble acquisitions of this revolution had been engulfed in hatreds, resistance to change, nepotism, and regional favoritism."[52] And in the New Year's speech of 1974, he cited the same themes, arguing for taking "revolution into one's own hands—everyone is responsible" while striving for "national harmony and peace" and for combating hatred.[53] A fuller articulation came on Independence Day 1974:

> Through its revolution at the end of 1959, Rwanda definitively rejected all forms of power built on the domination and exploitation of one part of the population by another. . . . The successes and benefits of our 1959 revolution were bestowed on the whole population during the first few years of this revolution. However, you know that little by

---

48. Guichaoua 2010: 44; Verwimp 2006.
49. Reyntjens 1994: 35.
50. De Lame 2005: 61; Reyntjens 1994: 32; Uvin 1998.
51. Guichaoua 2010: 44.
52. Habyarimana 1981a: 21.
53. Habyarimana 1974.

little the leaders lost view of their essential mission and of their responsibilities before the nation.[54]

In the same speech, Habyarimana went on to describe the cleavages, hatreds, persecutions, ostracism, terror, insecurity, and ethnic and regional discrimination that existed under Kayibanda. In other words, we have here a clear endorsement of the founding narrative of the Revolution. It ended "domination and exploitation." In the revolution, Rwandans "rediscovered their right to democracy and dignity, to justice and liberty, . . . that had been denied for a long time by the feudal-colonial regime," as he said on July 5, 1981.[55] But the revolution was endangered, prompting a need to renew it and to establish a new path of unity, harmony, and peace. The latter theme is also apparent in his July 5, 1977, speech in which he framed the coup as an effort of "national renewal" that would not "efface the past. . . . The new path . . . is destined to perfect the work of the liberation accomplished by the great majority of our people."[56]

The most full-throated articulation of these themes appeared in a long address on the twentieth anniversary of Rwandan independence, on July 1, 1982. For centuries, Habyarimana said, "the laboring and popular masses had to suffer . . . injustices, humiliations of all sorts, exploitation on the part of the feudal power alongside the deliberate complicity of the colonial power." The president claimed that the Bahutu Manifesto denounced the injustices publicly for the first time and how the revolution eventually facilitated a "democratic society, attentive to the interests of the popular masses." He saluted those who sacrificed their lives "in the just liberation of our people." But, the revolution having been undermined by the Kayibanda presidency, Habyarimana referred to his effort at a "moral revolution" to establish a "responsible democracy." His MRND "condemned all tendencies of a separatist or racial character, all attitudes of racial, ethnic, familial, regional, or religious superiority." He attested to the grounding values of peace, national harmony, tolerance, dialogue, and responsibility, and he claimed that "the few ethnic differences, far from being the object of separation, must be for us an element of enrichment of Rwandan society." He made reference to Tutsi refugees, who in the majority have integrated into host countries, but there is a "minority of activists and agitators who still want to reenter Rwanda by force and violence."[57] For those who want to return, Rwanda will respect international humanitarian law, the president said.

---

54. Habyarimana 1981a: 97
55. Habyarimana 1981a: 14.
56. Habyarimana 1977: 89.
57. Habyarimana 1982: 173, 175, 177, 179, 202, 203.

Such is the line that Habyarimana walked: He clearly endorsed a revolution that was violent and exclusionary, but he also promoted peace, harmony, and nondiscrimination. Tutsis could come back to Rwanda, but not by violence, and he encouraged many to integrate into their host countries.

His speech on the country's twenty-fifth anniversary, on July 1, 1987, emphasized many of these points but made an even stronger claim about ethnicity. "Our elders revolted against a feudal, minority power," he said, which allowed for the construction of a "democratic society" that is "Rwanda today." Proof of the "moral revolution," he said, lies in how "the majority of our youth today do not even understand how there could be division between our principal ethnic groups. . . . Our youth know today that our struggle was led against an outdated and hegemonic feudal system, but not against an ethnic group as such. . . . We are all Rwandans."[58] Again, Habyarimana endorsed the revolution, but in this speech he sought to distinguish feudalism from Tutsis.[59]

As one might expect from Habyarimana's stated ideals, the ethnic politics of the Habyarimana regime were mixed. Scholars who lived in Rwanda in the 1980s claim that Hutu-Tutsi tensions dissipated under Habyarimana. For example, Guichaoua writes that domestic ethnic tensions by the late 1980s were at their lowest level since the colonial period.[60] Danielle de Lame, a leading anthropologist of Rwanda, similarly found that ethnic discrimination decreased under Habyarimana even as regionalism increased.[61] Gasana talks of a rapprochement between Habyarimana and Tutsi elites in the country,[62] and memoirs by influential Tutsis confirm cordial relations between Habyarimana and such elites.[63]

Nonetheless, ethnicity clearly did not disappear from social life or from the political lexicon of the state. One of the central tools for regulating ethnicity was the introduction of ethnic and regional quotas. Called a policy of equilibrium, such policies limited representation of Tutsis in secondary schools, universities, and government posts to their official proportion in

---

58. Habyarimana 1987: 197, 200–201.

59. Throughout the archive of his speeches, Habyarimana articulates various versions of this story. He presents the Second Republic as a continuation of the project of the Revolution, but one that takes Rwanda in a new course focused on rural and economic development, popular mobilization, peace, and unity. His vision is not anti-Tutsi per se, but at the same time the foundation of the post-independence state remains that it had overthrown feudal minority power. For other representative speeches, consult the database of speeches.

60. Guichaoua 2010: 44.

61. De Lame 2005: 62; see also Gasana 2002: 54–55.

62. Gasana 2002: 27–28.

63. For instance, Kajeguhakwa 2001: 172.

the national population; they also served as a vehicle for the advancement of northerners. The idea was to redress Tutsi and southerners' overrepresenta-tion but to do so in a regulated fashion rather than the violent methods of 1973. According to one privileged Tutsi observer, Habyarimana and his close allies believed that they had brought peace to the Tutsi population. Officially, Tutsis were welcomed in the MRND and were considered citizens but with-out a place in the political sphere.[64] By the 1980s, the proportion of Tutsis in secondary schools, in government positions, in salaried employment, and in key sectors such as banking and insurance remained superior to their official population share.[65] Even in the Army, there was a Tutsi colonel, two Tutsi lieutenant colonels, and other Tutsi officers.[66] Before the crisis of the 1990s, there were token Tutsi ministers and one Tutsi prefect, even if there were no Tutsi burgomasters, who were the key local officials at the local level.

In sum, Habyarimana's policies continued to institutionalize and maintain ethnicity as a fundamental political and social category in Rwandan society. The regime remained, Guichaoua writes, "undeniably Hutu in the sense that its legitimacy depended on the exercise of power by the ethnic majority."[67] At the same time, the idea was to find space for Tutsi representation within the state, the party, and the society in line with the motto of "peace and national unity" that characterized Habyarimana's stated ideology. In an interview with the French-language magazine *Jeune Afrique*, Habyarimana defended the use of ethnic markers on national identity cards. His defense reveals much about official ethnicity in Rwanda:

> I suppose you know the history of our country. We had a monarchy based on a single ethnic group. We overturned it in 1959. To avoid reverting to that situation, we decided on a policy of equilibrium. . . . We are criticized for mentioning, on identity cards, Hutu, Tutsi, or Twa ethnicity. Simply doing away with the notation "Hutu" on my identity card does not automatically erase my membership in that ethnic group. To indicate that does not make a particular individual any more Rwan-dan than another. When your passport says that you are blond, blue-eyed, and so many centimeters tall, it's not discrimination: it's true. . . . Elsewhere they do not dare record it, we do. And then it's an old system; it already existed when my father was born.[68]

---

64. Kajeguhakwa 2001: 159, 172.
65. Munyantwali 1991; Uwizeyimana 1991.
66. Gasana 2002: 33.
67. Guichaoua 2010: 45.
68. Biloa 1989: 12.

Ethnic identity is biological reality for Habyarimana, analogous to height and hair color. Ethnicity is "true." But officially, for Habyarimana, ethnicity was not grounds for discrimination. Yet at the same time, the core founding narrative was a democratic majority that overthrew a "monarchy based on a single group." That encapsulates the internal tensions and contradictions of ethnic politics in Rwanda before the genocide, and it prefigures the narrative fluctuations that Habyarimana expressed during the crisis.

Into the Crisis

Even before the acute crisis in the 1990s, deep problems and fissures within the Habyarimana regime were apparent, especially in the second half of the 1980s. Local-level studies show increased disaffection with the direction of the country by the late 1980s and into the early 1990s. In the late 1980s there was a famine, general social degradation, and rises in banditry and insubordination.[69] De Lame found increasing inequality in rural areas with growing resentment of local elites who, often with connections to the party or state, manipulated their privilege for personal gain.[70] Other accounts similarly find an increased tension between urban elites and rural peasants.[71] Despite the claims to develop the countryside, the actual gains in rural areas were meager; there was a strong perception of corruption and elite favoritism.[72] At the national level, the core group surrounding the president became increasingly narrow and localized to the northwest, in particular the Gisenyi area, the home region of Habyarimana and his wife.[73] The shrinking of the core political elite further alienated Rwandan elites from other areas of the country. In short, as Guichaoua persuasively documents, by the end of the 1980s Rwanda was in a crisis, one in which there was a general sense of the end of an era—a perception of change that the hard core around the president prepared to combat step by step.[74]

Rwanda's crisis escalated sharply in the early 1990s with two twin direct threats to the ruling MRND elite and the network around the president. On the one hand, the ruling elite faced a threat from a newly legalized, primarily Hutu political opposition. On the other hand, the regime faced a significant armed threat from the newly formed Rwandan Patriotic Front (RPF). I focus on the latter first. Composed principally of Tutsi descendants of refugees who

---

69. Kimonyo 2008.
70. De Lame 2004.
71. Reyntjens 1994: 33.
72. Gasana 2002: 42–60.
73. Guichaoua 2010: 48; Reyntjens 1994: 33–35.
74. Guichaoua 2010: 53; Reyntjens 1994: 89.

had fled Rwanda in earlier episodes of violence, the RPF also critically came to include some high-level Hutu dissidents from the Habyarimana period and won recruits from the Rwandan domestic Tutsi population. The RPF attacked the country from northern Uganda in October 1990. The key military leadership in the RPF had experience fighting alongside Ugandan President Yoweri Museveni in his ultimately successful insurgency, and the Rwandan officers occupied key posts in the Ugandan intelligence and military institutions.[75] The RPF also benefited from a sophisticated system of contributions from the mostly Tutsi elite diaspora. In other words, the RPF constituted a motivated, experienced, decently financed, and ultimately disciplined fighting force.

However, their first major operation for the RPF ended poorly. The overall commander was killed on the second day of fighting, followed within the month by his two replacements. By the end of the first month the Rwandan army succeeded in a counter-attack, and the RPF insurgents scattered into a northern territory. In November, Major Paul Kagame returned from the United States where he had been training, pulled together the RPF's remaining forces in the northwest forest of Virunga, resupplied, and recruited Tutsis from neighboring states. Kagame also changed tactics to fight using guerilla tactics rather than a conventional approach. The RPF succeeded in launching attacks in 1991 and 1992.[76]

Meanwhile, the Rwandan army sizably increased its fighting forces and won military support from France and Zaire. While the RPF claimed to fight a nepotistic, corrupt, and authoritarian regime, key actors within the Habyarimana government countered by depicting the RPF as nostalgic Tutsis who would never accept the reality of the Social Revolution; they also made an implicit link between Tutsis on the interior as accomplices of Tutsis on the exterior. These arguments, which drew on the founding narrative of the Revolution, became the centerpiece of the propaganda against the RPF. The connections between internal and external Tutsis also translated into repression. After what is widely believed to be a staged attack on Kigali on the night of October 4, thousands of civilians were arrested, 90 percent of whom were Tutsi.[77] Tutsi civilians were also killed in northwest Rwanda in October 1990 and again in 1991 and 1992.[78]

Habyarimana struck multiple notes in his official speeches. On the one hand, he asserted that civilians would not be targeted on the basis of their ethnicity.[79] For example, in an interview published in *Jeune Afrique* on October 30,

---

75. Prunier 1998.
76. Guichaoua 2010: 55–83; Mamdani 2001: 159–84; Prunier 1993, 1998.
77. Guichaoua 2010: 77; Reyntjens 1994: 94.
78. Guichaoua 2010: 79; Straus 2006a: 192–94.
79. Reyntjens 1994: 94.

1990, he insisted that the war was "not an ethnic problem." He claimed that Tutsis were in the Army fighting the rebels and that his whole mission was to unite Rwandans, in contrast to Kayibanda. On the other hand, Habyarimana also invoked the principles of the Revolution. In an October 29, 1990, address to the nation, for example, he linked the RPF to the monarchy:

> The whole Rwandan people would rise as one man if direct negotiations were to be held with these aggressors who put the country to fire and sword while most despicably tarnishing its image as they have done while continuing to shoot at us and illegally to occupy our territory. Rather than giving up a single inch of our territory in response to a fait accompli from these deserters of a foreign army, the Rwandan people—all of us—[words indistinct] we will fight to the last man before allowing our country to be destroyed and the return of a feudal, elitist and royalist regime.[80]

In other words, Habyarimana clearly framed the stakes of the conflict through the terms of the founding narrative. The fight was between those would "fight to the last man" to protect the Revolution and those who wish to take it away.

A December 3, 1990, address to the MRND Central Committee showed these twin impulses. On the one hand, the Rwandan president reiterated that Rwandans should avoid resorting to a tribal conflict, but he also accused the attackers of not respecting democracy, a code word for the Revolution.[81] In a speech on December 7, 1990, Habyarimana spelled out a history of Rwanda where there had been Tutsi oppression that was overthrown in the name of democracy and the will of the majority in 1959. The original refugees, some of whom attacked, were "adversaries of a Republic that the majority of people had just installed. The enemy was against the will of the people and the majority, against democracy."[82] Again in these speeches, we see how the founding narrative shapes how Habyarimana interpreted and spoke about the nature of the military. The fight was no ordinary one. It was between those who would protect the revolution and those who would destroy it.

A particularly revealing episode was reported by state-owned Radio Rwanda when Habyarimana spoke to his party on April 28, 1991: "President Habyarimana started by requesting a one-minute silence in the memory

---

80. BBC Monitoring of Radio Rwanda 1990a.
81. BBC Monitoring of Radio Rwanda 1990b.
82. Habyarimana 1990.

of all those who have died due to the bullets of the enemy, both soldiers and civilians. He then reiterated his congratulations for the courage and determination of our armed forces who have saved us from falling back into the slavery of before 1959."[83]

Other speeches in 1991 similarly claimed that Rwandans had to fight the RPF in order to protect democracy against feudalism.[84] However, President Habyarimana also at times toned down his rhetoric.[85] Nonetheless, these few excerpts make clear that, upon facing armed attack from Tutsis, the president was quick to invoke the nationalist ideology of the Revolution.

Habyarimana was not alone. In the first two years of the war, 1990 and 1991, influential elites around the president not only invoked the Revolution but also linked internal Tutsis to external Tutsis. For example, following the arrest of Tutsi civilians in October 1990, the justice minister made it clear that ethnicity was a factor in who was detained.[86] In an interview on Radio Rwanda on October 21, Anastase Gasana, then described as a technical advisor to the MRND leadership, explained the origins of the attack in these terms: "The actual reasons are rather political, based on a monarchic and feudal regime that certain Rwandan refugees want to have restored in Rwanda whereas the majority of the people have objected to that . . . the Rwandan refugees never acknowledge the 1959 revolution, the democracy installed on 28 January 1961."[87] In other words, leading officials quickly returned to the founding narrative when faced with an armed threat, portraying the Tutsi attackers as enemies of democracy and nostalgic for the monarchy. In rural areas, De Lame found that the salience of ethnicity increased in 1988 following violence in Burundi but that the onset of armed conflict in Rwanda and local responses to it "crystallized rampant divisions."[88]

A key document in the runup to the genocide is the Military Commission report from late 1991. Called the "Bagosora Commission" after Colonel Bagosora, who chaired the committee, the Commission was convened by President Habyarimana. Composed of senior brass in the military, the group was tasked with establishing a plan to defeat the enemy on the military,

83. BBC Monitoring of Radio Rwanda 1991.

84. Bertrand 2000: 122.

85. Bertrand 2000: 123. See also the July 1992 Independence Day speech in which the president extended an invitation to Rwandan refugees to return, presumably as part of an effort to divide the exile community (Habyarimana 1992).

86. Reyntjens 1994: 94.

87. Gasana 1990.

88. De Lame 2004: 473.

media, and political fronts.[89] The report in turn commenced with a definition of the enemy, depicted as belonging to two categories:

1. The principal enemy is the Tutsi on the inside or outside [who is]
   extremist and nostalgic for power, who NEVER recognized and
   STILL DOES NOT recognize the realities of the Social Revolution of 1959 and who wants to reconquer power in Rwanda by any
   means, including arms.
2. The partisan of the ENI is any person who helps the principal ENI.

At the International Criminal Tribunal for Rwanda, where he was ques-
tioned about the document, Bagosora called the military commission an
effort to design a "strategy" to defeat the enemy.[90]

Some argue that the Commission report is a statement of genocidal intent,
present in the country as early as 1991. Like the ICTR decision in the Bagosora
case, I disagree.[91] Rather, the document shows the ways in which the founding
narrative of the Revolution explicitly shaped the thinking of military elites.
Even though the RPF was explicitly anti-monarchist, the government military
elites saw and presented the RPF attack through the lens of the Revolution—
the RPF was said to be seeking to overthrow the gains of the Revolution.
The founding narrative thus shapes how military elites define the stakes of the
conflict, for whom they are fighting and against whom they are fighting. The
narrative also shapes threat perception. The war is not a simple military one
between armed groups, but also a war between those who would take away
Hutu freedom and those who would protect it. Finally, the claim is also that
the Tutsis of the past want the same things as the Tutsis of the present. That
claim—Tutsis have the same preferences across generations—is essential to the
logic of genocide because it allows Tutsis to be constructed as unwinnable. As
we shall see, the logic of Tutsis wanting the same thing across generations and
specifically to overturn the Revolution will appear again and again.

Battlefield dynamics also mattered, and there the RPF showed itself to be
strong and getting stronger. In other words, the danger to the Revolution was
clear and present. Although the French initially helped repulse the RPF and

---

89. Excerpts of the report are available at *Rwanda de la guerre au génocide,* André Guichaoua's website for the primary documents of his 2010 book, available at http://rwandadelaguerreaugenocide.
univ-paris1.fr/?cat=20, accessed June 21, 2014.

90. « Transcript de l'interrogatoire principal de Théoneste Bagosora, procès Bagosora *et alii,*
TPIR, Arusha, » October 26 and 27, 2005, p. 20, available at http://rwandadelaguerreaugenocide.
univ-paris1.fr/wp-content/uploads/2010/01/Annexe_7.pdf, accessed June 23, 2014.

91. ICTR 2008.

later helped to train the Rwanda government's military forces, the RPF gained a foothold in the north of the country, and the rebels succeeded in launching significant attacks in 1991, 1992, and 1993, once they had regrouped under Paul Kagame's leadership. They also began recruiting from the internal Rwandan opponents of the regime, in particular resident Tutsis and Tutsis living in the diaspora. The rebels' strength is one reason why the terms of the 1993 peace agreement were as favorable to them as they were.[92]

But before coming to that peace agreement, known as the Arusha Accords, a key question to consider is the decision-making among the political opposition. More specifically, did the political opposition create a strong counter-narrative to the Revolution, one that could have influenced how the terms of the military fight were interpreted?

The legal political opposition that formed in 1991 fiercely opposed the MRND and the president, at least initially. The main opposition parties were the Mouvement Démocratique Républicaine (MDR), which was a Hutu-dominated party with a center of gravity in south-central Rwanda; the Parti social démocrate (PSD), whose base of support was the Butare Prefecture; and the Parti liberal (PL), which had strong support among Tutsis.

Of these parties, the most powerful was the MDR, which was a legacy party of Kayibanda's party of the same name. The MDR, rather than rejecting the Revolution, endorsed it. To be sure, the MDR had fractious voices within it. When the party appeared in 1991, there existed already a tension between those who idealized the Kayibanda era, casting the new MDR as a continuation of the old party, and those who wanted to emphasize national reconciliation. In the end, concludes a study of Rwandan opposition party dynamics by Jordane Bertrand, the party leadership chose to endorse continuity—to "re-launch and renovate" the old party, even while emphasizing that the party was against discrimination of all sorts. Nonetheless, Bertrand argues that subtle distinctions were often lost on the population, especially given the glorification of the Kayibanda regime. Indeed, when one influential MDR leader, Faustin Twagiramungu, sought to change slightly the name of the party to Mouvement Démocratique Rwandais—an effort to tack away from Kayibanda—the party leadership rejected the move. There was, Bernard concludes, a deliberate defense of the achievements of the Revolution.[93]

---

92. There are other reasons as well. The Habyarimana regime was in debt, and it faced pressure from donors to concede. By contrast, the RPF's base of support was outside the country, and it faced less pressure to concede. The dynamics are well laid out in a now declassified memo by Rick Ehrenreich of the U.S. State Department's intelligence program; see "Rwanda," United States Holocaust Memorial Museum, available at www.ushmm.org/confront-genocide/cases/rwanda, accessed June 21, 2014.

93. Bertrand 2000: 87, 88, 89, 91–92, 115.

By contrast, the PSD, with its core of support in Butare, a university town, clearly sought to distinguish itself from any association with ethnic exclusion. Bertrand argues that the PSD was the most intellectually open and least ethnically marked of the parties. Again in contrast to the MDR, PSD leaders refused any direct association with APROSOMA, which itself had a base of support in Butare but which was involved in the Revolution—its acronym stands for Association for the Promotion of the Masses—and thus connected to the founding narrative around the Revolution.[94]

In even greater contrast, the PL denounced the revolution—the only party that seems to have done so—but with Tutsis as key leaders the party quickly became tagged as a Tutsi party.[95]

Thus, as in Mali, Côte d'Ivoire, and Senegal, the political opening that occurred in the 1990s presented Rwandan political elites with an opportunity to reframe the founding narrative of the state and the nation. However, in contrast to Mali in particular, that did not happen. The most powerful opposition party in Rwanda in fact explicitly endorsed the legacy of the Revolution, even if seeking to move away from its excesses, and while another party disassociated itself from the Revolution, that move was not a centerpiece of its efforts. Rather, both the MDR and PSD opposition parties focused on a new, more representative parliament, institutionalizing multipartyism, liberalizing the media, criticizing one-party rule and Habyarimana, and negotiating with the RPF.[96] Only one party clearly rejected the Revolution, but that was the party in which the ethnic minority had the greatest representation.

The Arusha Accords, Hutu Power, and the Process of Escalation

This brings us to the Arusha Accords, which regional and international actors pushed and which brought together the three pillars of the domestic political arena: the president's camp, the political opposition, and the RPF. The Arusha process began in earnest in 1992. Throughout 1992 and the first half of 1993, Habyarimana struck a somewhat conciliatory tone; at least publicly, he invoked the importance of unity and reconciliation.[97] When the Accords

---

94. Bertrand 2000: 107–8.

95. Bertrand 2000: 110–11. A fourth opposition party, the Party Démocrate Chrétien (PDC), existed, but it was quite weak and poorly funded (Bertrand 2000: 113).

96. Bertrand 2000: 117–18.

97. See Habyarimana speeches on July 7, August 17, September 12, October 28, and December 1, 1992, January 25, April 30, May 13, and May 24, 1993. The main exception is a speech to the MRND party congress on November 15, 1992, in which he is alleged to have called Arusha "scraps

were signed in August 1993, he spoke of how Arusha represented "real reconciliation" and "compromise."[98] Throughout, Habyarimana presented himself publicly as above the fray, as a kingmaker who stood for the good of the country. Even as late as February 23, 1994, he spoke of the need for unity and dialogue: "Despite the political parties to which we belong, despite the various regions where we were born, despite our ethnic allegiances, we are all Rwandans, all equal, with the same rights and duties."

At the same time, it is clear that the peace process culminated in August 1993 with a major victory for the RPF and a defeat for the president's party.[99] The author of the most careful study of the Arusha process attributes the RPF's success to the discipline of its negotiating team as well as to its superior military position. Diplomatic efforts also favored democratization and multi-party governance.[100] The government side was weakened after it announced the creation of a multiparty coalition government in 1992, and indeed the government's delegation was initially led by an opposition figure.[101]

Under the terms of the agreement, the MRND only constituted 33 percent of the new Broad-Based Transitional Government; government forces were to constitute 50 percent of officers in the military and 60 percent of ordinary troops. Many influential figures in the party rejected the basic terms of the agreement. They saw the agreement as a sellout; many observers conclude that the terms of the agreement polarized and radicalized segments within the ruling party in particular.[102]

Even prior to the signing of the agreement, however, senior elites within the MRND began to develop a strategy to counter the gains that the RPF was making on the battlefield and in the negotiations. A central pillar was bipolarization. That is, the elite around the president—in particular, the inner core, or "akazu"[103]—sought to reduce the playing field in Rwanda to two: an anti-RPF, pro-Hutu bloc that defended the Revolution and a pro-RPF bloc that was against it. The basic intuition among the leaders, which was consistent with the

---

of paper," a phrase the opposition pounced upon. But in a text of the speech the main concern he articulated was who represented the government given that the then prime minister was from the opposition. Habyarimana said, "We support the negotiations that are being held in Arusha. . . . MRND supports the negotiations. I personally support the negotiations so that they can bring a true peace." But he goes on to say that he wants to make sure that the delegation represents Rwandans and to say what was agreed upon by the government.

98. See Habyarimana speeches on August 5 and 6, 1993.
99. Jones 2001.
100. Jones 2001.
101. Guichaoua 2010: 140.
102. Guichaoua 2010; Jones 2001: 103.
103. *Akazu* is a Kinyarwanda term that means "little house" and also signifies the insiders around the president and his wife.

country's founding narrative, is that the party's strength lay with the people. If the MRND could establish a "pro-Hutu" coalition, the party had an electoral advantage given the overwhelming demographic superiority of Hutus in the country.[104] There was a post-Arusha parliamentary political calculus as well: Faced with a minority of votes in parliament, if the MRND could "convert" politicians in opposition parties, it could reverse the math of the Accords to form a majority.[105] A central strategy became to divide the Hutu-dominant opposition parties into "pro-Hutu" and "pro-RPF" camps. This is the origin of the idea of "Hutu Power," the term for a political coalition of pro-Hutu parties.

Arusha hastened and reinforced the bipolarization strategy. It facilitated the strategy in that "Arusha made the worst fears of MRND come true" given how much power the ruling party formally lost.[106] Arusha also reinforced an electoral emphasis, given that MRND leaders thought that their comparative power lay with the electorate, rather than the battlefield or the negotiations process, which they felt the RPF had manipulated. Turning to the masses became a strategy to avoid the negative terms of peace deal.[107]

The bipolarization strategy ultimately worked. A key question is why. An important catalyst was Burundi. In October 1993, a few months after Arusha was signed, Tutsi officers assassinated the first Hutu president, Melchior Ndadaye, who had been democratically elected. His assassination galvanized Rwandan political elites, both in and outside Habyarimana's party, to claim in a variety of ways and in a variety of forums that Tutsis globally would refuse to accept democracy and do whatever they could to subvert the majority.[108]

A key speech occurred at a rally on October 29, 1993, just after Ndadaye's assassination. In the speech, a leader of the MDR, Froduald Karamira, rebaptized opposition parties as Hutu Power parties. In a rambling speech filled with animosity, he declared that the RPF had a hand in the assassination. Karamira refers to the leader of the RPF, Paul Kagame, as a "refugee who attacked Rwanda . . . has taken democracy away from the Burundians. The one who went on to deceive us in Arusha . . . you should be convinced that these people and all who support them, every Hutu living in Rwanda must rise up in turn, so that we do what needs to be done."

Karamira went on to advocate for "training." He castigated leading Hutu politicians who signed the Accords, claiming that they had betrayed the country. These problems concerned all Hutus: "Who is not a Parmehutu?" he said,

---

104. Guichaoua 2010: 116.
105. Guichaoua 2010: 186.
106. Guichaoua 2010: 149.
107. Guichaoua 2010: 146.
108. Guichaoua 2010: 173–74.

citing the independence-era party. "Which of you does not have Parmehutu blood flowing through his veins? Which of you did not benefit from Kayiban-da's generosity? So, are your eyes open?" He sought over and over again to rouse his audience. He warned them that "The enemy is in our midst," concluding:

> In short, dear militants. . . . Hutus should avoid arguing with each other, wherever they may be. Let us avoid attacking each other, while we are being attacked. Let us prevent the traitor from infiltrating our ranks and stealing our power. . . . We should demonstrate the power of every Hutu by going to the assistance of Burundi. . . . Unuhutu. . . . Power! Power! Power! MRND. . . . Power! Power! Power! CDR. . . . Power! Power! Power! MDR Power! Power! Power![109]

Karamira here articulates the foundation for a pan-Hutu coalition, one that was a central strategy of the ruling party to defeat the rebels and to shore up an electoral majority. The Burundi violence was an ingredient in forging this position: Burundi provided a demonstration for the pan-Hutu advocates that Tutsis would never share power. The RPF military gains as well as gains at the negotiating table also were a fixture, signaling a looming danger and a need to coalesce. Nonetheless, what brought these elements together into a coherent ideological position was the founding narrative. The Revolution acted as an ideological center of gravity, a framework that allowed elites to make sense of the crisis that they were in and to develop a strategy to overcome it. In this case, we see an MDR opposition party member invoking the Revolutionary party—Parmehutu—to make a case for Hutu unity and ultimately Hutu Power. The idea of Hutu Power is consistent with the Revolution—the Revolution was about Hutu Power—and here we see how that narrative pulls a key opposition figure back into a pro-Hutu coalition.

Would the development of Hutu Power have happened in the absence of the founding narrative? On the one hand, the ruling party had a strategic incentive to polarize the political field into two camps—one it would dominate and one that would claim a demographic majority—and arguably opposition Hutu figures would benefit more from being in a pan-Hutu coalition than being independent. On the other hand, the opposition Hutu parties could have rallied to the RPF, which was in fact stronger. In either case, what we see here is how the founding narrative facilitates the transition to a Hutu Power coalition and how the narrative grounds the idea of Hutu Power and makes Hutu Power seem continuous with the tenets of the opposition party whose legacy is the First Republic.

---

109. Discours Karamira Meeting Politique du 23 Octobre 1993, available at http://trim.unictr.org/webdrawer/rec/98211/.

In this speech, we also see how acute the sense of threat was and how that threat interacted with the founding narrative. The events in Burundi are pitched as a global threat to Hutu power and to Hutu rule, as a direct threat to the Revolution but also to "every Hutu." This is the process of escalation at work—a looming war, an armed rebel presence, a perception of vulnerability, and a founding narrative that frames the war as a fight between a majority identity group who should rule and a minority one who should not.

The Karamira speech—and the Hutu Power moment in general when the MRND broke off pro-Hutu factions from the opposition parties to form a new bloc—was a turning point in the process of escalation that preceded the genocide in April 1994. We can see similar themes developing at the major MRND rally in Kigali on January 16, 1994. In this rally, MRND officials gloated about how they have, through dividing the opposition parties, inverted the parliamentary and cabinet-level math of the Arusha Accords. But again, a strong rhetoric of the Revolution framed many of the speeches.

For example, consider MRND Minister André Ntagerura. He spoke just after Édouard Karemera, the MRND's first vice president. In his speech, Karemera revealed how the anti-MRND opposition had been outmaneuvered. Following that, Ntagerura declared that 1994 would be the year that the Revolution was saved: "I want to wish you a happy and good 1994, that it will be for us all who support democracy, sovereignty of the Republic, an occasion to reinforce our victory in inflicting defeat to all those who want to deprive us of the achievements of the Revolution of 59."[110] In other words, the MRND was in a battle with pro-Tutsi forces who wanted to take away the gains of the Revolution, and the political math that the MRND had done was in that service. Even more explicit was Mathieu Ngirumpatse, national party chairman of the MRND. His entire speech was an explicit effort to draw an historical parallel to the 1959 period, saying that the two periods "resembled each other despite the long distance that separated them." He compared the RPF to the ruling political authorities of the late 1950s who, he said, wanted to keep people in servitude. He made analogies to other dimensions of the two periods, including the role of the UN in both cases. He also claimed that Tutsis developed assassination lists in both cases: "We cannot claim that security reigns while we plan to establish lists of people to exterminate. The blood of President Habyarimana, of Justin Mugenzi, of Mathieu Ngirumpatse, of [Édouard] Karemera, of [Venantie] Kabageni, of [Joseph] Nzirorera and those of [other] MRND militants will not undermine the existence of the Republic.

---

110. RTLM/radio Rwabda 16/01/1994, "Broadcast RTLM-RTLM MRND K023-8108-8127," available at http://trim.unictr.org/webdrawer/rec/98110/.

What I only worry about, and what I repeat to these people, is that if ever blood is spilt, I think that they will gain nothing, just like in Burundi."[111]

Ngirumpatse was both invoking and making a threat. On the former, in essence, he claimed that the RPF had plans in place to assassinate MRND and allied leaders. He also connected them to Tutsis who wanted power in the past. On the latter, he warned that the effort will not work and that such efforts will result in violence for the Tutsis (as was the case in the 1950s and in Burundi).

In short, the founding narrative in Rwanda functioned like a funnel, shaping and coalescing positions among the influential elite and assimilating events into a broader framework by which politicians interpreted and responded to those events. Other dynamics were in play. Personalities and rivalries played a role in the splintering of the opposition, but my claim is the presence and character of the founding narrative played a significant part in why large elements of the opposition could quickly rally to a pro-Hutu coalition.

The RPF was the other big player in the process of escalation. The main claim of the MRND coalition was that the RPF wanted to take power by force. And, indeed, at some point—possibly triggered by the ways in which they were outmaneuvered politically—the RPF pursued, if not opted definitively for, a military solution. At a minimum, the RPF was pursuing both a diplomatic and a military option at the same time. For Guichaoua, in this late phase, the pro-Hutu coalition emphasized politics and the people; therein lay its comparative advantage, even if war started again. By contrast, the RPF's main approach was military.[112]

One other dimension that needs to be underlined is the way in which the state and the ruling party in particular, but not exclusively, invested in alternative institutions. These included a civilian defense force and militia training. The efforts were consistent with the idea that the MRND camp's advantage lay with the people and the idea that, through Arusha and the formation of coalition governments in 1992 and 1993, they had lost control of key institutions.[113] The same logic is true for the MRND's investments in an alternative radio station, Radio Télévision Milles Collines (RTLM), which became a font of pro-Hutu, anti-Tutsi rhetoric.

The documents that are available today, primarily through the work of the International Criminal Tribunal for Rwanda and scholars like Guichaoua, depict a period of intense distrust and the virtual collapse of government.

---

111. Broadcast RTLM-RTLM Number 0295 Clip "Ngirumpatse Speech Entire Tape and Transcript," available at http://trim.unictr.org/webdrawer/rec/98102/.

112. Guichaoua 2010: 189.

113. Guichaoua 2010: 175.

In particular, in the last few months of 1993 and the first three months of 1994, the state was effectively not functioning. Opposition parties boycotted a presidential swearing-in ceremony in December 1993. The prime minister, Agathe Uwilingiyimana, was from the opposition, but other members of her own MDR party did not recognize her. Other opposition parties were similarly deeply divided. The MRND leaders and the RPF were both preparing for war and accusing the other of doing the same. And the political rhetoric was foreboding and full of violent innuendo. The Ngirumpatse speech is one example of many. There were also high-level political assassinations of party leaders, both pro–Hutu Power and anti–Hutu Power. There were public rallies of militias and youth wings. The situation was exceptionally tense, and we have seen how a rhetoric of a threatened Hutu majority whose fundamental political project was in danger—a rhetoric informed and shaped by the founding narrative of the Revolution—had taken hold.[114]

The Onset of Genocide and Patterns of Violence

The catalyst that pushed the logic of violence to genocide was the assassination of President Habyarimana on April 6, 1994, and the quick resumption of war. Who killed Habyarimana remains hotly debated. In my 2006 book I argued that the RPF is responsible, a conclusion I still find persuasive as of this writing. They had the most incentive to assassinate the president; they were clearly more ready to fight and more committed to fighting than were the pro-MRND forces; the RPF favored a military strategy; their main plan was to launch a quick, decapitating strike and secure the country as quickly as possible. Indeed, that was what they did. Immediately following Habyarimana's death, RPF forces went on the offensive, principally from their positions in the north but also from their position in Kigali.

Meanwhile, from April 6, 1994, government forces were on the defensive. In the plane crash that killed the president, the pro-MRND camp not only lost the head of state but also other elite military leaders, including General Déogratias Nsabimana, the chief of staff of the Rwandan Army, and Colonel Élie Sagatwa, the head of the Army's elite Presidential Guard unit. The minister of defense, Augustin Bizimana, was out of the country. In short, the government military side faced a vacuum of leadership in both the political and military arenas.

---

114. To appreciate the depth of distrust and near collapse of formal institutions, see the primary documents from this period, available at http://rwandadelaguerreaugenocide.univ-paris1.fr/?cat=12, especially Annexes 35–42.

Into that vacuum jumped MRND hardliners and the key power brokers that had surrounded the president, many of whom were related to his wife, Agathe Habyarimana. A key figure was Théoneste Bagosora, a retired colonel who had chaired the military commission in 1991. Other major figures were Mathieu Ngirumpatse, Édouard Karemera, and Joseph Nzirorera on the MRND party side, as well as other actors, such as Protais Zigiranyirazo, the first lady's eldest brother. These actors made the principal decisions that set the genocide in motion.[115] They first orchestrated assassinations of leading opposition figures, including the prime minister; they engineered a new government composed uniquely of pro–MRND/Hutu Power politicians; and then they unleashed the force of the state to attack and murder Tutsi civilians across the territory still in government hands.

One alternative interpretation is that the MRND hardliners believed that Habyarimana had betrayed them and their political project by signing the Arusha Accords, given its negative terms for the ruling party. They thus removed the president, blamed his death on the RPF, and implemented a plan to eliminate the Tutsi threat once and for all. For several reasons, while plausible, this alternative interpretation remains weak—at least according to currently available information.

The central problems concern, first, the disorganization that characterizes those would-be planners immediately following the assassination. The hardliners did not develop a clear military response to the RPF; they sought to install a military government, but failed; and while they acted in a determined and vengeful fashion they did not appear to have a clearly worked-out plan in place ahead of time. Moreover, MRND officials were in hiding in this period; when people such as Jean Kambanda were named prime minister, they were often surprised; indeed, Kambanda had to be collected in a military vehicle, which suggests his lack of preparedness.[116] Second, Habyarimana was the party leader and standard-bearer. Killing him was a major blow to the political fortunes of the MRND, therefore to the party's future success, and killing him was likely a personal blow to his wife. There was no clear designate to succeed him among the would-be assassins from the hardliner camp. In these senses, assassinating Habyarimana would seem not to be in the interests of those who orchestrated the genocide. Third, if the plan was to defeat the RPF militarily, the assassination was a major strategic error. Habyarimana was the formal head of the military; moreover, on the plane were other military elites who would

---

115. This statement is made on the basis of the collected ICTR decisions to date, as well as the work of Guichaoua and my ongoing research into the Rwanda case.

116. Guichaoua 2010: 295, 304–5, 309, 322.

have been responsible for organizing the military defeat of the RPF, including Sagatwa who was the head of the Presidential Guard and himself a key insider of the regime. The military response overall was one of confusion, disarray, and division—at least initially and in sharp contrast to the clear military prepared-ness and organization on the RPF side.[117] Finally, the analysis that suggests that the Arusha Accords were the cause neglects the period following the signing of the agreement in which the MRND successfully undermined the politi-cal math of the Accords and divided the opposition. By early April, the RPF looked to have lost the political momentum, rather than the other way around. In short, I remain convinced that the RPF is responsible, but I also recognize that no undeniable evidence exists either way.

Whoever is responsible for killing Habyarimana, the events that followed are clear. Immediately after the president's death, the key actors within the presi-dential camp—the MRND leaders, members of the presidential family, and others in the "akazu"—set out to take control of the government. Bagosora was the lead public actor, acting both on behalf of the presidential family and seemingly with his own political ambitions. On the night of April 6, Bagosora pulled together a military crisis committee, which met on two occasions with the military high command. Bagosora sought to transform the crisis com-mittee into the country's ruling authority, in effect rupturing the terms of the Arusha Accords. However, the military leadership rejected the proposal, arguing that the committee's role should be limited to securing the country. Politically, they argued, the law should be followed and the terms of the Aru-sha Accords respected. The committee in turn rejected Bagosora and elected General Augustin Ndindiliyimana as head of the committee.[118]

Thwarted by the military high command, the hardliners associated with the presidential camp sought alternative means. In particular, on the night of April 6–7, they orchestrated the elimination of the main political rivals in the opposition, including Prime Minister Agathe Uwilingiyimana. The presi-dent's extended family apparently wanted revenge, and they also wanted to destroy any coalition coming to power that did not represent Hutu Power.[119] On that first evening, Tutsis were also killed as RPF accomplices in Kigali and Gisenyi.[120] Some interpret the shocking rapidity with which Tutsis were

---

117. The interpretation in this paragraph builds heavily on Guichaoua 2010, especially 241–353. It is also consistent with my 2006 book as well as the ICTR decisions in the Military I and MRND trials.

118. Guichaoua 2010: 247, 264–66; ICTR 2008.

119. Guichaoua 2010: 247, 255, 258–59, 281, 335–36.

120. ICTR 2008.

killed following the assassination as evidence of genocidal plan in place. But a generalized, nationwide campaign to murder Tutsis had not yet taken hold.

The political assassinations set the stage for the announcement of a new interim government, which the military high command formally accepted on the evening of April 8. The key players who organized the composition of the new government were the MRND leaders Karemera, Nzirorera, and Ngirumpatse, as well as Bagosora. The composition formally respected the terms of the Arusha Accords in the sense that it included members of the opposition in a broad-based government. But in reality the interim government was composed primarily of politicians from the Hutu Power factions of all the non-MRND parties. Kambanda was named prime minister. Théodore Sindikubwabo, an MRND politician from the south, was named president. Guichaoua concludes that the whole process was "a putsch by the military officers of the presidential clan and by the leaders of the MRND." As a Hutu Power government, the interim government embodied the political logic that the MRND had developed to win—that of reconstituting national unity around the "majority people" and to end intra-Hutu rivalries.[121]

Meanwhile, moderates within the military high command sought to stop the killings and achieve a ceasefire with the RPF, best represented by the public communiqué of April 12.[122] The interim government rejected this initial gesture from the military officers, but so did the RPF, which by this stage was committed to a military path.[123] In short, efforts at a ceasefire failed, the moderates were sidelined, and the situation escalated into a direct military confrontation between an advancing and determined RPF and a hardliner government flanked by a military with significant internal divisions.[124] In that context, the interim government fled Kigali to find a more secure location, setting up shop in Gitarama to the south.

April 12 was also the turning point in the formal policy of genocide. Until that day, the state's direction was ambiguous.[125] Leaders of the military high command called for moderation and the absence of killing; even the coalition of Hutu Power parties issued a communiqué on April 10 encouraging the population to stop massacres;[126] political party leaders—both Hutu

---

121. Guichaoua 2010: 310–12, 314, 324.
122. See "Annexe 70," http://rwandadelaguerreaugenocide.univ-paris1.fr/wp-content/uploads/2010/01/Annexe_70.pdf.
123. See ibid, especially General Romeo Dallaire's deposition, and Guichaoua 2010: 342.
124. Guichaoua 2010: 346.
125. Guichaoua 2010: 414.
126. See "Annexe 89," at http://rwandadelaguerreaugenocide.univ-paris1.fr/wp-content/uploads/2010/01/Annexe_89.pdf.

and Tutsi—were being killed. Who was in control and what the state's policies were—the answers to these questions were in at least some doubt. But
after the moderates failed on April 12, it became clear that the hardliners
associated with the MRND and the Hutu Power wings had the upper hand
and were in charge.[127] They distributed weapons on that day. For them, the
strategy became twofold: Turn to the population as a last resort to defeat the
RPF and impose massive collective punishment on the Tutsis.[128] In other
words, according to Guichaoua, the logic was to ensure that even if the RPF
won militarily, they would lose their base and achieve the smallest benefit
possible.[129] The government wanted to make the RPF pay for their victory
and to destroy the RPF's base of support.[130] From April 12 forward, on
the government side, that strategy dominated, and it was one to which the
MRND leadership and interim government committed themselves.[131]

By April 12, those in government and the MRND began to call on the
population to attack Tutsi civilians. In a broadcast aired on state radio and
approved by the Ministry of Defense, soldiers, gendarmes, and "all Rwandans"
were instructed to "unite against the enemy, the only enemy and this is the
enemy that we have always known . . . it's the enemy who wants to reinstate
the former feudal monarchy".[132] By April 14, violence against Tutsis had
started in most parts of the country. The main holdout areas were Butare and
Gitarama Prefectures, where there was considerable resistance from Hutus
and Tutsis to starting the violence. The hardliners ultimately removed the prefect (the leading regional-level administrative authority) in Butare, deployed
the interim president and prime minister to both prefectures, and threatened
any Hutus who refused to join the fight against Tutsis. By April 21, widespread and systematic violence against Tutsi civilians had become the norm in
almost every area of the country that had not yet fallen to the rebels.

For the next eleven weeks, the conflict's broad outlines did not change.
In areas under the government's control, genocide was the order of the day.
However, the RPF rebels steadily advanced. By late April, the RPF rebels
controlled most of north-central and eastern Rwanda. By the end of May,
they controlled most of central Rwanda (though not Kigali, which did not
fall until July 4). By mid-July the rout was complete: Three months after

---

127. Guichaoua 2010: 415.
128. Guichaoua 2010: 345, 427, 441, 453.
129. Guichaoua 2010: 345.
130. Guichaoua 2010: 346, 447.
131. Militia leaders consistently claim they had high-level support, especially from the MRND.
See Guichaoua 2010: 426 and Annexes 40, 53, 87, and 91.
132. ICTR 1998: 20; see also Des Forges 1999: 202–3.

Habyarimana's assassination and the resumption of war, the rump genocidal regime fled into what was then Zaire, taking with them the remnants of the army, the militia, the civilian administration and more than one million civilians, most of them Hutus. Close to another million fled eastward into Tanzania.

Patterns of Mobilization and Violence at the Local Level

Authorities at the top initiated and encouraged widespread violence against Tutsis, and national-level institutions such as the military, the government, the gendarmerie, and media institutions played key roles in directly carrying out the violence or in encouraging local actors to attack Tutsi civilians during the genocide period.[133] However, the violence would not have succeeded or taken the form that it did without local-level intermediaries and participants.

In examining the country as a whole, there is evident variation in when the violence began in different regions and in the coalitions of actors who led the violence at the local level. With regards to the timing of when the violence started, in general the areas where the violence against Tutsis started earliest were those regions where the ruling MRND was strongest and in particular where Habyarimana and hardliners in the regime had the greatest political support. Also significant was proximity to war fighting; that is, areas that were closest to RPF positions in April in general tended on average to start the violence the soonest. Thus, the violence started earliest in Kigali, Rural-Kigali, Gisenyi, Ruhengeri, and Byumba Prefectures. By contrast, in general the areas that had less support for the MRND and were farther from RPF military positions initiated the violence later, such as Butare and Gitarama Prefectures and parts of Kibuye Prefecture.

As for patterns of mobilization, in general the leaders at the national (or prefectural) level in the government, ruling party, and military advocated or encouraged violence against the "Tutsi enemy." They did so in the name of fighting a war and in the name of self-defense—in the name of security, even if the actual war fighting was some distance from where they were located. The channels of communication were through military, state, and political party networks as well as through face-to-face meetings. National leaders also fanned out into the countryside and called public meetings or held private meetings with local leaders. National actors also communicated their message through calls on the radio for vigilance and citizen participation in the war effort.

---

133. This section draws heavily on Straus 2006b, ch. 3.

In describing the enemy and orienting the population, the authorities used different terms. They referred variously to the "enemy," the "Tutsi enemy," the *Inyenzi*, or the *Inkotanyi*. The latter formally refers to the RPF; *Inyenzi* is a more pejorative term that translates as "cockroaches." In the context of the genocide in 1994, there was widespread understanding among the population that when authorities referred to the "enemy," to the *Inkotanyi*, or to the *Inyenzi*, they were in fact referring to the entire Tutsi population. In interview after interview that I conducted with perpetrators in Rwanda, this association between the Tutsi enemy/RPF and the entire Tutsi population was clear.

At the subnational level in rural areas, the crisis triggered different responses. As suggested above, in areas with strong support for the deceased president, for the ruling party, or even for Hutu Power, coalitions of local hardliners quickly formed and initiated violence against Tutsi civilians. In other areas, moderates sought to prevent violence from starting. Over time, however, in all areas not yet lost to rebels, hardliners succeeded in undermining moderates, eventually consolidating control. Once they did so, communities switched from a period of heightened anxiety and confusion due to the president's assassination and resumption of civil war to a period of participatory and exterminatory violence.

The general pattern of mobilization at the local level is that at the top was a coalition of rural local elites. Rural elites in Rwanda are generally those with positions of status, authority, or wealth in the community or some combination of the three. Positions of status were generated from being a part of the local state hierarchy, the local political party structure, the clergy, business, or the education and health sector. In general, the rural elite had comparatively high levels of education (some high school education or greater), had salaried income or business income, and were in some position of authority or influence prior to the genocide. Sometimes the rural elite came from well-to-do families or families with representation in the upper echelons of government. In general, a rural elite formed the core leadership in rural communities during the genocide. In contrast to the rural elite were ordinary farmers and shepherds, who formed roughly 90 to 95 percent (sometimes even more) of the rural population. In general, these Rwandans have little education and little social power.

Alongside the rural elite were those actors who specialized in violence. These could be former army reservists, militia leaders, or even young toughs who during the genocide rose to the top of the genocide hierarchy because of their prowess for violence. In most communities, the rural local elite and the young toughs formed the core nucleus of the genocidal violence. Once that coalition formed, they traversed their communities, recruiting a large number of Hutu men to participate in manhunts of Tutsis or to participate in other forms of "self-defense," such as manning roadblocks. They sometimes referred to the attacks and patrols as "work," in reference to a communal work program in Rwanda called *umuganda*, which in non-emergency periods entailed fixing roads, digging ditches, and building schools, among other projects. The recruiting most often was done house-to-house, at markets or rural commercial centers, at rural bars, or at meetings called by local authorities. Eventually, through these recruiting efforts and the general dynamics of violence in this period, hundreds of thousands of ordinary Rwandan citizens who had no prior history of violence came to participate in the genocidal violence.

Once the violence started, civilians were killed in four main locations: (1) at roadblocks, on roads, and at public meeting points, such as commercial centers, where Tutsis' identification cards were inspected or where Tutsis were otherwise identified; (2) in or just outside homes where Tutsis lived or had sought refuge; (3) in fields, marshes, or other places, such as banana plantations, where Tutsis hid; and (4) at central congregation points, such as churches, schools, government buildings, and hilltops where Tutsis had fled for safety and where they sometimes sought to resist. The largest massacres—numbering in the hundreds and even thousands of civilians—occurred at the central congregation points, and they often involved military or paramilitary actors who had modern firearms and grenades.

It is difficult to establish a precise number of how many civilians were killed. Many people were killed in a very short period of time, and no one counted the number of dead as they were killed. During the genocide and war, as well as afterward, many Rwandans fled the country. After the RPF won control, many Tutsi exiles who had lived abroad returned to the country. Moreover, the numbers killed is controversial, both in the country and outside it, and statistical records in Rwanda before the genocide and afterward, as in many African states, have validity problems. That said, I shall try to summarize the existing data.

The standard international estimate in journalistic and United Nations reports is 800,000 killed.[134] However, according to the last government census taken before the genocide (in 1991), only 600,000 Tutsis were living in Rwanda.[135] Given Rwanda's population growth, there may have been as many as 660,000 Tutsis in Rwanda at the time of the genocide.[136] It is possible that government officials or Tutsis themselves disguised the true number of Tutsis,

---

134. ICTR 1998: 20; OAU 2000, p. 8. For a higher estimate of 934,218 killed, see République Rwandaise 2001: 7.

135. République du Rwanda 1994: 124.

136. République Rwandaise 2001: 12. The reported annual growth rate is 3.1%.

but there is limited evidence of widespread and systematic falsification, and the 1991 census data correspond to data in the last census conducted in the colonial period.[137]

In my view, the best aggregate estimate of the number killed during the genocide comes from historian and human rights activist Alison Des Forges, who triangulates data from three sources and estimates that at least 500,000 Tutsi civilians were killed in the genocide. That sum amounts to roughly three-quarters of Rwanda's pre-genocide Tutsi population.[138] An estimate of 75 percent killed of the resident Tutsi population is consistent with a dictionary of names of people killed produced by the survivor organization Ibuka. That book lists 59,050 names of people killed in Kibuye Prefecture; that number is equivalent to about 78 percent of the Tutsi population in the region.[139] Similarly, a detailed study of demographic data from Gikongoro Prefecture similarly found a death rate during the genocide period of 75 percent; that same study, however, found evidence of underreporting in the 1991 census of the number of Tutsi living in Rwanda. Estimating a series of different scenarios, that study concluded that the number of Tutsi civilians killed to be between 600,000 and 800,000 in 1994.[140] In sum, I would estimate between 500,000 and 800,000 Tutsis killed in three months, roughly 75 percent of the domestic Tutsi population.

Tutsis were not the only civilians killed in this period. The pro-genocide forces also targeted and sometimes killed other Hutus. How many they killed is difficult to say given poor data on the subject. Hutus who refused to participate in the violence against Tutsis were punished and beaten. Sometimes Hutus fought over spoils of looted property. Some Hutus were killed as examples, for repeatedly resisting the killing, and for personal vendettas, but not as a rule. Judging from field research I conducted and from other field-based studies, the level of such intra-Hutu violence is on a scale that is considerably lower than the genocidal violence or that of the RPF violence. The RPF also killed MRND political leaders and Hutu civilians as they advanced; again, the number is not known.[141] Des Forges cites two estimates ranging from 25,000 to 60,000.[142]

---

137. Des Forges 1999: 15.
138. Des Forges 1999: 15–16.
139. See Straus 2006b.
140. Verpoorten 2005.
141. Verwimp 2003.
142. The latter figure includes estimates of Hutus killed through August 1995.

Sources of Escalation and the Logic of Genocide

The question still remains as to why the elite decision-makers who took effective control of the state in this period set Rwanda down a path of genocide. Throughout this period, including the period after the president was assassinated and the rebels advanced, several options remained possible. The authorities could have instructed their supporters not to kill civilians and insisted on obedience on the point. They could have authorized some massacres as a deterrent to the RPF but restrained the use of such violence once it became clear that coercive violence was not working. They could have fled. They could have stood down. They could have insisted on international mediation and intervention. Or they could have pursued some combination thereof. However, instead, they chose a path of maximum violence—of declaring the entire Tutsi civilian population to be accomplices of the RPF who in turn had to be destroyed.

Why did they do so? Guichaoua argues that given the military superiority of the RPF, the hardliners judged that the state's comparative strength lay in its overwhelming demographic majority. He argues that if the local Tutsis were eliminated, the RPF could not govern the country or, at a minimum, their victory would be so painful and punishing that they would not be able to savor it. Government forces were in a position to harm Tutsi civilians, but not so the rebel army; they thus killed whomever they could.[143] These are plausible interpretations. In some ways, the genocide was the card that an outmaneuvered, vengeful, and ideologically committed hardliner elite played as a response to their imminent defeat, their sense of betrayal, and their outrage at the killing of their leader. Having been outplayed, they detonated their version of a nuclear bomb: Inflict the maximum damage that they could on their enemies.

That still begs the question as to why that response was thinkable, even legitimate, in the minds of those who fostered it. The move was not instrumentally "strategic" in the sense that it did not improve their chances of defeating the RPF and retaining power. Moreover, the scale of violence was so dramatic that the genocide, over time, completely discredited all Hutu movements associated with it, thereby bankrupting the Hutu Power movement of any international legitimacy—a move from which it still suffers as of this writing. While I have argued and remain convinced that the genocide as such was not a completely thought out and planned strategy in advance—prior to April 1994[144]—a position

---

143. Guichaoua 2010: 250, 345.
144. Straus 2006b.

that Guichaoua shares,[145] the policy of mass violence against Tutsis was not completely spontaneous: It was an extension of the process of escalation in the four years, especially the final eight months, that preceded the downing of the plane and the formation of a Hutu Power government.

Fundamental to that logic were the main drivers of mass categorical violence: a sense of acute threat framed as an existential struggle between two identity groups, one that deserved to rule and in whose name the state ruled and one that did not deserve to rule and whose interests lay in taking away the freedoms of the first group. The undeserving group was furthermore constructed as an unwinnable population category, a group whose interests were relatively uniform and unchanging over time. The reason that the threat was framed in such a way is the country's founding narrative, which held that the Hutu majority had won a hard-fought freedom from the oppressive Tutsi minority and that the post-independence state was about achieving that political reality.

Clearly, the state faced an acute threat. The president had been assassinated, and the rebels were advancing. Almost every communiqué from this period is about security. Interviewed perpetrators consistently narrate the logic of committing violence against Tutsis as a measure of protection and security.[146] With regard to the framing, the Tutsi population was described as a permanent—that is, unwinnable—enemy that was committed to destroying the Hutu political freedom that had been achieved at independence. In other words, the terms and stakes of the fight were framed according to the parameters of Rwanda's post-independence founding narrative. Thus, even if Guichaoua is correct that the strategy was to make Rwanda ungovernable or to impose a pyrrhic victory, the premise underpinning that strategy is that the RPF and their Tutsi supporters were antithetical to the legitimate ethnic majority and the state's founding political project.

As evidence, consider the April 12 tract that Karemera wrote, printed at the Ministry of Defense and initially intended to be distributed across the country. The distribution was in fact stopped by the acting minister of defense, Marcel Gatsinzi, one of the officers advocating a ceasefire; he was deposed shortly after halting the tract's distribution.[147] Nonetheless, the logic of the tract represents the rationale that I am describing:

> Rwandans, all citizens of Rwanda, be reassured, protect the Republic and Democracy, which you achieved with the 1959 "Popular

---

145. Guichaoua 2010: 449.
146. Lyons and Straus 2006; McDoom 2009; Straus 2006b.
147. Guichaoua 2010: 331–32.

Revolution;" the Inkotanyi want to erase your achievements and return you to servitude.

You, commune leaders, heads of political parties, you, heads of communal councils and members of cell committees, be active, organize meetings, warn the population, a great danger is at its gates.

Rwandans, put aside your divisions, unite your forces so that you can face the grandchildren of UNAR that have decided to submit you once again to servitude.

In their respective cells, the population is asked immediately to study the ways and means to organize adequate patrols and to put up roadblocks so as to cut the enemy's route. When the situation is difficult, the population must alert the armed forces.[148]

In the first paragraph, Karemera sets out the terms of the struggle, which are in fact directly derived from the founding narrative: The RPF wants to erase the achievements of the Revolution. The founding narrative framed how elites thought about and framed the terms of the threat—in this case, the RPF would return Hutus to "servitude." In the second paragraph, Karemera repeats the notion of threat: "a great danger is at your gates." But the response is to mobilize the population through the civilian administration. Here Karemera is relying on the fact that the Rwandan state had an extensive administrative apparatus, which, even if the state was in deep turmoil, still was in place and could be used to mobilize the citizenry. His logic of mobilizing the population is also consistent with the revolution: The state was grounded in the Hutu masses. In the third paragraph, Karemera reiterates the threat, but here he characterizes Tutsis as unwinnable: They are the "grandchildren of UNAR." In other words, their intent is the same across time; they are unwinnable and committed to the oppression of Hutus. And again in the final paragraph, the idea is that the population is, as Karemera later said, "the last asset against the enemy."[149]

The general rationale is clear from the public speeches that leaders of Rwanda's interim government leaders made from April 12 forward. To cite one example, consider the text of a memorandum that Prime Minister Jean Kambanda sent out to local administrative officials. While saying that the government was seeking to negotiate a return to the Arusha Accords, Kambanda emphasized the need for popular support to defeat the enemy and achieve security:

The enemy that attacked Rwanda is known; it is the RPF-Inkotanyi. We thus ask you to explain to the citizens that they must guard against

---

148. Guichaoua 2010, see note 9 in chapter 3 of this book.
149. Guichaoua 2010: 333.

all who start troubles amongst themselves under the pretext of ethnicity, region, religions, political parties, hatreds, etc because all these
troubles in the population constitute openings for the enemy. Nonetheless, the population must remain vigilant to unmask the enemy and
his accomplices and to bring them to the authorities and to help the
national army when it needs help. The communal, sectoral, and cell
authorities, helped by the national army where possible, are asked to
designate places where roadblocks can continued to be placed so that
the enemy does not find any openings to infiltrate.[150]

Throughout Rwanda, this call and similar ones were widely interpreted
as calls to attack the Tutsi civilian population as "accomplices" of the RPF.
Although Kambanda did not spell out the rationale for genocide, he made
it clear that the country and the people are under severe attack. That threat
required popular "vigilance," and indeed we see here the ways in which the
decision-making elites sought to use the civilian administration and threat to
mobilize participation.

Perhaps the most chilling rationale for the genocide was put forth in a
manuscript that Bagosora wrote in 1995 while he was in exile. The manuscript is his version of events, one that clearly seeks to paint his actions in
a favorable light, but it also is a window into the thinking of a key high-
ranking official whose actions clearly shaped the course of events.

This is how Bagosora begins his introduction:

> The Hutu people have their backs against the wall and beg the inter-
> national community for help. For the past five years, this people
> demonized by its Tutsi detractors and their allies and betrayed para-
> doxically by its own political leaders who just lost about 2 million
> people who are now are nearly a third their size before the war of
> October 1, 1990 [when the RPF attacked to start the civil war] and
> risk disappearing if nothing is quickly done to help them. The Hutu
> leaders, who should be most concerned by this cry for help, must
> now change their behavior, recognizing their errors of the past and
> correcting them without delay in order to develop a common strat-
> egy that privileges all those who can take this people out of their
> disarray.[151]

---

150. See Annex 92, including both Kambanda's communiqué and other MRND official
statements: http://rwandadelaguerreaugenocide.univ-paris1.fr/wp-content/uploads/2010/01/
Annexe_92.pdf.

151. Bagosora 1995, p. 6.

Here Bagosora sets out the stakes of the issue, a presentation that is consistent with his actions at the start of the genocide. In effect, he writes, the Hutus are at risk of disappearing. Moreover, he clearly frames the struggle as one between Hutus and Tutsis: The Tutsis are those who threaten the Hutu people, aided in this case by Hutu disunity. Bagosora continues by framing the fight as one that is a legacy of the past, in particular the Revolution:

> For the record, the Hutu leaders know well that the RPF emanates from the political party UNAR (the Rwandan National Union) and its *Inyenzi* militia that between 1960 and 1967 had tried time and time again to recapture power by force but without success. The Tutsi minority had lost this power that it had held for nearly four centuries following the 1959 Social Revolution of the Hutu people. The Hutu leaders will thus not ignore that the UNAR-Inyenzi rebaptized the RPF-Inkotanyi have returned with the same objective.

And he continues on the next page: "Do we need to remind ourselves that the Hutu-Tutsi conflict was not evoked during the Arusha negotiations even though everyone knows that the October 1 war was a war of revenge to recapture power that they had lost after the revolution of the Hutu people in 1959?"[152] There are two key points here. The first is that the conflict is clearly framed, again, as a fight between Hutu and Tutsi. Bagosora felt the need to remind his audience that despite what everyone may say the real story is that the Tutsis who lost power in the Revolution are now fighting to recapture power by force. In other words, the founding narrative shapes how he frames and understands the conflict and the enemy that he faces. The second key point is that the Tutsis are presented as unitary actors who across generations want the same thing. The RPF are the UNAR are the Tutsis, and all of them stand for oppressing Hutus. They are both unitary and unwinnable—that is, as I have argued, one of the conditions that make the logic of genocide possible. He proceeded over the next few pages to describe the Tutsis as cunning, manipulative, lying Nilotics who are "conceited and arrogant [and] inclined to impose their supremacy" and committed to "cruel and bloody" rule over Hutus; by contrast, the Hutus are portrayed as naive and divided. The Tutsis never share power, he argues, and that is why the Revolution occurred.[153] Such is the lead-in to the genocide period:

> One has to think of the assassination of Presidents Habyarimana of Rwanda and Ntaryamira of Burundi as the ultimate provocation that

---

152. Bagosora 1995, pp. 7–8.
153. Bagosora 1995, pp. 9–16.

expose to all that a logic of war that held in all ranks of the RPF for four years. . . . This is the Rwandan drama. . . . The Tutsi minority wants to seize power at all costs and the Hutu majority disagrees. . . . In effect, the Tutsis, at once conceited, arrogant, conniving, and perfidious remain convinced that the good Tutsi is a Tutsi in power and that the good Hutu is the so-called moderate Hutu who serves the interests of Tutsis unconditionally. On the other hand is the Hutu who is at once modest, candid, loyal, independent, and impulsive who since the social Revolution of 1959 no longer wants to hear of Tutsi domination.[154]

In other words, the conflict that shaped the genocide period is an epic one, between Tutsi domination and Hutu freedom, and the enemy, as seen through Rwanda's founding narrative, is committed to a "logic of war." He continues in this vein for some time, arguing: "The assassination of Habyarimana was the ultimate operation of the RPF-Inkotanyi for reconquering power but the strategy behind it included a major mistake in not appreciating the consequences of such a decision or they had to close their eyes before the price."[155]

Here again it is clear that Bagosora's understanding of the past—of what his Rwanda stands for, of what the nature of the struggle is—shapes his interpretation of events. The assassination of the president was seen as the "ultimate operation" of the very same Tutsis who would never give up power and never recognize the Revolution. And the consequences, he argues, were misjudged—in effect, mass killing of Tutsis, which he suggests is the natural consequence of the RPF's actions.[156]

In sum, Rwanda had the two main ingredients that drive mass categorical violence and genocide: a major, material military threat and a nationalist founding narrative that framed the war as a fight between two identity groups, one of which deserved to rule and the other of which did not. How decision-making elites understood what Rwanda was for—in this case, for the freedom of Hutus in the name of the Revolution—influenced how they interpreted the actions of their opponents in war and how they developed what they considered to be appropriate responses. Their opponents in this case were advancing militarily, and they were likely responsible for killing the president. They were militarily superior and threatening. But what that

---

154. Bagosora 1995, p. 18.
155. Bagosora 1995, p. 20.
156. See also excerpts from his 2005 interrogation before the International Criminal Tribunal for Rwanda in 2005 where he articulated a similar logic and defended the 1991 Military Commission that identified the enemy as those who opposed the Revolution: http://rwandadelaguerreaugenocide. univ-paris1.fr/wp-content/uploads/2010/01/Annexe_7.pdf.

meant and how it was understood, and in turn what was perceived as a legitimate counter-strategy—these were influenced by the dominant narrative in decision-makers' heads.

Like Guichaoua and others, I believe that the policy of genocide emerged over time, in response to events. I am not convinced that the policy was a well-thought-out strategy. But the logic of violence reflected the idea that the principal political community was facing a dire, existential threat and that the enemy was an unwinnable and uncontainable identity group. Whether the elites thought that mass violence would help them win, impose a pyrrhic victory, or allow them to win in a future round of fighting is difficult to know. All three strategies may have been present, as may have been collective revenge. But the violence had a logic of its own, one that was an expression of how elites framed it—in particular, as an epic struggle between the majority people and a minority bent on their oppression, a framing that was a direct consequence of the country's founding narrative.

Rwanda had other elements that made the perpetration of mass violence possible. First, the state had the organizational capacity and territorial domination to exercise violence in a sustained fashion across time and space. In this case, the means occurred through a centralized state with a penetrating local administration and deep institutions and expectations around popular mobilization. Although the state was deeply contested in the multiparty era, the administrative structures and the idea of the state remained very strong in the countryside. Moreover, there was a war, an advancing army, a dead president and prime minister, and violence all around. This combination of acute insecurity and an extensive administration, coupled with a broad awareness of identity categories and their salience, drove widespread participation. Rwanda's founding narrative did not motivate most perpetrators, but the terms that they were asked to mobilize around—Hutu self-protection in the context of Tutsi aggression—built on familiar tropes in the society. They resonated, especially in the context of a state telling people that Hutus were in danger and using an effective administration to enforce participation.[157]

By the same token, other restraint mechanisms were limited. An international peacekeeping force existed, but the peacekeeping force was famously ill prepared and under-mandated to stand as an interposition forces between the two sides. Moreover, after ten Belgian peacekeepers were killed on April 7 and with the precedent of an international fiasco in Somalia less than a year earlier, key international actors and the United Nations Department of Peacekeeping Office moved to emasculate the international force rather than

---

157. This paragraph builds on the argument and evidence presented in Straus 2006b.

to buttress it.[158] In short, the international peacekeeping force was too weak to restrain the rapid escalation of violence following the resumption of war and in the period just prior to April 1994.

Like Côte d'Ivoire, agricultural exports—chiefly coffee and tea—were among the central sources of foreign currency in the country. In Rwanda, too, the production of coffee and tea took place on smallholder plots, as well as some larger state-run estates. Both Hutus and Tutsis grew the crops. Yet in contrast to Côte d'Ivoire, the size of the Rwandan sector was small. Côte d'Ivoire is a global giant in the growth of these crops, and the economic success that they have bestowed on Côte d'Ivoire looms large in the Ivoirian imagination and indeed in the nationalist narrative of that country. In Rwanda, the chief economic sectors were too weak to serve as a major bulwark against violence. The genocide did devastate production: The four-year average between 1989 and 1993 for Rwanda was 35,000 tons of green coffee and 13,000 tons of tea. In 1994, coffee exports fell to 1,274 tons and tea to 4,136 tons, according to the Food and Agricultural Organization. By contrast, in the decade from 1999 to 2008, Côte d'Ivoire averaged 1.3 million tons of cocoa and nearly 200,000 tons of coffee.[159] Similarly, Rwanda had a tiny middle class. A recent African Development Bank report put the figure at 2.6 percent of the population, compared to Côte d'Ivoire's 18.9 percent.[160]

While there was a small human rights and non-affiliated civil society in Rwanda, the NGO sector was no match for the ruling party, the state, and the military. Moreover, as discussed in chapter 2, the churches were key civil society institutions, but the leadership in the Catholic Church in particular was close to the ruling party and even, as Timothy Longman argues, facilitated the genocide. In sum, we have little in the way of strong restraint factors in the Rwandan case.

To conclude, I wish to make two points. First, I have presented a case study that pinpoints dynamic developments and processes, ones that eventually shaped a genocide against the Rwandan Tutsi population. I have highlighted the ways in which a founding narrative was forged at independence, maintained during the first and second republics, and then invoked to counter a military threat. However, nothing about these processes was inevitable. The founding narrative of the state did not have to be Hutu majoritarian democracy. History influenced that choice, in particular the ways in which the

158. On the international dimensions, see Barnett 2002; Dallaire and Beardsley 2005; Melvern 2000.
159. All of these data come from the FAO: http://faostat.fao.org/.
160. The percentages represent the lower and upper middle-class categories in the AFDB report (but not the "floating" middle class). African Development Bank 2011.

colonialists had interpreted the society they had encountered and established a governing structure. But the actions of the Tutsi elite, the Hutu counter-elite, and the Belgian authorities at the time shaped a course of events that produced a specific nationalist synthesis. In other words, the actors and the dynamics of action and counter-reaction were decisive. Similarly, at every step of Rwanda's postcolonial history, political actors could have decisively tacked away from the Revolution as the founding narrative. Yet on the whole they did not. And in the crucial period in April 1994 when facing a political void and a raging war, several options remained on the table. The force of the revolutionary ideology coupled with the intensity of war influenced the course of events, but they were not deterministic. Political and military elites made choices, ones that had devastating consequences.

The final point concerns contemporary Rwanda. The RPF has controlled the Rwandan state since the genocide. They have established a new founding narrative, one that eliminates ethnicity from public discourse, modernizes the economy, and overall seeks to remake the country in a new image.[161] One specific element of the new founding narrative is to claim that the former regimes in Rwanda were animated by a "genocide ideology," and indeed, the parliament has passed laws that criminalize the use of "genocide ideology." That law in turn has been used to muzzle the opposition, the human rights community, and the press.[162] My analysis in this chapter and throughout the book is not inconsistent with the idea of a "genocidal ideology." However, there are crucial differences. My argument is that particular ways of framing the nation and the state's main political project lend themselves to a logic of genocide. Rwanda had that. But such violence occurs in particular circumstances, in particular during intense wars, in which the founding narrative shapes how decision-making elites respond to and frame the threats that they face. Without war, and probably without a devastating shock like the presidential assassination, genocide would not have occurred in Rwanda. Moreover, mass categorical violence and genocide require political actors who are committed to it. There is agency. In short, a founding narrative of the type I have described is not the same as genocide, and certainly the idea of distinct ethnic groups—a claim that has been used to brandish charges of "genocide ideology"—is not the same as genocide. And perhaps it goes without saying: Criminalizing political narratives that could, in some circumstances, lead to mass categorical violence and genocide is not the most effective and certainly not the most democratic way to handle their existence.

---

161. Straus and Waldorf 2011.
162. Longman 2011; Waldorf 2011.

Conclusion
Making Nations and Preventing Their Unmaking

This chapter addresses some loose ends in the book. Two in particular: the policy implications of my findings and the theoretical implications of my emphasis on the legacy of political ideas.

Like other areas of research, genocide studies sits uncomfortably between scholarship and prescription. To understand the drivers of genocide, some analysts put research questions and evidence first. My book is clearly in that camp. The book does not let the art of the politically possible shape my explanation. But my topic is *genocide*, and, like other scholars, I hope the research will aid policy designed to lessen the likelihood of the phenomenon.

I see two sets of policy implications. The first concerns diagnostic frameworks. Policymakers, civil society actors, and concerned citizens place a premium on "early warning" systems to predict where genocide is likely to occur. Most early warning diagnostic tools take existing theory and create quantitative models to forecast which countries are at risk of genocide.

The emphasis on prediction makes good sense. In the fast-paced rhythm of the policy world, assessments that clearly and quickly sort cases into genocide-likely and genocide-unlikely are very valuable. However, as discussed in the introduction, current models lead to a large number of "false positives" or cases that appear at risk of genocide but that do not result in genocide.

My findings could translate into quantitative variables. However, I think they are better equipped for country-specific, qualitative assessments, which would complement quantitative forecasting models. In the appendix, I translate the book's various claims into three sets of questions that policymakers and others can ask of specific situations. The questions concern (1) broad risk factors, (2) short-term dynamics of escalation, and (3) patterns of violence that indicate the onset of genocide or mass categorical violence. These diagnostic questions should help analysts determine whether a country is likely to move from a country at risk of genocide to one where genocide is probable or is in the beginning stages.

My arguments also have implications for how to prevent and respond to genocide, for both domestic and international actors. Scholars, like me, with limited direct policy-making experience are not ideally positioned to craft specific recommendations for what to do. Moreover, every situation is different, and what is possible in different situations will vary considerably. My approach, then, is to propose policy principles that should help reduce the long-term risk of genocide or mitigate escalation once genocide starts.

Preventing and Responding to Genocide

I afford a central role to political agency in the process of "making nations." In the African context, most states are ethnically and religiously heterogeneous. The long-term best asset against the risk of genocide and mass categorical violence is to craft a political vision that incorporates a role for multiple identities as fundamental to the project of the state. Leaders often rule with narrow and particularistic interests, to be sure, and there is no reason to be naive about their willingness to embrace or instill pluralism. Yet many political elites want to do right by their country, and they have some autonomy in how they construct the nation and, ultimately, in how they allocate power and goods. Multiethnic nations can be made. In the end, articulating a nationalist narrative of pluralism and inclusion provides the greatest source of restraint.

Banning identity, which the post-genocide state in Rwanda has done, is not the solution. Simply eliminating references to categorical identities by fiat will not destroy their resonance. Rather, the idea is to create a nationalist vision—to make nations—in a way that recognizes the fundamentally multi-identity character of the population. Practice also matters hugely. A beautifully crafted, pluralist narrative that masks the total domination of one or two groups at the expense of others will not do the trick. Even in low-information settings that characterize poor countries, citizens are not dummies. They know whom the state serves.

In the book, Léopold Senghor and Alpha Oumar Konaré are heroes. At transition moments, they created, defended, defended again, and practiced a pluralist vision of their nation, one rooted in the local realities and cultures of Senegal and Mali, respectively. Felix Houphouët-Boigny was more instrumentally pluralist. He also favored his own group as superior, but nonetheless he practiced and preached a vision of a tolerant, unified, peaceful, multiethnic Côte d'Ivoire. And he backed that with enormous gains for his country.

These men were not alone, in Africa or beyond. Julius Nyerere in Tanzania created a lasting pluralist legacy in his country; he sought and practiced a nationalist vision that strongly deemphasized particularistic ethnic and religious identities. In South Africa, Nelson Mandela articulated a founding narrative of a "Rainbow" nation, as good a metaphor as any for multiethnicity and pluralism and one that would be a strong bulwark against any future leaders who wanted to escalate violence in that country.

Charismatic, visionary leaders like Mandela, Nyerere, Senghor, Konaré, and Houphouët are few and far between. But even in places as diverse and challenging as postwar Nigeria, leaders have made sustained efforts to build multiethnic coalitions and institutionalize them in ways that have reduced the risk of a return to mass categorical violence and genocide in those places.

Making nations is not a uniquely African problem in the contemporary world. Many states—low-income and high-income—face questions about how to manage diversity. Many states in the world govern multiethnic and multireligious states. The question is how to recognize diversity while not inherently making the state the political territory of one group at the expense of another.

There are role models outside Africa too. Mahatma Gandhi created an integrationist vision for his country and his party that created a reserve of restraint against the escalation of mass violence. This does not mean that India is without identity-based violence, and indeed counternarratives, such as Hindu nationalism, remain powerful in that country. But Gandhi's vision and its legacy in India's Congress Party serves as a robust counterbalance to any efforts to escalate violence on a group-selective basis.

Another long-term domestic prevention measure is to find ways to avoid or end armed conflict. The outbreak of war and the attendant threats that accompany war remain the single largest influence on the occurrence of mass categorical violence and genocide. There are exceptions to what is nearly a rule of thumb—"no war, no genocide"—but even those, as I have shown, reveal how elites perceive themselves to be at war. In short, domestic leaders who wish to avoid genocide and mass categorical violence should work very hard to avoid war. Should war occur, they should find ways to reach a negotiated settlement. Conflict management is a major form of genocide prevention.

Of course, ending wars is not easy, and the military and political elites who are willing to commit mass violence are not likely to back down quickly in the face of armed challenges to their rule. Nonetheless, as a general rule of thumb, finding ways to avoid or mitigate armed conflict remains an imperative—one that has long-term developmental benefits as well.[1]

Diversifying economies, especially those that are reliant on high-value, enclaved mineral exports, is also a long-term mechanism to reduce the risk of mass categorical violence and genocide. The greater the domestic costs to escalation, the greater will be the domestic restraint against mass violence.

Diversified economies are not firewalls against genocide, and clever leaders can find ways to turn war and violence into sources of domestic economic rents. But in general diversified economies create domestic incentives and pressure to moderate violence.

Many economic sectors are vulnerable to the disruption that mass violence causes, including export agriculture, most manufacturing, and many services. Snapping one's fingers and producing such economies is a pipe dream, but the arguments in this book provide an additional rationale (beyond economics and welfare) for investments in diversified economies. In sum, diversified economic development is a form of genocide prevention.

The same logic applies to the need for robust and independent civil societies. Like economic restraints, civil society restraints can be overcome by determined military and political elites. However, the more diversified the political and social space, the greater will be the domestic restraint against the escalation of violence. Again, one should not be naive about domestic civil society, which is often an appendage of ruling authorities, adheres to international donors and has weak domestic roots, or is illiberal itself (militias can be seen as a form of civil society). Nonetheless, in theory, a robust and independent civil society can articulate counternarratives to the escalation of violence.

Finally, ensuring accountability for past human rights violations sends a signal that such violence, even if committed in the name of a higher purpose, is not acceptable. Threat and founding narratives provide elites and followers with a rationale for committing violence against certain groups. But the premise of human rights is that certain kinds of violations are never acceptable.

---

1. As the World Bank's 2011 World Development Report showed.

Building a credible record around human rights claims is therefore one way to undermine the "thinkability" of genocide and mass categorical violence.

Especially important is when accountability is not one-sided. Political justice—that is, justice that amounts to winners using courts and other accountability means to disenfranchise losers—does not send a signal that human rights violations are wrong. The message there is about the importance of winning. But justice that stings even those who are in power sends a strong message about the unacceptability of violence against civilians.

In the long run, I conclude that domestic actors are likely to be more effective than international ones at prevention. Ultimately, the dynamics that give rise to the escalation of mass violence emanate from domestic decision-making, leadership, and political bargains about the distribution of power and opportunity.

That said, international actors can play a supporting role. They can reward and encourage each of these measures through a variety of diplomatic and material measures. They can build personal relationships and professional networks with domestic actors through training and exchange programs, education, and diplomacy. However, it is very difficult, if not impossible, for international actors to impose new political narratives or to impose peace on ruling elites who do not want to compromise.

When war does persist, international actors should act to mitigate threat. Acute security fears animate genocide, and where possible international actors should encourage belligerents to clarify their objectives and to make promises not to harm or disenfranchise whole categories of civilians. International actors should look to mediate disputes and provide reliable, third-party information to all sides in a conflict.

International actors can also deploy peacekeepers to conflict environments. Once there, they should be aware of the dangers at hand; they should have sufficient force strength and equipment to serve as a real deterrent; they should have backing from a major international power; they should engage in organizational learning and be sensitive to local dynamics; they should seek to remain neutral and transparent and do everything possible to disassociate themselves from one party or another; and they should develop a network of domestic actors whom they can lobby should the violence begin to escalate.[2] Of particular value is where international peacekeepers can physically separate armed actors and have the capacity to enforce that separation—to create an interposition force—as they did in Côte d'Ivoire.

---

2. The recommendations here are a synthesis of Autesserre 2010; Dallaire and Beardsley 2005; Fortna 2008; and Howard 2008.

Such measures will not work in every case. Narrow interests often undermine capacious ideals. Ruling elites may favor exclusion, armed conflict, mineral economies, weak or coopted civil society, impunity, and feckless international intervention. I also recognize how practically difficult implementing these suggestions are. Nonetheless the book's findings provide a theoretical foundation for why these principles should work to reduce the long-term risk of genocide and mass categorical violence.

Response Measures

A different set of dynamics applies when mass violence is under way. All the options listed above remain open: Political leaders can emphasize a pluralist narrative, they can opt for peace, they can seek accountability for human rights violations, and they can encourage civil society actors. However, if the situation is one where political and military authorities are pushing their polities and militaries toward escalation, then the chances that such measures will be pursued are slim. As a consequence, the onus for action shifts from domestic actors to external ones.

That said, there are exceptions to that rule, in particular around the question of resistance. Domestic actors do not have to remain passive to the escalation of violence.

In chapter 3, I argued that political and military leaders must forge three consolidation nodes to succeed with their policies: at the elite, subnational, and popular (individual) levels. In theory, spirited domestic actors can seek to disrupt these processes. They can lobby elites inside a potential coalition of perpetrators to oppose the escalation of violence. Even in the face of a determined set of authorities, policies of genocide and mass categorical violence are hard to sustain in the absence of an elite consensus. The same is true for subnational actors and ordinary civilians. Depending on the circumstances, they may experience themselves to be relatively powerless. But my arguments suggest that their participation (in the case of subnational actors) and acquiescence (in the case of the public) are critical for the consolidation of a policy of mass categorical violence and genocide. By consequence, their resistance could decrease the likelihood of such events.

Would-be victims also have choices. They should find mechanisms to avoid perpetrators' control over them. I have argued that a component of capacity is effective domination of would-be perpetrators over would-be victims. If the latter worry about escalation, they should look for ways to increase the chances of evasion and exit—through accumulating cash reserves, developing underground escape networks, and the like. Self-arming is risky. If would-be perpetrators claim that target groups are part of the threat structure, arming could increase such perceptions, even if the weaponry might have the effect of decreasing would-be perpetrators' control over such groups.

In contrast to domestic actors caught in the vortex of escalation, international actors have a greater range of action. In the late stages of escalation, my analysis suggests that international actors should keep three broad principles in mind: reduce threats, impose costs, and decrease the capacity to inflict violence.

If a conflict deteriorates and two sides prepare to fight each other, the task of reducing threat is not an easy one. Peacekeepers are not hardwired for combat. Yet at some level, external military actors should try to intervene in situations where there is a risk of escalation to mass categorical violence and genocide. In such situations, they should be equipped to stand in the way of those who would escalate an armed conflict.

Barring that, they should develop mechanisms for reducing perceptions of threat. They should work with belligerents to communicate goals that might alleviate the fears of the opposing side, and they should work with belligerents to demonstrate that they will protect civilians.

The second main arena where external actors should be effective is in the realm of imposing costs. My analysis suggests that domestic actors who favor the escalation of violence make conscious decisions. They may not have fully worked out strategies or tactics in mind, but they make decisions to escalate or not and to unleash maximum violence or not. In making those decisions, they analyze their playing field, looking at the international environment, the domestic costs, and their ability to win over key elite, subnational, and popular segments of the society. External actors can influence that decision-making process. They can credibly threaten criminal prosecution, they can impose targeted sanctions, they can institute travel bans, and they can withhold present and future assistance.

The book's discussion of domestic restraints suggests that different places and leaders will be more and less receptive to the imposition of such costs. In places such as Côte d'Ivoire and Kenya, where state revenue depends on international markets and trade, where large middle classes with international profiles exist, and where ruling elites have been educated or have children being educated abroad, the effectiveness of imposing costs is likely to be greater. More international integration means that the withholding of international benefits will be felt more sharply. Nonetheless, a clear implication of the book is that imposing costs on would-be perpetrators should have an effect, at least at the margins.

The last set of options open to external actors is to disrupt capacity. I have outlined the ways in which perpetrators forge the capacity to sustain large-scale violence against civilians. In principle, at least three of the dimensions of capacity should be open to disruption. International actors could seek to interrupt multi-agency coordination through direct actions such as jamming communication or indirect action such as lobbying key actors across an elite coalition. If public media are a mechanism for achieving coordination, then external actors might jam or take out those media.

International actors could also seek to decrease the capacity of perpetrators to control victim groups. The main action should be to use force to protect civilians or to use force to create safe areas that can be reliably defended. If the execution of mass violence requires access to target populations, external actors can disrupt that process.

Finally, international actors can seek to disrupt the capacity to inflict violence. They can seek to seize weapons stocks or otherwise take away the capacity of perpetrators to harm civilian groups. They might interrupt weapons shipments. In the last resort scenario, international actors can intervene militarily to defeat the perpetrators.

Again, none of these measures is easy or palatable. Sometimes they will not work. Each carries risk. Many of these measures are coercive, and some international actors will object to the ways in which coercive military actions override sovereignty. That, however, is a debate for another place. The main purpose here is to derive practical principles from the theoretical arguments that I develop in the book. The politics of those principles is a separate—and complicated—question.

Ideas and Politics

Beyond the role of restraint, the most theoretically distinctive dimension of my argument concerns the ways in which ideas and ideology shape strategic behavior in war. In general, the political science literature on violence has come to downplay the role of ideology and even identity in explaining the onset, duration, and variation in different forms of political violence.[3] My in-depth research shows, by contrast, that strategies of violence have ideational foundations.

Genocide and mass categorical violence are specific outcomes. The outcomes may be outliers in terms of thinking through the role of ideas in

---

3. For a recent exception, see Gutiérrez Sanín and Wood 2014.

shaping political processes. But perhaps not. While aware that ideational arguments risk circularity, I emerge from this book convinced that political culture and ideology shape decision-making in subtle but often profound ways. If part of the social scientist's task is to explain processes and outcomes, in particular comparatively, we would be remiss if we neglect the role of ideas in influencing political decision-making and structuring variation across countries.

Two questions, at least, about the role of ideas in politics remain. One concerns the origins of the founding narratives whose causal impact I insist upon. Are those narratives endogenous to some other factor that is "really" what shapes genocide?

Looking comparatively, I do not see some structural or strategic reason why political leaders in some places but not others sought to ground their nations and states around a core identity group—with perhaps one exception.

For example, the number of ethnic groups does not cause more inclusive or pluralist narratives. One could imagine that a pluralist founding narrative derives from a strategy of building a minimum winning coalition.[4] In this case, political elites might look for an ideology that reflects a cold strategy of finding a majority of 50 percent but not one that is so large as to share political spoils.

But that is not the case. If that logic were operative in Côte d'Ivoire, one might imagine Houphouët at independence to have sought a Christian coalition of southerners, rather than to build a multiethnic nation that clearly included a role for northern Muslims. In Mali, one might have expected a Mandé coalition (and ideology), yet the 1990s leaders sought to craft an inclusive vision of the state.

Another claim could be that majoritarian narratives built around a primary political community develop in states where there is overwhelming demographic dominance of one ethnic group. Such is the case in Rwanda and Burundi. But that is not the case in Sudan, where the state has dozens and dozens of ethnic groups but where northern elites have consistently favored Arab-Islamic nationalism.

Moreover, narratives built around overwhelming majorities were, in principle, available to political elites in Senegal and Mali, respectively. Senegal could have developed a Muslim-oriented nationalist narrative. Senghor could well not have become the first independence leader. The same is true for Mali, where political elites could have favored a southern, sedentary, or

---

4. The argument would be derivative of the claims in Posner 2005 and Christia 2012.

Bambaran-language majority, to the exclusion of the minority Tuaregs and Arabs. But this did not happen.

Yet another argument could be that the economic value of the would-be downgraded group matters. Perhaps in Côte d'Ivoire Houphouët developed an inclusionary narrative because he needed the labor of Muslims and northerners, for example. Inclusionary narratives are a function of the economic value of the would-be excluded groups.

But that argument does not travel. In Mali, the Tuaregs and Arabs were marginal to the economy, as were the Joola in Senegal. By contrast, the Tutsi were the most powerful economically in Rwanda at independence.

In sum, while I may be unaware of some missing variable, I do not see some underlying political economy or mathematical explanation for why some founding narratives are inclusive and pluralist while others are hierarchical and built around one primary community to the detriment of others.

The main influence is history. When crafting founding narratives, political elites worked from the raw material of their societies. They grounded the stories of their states and nations on the social, cultural, and often political elements around them. If they did not—if they created narratives that had little social, cultural, or political resonance—then the founding narratives would have had little staying power. There is autonomy; other leaders using similar raw material could have chosen otherwise. Nonetheless, context matters.

Especially important are the historically determined frames of reference at the point when political elites craft narratives. Political elites do not invent terms and narratives from whole cloth. They synthesize, emphasize, and shape what is around them.

At independence, the colonial legacy was highly significant. In Rwanda, the colonial political system and the colonial-era political discourse around race formed the raw material that went into the Hutu Revolution. The same is true in Sudan. Would the northern elites have imagined a fundamentally Arab-Islamic character to their nation in the absence of a history of slave-running, exploitation, and institutional developments that occurred under Ottoman rule? Probably not. Sudanese nationalism and resistance to it would have looked differently had the British not colonized and administered Sudan differently.

By the same token, it is probably no accident that the main negative cases in the book were former French colonies. As a general statement, France ruled its African colonies with a more fluid sense of identity than did the British, the Portuguese, and the Belgians. The French had an integrationist approach to colonialism; their vision was that Africans could become French even while retaining their tribal roots. In the terminal colonial period, African leaders also joined the French parliamentary system—indeed, Senghor and Houphouët both participated in it. In short, it is likely that the French integrationist model created a more fluid and plausibly plural sense of identity than did other European colonial models of rule and identity.

That is not an ironclad rule. In the African context, Julius Nyerere and Nelson Mandela—to name two pluralist visionaries—come from Anglophone contexts. One cannot also forget that France was an ally of the Habyarimana government in Rwanda, that Chad with its problems is a former French colony, as was Cambodia. In other words, I am not applauding French colonialism or French actions in Africa in some blanket way. But, in contrast to other European ex-colonial states, at independence the idea of building nations on the basis of a primary ethnic or religious political community, to the detriment of another community, was less thinkable in a French context than in other contexts.

The determinants of variation among African nationalists clearly deserve greater research. An early generation of Africanist scholarship focused on the determinants of nationalism but framed the question around the quest for self-rule. But less research exists that explains variation in the underlying character of visions of the national political community and the purpose of the state.

The last question about the legacy of political ideas is a broader one: Do ideas independently shape big political outcomes? I suspect I will have convinced few skeptics or, if I have, I will have convinced them that ideas matter for extreme, rare, normally unthinkable events such as genocide. But beyond that, their skepticism may remain.

As a recovering skeptic, I am not so sure. I understand why economistic, rationalist, and institutionalist models have become dominant in the social sciences. They often provide clear causal pathways; they provide the basis for predictions; and there is something deeply satisfying about seeing an underlying mathematical logic to otherwise complex political processes.

Ideology and culture are messier. They are harder to measure. The logic can feel circular. But this study nonetheless has convinced me that political ideas are independent forces that shape outcomes in ways that are both visible and invisible. When social scientists look to explain outcomes, and variation among outcomes, we are remiss if we ignore how ideas influence politics.

APPENDIX

Identifying the Risk of Genocide and Mass Categorical Violence

Broad Risk Factors

Broad risk factors refer to structural conditions that I have argued are the conditions that generally need to be present in order for genocide or mass categorical violence to be the strategic choice of a political or military elite.

1. **Acute Threat:** Is there evidence that the leadership of a state (or another organization capable of committing mass atrocities) experiences a heightened security risk?
   a. Is the country engaged in an armed conflict?
      i. If not, is there some organized resistance to existing authorities that those authorities interpret as an elevated security risk?
   b. If so, what are the military capabilities of the armed resistance?
      i. Do they have now or could they have the military capability to unseat the existing authorities?
      ii. Does the armed resistance have, or are they interpreted to have, a powerful ally who has an adversarial relationship to existing authorities?
      iii. In the ways that political and military elites describe the conflict, do they claim that they face a highly dangerous foe?

c. Do existing authorities experience acute vulnerability tied to the armed conflict?

   i. What are the military capabilities of the authorities?

   ii. Is the ruling coalition significantly divided and fractured?

   iii. Is the army loyal to the political authorities?

   iv. Does the ruling coalition represent a minority ethnic or religious group fighting armed elements associated with the majority, that is, is there a demographic vulnerability?

   v. In the ways that political and military elites describe the conflict, do they claim that they are acutely vulnerable and being undermined from within?

2. **Founding Narratives:** Does a grounding ideology posit a primary ethnic, religious, or other political community in a plural state or a core mission of transformation that identifies a specific community as the enemy of that transformation?

a. Is there a founding narrative of the state that was promulgated when that state came into existence or at key transitions thereafter?

   i. If so, what is the core vision of the state and nation?

      1. Does the founding narrative create a primary political community in whose interests the state serves?

      2. Does the founding narrative indicate that one identity group should rule while another should not?

      3. Does the founding narrative seek to transform the society away from a past associated with a particular identity group, such as an ethnic group, a social class, or a group associated with the former regime?

      4. Does the founding narrative hold that the state serves to protect the interests of a minority who are threatened by a majority?

      5. Is or was the founding narrative articulated by a highly influential figure and inculcated through official media?

b. Is there any past political behavior on the part of the would-be perpetrators that suggests a willingness to use violence to defend the core mission of the state?

      1. Have political authorities used the founding narrative in the past to justify preexisting violence against civilians?

      2. Has violence been committed in the past against the would-be victim group in the name of founding narrative?

      3. Has there been any criminal or political accountability for violence committed in the name of the founding narrative?

   c. If there is a founding narrative that exists along these lines, is there a counter-narrative that runs contrary to the tenets of exclusion?

      i. Is there a counter-narrative that defines the national community as fundamentally plural?

      ii. Is there a counter-narrative that defines the national community as being fundamentally not about identity?

      iii. Is there a counter-narrative that defines the core values of the state around inclusion, accommodation, dialogue, harmony, and peace?

3. **Other Factors of Restraint:** Are there domestic or international structures in place that would encourage the deescalation or non-escalation of violence, and, if so, how strong are such structures?

   a. Is the dominant economic sector in the country on which the state depends for revenue sensitive to the escalation of violence?

      i. Would the escalation of violence disrupt significant revenue to the state or jeopardize the main income source of influential elites in the society?

         1. Are the would-be targets of violence essential to the continued vitality of the dominant economic sector?

         2. Does the industry depend on widespread social stability in order to produce and deliver to market the goods in question?

         3. Is the area in which the dominant economic sector exists large or small, that is, is it enclaved?

      ii. Is there a significant number of economic elites in the country who would be negatively impacted by the escalation of violence?

         1. Are the economic elites who benefit from the violence-sensitive industry connected to the ruling military or the political elite?

         2. Do the economic elites who benefit have institutional mechanisms to articulate their concerns about the economic risks of escalation?

   b. Is there a significantly large civil society with interests and political views that are independent of the would-be perpetrators of violence?

      i. Is the civil society organized enough to articulate their views in the face of possible state repression?

      ii. Do civil society actors have connections to international civil society networks?

iii. Are there local civil society mechanisms that are strong enough to resist the escalation of violence in their communities?

c. Is there external collective action to respond to the risk of escalation of violence?

   i. Is there a military interposition force that can protect civilians or separate armed actors?

     1. Does the military interposition force have the mandate, equipment, and intelligence to act decisively in the face of an escalation of violence?

     2. Does the military interposition force provide reliable information to both sides in the armed conflict about the military preparations of the adversaries?

     3. In the event of a United Nations operation, does the military interposition force have a strong, Permanent Five member backing the force?

   ii. Is there a regional organization that has acted clearly to tamp down the escalation of violence?

     1. Has the regional organization legitimized the operation of a military interposition force?

   iii. Are there other sources of domestic or external restraint that would present a significant obstacle to the escalation of group-selective violence?

     1. For example, are there widespread norms of interpersonal institutions of intergroup reciprocity that would need to be overcome for the escalation of violence to succeed?

4. **Capacity for Violence:** Do would-be perpetrators have the capacity to inflict violence across time and space against a target group?

a. Do perpetrators have the capacity to coordinate a coalition of actors at both the national and local levels?

   i. Do perpetrators have the loyalty of at least a significant segment of the national military and national government?

     1. Will they be able to achieve horizontal coordination among elites?

   ii. Do perpetrators have the loyalty of subnational, local armed actors?

     1. Would national-local (vertical) coordination be achieved through an existing bureaucracy, that is, through a civilian administration?

    2. Would national-local coordination be achieved through decentralized mechanisms, such as an alliance of interests?

  b. Do perpetrators have the capacity to identify would-be targets of violence?

    i. Do perpetrators have the ability to sort target populations?

      1. Are there identifiable markers or other instruments that perpetrators can use to identify specific targets of violence?

        a. Have they created such markers?

      2. Are there local actors allied with perpetrators who know who is who?

    ii. Is the would-be target group highly concentrated in a region, such that group identity markers are unnecessary?

  c. Do perpetrators have the capacity to control the would-be target populations?

    i. Are would-be victim groups physically accessible to would-be perpetrator groups?

    ii. Do would-be perpetrators have the capacity to control the movement of would-be victim groups?

    iii. Do would-be perpetrators have the ability to overcome any resistance on the part of would-be victim groups?

  d. Do perpetrators have the capacity to inflict violence across time and space?

    i. Beyond the capacity to coordinate coalitions over space and time, is there sufficient weaponry to inflict violence in a sustained way against the victim group?

  e. Do perpetrators have the capacity to insure, at a minimum, popular quiescence?

    i. That is, can perpetrators insure that they will not face a popular resistance movement to their campaign of violence?

These are the primary indicators that flow from the arguments in the book. The list here is designed not to be comprehensive but to translate how the arguments that I have made would translate into specific indicators.

Short-Term Dynamics of Escalation

While broad risk factors are helpful in assessing whether a particular place has the general ingredients for the escalation of group-selective violence, the framework does not provide insight into the timing of when such a risk is particularly high. As a general rule, my research suggests that the risk of such violence increases (or decreases) when there is movement on the four main axes identified in the previous section. More specifically:

1. **Is there evidence of increased threat perception?**
   a. Are there events or battlefield changes that significantly increase threat?
      i. Is there a sudden military advance against the would-be perpetrators?
      ii. Is there a game-changing event, such as a high-level assassination or coup attempt, against the would-be perpetrator coalition?
      iii. Is there an entry into the war of a third party who will ally with the would-be perpetrators' enemy?
      iv. Have the would-be perpetrators seized control of territory but found itself with a population it fears it cannot control?
      v. Is there a sharp deterioration of relations between opposing armed actors, such that would-be perpetrators may fear a renewed attack?
         1. Is there a breakdown of peace negotiations?
         2. Is there a breakdown of an electoral process?
      vi. Are there other events that crystallize threat?
   b. Is there an intensification of political rhetoric justifying harm in the name of imminent danger?
      i. Is there evidence of apocalyptic and existential political rhetoric, such as "if this happens, all is lost," "we are on the brink of disaster," "our very existence is threatened," and the like?
      ii. Is there political rhetoric conveying immediate danger from a group, such as "they want to destroy us," "they want to enslave us," "they want to bring us back to some era during which we suffered"?
      iii. Is there political rhetoric that incites a willingness to use violence for self-protection, such as "we must protect ourselves," "don't turn a blind eye," "act now or it will be too late"?
      iv. Is there political rhetoric suggesting that the would-be victim group is unwinnable and uncontainable?
   c. Is there any low-level violence that is justified in the name of threat perception?
2. **Is there an intensified move to an exclusionary founding narrative?**
   a. Is there an effort to create a coalition of "hardliners" who hold fast to the tenets of an exclusionary founding narrative?
      i. Are "moderates" or those who espouse a counter-narrative removed from a coalition of actors or otherwise sidelined?

    ii. Are there attacks or other harmful actions against moderates or those who espouse a counter-narrative?

  b. Is there a renewed rhetorical emphasis on the founding narrative?

    i. Are those in positions of power and influence laying new or special emphasis on the core mission of the state that implies the protection of one group in the face of another?

    ii. Is there a move to hail the founding fathers (or mothers) who once espoused the founding narrative?

  c. Are there any low-level acts of violence against non-core populations?

    i. Have those acts of violence been punished, either politically or criminally?

    ii. Have political and military elites justified the acts of violence in the name of the state's founding narrative?

3. Is there an effort to weaken or overcome any existing restraints, domestic or international?

  a. If a robust civil society exists, are key actors within civil society imprisoned or intimidated?

  b. If there are local-level mechanisms of intergroup dependence, are those disrupted, for example by forbidding intermarriage?

  c. Are there attacks against civilians that go unpunished, thereby indicating the political acceptability of such violence?

  d. If an international force exists, are there efforts to either constrain it or to evade it?

4. Is there an increase in the capacity for group-selective violence?

  a. Is there evidence of the creation of a multi-actor coalition capable of committing large-scale violence?

    i. Is there evidence of the creation of organizations that specialize in or are adept at targeting civilians, for instance the formation of paramilitary or militia groups?

      1. Do those groups have access to local populations?

    ii. Is there evidence of integrating actors in different paramilitary groups or integrating paramilitary groups with national institutions, such as the Army?

    iii. Is there evidence of dismissing officers considered to be disloyal?

  b. Are there efforts to increase the visibility or identification of would-be victim groups?

    i. Are members of a civilian group physically segregated?

    ii. Are members of a civilian group required to wear certain garb or to carry cards that identify them?

    iii. Are members of a specific group labeled "unpatriotic" or "enemies"?

    c. Is there an effort to increase access to the would-be target group?

      i. Are members of the would-be victim group disarmed?

      ii. Are members of the would-be victim group removed from positions of authority, the police, or the military?

      iii. Have would-be perpetrators increased their surveillance over would-be victim groups?

    d. Is there evidence of increased capacity to inflict violence?

      i. As above, have groups specialized in harming or monitoring civilians been formed, for instance paramilitaries?

      ii. Is there evidence of the accumulation of weapons that could be used against civilians?

      iii. Is there evidence of the distribution of weapons, especially to groups or locations where would-be victims would likely to be targeted?

The sets of indicators that I have provided will not perfectly predict the onset of mass categorical violence and genocide. However, the indicators are theoretically driven, and if the arguments that I have presented in this book are correct, the indicators should produce fewer false positives than existing frameworks suggest. But at the same time, it is also true that many indicators that I list here are not unique to mass categorical violence and genocide. Accumulating weapons, for example, is consistent with waging war. Falling back on a nationalist narrative, to take another example, can be consistent with building a minimum winning coalition in an electoral contest. The indicators are not jointly necessary. Not every one needs to be checked off for the risk of mass categorical violence and genocide to be exceptionally high. But, as a general statement, the more that do exist, the higher the risk of this type of violence.

Patterns of Violence Indicating the Onset of Group-Selective Violence and Genocide

In the previous two sections, I have listed criteria that would help observers determine the relative risk of the onset of mass categorical violence and genocide. In this section, I list criteria for helping to determine whether such violence is under way.

1. Indicators of Group-Selective Violence

    a. Are civilians deliberately targeted?

i. Is there evidence of shelling, bombing, sweeps, or raids of civilian neighborhoods?

ii. Is there evidence of large-scale detentions and/or disappearance of civilians?

iii. Is there evidence of large-scale relocations of civilians?

iv. Are there mass graves in or near civilian neighborhoods?

v. Are civilians clearly not engaged in conflict being killed, such as the elderly, women, children, or civilians physically far from the fighting?

vi. Are large numbers of civilians fleeing?

    1. If so, do refugee interviews indicate deliberate targeting of civilians?

b. Are groups being deliberately targeted?

i. Are those civilians targeted for violence being primarily identified on the basis of their ostensible group membership?

ii. Are there attacks on group markers, such as religious institutions, commercial institutions associated with a group, graves, and so forth?

iii. Are physical group markers such as diet, phenotype, height, hair color or length, name, and dress used by perpetrators in selecting targets of the violence?

2. Indicators of "Mass" or Large-Scale Violence

a. In the commission of violence, is there collaboration between different agencies or groups, especially collaboration between political administration, military, paramilitary, and new civilian recruits?

b. Is there evidence that the violence is widespread?

i. Is there evidence of "extra-local" violence, that is, violence that in occurs in a similar way in multiple locations?

c. Is there evidence that the violence is sustained?

i. Does the violence recur in a patterned way at multiple points in time?

d. Is there evidence of additional weapons accumulation or distribution?

3. Indicators of Group-Destructive violence

a. In addition to murder, is there evidence of attacks against structures of group survival, for instance food stocks, water sources, shelter, and health centers?

b. Is there evidence of deliberate targeting of those who would reproduce the victim group, such as children and women of child-bearing age?

   c. Is there political rhetoric indicating the need to eliminate the group?

      i. Is there political rhetoric about the ways in which the group will never change its behavior and cannot be trusted?

      ii. In the commission of violence, do perpetrators cite previous episodes of violence that were ineffective?

      iii. Is there political rhetoric indicating that the target group poses a permanent and existential threat?

References

Abdalla, Muna A. 2009. "Understanding of the Natural Resource Conflict Dynamics: The Case of Tuareg in North Africa and the Sahel." *Institute for Security Studies* 194 (August): 1–16.

'Abd Al-Rahim, Muddathir. 1969. *Imperialism and Nationalism in the Sudan: A Study in Constitutional and Political Development, 1899–1956.* Oxford: Clarendon Press.

———. 1973. "Arabism, Africanism, and Self-Identification in the Sudan." In *The Southern Sudan Question: The Problem of National Integration,* ed. Dunstan Wai, 29–46. London: Frank Cass.

Abdelhay, Ashraf Kamal. 2007. *The Politics of Language Planning in the Sudan: The Case of the Naivasha Language Policy.* PhD dissertation, Department of Linguistics and English Language, University of Edinburgh.

Acemoglu, Daron, and James Robinson. 2006. *Economic Origins of Dictatorship and Democracy.* New York: Cambridge University Press.

Adamolekun, Ladipo. 1976. *Sékou Touré's Guinea: An Experiment in Nation Building.* London: Methuen.

Africa Watch. 1990a. *Denying "The Honor of Living": Sudan, a Human Rights Disaster.* New York: Africa Watch.

———. 1990b. *Somalia: A Government at War with Its Own People: Testimonies about the Killing and the Conflict in the North.* New York: Africa Watch.

———. 1991. *Evil Days: Thirty Years of War and Famine in Ethiopia.* New York: Africa Watch.

African Development Bank. 2011. *The Middle of the Pyramid: Dynamics of the Middle Class in Africa.* April 20.

African Rights. 1995. *Facing Genocide: The Nuba of Sudan.* London: African Rights.

Ag Baye, Cheick. 1993. "The Process of a Peace Agreement: Between the Movements and the United Fronts of Azawad and the Government of Mali." In *"Never Drink from the Same Cup": Proceedings of the Conference on Indigenous Peoples in Africa,* ed. Hanne Veber, Jens Dahl, Fiona Wilson and Espen Waehle, 247–56. Tune, Denmark: IWGA Document 74.

Ag Mohamed, Alassane, Chéibane Coulibaly, and Gaoussou Drabo. 1995. *Nord du Mali: de la Tragédie à l'Espoir (1990–1995).* Bamako, Mali: Université Mande Bukari.

Airault, Pascal. 2010. "Le système Gbagbo." *Jeune Afrique,* September 28.

Akçam, Taner. 2006. *A Shameful Act: The Armenian Genocide and the Question of Turkish Responsibility.* New York: Henry Holt.

Akhavan, Payam. 2009. "Are International Criminal Tribunals a Disincentive to Peace? Reconciling Judicial Romanticism with Political Realism." *Human Rights Quarterly* 31 (August): 624–54.

Akindès, Francis. 2004 *The Roots of the Military-Political Crises in Côte d'Ivoire*. Uppsala, Sweden: Nordiska Afrikainstitutet.

———. 2009. "Côte d'Ivoire since 1993: The Risky Reinvention of a Nation." In *Turning Points in African Democracy*, ed. Abdul Raufu Mustapha and Lindsay Whitfield, 31–49. Suffolk, U.K.: James Currey.

Alaily, Jihan. 2004. "Militia Chief Denies Darfur Atrocities." BBC.com. August 23, accessed August 30, 2004.

Alier, Abel. 1973. "The Southern Sudan Question." In *The Southern Sudan Question: The Problem of National Integration,* ed. Dunstan Wai, 11–28. London: Frank Cass.

Alvarez, Alex. 2010. *Genocidal Crimes*. New York: Routledge.

Amnesty International. 1978. *Human Rights in Uganda: Report*. London, AFR 59/05/78.

———. 1982. *Human Rights Violations in the Popular and Revolutionary Republic of Guinea: An Account of "Disappearances," Extrajudicial Executions, Torture, and Incommunicado Detentions*. New York.

———. 1990. "Torture in Senegal: The Casmance Case." May 23, AFR 49/02/90.

———. 1991. "Republic of Guinea: Summary of Amnesty International's concerns since April 1984." March 29, AFR 29/03/9.

———. 1992. "Burundi: Sectarian Security Forces Violate Human Rights with Impunity." November 27, AFR 16/010/1992.

———. 1993. "Chad: Never Again? Killings Continue into the 1990s." March 31.

———. 1994. "Mali: Ethnic Conflict and Killings of Civilians." AFR 37/08/94, September 21.

———. 1998a. "Rwanda: The Hidden Violence: 'Disappearances' and Killings Continue." June 23, AI Index: AFR 47/23/98.

———. 1998b. *Senegal: Climate of Terror in Casamance*. AFR 49/01/98.

———. 2004. *Sudan, Darfur: Rape as a Weapon of War: Sexual Violence and Its Consequences*. London, July.

Amondji, Marcel. 1986. *Côte-d'Ivoire, le P.D.C.I. et la vie politique de 1944 à 1985*. Paris: L'Harmattan.

Amselle, Jean-Loup. 1978. "La conscience paysanne: La révolte de Ouolossébougou (juin 1968, Mali)." *Canadian Journal of African Studies* 12 (3): 339–55.

———. 1998. *Mestizo Logics: Anthropology of Identity in Africa and Elsewhere*. Trans. Claudia Royal. Palo Alto: Stanford University Press.

Arnaut, Karel. 2004. "'Out of the Race': The Poesis of Genocide in Mass Media Discourse in Côte d'Ivoire." In *Grammars of Identity/Alterity: A Structural Approach,* ed. Gerd Baumann and Andre Gingrich, 112–41. New York: Bergahn Books.

———. 2005. "Re-Generating the Nation: Youth, Revolution, and the Politics of History in Côte d'Ivoire." In *Vanguard or Vandals: Youth, Politics, and Conflict in Africa,* ed. Jon Abbink and Ineke van Kessel, 110–42. Brill, the Netherlands: Leiden.

Arnoldi, Mary Jo. 2007. "Bamako, Mali: Monuments and Modernity in the Urban Imagination." *Africa Today* 54 (2): 3–24.

Artucio, Alejandro. 1979. *The Trial of Macias in Equatorial Guinea: The Story of a Dictatorship*. Geneva: International Commission of Jurists.

Asprey, Robert. 2002. *War in the Shadows: The Guerrilla in History*. Vol. 1. Lincoln, NE: IUniverse.

Austen, Ralph. 1999. *In Search of Sunjata: The Mande Oral Epic as History, Literature, and Performance.* Bloomington: Indiana University Press.

Autesserre, Séverine. 2010. *The Trouble with the Congo: Local Violence and the Failure of International Peacebuilding.* New York: Cambridge University Press.

Axelrod, Robert. 1984. *The Evolution of Cooperation.* New York: Basic Books.

Azam, Jean-Paul. 1995. "How to Pay for the Peace? A Theoretical Framework with References to African Countries." *Public Choice* 83 (1–2): 173–84.

———. 2001. "The Redistributive State and Conflicts in Africa." *Journal of Peace Research* 38 (4): 429–44.

Azam, Jean-Paul, and Christian Morrisson. 1994. *The Political Feasibility of Adjustment in Côte d'Ivoire and Morocco.* Paris: OECD.

Azam, Jean-Paul, and Christian Morrisson with Sophie Chauvin and Sandrine Rospabé. 1999. *Conflict and Growth in Africa, Vol. 1: The Sahel.* Paris: OECD.

Ba Konaré, Adame. 2000a. *L'Os de la Parole: Cosmologie du pouvoir.* Paris: Présence Africaine.

———. 2000b. "Perspectives on History and Culture: The Case of Mali." In *Democracy and Development in Mali,* ed. James Bingen, David Robinson, and John Staatz, 15–22. East Lansing: Michigan State University.

———. 2001. "La tradition orale au Mali: une approche analytique de l'épopée du pays Dò selon le récit de Jali Bakari Koné." In *Les historiens africains et la mondialisation: Actes du 3e congrès international des Historiens africaines (Bamako, 2001),* ed. Isiiaka Mandé and Blandine Stefanson, 391–98. Paris: Karthala.

———. 2004. "Discours inaugural." In *L'Afrique: Les Rendez-vous de l'Histoire,* 9–27. Nantes: Editions Pleins Feux.

Babo, Alfred. 2013. *L'étranger en Côte d'Ivoire: crises et controverses autour d'une catégorie sociale.* Paris: L'Harmattan.

Bagosora, Théoneste. 1995. *L'assassinat du Président Habyarimana ou L'ultime opération du TUTSI pour sa reconquête du pouvoir par la force au Rwanda.* Unpublished manuscript, Defense Exhibit DB 278, Case ICTR-98-41-T.

Bagayogo, Shaka. 1978. "L'État au Mali: Représentation, autonomie, et mode de fonctionnement." In *L'État contemporain en Afrique,* ed. Emannuel Terray, 91–122. Paris: L'Harmattan.

———. 1989. "Lieux et théorie du pouvoir dans le monde mandé: passé et présent." *Cahiers Sciences Humaines* 25 (4): 445–60.

Bailly, Séry. 2005. *Ne Pas Perdre le Nord.* Abidjan: Éditions Universitaires de Côte d'Ivoire.

Bakary, Tessilimi. 1984. "Elite Transformation and Political Succession." In *The Political Economy of Ivory Coast,* ed. I. William Zartman and Cristopher Delgado, 21–55. New York: Praeger.

Balakian, Peter. 2003. *The Burning Tigris: The Armenian Genocide and America's Response.* New York: HarperCollins.

Balint-Kurti, Daniel. 2007. "Côte d'Ivoire's Forces Nouvelles." Chatham House, Programme Paper, London, September.

Banegas, Richard. 2006. "Côte d'Ivoire: Patriotism, Ethnonationalism, and other African Modes of Self-Writing." *African Affairs* 105 (421): 535–52.

———. 2007. "Côte d'Ivoire: Les jeunes 'se levent en hommes' Antocolonialisme et ultranationalisme chez les Jeunes patriotes d'Abidjan." Les Érudes du CERI, No. 137, July.

Banegas, Richard, and Ruth Marshall-Fratani. 2007. "Côte d'Ivoire: Negotiating Identity and Citizenship." In *African Guerillas: Raging against the Machine,* ed. Morten Boas and Kevin Dunn, 81–122. Boulder, CO: Lynne Rienner.

Bankier, David. 1992. *The Germans and the Final Solution: Public Opinion under Nazism.* Oxford: Blackwell Publishers.

Baqué, Philippe. 1995. "Derapages de la repression, eclatement de la rebellion: Nouvel enlisement des espoirs de paix dans le conflit touareg au Mali." *Le Monde Diplomatique,* April, pp. 30–31.

Barbier-Wiesser, François George, ed. 1994. *Comprendre la Casamance: Chronique d'une integration contrastée.* Paris: Karthala.

Barnett, Michael. 2002. *Eyewitness to a Genocide: The United Nations and Rwanda.* Ithaca, NY: Cornell University Press.

Bassett, Thomas. 2003. "'Nord musulman et Sud chrétien': les moules médiatiques de la crise ivoirienne." *Afrique Contemporaine* 206 (Summer): 13–27.

———. 2011. "Winning Coalition, Sore Loser: The 2010 Presidential Elections in Côte d'Ivoire." *African Affairs* 110 (440): 457–68.

Bassett, Thomas, and Scott Straus. 2011. "Defending Democracy in Côte d'Ivoire: Africa Takes a Stand." *Foreign Affairs* 90 (4): 130–40.

Bauman, Zygmunt. 1989. *Modernity and the Holocaust.* Ithaca, NY: Cornell University Press.

Bayart, Jean-François. 2010. *L'Islam Républicain: Ankara, Téhéran, Dakar.* Paris: Albin Michel.

BBC Summary of World Broadcasts. 1994a. "Demonstrators in Bamako Reportedly Attack Tuareg and Arabs." August 2.

———. 1994b. "President Konaré Interviewed on Politics, Problems with Tuareg Rebels." December 1.

Beck, Linda. 2008. *Brokering Democracy in Africa: The Rise of Clientelist Democracy in Senegal.* New York: Palgrave MacMillan.

Becker, Felicitas. 2004. "Traders, 'Big Men,' and Prophets: Political Continuity and Crisis in the Maji Maji Rebellion in Southeast Tanzania." *Journal of African History* 45 (March): 1–22.

Bédié, Henri Konan. 2000. "Voici ma part de la vérité." *Le Monde,* January 15.

Beissinger, Mark. 2001. "Violence." In *Encyclopedia of Nationalism.* Vol. 1. San Diego: Academic Press.

Bellamy, Alex. 2011. "Mass Atrocities and Armed Conflict: Links, Distinctions, and Implications for the Responsibility to Protect." Stanley Foundation, February.

Benjaminsen, Tor. 2008. "Does Supply-Induced Scarcity Drive Violent Conflicts in the African Sahel? The Case of the Tuareg Rebellion in Northern Mali." *Journal of Peace Research* 45 (6): 819–36.

Benjaminsen, Tor, and Boubacar Ba. 2009. "Farmer-Herder Conflicts, Pastoral Marginalisation and Corruption: A Case Study from the Inland Niger Delta of Mali." *Geographical Journal* 175 (1): 71–81.

Bergen, Doris. 2009. *War and Genocide: A Concise History of the Holocaust.* 2d ed. Lanham, MD: Rowman and Littlefield.

Berman, Sheri. 1998. *The Social Democratic Moment: Ideas and Politics in the Making of Interwar Europe.* Cambridge, MA: Harvard University Press.

Bernus, Edmond. 1992. "Être Touareg au Mali." *Politique Africaine* 47 (October): 23–30.

Bertrand, Jordane. 2000. *Rwanda, Le Piège De L'histoire: L'opposition Démocratique Avant Le Génocide, 1990–1994*. Paris: Karthala.

Besteman, Catherine. 1999. *Unraveling Somalia: Race, Violence, and the Legacy of Slavery*. Philadelphia: Pennsylvania University Press.

Beugré, Joachim. 2011. *Côte d'Ivoire: Coup d'État de 1999. La vérité, enfin!* Abidjan: CERAP.

Blattman, Christopher, and Edward Miguel. 2010. "Civil War." *Journal of Economic Literature* 48 (1): 3–57.

Blé Goudé, Charles. 2006. *Crise ivoirienne: Ma part de vérité*. Abidjan: Frat Mat Editions.

Bleck, Jaimie, and Kristen Michel. 2014. "Capturing the Airwaves, Capturing the Nation: Citizen Response to Putchist-Controlled Radio." Working Paper, University of Notre Dame, May 1.

Bley, Helmut. 1971. *South-West Africa under German Rule, 1894–1914*. Trans. Hugh Ridley. Evanston, IL: Northwestern University Press.

Blingen, R. James, David Robinson, and John Staatz, eds. 2000. *Democracy and Development in Mali*. East Lansing: Michigan State University Press.

Bloxham, Donald. 2005. *The Great Game of Genocide: Imperialism, Nationalism, and the Destruction of the Ottoman Armenians*. Oxford: Oxford University Press.

——. 2009. *The Final Solution: A Genocide*. Oxford: Oxford University Press.

Bloxham, Donald, and A. Dirk Moses. 2010. *The Oxford Handbook of Genocide Studies*. Oxford: Oxford University Press.

Blumer, Herbert. 1958. "Race Prejudice as a Sense of Group Position." *Pacific Sociological Review* 1 (Spring): 3–7.

Boilley, Pierre. 1994. "La démocratisation au Mali: un processus exemplaire." *Relations Internationales et Stratégiques* 14 (Summer): 119–21.

——. 1999. *Les Touaregs Kel Adagh: Dépendances et révoltes: du Soudan Français au Mali Contemporain*. Paris: Karthala.

Boone, Catherine. 1990. "State Crisis and Economic Power in Senegal." *Comparative Politics* 22 (3): 341–57.

——. 1995. "The Social Origins of Ivoirian Exceptionalism: Rural Society and State Formation." *Comparative Politics* 27 (4): 445–63.

——. 2003. *Political Topographies of the African State: Territorial Authority and Institutional Choice*. New York: Cambridge University Press.

Bouquet, Christian. 1982. *Tchad: Gènese d'un conflit*. Paris: L'Harmattan.

——. 2005. *Géopolitique de la Côte d'Ivoire. Le désespoir de Kourouma*. Paris: Armand Colin.

Bourgeot, André. 1994. "Révoltes et rébellions en pays touareg." *Afrique Contemporaine* 170 (2nd trimester): 3–19.

——. 1995. *Les sociéties touarègues: Nomadisme, identité, resistances*. Paris: Karthala.

——. 1996. "Les rébelions touarèges: une cause perdue?" *Afrique Contemporaine* 180 (October–December): 99–115.

Boyer, Allison. 1992. "An Exemplary Transition." *Africa Report* 37 (4): 40–42.

Boyer, Timothy. 2006. "Ivory Coast: A Case study in Intervention and Prevention of Genocide." Air Command and Staff College, Maxwell Air Force Base, Alabama. AU/ACSC/1998/AY06.

Bringa, Tone. 1995. *Being Muslim the Bosnian Way: Identity and Community in a Central Bosnian Village*. Princeton, NJ: Princeton University Press.

Browning, Christopher. 1992. *Ordinary Men: Reserve Police Battalion 101 and the Final Solution in Poland*. New York: Harper Perennial.

Browning, Christopher, with Jurgen Matthaus. 2004. *The Origins of the Final Solution: The Evolution of Nazi Jewish Policy, September 1939–1942*. Lincoln and Jerusalem: University of Nebraska Press/Yad Vashem.

Brubaker, Rogers. 2004. *Ethnicity without Groups*. Cambridge, MA: Harvard University Press.

Buijtenhuijs, Robert. 1987. *Le Frolinat et les guerres civiles du Tchad*. Paris: Karthala.

Burr, Millard. 1998. *Working Document II: Quantifying Genocide in Southern Sudan and the Nuba Mountains, 1983–1998*. Washington, DC: U.S. Committee for Refugees.

Burr, J. Millard, and Robert O. Collins. 2006. *Darfur: The Long Road to Disaster*. Princeton, NJ: Markus Weiner Publishers.

Camara, Sory. 1976. *Gens de la parole: Essai sur la condition et le rôte des griots dans la société Malinké*. Paris: Mouton.

Campbell, Bonnie. 1987. "The State and Capitalist Development in Ivory Coast." In *The African Bourgeoisie: Capitalist Development in Nigeria, Kenya, and the Ivory Coast,* ed. Paul Lubeck, 281–306. Boulder, CO: Lynne Rienner.

Carver, Richard. 1991. *When Silence Rules: The Suppression of Dissent in Malawi*. New York: Human Rights Watch.

Catholic Commission for Justice and Peace in Zimbabwe. 2008. *Gukurahundi in Zimbabwe: A Report on the Disturbances in Matabeleland and the Midlands, 1980–1988*. New York: Columbia University Press.

Cattanéo, Bernard. 2004. *Alpha Oumar Konaré: Un Africain du Mali*. Paris, France: Cauris Editions.

Centre Djoliba. 2002. *26 mars 1991–26 mars 2001 Xeme anniversaire: Bâtissons la mémoire du Mali démocratique*. Bamako, Mali: Association Djoliba.

Chalk, Frank, and Kurt Jonassohn. 1990. *The History and Sociology of Genocide: Analyses and Case Studies*. New Haven, CT: Yale University Press.

Chambers, Simone, and Jeffrey Kopstein. 2001. "Bad Civil Society." *Political Theory* 29 (6): 837–65.

Chandler, David. 1992. *Brother Number One: A Political Biography of Pol Pot*. Boulder, CO: Westview Press.

——. 1999. *Voices from S-21 Terror and History in Pol Pot's Secret Prison*. Berkeley: University of California Press.

Chandra, Kanchan. 2006. "What Is Ethnicity and Does It Matter?" *Annual Review of Political Science* 9: 397–424.

Charny, Israel. 1982. *How Can We Commit the Unthinkable: Genocide, the Human Cancer*. Boulder, CO: Westview.

Chauveau, Jean-Pierre. 2002. "La loi ivoirienne de 1998 sur le domaine foncier rural et l'agriculture de plantation villageoise : une mise en perspective historique et sociologique." *Réforme Agraire, Colonisation et Coopératives Agricoles* (1), 62–79

——. 2006. "How Does an Institution Evolve? Land, Politics, Intergenerational Relations, and the Institution of the Tutorat amongst Autochthones and Immigrants (Gban Region, Côte d'Ivoire)." In *Land and the Politics of Belonging in West Africa,* ed. Richard Kuba and Carola Lentz, 213–40. Brill, the Netherlands: Leiden.

——. 2008. "La loi de 1998 sur les droits fonciers coutumiers dans l'histoire des politiques foncières en Côte d'Ivoire: une économie politique des transferts de droits entre 'autochtones' et 'étrangers' en zone forestière." In *Law, Land Use, and the Environment*, ed. Christoph Eberhard, 155–90. Afro-Indian Dialogues. Institute Français de Pondicherry, Pondicherry, India.

Chauveau, Jean-Pierre, and Koffi Samuel Bobo. 2008. "La crise de la ruralité en Côte d'Ivoire." In *Frontiers de la citoyenneté et violence politique en Côte d'Ivoire,* ed. Jean-Bernard Ouédraogo and Ebrima Sall, 105–23. Dakar: Codesria.

Chauveau, Jean-Pierre, and Eric Léonard. 1996. "Côte d'Ivoire's Pioneer Fronts: Historical and Political Determinants of the Spread of Cocoa Cultivation." In *Cocoa Pioneer Fronts since 1800: The Role of Smallholders, Planters, and Merchants,* ed. William Gervase Clarence-Smith, 176–94. London: MacMillan.

Chauveau, Jean-Pierre, and Paul Richards. 2008. "West African Insurgencies in Agrarian Perspective: Côte d'Ivoire and Sierra Leone Compared." *Journal of Agrarian Change* 8 (4): 515–52.

Chege, Michael. 1979. "The Revolution Betrayed: Ethiopia, 1974–9." *Journal of Modern African Studies* 17 (3): 359–80.

Chirot, Daniel. 2005. "What Provokes Violent Ethnic Conflict? Political Choice in One African and Two Balkan Cases." In *Ethnic Politics after Communism,* ed. Zoltan Barany and Robert Moser, 140–65. Ithaca, NY: Cornell University Press.

Chirot, Daniel, and Clark McCauley. 2006. *Why Not Kill Them All? The Logic and Prevention of Mass Political Murder.* Princeton, NJ: Princeton University Press.

Chorbajian, Levon, and George Shirinian, eds. 1999. *Studies in Comparative Genocide.* New York: Macmillan.

Chrétien, Jean-Pierre. 1995. *Rwanda, les médias du génocide.* Paris: Karthala.

——. 2003. *The Great Lakes of Africa: Two Thousand Years of History.* Trans. Scott Straus. New York: Zone Books/MIT Press.

Chrétien, Jean-Pierre, and Jean-François Dupaquier. 2007. *Burundi 1972: Au bord des genocides.* Paris: Khartala.

Clark, Andrew. 2000. "From Military Dictatorship to Democracy: The Democratization Process in Mali." In *Democracy and Development in Mali,* ed. James Bingen, David Robinson, and John M. Staatz, 251–64. East Lansing: Michigan State University.

Claudot-Hawad, Hélene. 1992. "Bandits, Rebelles et Partisans: Vision Plurielle de Evenements Touaregs, 1990–1992." *Politique Africaine* 46:143–49.

——. 1994. "La Question touarègue, un silence eloquent." *La République des Lettres,* December 1.

——. 1995. "'Négrafricanisme' et racisme." *Le Monde Diplomatique,* April, p. 30.

Coalition for International Justice. 2005. "New Analysis Claims Darfur Deaths near 400,000." Washington, DC, April 21.

Cockett, Richard. 2010. *Sudan: Darfur and the Failure of an African State.* London: Yale University Press.

Cohen, Roger. 2008. "How Kofi Annan Rescued Kenya." *New York Review of Books,* August 14, pp. 51–53.

Coleman, James. 1958. *Nigeria: Background to Nationalism.* Berkeley and Los Angeles: University of California Press.

Colin, Jean-Philippe, Georges Kouamé, and Débégnoun Soro. 2007. "Outside the Autochthon-Migrant Configuration: Access to Land, Land Conflicts, and Inter-Ethnic Relationships in a Former Pioneer Area of Lower Côte d'Ivoire." *Journal of Modern African Studies* 45 (1): 1–27.

Collier, Paul, and Anke Hoeffler. 2001. "Greed and Grievance in Civil War." World Bank, October 21.

Collier, Paul, and Nicholas Sambanis, eds. 2005. *Understanding Civil War: Evidence and Analysis, Volume 1: Africa.* Washington, DC: The World Bank.

Collins, Randall. 2008. *Violence: A Micro-Sociological Theory.* Princeton, NJ: Princeton University Press.

Coloroso, Barbara. 2007. *Extraordinary Evil: A Short Walk to Genocide.* New York: Nation Books.

Commission d'enquête nationale (CEN). 1993. *Les crimes et détournements de l'ex-président Habré et de ses complices: rapport de la Commission d'enquête nationale.* Paris: L'Harmattan.

Commission of Inquiry (COI). 2005. *Report of the International Commission of Inquiry on Darfur to the United Nations Secretary-General.* Geneva, January 25.

Cook, Susan, ed. 2006. *Genocide in Cambodia and Rwanda: New Perspectives.* New Brunswick, NJ: Transaction.

Costa, Dora, and Matthew Kahn. 2008. *Heroes and Cowards: The Social Face of War.* Princeton, NJ: Princeton University Press.

Coulibaly, Chéibane. 2000. *Comme un petit air de démocratie bananière.* Bamako, Mali: Editions Le Cauri d'Or.

Couloubaly, Pascal Baba. 2004. *Le Mali d'Alpha Oumar Konaré: Ombres et lumières d'une démocratie en gestation.* Paris: L'Harmattan.

Cronjé, Suzanne. 1976. *Equatorial Guinea: The Forgotten Dictatorship.* London: Anti-Slavery Society.

Crook, Richard. 1990. "Politics, the Cocoa Crisis, and Administration in Côte d'Ivoire." *Journal of Modern African Studies* 28 (4): 649–69.

Crompton, D. Elizabeth, and Iain Christie. 2003. "Senegal: Tourism Sector Study." Africa Region Working Paper Series No. 46.

CURDIPHE. 2000. "L'Ivoirité ou l'esprit du nouveau contrat social du Président H.K. Bédié." *Politique Africaine* 78 (July): 65–69.

Dadrian, Vahakn. 2003. [1995]. *The History of the Armenian Genocide: Ethnic Conflict from the Balkans to Anatolia to the Caucasus.* New York: Berghahn Books.

Dagne, Ted. 2004. "Sudan: The Crisis in Darfur." Congressional Research Service, Washington D.C., RS21862, June 16.

Dallaire, Roméo, and Brent Beardsley. 2005. *Shake Hands with the Devil: The Failure of Humanity in Rwanda.* New York: Carroll & Graf.

Daly, M. W. 1993. "Broken Bridge and Empty Basket: The Political and Economic Background of the Sudanese Civil War." In *Civil War in the Sudan,* ed. M. W. Daly and Ahmad Alawad Sikainga, 1–26. London: British Academic Press.

———. 2007. *Darfur's Sorrow: A History of Destruction and Genocide.* New York: Cambridge University Press.

Darbon, Dominique. 1988. *L'Administration et le paysan en Casamance.* Paris: Editions A. Pedone.

Dash, Leon. 1983. "Senegal's Vote Stirs Foes of Traditional Politics." *Washington Post*, May 29, p. A27.

De Jong, Ferdinand. 2005. "A Joking Nation: Conflict Resolution in Senegal." *Canadian Journal of African Studies* 39 (2): 389–413.

De Jorio, Rosa. 2003. "Narratives of the Nation and Democracy in Mali: A View from Modibo Keita's Memorial." *Cahiers d'Études Africaines* 172 (4): 827–55.

———. 2006. "Politics of Remembering and Forgetting: The Struggle over Colonial Monuments in Mali." *Africa Today* 52 (4): 79–106.

De Lame, Danielle. 2005. *A Hill among a Thousand: Transformations and Ruptures in Rural Rwanda*. Trans. Helen Arnold. Madison: University of Wisconsin Press.

De St. Jorre, John. 1970. *The Nigerian Civil War*. London: Hodder and Stoughton.

De Waal, Alex. 1993. "Some Comments on Militias in the Contemporary Sudan." In *Civil War in the Sudan*, ed. M.W. Daly and Ahmad Alawad Sikainga, 142–56. London: British Academic Press.

———. 1997. *Famine Crimes: Politics and the Disaster Relief Industry in Africa*. London: African Rights and the International African Institute in association with James Currey, Oxford and Indiana University Press, Bloomington.

———. 2004. "Darfur: Counter-Insurgency on the Cheap." *London Review of Books* 26 (15): 25.

———. 2007. "Sudan: The Turbulent State." In *War in Darfur and the Search for Peace*, ed. Alex de Waal, 1–38. Cambridge, MA: Global Equity Initiative/Harvard University.

Decalo, Samuel. 1987. *Historical Dictionary of Chad*. 2d ed. Metuchen, NJ: Scarecrow Press.

Dembélé, Ousmane. 2002. "La construction économique et politique de la catégorie 'étranger' en Côte d'Ivoire." In *Côte d'Ivoire: L'Année terrible 1999–2000*, ed. Marc le Pape and Claudine Vidal, 123–71. Paris: Karthala.

Deng, Francis. 1995. *War of Visions: Conflict of Identities in the Sudan*. Washington, DC: Brookings Institution.

Des Forges, Alison. 1986. "'The Drum Is Greater than the Shout': The 1912 Rebellion in Northern Rwanda." In *Banditry, Rebellion, and Social Protest in Africa*, ed. Donald Crummey, 311–32. London: James Currey.

———. 1999. *Leave None to Tell the Story: Genocide in Rwanda*. New York: Human Rights Watch.

Des Forges, Alison, and David Newbury. 2011. *Defeat Is the Only Bad News: Rwanda under Musinga, 1896–1931*. Madison: University of Wisconsin Press.

Destexhe, Alain. 1995. *Rwanda and Genocide in the Twentieth Century*. Trans. Alison Marschner. New York: New York University Press.

Diallo, Boucounta. 2009. *La Crise Casamançaise: Problématique et voies de solutions*. Paris: L'Harmattan.

Diamond, Larry. 1988. *Class, Ethnicity, and Democracy in Nigeria: The Failure of the First Republic*. Syracuse, NY: Syracuse University Press.

Diarrah, Cheick Oumar. 1986. *Le Mali de Modibo Keita*. Paris: L'Harmattan.

———. 1996. *Le défi démocratique au Mali*. Paris: L'Harmattan.

Diawara, Mamadou. 1999. "Searching for the Historical Ancestor: The Paradigm of Sunjata in Oral Traditions of the Sahel (13th–19th Centuries)." In *In Search of Sunjata: The Mande Oral Epic as History, Literature and Performance*, ed. Ralph Austen, 111–140. Bloomington, IN: University of Indiana Press.

Diédhiou, Paul. 2011. *L'identité Jóola en question (Casamance)*. Paris: Karthala.

Diop, Momar-Coumba. 2002. "Léopold Sédar Senghor, Abdou Diouf, Abdoulaye Wade, et après?" In *La Construction de l'etat au Sénégal*, ed. Donal Cruise O'Brien, Momar-Coumba Diop, and Mohammed Diouf, 101–41. Paris: Karthala.

Diop, Momar-Coumba, and Mamadou Diouf. 1990. *Le Sénégal sous Abdou Diouf*. Paris: Karthala.

Diouf, Makhtar. 1994. *Sénégal: les ethnies et la nation*. Paris: l'Harmattan.

Diouf, Mamadou. 2001. *Histoire du Sénégal: le modèle Islamo-Wolof et ses périphéries*. Paris: Maisonneuve et Larose.

——. 2002. "Culture politique et administrative et réformes économiques." In *La Construction de l'etat au Sénégal*, ed. Donal Cruise O'Brien, Momar-Coumba Diop, and Mohammed Diouf, 49–82. Paris: Karthala.

Dobkowski, Isidor, and Michael Wallimann. 1987. *Genocide and the Modern Age: Etiology and Case Studies of Mass Death*. New York: Greenwood Press.

Docking, Timothy. 1997. "Mali: The Roots of Democracy's 'Success.'" In *L'Afrique Politique: Revendications populaires et recompositions politiques*, ed. Centre d'étude d'Afrique Noir, 191–212. Paris: Karthala.

Downes, Alexander. 2008. *Targeting Civilians in War*. Ithaca, NY: Cornell University Press.

Dozon, Jean-Pierre. 1985. "Les Bété: une création coloniale." In *Au cœur de l'ethnie: Ethnie, tribalisme, et État en Afrique*, ed. Jean-Loup Amselle et Elikia M'Boloko, 49–86. Paris: La Découverte.

——. 1997. "L'étranger et l'allochtone en Côte-d'Ivoire." In *Le modèle ivoirien en questions: Crises ajustements, recompositions*, ed. Bernard Contamin and Harris Memel-Fotê, 779–801. Paris: Karthala.

——. 2000. "La Côte d'Ivoire au péru de l'ivoirité': Genèse d'un coup d'Etat." *Afrique Contemporaine* 193:13–23.

Dudley, B. J. 1973. *Instability and Political Order: Politics and Crisis in Nigeria*. Ibadan, Nigeria: Ibadan University Press.

Dumitru, Diana, and Chris Johnson. 2011. "Constructing Interethnic Conflict and Cooperation: Why Some People Harmed Jews and Others Helped Them During the Holocaust in Romania." *World Politics* 63 (1): 1–42.

Dunning, Thad, and Lauren Harrison. 2010. "Cross-Cutting Cleavages and Ethnic Voting: An Experimental Study of Cousinage in Mali." *American Political Science Review* 104 (1): 21–39.

Eck, Kristine, and Lisa Hultman. 2007. "One-Sided Violence against Civilians in War: Insights from New Fatality Data." *Journal of Peace Research* 44 (2): 233–46.

Economist Intelligence Unit. 2008. "Côte d'Ivoire: Country Profile." London.

Ekwe-Ekwe, Herbert. 1990. *The Biafra War: Nigeria and the Aftermath*. Lewiston, NY: Edwin Mellen Press.

El-Affendi, Abdelwahab. 1991. *Turabi's Revolution: Islam and Power in Sudan*. London: Grey Seal.

Elkins, Caroline. 2005. *Imperial Reckoning: The Untold Story of Britain's Gulag in Kenya*. New York: Henry Holt.

Emizet, Kisangani. 2000. "The Massacre of Refugees in Congo: A Case of UN Peacekeeping Failure and International Law." *Journal of Modern African Studies* 38 (2): 163–202.

Erny, Pierre. 1994. *Rwanda: Clés pour comprendre le calvaire d'un peuple.* Paris: L'Harmattan.

Evans, Gareth. 2008. *The Responsibility to Protect: Ending Mass Atrocity Crimes Once and For All.* Washington, DC: Brookings Institution Press.

Evans, Martin. 2000. "Senegal: Wade and the Casamance Dossier." *African Affairs* 99 (397): 649–58.

———. 2003. "Ni Paix Ni Guerre: The Political Economy of Low-Level Conflict in the Casamance." HPG Background Paper, Overseas Development Institute.

Extraordinary Chambers in the Courts of Cambodia (ECCC). 2010. *Kaing Guek Eav alias Duch Judgment,* Phnom Penh, Cambodia.

Fargues, Phillippe. 1986. "Mobilité du Travail et Croissance d'une Économie Agricole: La Côte d'Ivoire." *Revue Tiers Monde* 27 (105): 195–211.

Fatton, Robert. 1987. *The Making of a Liberal Democracy: Senegal's Passive Revolution, 1975–1985.* Boulder, CO: Lynne Rienner.

Fauré, Y. A. 1982. "Le Complexe Politico-Économique." In *État et bourgeoisie en Côte d'Ivoire,* ed. Y. A. Fauré and J. F. Médard, 21–60. Paris: Karthala.

Fearon, James. 1995. "Rationalist Explanations for War." *International Organization* 49 (3): 379–414.

———. 2003. "Ethnic and Cultural Diversity by Country." *Journal of Economic Growth* 8:195–222.

Fearon, James, and David Laitin. 1996. "Explaining Interethnic Cooperation." *American Political Science Review* 90 (4): 715–35.

———. 2003. "Ethnicity, Insurgency, and Civil War." *American Political Science Review* 97 (1): 75–90.

Fegley, Randall. 1989. *Equatorial Guinea: An African Tragedy.* New York: Peter Lang.

Fein, Helen. 1979. *Accounting for Genocide: National Responses and Jewish Victimization during the Holocaust.* Chicago: University of Chicago Press.

———. 1990. "Genocide: A Sociological Perspective." *Current Sociology* 38 (1): 1–126.

Feinstein, Lee. 2007. *Darfur and Beyond: What Is Needed to Prevent Mass Atrocities.* New York: Council on Foreign Relations.

Finkel, Evgeny, and Scott Straus. 2012. "Micro, Meso, and Macro Theories of Genocide: Gains, Shortcomings, and Future Areas of Inquiry." *Genocide Studies and Prevention* 7 (1): 56–67.

Flint, Julie, and Alex de Waal. 2008. *Darfur: A Short History of a Long War.* New York and London: Zed Books.

Forsyth, Frederick. 1969. *The Biafra Story.* Middlesex, U.K.: Penguin.

Fortna, Virginia Page. 2008. *Does Peacekeeping Work? Shaping Belligerents' Choices after Civil War.* Princeton, NJ: Princeton University Press.

Foucher, Vincent. 2003. "Pas d'alternance en Casamance? Le Nouveau pouvoir Sénégalaise face à la revendication séparatiste Casamançaise." *Politique Africaine* 91:101–19.

———. 2007. "Senegal: The Resilient Weakness of Casamançais Separatists." In *African Guerillas: Raging against the Machine,* ed. Morten Boas and Kevin Dunn, 171–97. Boulder, CO: Lynne Rienner.

———. 2009. "'La Guerre par d'autre moyens'? La société civile dans le processus de paix en Casamance." *Raisons Politiques* 35:143–65.

French, Howard. 1995. "In a Fabled Faraway Place, No Escape from Fear." *New York Times,* January 30, p. A4.

——. 2004. *A Continent for the Taking: The Tragedy and Hope of Africa.* New York: Alfred A. Knopf.

Friedlander, Saul. 1997. *Nazi Germany and the Jews: Volume 1: The Years of Persecution, 1933–1939.* New York: HarperCollins.

Front Populaire Ivoirien. 2000. *Gouverner autrement la Côte d'Ivoire: Programme de gouvernement adopté au Congrès des 9-10-11 juillet 1999.* Paris: L'Harmattan.

Fujii, Lee Ann. 2009. *Killing Neighbors: Webs of Violence in Rwanda.* Ithaca, NY: Cornell University Press.

——. 2013. "The Puzzle of Extra-Lethal Violence," *Perspectives on Politics* 11 (2): 410–426.

Gagnon, V. P. 2004. *The Myth of Ethnic War: Serbia and Croatia in the 1990s.* Ithaca: Cornell University Press.

Galvan, Dennis. 2004. *The State Must Be our Master of Fire: How Peasants Craft Sustainable Development in Senegal.* Berkeley and Los Angeles: University of California Press.

Gasana, James. 2002. *Rwanda: du parti-état à l'état-garnison.* Paris: L'Harmattan.

Gatta, Gali Ngothé. 1985. *Tchad: Guerre Civile et Désagrégation de l'État.* Dakar and Paris: Présence Africaine.

Gbagbo, Laurent. 1995. *Le Temps de l'Espoir: Entretiens avec Honoré De Sumo.* Johannesburg: Les Editions Continentales.

——. 2000. *Mon ambition pour la Côte d'Ivoire: fonder une nation prospère, démocratique, et solidaire.* No publication data.

Gbetibouo, Mathurin, and Christopher Delgado. 1984. "Lessons and Constraints of Export Crop-Led Growth: Cocoa in Ivory Coast." In *The Political Economy of Ivory Coast,* ed. William Zartman and Christopher Delgado, 115–47. New York: Praeger.

Gellately, Robert, and Ben Kiernan, eds. 2003. *The Specter of Genocide: Mass Murder in Historical Perspective.* New York: Cambridge University Press.

Genocide Prevention Task Force. 2008. *Genocide Prevention Task Force Report.* Washington, DC: United States Institute of Peace.

Genocide Watch. 2002. "Crisis in Côte d'Ivoire." December 11.

George, Alexander, and Andrew Bennett. 2004. *Case Studies and Theory Development in the Social Sciences.* Cambridge, MA: Harvard University/MIT Press.

Gerlach, Christian. 2000. "The Wannsee Conference, the Fate of German Jews, and Hitler's Decision in Principle to Exterminate All European Jews." In *The Holocaust: Origins, Implementation, Aftermath,* ed. Omer Bartov, 106–61. London: Routledge.

——. 2010. *Extremely Violence Societies: Mass Violence in the Twentieth-Century World.* Cambridge, U.K.: Cambridge University Press.

Gerring, John. 1997. "Ideology: A Definitional Analysis." *Political Research Quarterly* 50 (4): 957–94.

——. 2007. *Case Study Research: Principles and Practices.* New York: Cambridge University Press.

Gewald, Jan-Bart. 1999. *Herero Heroes: A Socio-Political History of the Herero of Namibia, 1890–1923.* Oxford: James Currey.

Glassman, Jonathon. 2011. *War of Words, War of Stones: Racial Thought and Violence in Colonial Zanzibar.* Bloomington: Indiana University Press.

Goddard, Stacie. 2010. *Indivisible Territory and the Politics of Legitimacy: Jerusalem and Northern Ireland.* New York: Cambridge University Press.

Goldsmith, Benjamin, Charles Butcher, Dimitri Semenovich, and Arcot Sowmya. 2013. "Forecasting the Onset of Genocide and Politicide: Annual Out-of-Sample Forecasts on a Global Dataset, 1988–2003." *Journal of Peace Research* 50 (4): 437–452.

Gnakalé, Viviane. 2006. *Laurent Gbagbo: Pour l'avenir de la Côte d'Ivoire.* Paris: L'Harmattan.

Goldhagen, Daniel. 1996. *Hitler's Willing Executioners: Ordinary Germans and the Holocaust.* New York: Knopf.

——. 2009. *Worse than War: Genocide, Eliminationism, and the Ongoing Assault on Humanity.* New York: PublicAffairs.

Goudie, Andrew, and Bilin Neyapti. 1999. *Conflict and Growth in Africa: Vol. 3, Southern Africa.* Paris: OECD.

Government Accounting Office. 2006. *Darfur Crisis: Death Estimates Demonstrate Severity of Crisis, but Their Accuracy and Credibility Could be Enhanced,* November.

Greif, Avner. 2006. *Institutions and the Path to the Modern Economy: Lessons from Medieval Trade.* New York: Cambridge University Press.

Grémont, Charles, André Marty, Rhissa ag Mossa, and Younoussa Hamara Touré. 2004. *Les liens sociaux au Nord-Mali: Entre fleuve et dunes.* Paris: Karthala.

Grigoryan, Arman. 2010. "Third-Party Intervention and the Escalation of State-Minority Conflicts." *International Studies Quarterly* 54 (3): 1143–74.

Guichaoua, André. 2010. *Rwanda: de la guerre au génocide. Les politiques criminelles au Rwanda (1990–1994).* Paris: La Découverte.

Haggar, Ali. 2007. "The Origins and Organization of the Janjawiid in Darfur." In *War in Darfur and the Search for Peace,* ed. Alex de Waal, 113–39. Cambridge, MA: Global Equity Initiative/Harvard University.

Hagan, John, and Alberto Palloni. 2006. "Death in Darfur." *Science* 313:1578–79.

Hagan, John, and Wenona Rymond-Richmond. 2009. *Darfur and the Crime of Genocide.* New York: Cambridge University Press.

Hale, Henry. 2008. *The Foundations of Ethnic Politics: Separatism of States and Nations in Eurasia and the World.* New York: Cambridge University Press.

Hall, Bruce. 2005. "The Question of 'Race' in the Pre-colonial Southern Sahara." *Journal of North African Studies* 10 (3–4): 339–67.

——. 2011. *History of Race in Muslim West Africa.* Cambridge, U.K.: Cambridge University Press.

Hall, Margaret. 1999. *The Casamance Conflict 1982–1999.* London: Africa Research Group, Foreign and Commonwealth Office.

Halliday, Fred, and Maxine Molyneux. 1981. *The Ethiopian Revolution.* London, U.K.: Verso.

Hamilton, Rebecca. 2011. *Fighting for Darfur: Public Action and the Struggle to Stop Genocide.* New York: Palgrave MacMillan.

Hanson, Stephen. 2003. "From Culture to Ideology in Comparative Politics." *Comparative Politics* 35 (3): 355–76.

——. 2010. *Post-Imperial Democracies: Ideology and Party Formation in Third Republic France, Weimar Germany, and Post-Soviet Russia.* New York: Cambridge University Press.

Harbom, Lotta. 2005. *States in Armed Conflict 2004.* Uppsala, Sweden: Uppsala University Press.

Harden, Blaine. 1988. "Burundi Lays Blame in Massacre." *Washington Post*, August 25.

Harff, Barbara. 1987. "The Etiology of Genocides." In *Genocide and the Modern Age: Etiology and Case Studies of Mass Death,* ed. Isidor Walliman and Michael Dobkowski, 41–59. Westport, CT: Greenwood Press.

———. 2003. "No Lessons Learned from the Holocaust? Assessing Risks of Genocide and Political Mass Murder since 1955." *American Political Science Review* 97 (1): 57–73.

Harroy, Jean Paul. 1984. *Rwanda: Souvenirs d'un Compagnon de la Marche du Rwanda Vers la Démocratie et L'indépendance.* Brussels: Hayez.

Hathaway, Oona. 2002. "Do Human Rights Treaties Make a Difference?" *Yale Law Journal*, pp. 1935–2042.

Hecht, Robert. 1985. "Immigration, Land Transfer, and Tenure Changes in Divo, Ivory Coast, 1940–1980." *Africa* 55 (3): 319–36.

Hegre, Havard, Tanja Ellingsen, Scott Gates, and Nils Petter Gleditsch. 2001. "Toward a Democratic Civil Peace? Democracy, Political Change, and Civil War, 1816–1992." *American Political Science Review* 95 (1): 33–48.

Herbst, Jeffrey. 2000. "Economic Incentives, Natural Resources, and Conflict in Africa." *Journal of African Economies* 9 (3): 270–94.

———. 2004. "African Militaries and Rebellion: The Political Economy of Threat and Combat Effectiveness." *Journal of Peace Research* 41 (3): 357–69.

Herrmann, Richard. 2013. "Perceptions and Image Theory in International Relations." In *The Oxford Handbook of Political Psychology,* ed. Leonie Huddy, David Sears, and Jack Levy, 2d ed. 334–63.

Herrmann, Richard, and Michael Fischerkeller, 1995. "Beyond the Enemy Image and Spiral Model: Cognitive-Strategic Research after the Cold War." *International Organization* 49 (3): 415–50.

Hiebert, Maureen. 2008. "Theorizing Destruction: Reflections on the State of Comparative Genocide Theory." *Genocide Studies and Prevention* 3 (3): 309–39.

Hilberg, Raul. 2003. *The Destruction of the European Jews.* 3d ed. New Haven, CT: Yale University Press.

Hinton, Alexander. 2005. *Why Did They Kill? Cambodia in the Shadow of Genocide.* Berkeley and Los Angeles: University of California Press.

Horowitz, Irving Louis. 1976. *Genocide: State Power and Mass Murder.* New Brunswick, NJ: Transaction.

Horowitz, Donald. 1985. *Ethnic Groups in Conflict.* Berkeley: University of California Press.

———. 2001. *The Deadly Ethnic Riot.* Berkeley: University of California Press.

Hovannisian, Richard, ed. 1986. *The Armenian Genocide in Perspective.* New Brunswick, NJ: Transaction.

Howard, Lise Morjé. 2008. *UN Peacekeeping in Civil Wars.* New York: Cambridge University Press.

Hoyt, Michael. 1972. *Messages concerning the Burundi Massacres to and from American Embassy, Bujumbura, April 29 to August 29, 1972.* Microfiche.

Huband, Mark. 1998. *The Liberian Civil War.* London: Frank Cass.

Hull, Isabel. 2005. *Absolute Destruction: Military Culture and the Practices of War in Imperial Germany.* Ithaca and New York: Cornell University Press.

Human Rights Watch. 1995. *Somalia Faces the Future: Human Rights in a Fragmented Society.* New York: Human Rights Watch.

———. 2001. *The New Racism: The Political Manipulation of Ethnicity in Côte d'Ivoire.* New York: Human Rights Watch.

———. 2002. *Government Abuses in Response to Army Revolt.* New York: Human Rights Watch.

———. 2003. *Trapped Between Two Wars: Violence against Civilians in Western Côte d'Ivoire.* New York: Human Rights Watch.

———. 2004. *Darfur Destroyed: Ethnic Cleansing by Government Militia Forces in Western Sudan.* New York: Human Rights Watch.

———. 2005. *The Victims of Hissène Habré Still Awaiting Justice.* New York: Human Rights Watch.

———. 2008a. *"The Best School": Student Violence, Impunity, and the Crisis in Côte d'Ivoire.* New York: Human Rights Watch.

———. 2008b. *Collective Punishment: War Crimes and Crimes against Humanity in the Ogaden Area of Ethiopia's Somali Regional State.* New York: Human Rights Watch.

———. 2011a. "Côte d'Ivoire: Crimes against Humanity by Gbagbo Forces." March 15.

———. 2011b. "Côte d'Ivoire: Violence Campaign by Security Forces, Militias." January 26.

———. 2011c. "'We Have Lived in Darkness': A Human Rights Agenda for Guinea's New Government." May.

Human Security Centre. 2005. *Human Security Report 2005: War and Peace in the 21st Century.* New York: Oxford University Press.

Humphreys, Macartan, and Habaye Ag Mohamed. 2005. "Senegal and Mali." In *Understanding Civil War: Africa,* ed. Paul Collier and Nicholas Sambanis, 247–302. Washington, DC: World Bank Publications.

Humphreys, Macartan, and Jeremy Weinstein. 2006. "Handling and Manhandling Civilians in Civil War: Determinants of the Strategies of Warring Factions." *American Political Science Review* 100 (3): 429–48.

———. 2008. "Who Fights? The Determinants of Participation in Civil War." *American Journal of Political Science* 52 (2): 436–55.

Iliffe, John. 1979. *A Modern History of Tanganyika.* London: Cambridge University Press.

International Cocoa Organization. 1998–2010. *Annual Reports.* Available at www. icco.org/about/anualreport.aspx, accessed November 2011.

International Criminal Tribunal for Rwanda (ICTR). 1998. "The Prosecutor vs. Jean-Paul Akayesu." Case No. ICTR-96-4-T.

———. 1999. "The Prosecutor against Théoneste Bagosora." Amended Indictment, August 12, 1999, Case No. ICTR-96-7-I.

———. 2008. "The Prosecutor vs. Théoneste Bagosora, Gratien Kabiligi, Aloys Ntabakuze, and Analtole Nsengiyumva, Judgment and Sentence." Case No. ICTR-98-41-T.

———. 2012. "The Prosecutor v. Édouard Karemera and Matthieu Ngirumpatse." Judgment and Sentence, Case No. ICTR-98-44-T.

International Criminal Court for the former Yugoslavia (ICTY). 2004. "Prosecutor v. Radislav Krstic." Appeals Chamber, Judgment, Case No. IT-98-33-A.

International Crisis Group. 2011a. "Côte d'Ivoire: Is War the Only Option?" March 3.

———. 2011b. "Open Letter to the UN Security Council on the Situation in Côte d'Ivoire, March 25.

IRIN. 2005. "Nigeria: 30 Killed in Clashes between Farmers and Herdsmen in Adamawa State." Available at www.irinnews.org/report.aspx?reportid=52944, accessed June 23, 2014.

Institut National de la Statistique. 2001a. *Recensement Général de la Population et de l'Habitation de 1998, Volume IV: Analyses des Résultats, Tome 1: État et Structure de la Population.* Abidjan

———. 2001b. *Recensement Général de la Population et de l'Habitation de 1998, Volume IV: Analyses des Résultats, Tome 7: Activités Économiques.* Abidjan.

———. 2007. *Rapport de Collecte et d'Analyse des Statistiques de l'Etat Civile de la Ville d'Abidjan 2005.* Abidjan.

———. 2008a. *Annuaire des Statistiques 2006.* No. 9, Abidjan.

———. 2008b. *Comptes de la Nation 2006.* Abidjan.

Institut National de la Statistique. 2011. *Recensement Général de la Population et de l'Habitat du Mali* (RGPH-2009): Analyse des Résultats Définitifs. Bamako.

Jacob Blaustein Institute for the Advancement of Human Rights with Special Adviser on the Prevention of Genocide, United Nations. 2011. *Compilation of Risk Factors and Legal Norms for the Prevention of Genocide.* New York: JBIAHR.

Jacobs, Dan. 1987. *The Brutality of Nations.* New York: Alfred Knopf.

Jeanjean, Maurice. 2005. *Sékou Touré: Un totalitarisme africaine.* Paris: L'Harmattan.

Jha, Saumitra. 2008. "Trade, Institutions, and Religious Tolerance: Evidence from India." Research Paper No. 2004, Palo Alto, Stanford Graduate School of Business.

Johnson, Douglas. 2003. *The Root Causes of Sudan's Civil Wars.* 2d ed. Bloomington: Indiana University Press.

Jok, Jok Madut. 2007. *Sudan: Race, Religion, and Violence.* Oxford: Oneworld Publications.

Jolivet, Elen. 2003. *L'Ivoirité: De la conceptualization à la manipulation de l'identité ivoirienne.* Memoire, Science Po, University of Rennes.

Jonassohn, Kurt, with Karin Solveig Bjornson. 1998. *Genocide and Gross Human Rights Violations.* New Brunswick, NJ: Transaction.

Jones, Bruce. 2001. *Peacemaking in Rwanda: The Dynamics of Failure.* Boulder, CO: Lynne Rienner.

Kaba, Lansiné. 1988. "From Colonialism to Autocracy: Guinea under Sékou Touré." In *Decolonization and African Independence,* ed. Prosser Gifford and William Roger Louis, 225–44. New Haven, CT: Yale University Press.

Kahl, Colin. 2006. *States, Scarcity, and Civil Strife in the Developing World.* Princeton, NJ: Princeton University Press.

Kajeguhakwa, Valens. 2001. *Rwanda: de la terre de paix à la terre de sang et après?* Paris: Éditions Remi Perrin.

Kalyvas, Stathis. 2003. "The Ontology of Political Violence." *Perspectives on Politics* 1 (3): 475–94.

———. 2006. *The Logic of Violence in Civil War.* New York: Cambridge University Press.

Kapteijns, Lidwein. 1985. *Mahdist Faith and Sudanic Tradition: The History of the Masalit Sultanate, 1870–1930.* London: KPI Limited.

Kasozi, A. B. K. 1999 [1994]. *The Social Origins of Violence in Uganda, 1964–1985.* Kampala, Uganda: Fountain Publishers.

Kayibanda, Grégoire. 1964. *Le Président Kayibanda Vous Parle.* Kigali: République du Rwanda.

Keck, Margaret, and Kathryn Sikkink. 1998. *Activists beyond Borders: Advocacy Networks in International Politics*. Ithaca, NY: Cornell University Press.

Keita, Naffet. 2005. "De l'identitaire au problem de la territoritalité. L'OCRS et les societies Kel Tamacheq du Mali." In *Mali-France: Regards sur une histoire partagée*, ed. Christian Connan. Paris: Karthala.

———. 2010. "Problematique des conflits et mécanismes de gestion des crise intra et interethnique en Afrique: L'exemple des 'révoltes et rebellions' Touareg au Mali en question." Unpublished manuscript.

Keller, Edmond. 1988. *Revolutionary Ethiopia: From Empire to People's Republic*. Bloomington: Indiana University Press.

Kershaw, Ian. 2000. *The Nazi Dictatorship: Problems and Perspectives of Interpretation*. 4th ed. London: Arnold.

Kiernan, Ben. 1996. *The Pol Pot Regime: Race, Power, and Genocide in Cambodia under the Khmer Rouge, 1975–79*. New Haven, CT: Yale University Press.

———. 2007. *Blood and Soil: A World History of Genocide and Extermination from Sparta to Darfur*. New Haven, CT: Yale University Press.

Kimonyo, Jean-Paul. 2008. *Rwanda: Un génocide populaire*. Paris: Karthala.

King, Charles. 2004. "The Micropolitics of Social Violence." *World Politics* 56 (3): 431–55.

Kiraranganya, Boniface. 1977. *La vérité sur le Burundi: Témoignage*. Quebec: Editions Naaman.

Kirk-Greene, A. H. M. 1971. *Crisis and Conflict in Nigeria: A Documentary Source-Book*. London: Oxford University Press.

Klopp, Jacqueline, and Elke Zuern. 2007. "The Politics of Violence in Democratization: Lessons from Kenya and South Africa." *Comparative Politics* 39 (1): 127–46.

Klugman, Jeni, Bilin Neyapti, and Frances Stewart. 1999. *Conflict and Growth in Africa: Vol. 2 Kenya, Tanzania, and Uganda*. Paris: OECD.

Konaré, Alpha Oumar. 2005. "Allocation d'ouverture." In *Des frontières en Afrique du XIIe au XXe Siècle*, 27–33. Paris: UNESCO.

Konaté, Doulaye. 1999. "Les fondements endogènes d'une culture du paix au Mali: Les mécanismes traditionnels de prevention et de resolution des conflits." In *Les fondements endogènes d'une culture du paix en Afrique: Mécanismes traditionnels de prevention et de resolution des conflits*, ed. Edouard Matoko, 27–48. Paris: UNESCO.

———. 2006. *Travail de mémoire et construction nationale au Mali*. Paris: L'Harmattan.

Kouassi, Moïse Lida. 2010. *Témoignage sur la crise ivoirienne: De la lutte pour la démocratie à l'épreuve de la rébellion*. Paris: L'Harmattan.

Krain, Matthew. 1997. "State-Sponsored Mass Murder: The Onset and Severity of Genocides and Politicides." *Journal of Conflict Resolution* 41 (3): 331–60.

Kramer, Alan. 2007. *Dynamic of Destruction: Culture and Mass Killing in the First World War*. Oxford: Oxford University Press.

Krings, Thomas. 1995. "Marginalisation and Revolt among the Tuareg in Mali and Niger." *GeoJournal* 36 (1): 57–63.

Kuper, Leo. 1981. *Genocide: Its Political Use in the Twentieth Century*. New Haven, CT: Yale University Press.

Kuperman, Alan. 2001. *The Limits of Humanitarian Intervention: Genocide in Rwanda*. Washington, DC: Brookings Institution.

——. 2008. "The Moral Hazard of Humanitarian Intervention: Lessons from the Balkans." *International Studies Quarterly* 52 (1): 49–80.

Kydd, Andrew. 2010. "Rationalist Approaches to Conflict Prevention and Resolution." *Annual Review of Political Science* 13: 101–21.

Kydd, Andrew, and Scott Straus. 2013. "The Road to Hell? Third Party Intervention to Prevent Atrocities." *American Journal of Political Science*, 57 (3): 673–84.

Lacina, Bethany, and Nils Petter Gleditsch. 2005. "Monitoring Trends in Global Combat: A New Dataset of Battle Deaths." *European Journal of Population* 21:145–66.

Laitin, David. 2004. "Ethnic Unmixing and Civil War." *Security Studies* 12 (4): 136–75.

Lakoff, George. 2002. *Moral Politics: How Liberals and Conservatives Think.* 2d ed. Chicago: University of Chicago Press.

Lambert, Michael. 1998. "Violence and the War of Words: Ethnicity v. Nationalism in the Casamance." *Africa* 68 (4): 585–602.

Langer, Arnim. 2007. "When Do Horizontal Inequalities Lead to Conflict? Lessons from a Comparative Study of Ghana and Côte d'Ivoire." In *Horizontal Inequalities and Conflict: Understanding Group Violence in Multiethnic Societies,* ed. Frances Stewart, 163–89. New York: Palgrave MacMillan.

Lanne, Bernard. 1981. "Le sud du Tchad dans la guerre civile (1979–1980)." *Politique Africaine* 3:75–89.

Lecocq, Baz. 2002. *"That Desert is Our Country": Tuareg Rebellions and Competing Nationalisms in Contemporary Mali (1946–1996).* PhD dissertation, University of Amsterdam.

——. 2005. "The Bellah Question: Slave Emancipation, Race, and Social Categories in Late Twentieth-Century Northern Mali." *Canadian Journal of African History* 39:1, pp. 42–68.

Leitenberg, Milton. 2006. *Deaths in Wars and Conflicts in the 20th Century.* 3d ed. Occasional Paper No. 29, Cornell University Peace Studies Program, Ithaca, New York.

Lemarchand, René. 1970. *Rwanda and Burundi.* London: Pall Mall.

——. 1986. "The Misadventures of the North-South Dialectic." *African Studies Review* 29 (3): 27–41.

——. 1989. "Burundi: The Killing Fields Revisited." *Issue* 18 (1): 22–28.

——. 1994. *Burundi: Ethnic Conflict and Genocide.* Cambridge and New York: Cambridge University Press and Woodrow Wilson Center.

——. 2002. "Le génocide de 1972 au Burundi: Les silences de l'histoire." *Cahiers d'Etudes Africaines* 167 (42–3): 551–67.

——. 2008. "The Burundi Killings of 1972." Online Encyclopedia of Mass Violence. Available at www.massviolence.org/Article?id_article=138, accessed June 23, 2014.

——. 2009. *The Dynamics of Violence in Central Africa.* Philadelphia: University of Pennsylvania Press.

Lemarchand, René, and David Martin. 1974. *Selective Genocide in Burundi.* London: Minority Rights.

Lemkin, Raphael. 1944. *Axis Rule in Occupied Europe.* Washington, DC: Carnegie Endowment for International Peace.

——. 1947. "Genocide as a Crime under International Law." *American Journal of International Law* 41 (1): 145–51.

Lemkin, Robert, and Sambath Thet. 2009. *Enemies of the People a Personal Journey into the Heart of the Killing Fields.* Oxford: Old Street Films. Video documentary.

Leonard, David, and Scott Straus. 2003. *Africa's Stalled Development: International Causes and Cures.* Boulder, CO: Lynne Rienner.

Leonard, E., and M. Oswald. 1995. "Cocoa Smallholders Facing a Double Structural Adjustment in Côte d'Ivoire: Responses to a Predicted Crisis." In *Cocoa Cycles: The Economics of Cocoa Supply,* ed. François Ruf and P. S. Siswoputranto, 125–60. Cambridge, U.K.: Woodhead.

Lesch, Ann Mosely. 1998. *The Sudan: Contested National Identities.* Bloomington: Indiana University Press.

Levene, Mark. 2005. *Genocide in the Age of the Nation State.* 2 vols. London: I.B. Tauris.

Levitsky, Steven, and Lucan Way. 2010. *Competitive Authoritarianism: Hybrid Regimes after the Cold War.* New York: Cambridge University Press.

Lewis, Paul. 1988. "Burundi President Presents Its Side of Story." *New York Times,* August 29.

Lieberman, Evan. 2005. "Nested Analysis as a Mixed-Method Strategy for Comparative Research." *American Political Science Review* 99 (3): 435–52.

———. 2009. *Boundaries of Contagion: How Ethnic Politics Have Shaped Government Responses to AIDS.* Princeton, NJ: Princeton University Press.

Liniger-Goumaz, Max. 1983. *De la Guinée Equatoriale Nguemiste: Elements pour le dossier de l'Afro-Fascisme.* Geneva: Les editions du temps.

———. 1988. *Small Is Not Always Beautiful: The Story of Equatorial Guinea.* Trans. John Wood. London: Hurst.

Lipset, Seymour, and Stein Rokkan. 1967. *Party Systems and Voter Alignments: Cross-National Perspectives.* New York: Free Press.

Lode, Kare. 1997a. *Civil Society Takes Responsibility: Popular Involvement in the Peace Process in Mali.* Oslo, PRIO Report, May.

———. 1997b. "The Peace Process in Mali: Oiling the Works?" *Security Dialogue* 28 (4): 409–24.

———. 2002. "Mali's Peace Process: Context, Analysis, and Evaluation." Available at www.c-r.org/our-work/accord/public-participation/malis-peace-process. php, accessed March 24, 2010.

Lofchie, Michael. 1970. "The Zanzibari Revolution: African Protest in a Racially Plural Society." In *Protest and Power in Black Africa,* ed. Robert Rotberg and Ali Mazrui, 924–67. New York: Oxford University Press.

Logiest, Guy. 1988. *Mission au Rwanda.* Brussels: Didier Hatier.

Longerich, Peter. 1999. *Policy of Destruction: Nazi Anti-Jewish Policy and the Genesis of the Final Solution.* Washington, DC: Holocaust Museum.

———. 2010. *Holocaust: The Nazi Persecution and Murder of the Jews.* New York: Oxford University Press.

Longman, Timothy. 2010. *Christianity and Genocide in Rwanda.* New York: Cambridge University Press.

Lugan, Bernard. 1997. *Histoire du Rwanda: De la Préhistoire à nos jours.* Paris: Bartillat.

Lyall, Jason, Graeme Blair, and Kosuke Imai. 2013. "Explaining Support for Combatants during Wartime: A Survey Experiment in Afghanistan." *American Political Science Review* 107 (4): 679–705.

Lynch, Meghan. 2013. *The Escalation of Mass Violence against Civilians.* PhD dissertation, Department of Political Science, Yale University.

MacDonald, Mairi. 2009. *The Challenge of Guinean Independence, 1958–1971.* PhD dissertation, Graduate Department of History, University of Toronto.

———. 2012. "Guinea's Political Prisoners: Colonial Models, Postcolonial Innovation." *Comparative Studies in Society and History* 54 (2): 890–913.

Mahoney, James, and Gary Goertz. 2004. "The Possibility Principle: Choosing Negative Cases in Qualitative Research." *American Political Science Review* 98 (4): 653–70.

Maïga, Mohamed Tiessa-Farma. 1997. *Le Mali: De la secheresse à la rebellion nomade: Chronique et analyse d'un double phénonomène du contre-développement en Afrique sahélienne.* Paris: L'Harmattan.

Malwal, Bona. 1981. *People and Power in Sudan.* London: Ithaca Press.

Mamdani, Mahmood. 1996. *Citizen and Subject: Contemporary Africa and the Legacy of Late Colonialism.* Princeton, NJ: Princeton University Press.

———. 2001. *When Victims Become Killers: Colonialism, Nativism, and the Genocide in Rwanda.* Princeton, NJ: Princeton University Press.

Mampilly, Zachariah. 2011. *Rebel Rulers: Insurgent Governance and Civilian Life during War.* Ithaca, NY: Cornell University Press.

Mann, Michael. 2005. *The Dark Side of Democracy: Explaining Ethnic Cleansing.* New York: Cambridge University Press.

Mapuri, Omar. 1996. *The 1964 Revolution: Achievements and Prospects.* Dar es Salaam: Tema Publishers.

Mark, Peter. 1985. *A Cultural, Economic, and Religious History of the Basse Casamance since 1500.* Stuttgart: Franz Steiner Verlag Wiesbaden.

Marshall, Monty, and Ted Robert Gurr. 2005. *Peace and Conflict 2005.* Center for International Development and Conflict Management.

Marshall-Fratani, Ruth. 2006. "The War of 'Who Is Who': Autochthony, Nationalism, and Citizenship in the Ivoirian Crisis." *African Studies Review* 49 (2): 9–43.

Marut, Jean-Claude. 1995. "Solution militaire en Casamance." *Politique Africaine* 58:163–69.

———. 2010. *Le conflit de Casamance: Ce que disent les armes.* Paris: Karthala.

May, Larry. 2010. *Genocide: A Normative Account.* New York: Cambridge University Press.

Mazower, Mark. 2009. *No Enchanted Palace: The End of Empire and the Ideological Origins of the United Nations.* Princeton, NJ: Princeton University Press.

McAdam, Doug, and Sidney Tarrow. 2010. "Ballots and Barricades: On the Reciprocal Relationship between Elections and Social Movements." *Perspectives on Politics* 8 (2): 529–42.

McDoom, Omar. 2009. *The Micro-Politics of Mass Violence: Security, Authority, and Opportunity in Rwanda's Genocide.* Ph.D. Thesis, London School of Economics, Development Studies.

McDoom, Opheera. 2004. "Darfur Rebels Use Human Shields-Sudan." Reuters, October 18.

McGovern, Mike. 2011. *Making War in Côte d'Ivoire.* Chicago: Chicago University Press.

McMahon, Patrice. 2007. *Taming Ethnic Hatred: Ethnic Cooperation and Transnational Networks in Eastern Europe.* Syracuse, NY: Syracuse University Press.

Médard, J. F. 1982. "La regulation socio-politique." In *État et bourgeoisie en Côte d'Ivoire*, ed. Y. A. Fauré and J. F. Médard, 61–88. Paris: Karthala.

Meierhenrich, Jens. 2008. *The Legacies of Law: Long-Run Consequences of Legal Development in South Africa, 1652–2000*. New York: Cambridge University Press.

Melady, Thomas. 1974. *Burundi: The Tragic Years*. Maryknoll, NY: Orbis Books.

Melson, Robert. 1992. *Revolution and Genocide: On the Origins of the Armenian Genocide and the Holocaust*. Chicago: Chicago University Press.

Melvern, Linda. 2000. *A People Betrayed: The Role of the West In Rwanda's Genocide*. London: Zed Books.

———. 2004. *Conspiracy to Murder: The Rwandan Genocide*. London: Verso.

Memel-Fotê, Harris. 1998. *Fonder une Nation Africaine démocratique et socialiste en Côte d'Ivoire*. Paris: L'Harmattan.

Merrill, Austin. 2005. "Duékoué Dispatch: Citizen Soldiers." *New Republic*, October 17.

Mitchell, Matthew. 2012. "Migration, Citizenship, Autochthony: Strategies and Challengers for State-Building in Côte d'Ivoire." *Journal of Contemporary African Studies* 30 (2): 267–87.

Moses, A. Dirk, ed. 2008. *Empire, Colony, Genocide: Conquest, Occupation, and Subaltern Resistance in World History*. New York: Bergahn Books.

Midlarsky, Manus. 2005. *The Killing Trap: Genocide in the Twentieth Century*. Cambridge, U.K.: Cambridge University Press.

Mieu, Baudelaire. 2009. "Nady, l'atout nordiste du president Gbagbo." *Jeune Afrique*, October 30.

Miguel, Edward, Shanker Satyanath, and Ernest Sergenti. 2004. "Economic Shocks and Civil Conflict: An Instrumental Variables Approach." *Journal of Political Economy* 112 (4): 725–53.

Milgram, Stanley. 1974. *Obedience to Authority: An Experimental View*. New York: Harper and Row.

Monroe, Kristen Renwick. 2011. *Ethics in an Age of Terror and Genocide*. Princeton, NJ: Princeton University Press.

Monson, Jamie. 1998. "Relocating Maji-Maji: The Politics of Alliance and Authority in the Southern Highlands of Tanzania, 1870–1918." *Journal of African History* 39:95–120.

Moore, Barrington. 1966. *Social Origins of Dictatorship and Democracy: Lord and Peasant in the Making of the Modern World*. Boston: Beacon Press.

Mouvement Ivoirien des Droits Humains (MIDH). 2001. *Rapport sur les événements des 04 décembre et 05 décembre 2000*. Abidjan: MIDH.

———. 2004a. *Rapport d'enquête sur les exactions à l'ouest de la Côte d'Ivoire*. Abidjan: MIDH.

———. 2004b. *Repression violente de la marche d'opposition politique*. Abidjan: MIDH.

Munyantwali, Eustache. 1991. "La Politique d'equilibre dans l'enseignement." In *Les relations interethniques au Rwanda à la lumière de l'aggression d'Octobre 1990*, ed. F. X. Bangamwabo et al., 300–322. Ruhengeri: Editions Universitaires du Rwanda.

Mylonas, Harris. 2012. *The Politics of Nation-Building: Making Co-Nationals, Refugees, and Minorities*. New York: Cambridge University Press.

Naimark, Norman. 2001. *Fires of Hatred: Ethnic Cleansing in Twentieth-Century Europe*. Cambridge, MA: Harvard University Press.

——. 2007. "War and Genocide on the Eastern Front, 1941–1945." *Contemporary European History* 16 (2): 259–74.

——. 2010. *Stalin's Genocides*. Princeton, NJ: Princeton University Press.

Ndiaye, A. Raphael. 1993. "Ethno-Patronymic Correspondences and Jocular Kinship: A Large-Scale Problem of Integration." *African Environment* 8 (3–4): 93–124.

Newbury, Catharine M. 1978. "Ethnicity in Rwanda: The Case of Kinyaga." *Africa* 48 (1): 17–29.

——. 1988. *The Cohesion of Oppression: Clientship and Ethnicity in Rwanda, 1860–1960*. New York: Columbia University Press.

Newbury, David. 2001. "Precolonial Burundi and Rwanda: Local Loyalties, Regional Royalties." *International Journal of African Historical Studies* 34 (2): 255–314.

Newman, Leonard, and Ralph Erber, eds. 2002. *Understanding Genocide: The Social Psychology of the Holocaust*. Oxford: Oxford University Press.

New York Times. 2000. "Attempts to Reconcile Ivory Coast Ends in Shouts and Accusations." November 10.

Niane, Djibril. 1985. "Le Mali et la deuxième expansion mandé." In *Histoire Génerale de l'Afrique IV: L'Afrique di XIIe au XVIe siècle*, ed. D. T. Niane, 141–96. Paris: UNESCO.

Niremberg, David. 1996. *Communities of Violence: Persecution of Minorities in the Middle Ages*. Princeton, NJ: Princeton University Press.

Nkundabagenzi, Fidèle. 1961. *Rwanda Politique*. Brussels: The Centre.

Nolutshungu, Sam. 1996. *Limits of Anarchy: Intervention and State Formation in Chad*. Charlottesville: University Press of Virginia.

O'Brien, Conor Cruise. 1967. "The Tragedy of Biafra: A Condemned People." *New York Review of Books*, December 21, pp. 14–20.

——. 1969. "Biafra Revisited." *New York Review of Books*, May 22, pp. 15–27.

O'Brien, Donal Cruise. 1992. "Le contrat social sénégalais à l'épreuve." *Politique Africaine* 45:9–20.

——. 1998. "The Shadow-Politics of Wolofisation." *Journal of Modern African Studies* 36 (1): 25–46.

——. 2002. "Langue et nationalité au Sénégal. L'enjeu politique de la wolofisation." In *La construction de l'État au Sénégal,* ed. Donal Cruise O'Brien, Momar-Coumba Diop, and Mamadou Diouf, 143–55. Paris: Karthala.

Observer Team. 1968. "Report on Activities during the Period 24th September to 23rd November 1968." In *No Genocide*, Federal Ministry of Information, Apapa, Nigeria.

Okocha, Emma. 1994. *Blood on the Niger: An Untold Story of the Nigerian Civil War*. Lagos: Sunray Publications.

Omara-Otunnu, Amii. 1987. *Politics and the Military in Uganda, 1890–1985*. London: Macmillan Press.

Organization of African Unity. 1968. "Final Report of the First Phase from 5th October to 10th December by the Organization of African Unity Observers in Nigeria, December, 1968." In *No Genocide*, Federal Ministry of Information, Apapa, Nigeria.

Organization of African Unity. 2000. *Rwanda: The Preventable Genocide*. International Panel of Eminent Personalities.

Orjibta, Ikechukwu. 2000. *The Death of Biafra*. Enugu, Nigeria: Snaap Press.

Orth, Richard. 2004. "Rwanda's Hutu Extremist Insurgency: An Eyewitness Account." MacMillan Center Working Paper, Yale University.

Osiel, Mark. 2009. *Making Sense of Mass Atrocity.* Oxford: Oxford University Press.

Ostein, Philip. 2009. "Jonah Jang and the Jasawa: Ethno-Religious Conflict in Jos, Nigeria." Available at www.sharia-in-africa.net/pages/publications.php, accessed October 2011.

Ouattara, Azoumana. 2011. "Le coup d'état de décembre 1999 ou la fin de l'"exception militaire ivoirienne': les mutations d l'armée ivoirienne depuis 1960." In *Côte d'Ivoire: la reinvention de soi dans la violence,* ed. Francis Akindès, 169–212. Dakar: CODESRIA.

Oyserman, Daphna, and Armand Lauffer. 2010. "Examining the Implications of Cultural Frames on Social Movements and Group Action." In *Understanding Genocide: The Social Psychology of the Holocaust,* ed. Leonard Newman and Ralph Erber, 162–87. Oxford: Oxford University Press.

Özdemir, Hilmet, and Yusuf Sarinay. 2007. *Turkish-Armenian Conflict Documents.* TBMM Kültür, Sanat ve Yayin Kurulu Yayinlaru, No. 126, Ankara: Egemenlik Kayitsiz Şartsiz Milletindir.

Quillian, Lincoln. 1995. "Prejudice as a Response to Perceived Group Threat: Population Competition and Anti-Immigrant and Racial Prejudice in Europe." *American Sociological Review* 60 (4): 586–611.

Packer, George. 2003. "Gangsta War: Letter from Ivory Coast." *New Yorker,* September 20, pp. 68–81.

Panter-Brick, Samuel. 1970. *Nigerian Politics and Military Rule: Prelude to the Civil War.* London: Athlone Press.

Pape, Marc Le and Claudine Vidal. 2002. *Côte D'ivoire: L'année Terrible, 1999–2000.* Paris: Karthala

Paternostre de La Mairieu, Baudouin. 1994. *Toute Ma Vie Pour Vous, Mes Frères! Vie de Grégoire Kayibanda, Premier Président Élu du Rwanda.* Paris: P. Téqui.

Payne, Leigh. 2000. *Uncivil Movements: The Armed Right Wing and Democracy In Latin America.* Baltimore: Johns Hopkins University Press.

Peskin, Victor. 2008. *International Justice in Rwanda and the Balkans: Virtual Trials and State Cooperation.* New York: Cambridge University Press.

Petersen, Roger. 2001. *Resistance and Rebellion: Lessons from Eastern Europe.* Cambridge, U.K.: Cambridge University Press.

Piccolino, Giulia. 2012. "David against Goliath in Côte d'Ivoire? Laurent Gbabgo's War against Global Governance." *African Affairs* 111 (442): 1–23.

Political Instability Task Force. 2001. *Internal Wars and Failures of Governance, 1955–2004, Problem Set and Codebook.* Accessed online at http://globalpolicy.gmu.edu/pitf/pitfcode.htm.

Porter, Jack Nusan. 2005. *The Genocidal Mind: Sociological and Sexual Perspectives.* Lanham, MD: University Press of America.

Posen, Barry. 1993. "The Security Dilemma and Ethnic Conflict." *Survival* 35 (1): 27–47.

Poulton, Robin-Edward, and Ibrahim ag Youssouf. 1998. *A Peace of Timbuktu: Democratic Governance, Development, and African Peacekeeping.* Geneva: United Nations Institute for Democratic Research.

Power, Samantha. 2002. *"A Problem from Hell": America and the Age of Genocide.* New York: PublicAffairs.

——. 2004. "Dying in Darfur." *New Yorker*, August 30, pp. 56–83.

Présidence Mali. 2006. "Déclaration à S.E.M. de la République sur la Situation à Kidal." May 23. Available at www.koulouba.pr.ml/spip.php?article854, accessed March 16, 2012.

——. 2012. "Situation au Nord: Declaration du Président Amadou Toumani Touré, Chef de l'Etat." February 1. Available at www.journaldumali.com/article. php?aid=4186, accessed March 16, 2012.

Press, Daryl. 2005. *Calculating Credibility: How Leaders Assess Military Threats.* Ithaca, NY: Cornell University Press.

Pringle, Robert. 2006. *Democratization in Mali: Putting History to Work.* Peaceworks 58. Washington, DC: United States Institute of Peace.

Prunier, Gérard. 1993. "Élements pour une histoire du Front patriote rwandais." *Politique Africaine* 51:121–38.

——. 1995. *The Rwanda Crisis: History of a Genocide.* New York: Columbia University Press.

——. 1998. "The Rwandan Patriotic Front." In *African Guerrillas,* ed. Christopher Clapham, 119–33. Oxford: James Currey.

——. 2005. *Darfur: A 21st-Century Genocide.* Ithaca: Cornell University Press.

——. 2009. *Africa's World War: Congo, the Rwandan Genocide, and the Making of a Continental Catastrophe.* Oxford: Oxford University Press.

Radio France International. http://senegal.france24.com/2012/03/26/entretien-avec-macky-sall-je-suis-un-senegalais-de-synthese-un-pulaar-de-culture-serere/, accessed May 2, 2012.

République du Sénégal (RDS). 2008. *Sénégal: Résultats définitifs du Troisième Recensement Général de la Population et de l'Habitat-(2002).* Dakar: Agence Nationale de la Statistique et de la Démographie.

Reno, Will. 2011. *Warfare in Independent Africa.* New York: Cambridge University Press.

République du Rwanda. 1994. *Recensement général de la population et de l'habitat au 15 aout 1991: Analyse des résultats définitifs.* Kigali, April.

République Rwandaise. 2001. "Dénombrement des victimes du génocide: Analyse des resultats, draft." *Kigali: Ministère de l'administration locale et des affaires sociales.*

Reyntjens, Filip. 1985. *Pouvoir et droit au Rwanda. Droit public et évolution politique, 1916–1973.* Tervuren, Belgium: Musée Royal de l'Afrique Centrale.

——. 1994. *L'Afrique des grands lacs en crise: Rwanda, Burundi: 1988–1994.* Paris: Karthala.

——. 2009. *The Great African War: Congo and Regional Geopolitics, 1996–2006.* New York: Cambridge University Press.

——. 2011. "Waging (Civil) War Abroad: Rwanda and the DRC." In *Remaking Rwanda: State Building and Human Rights after Mass Violence,* ed. Scott Straus and Lars Waldorf, 132–51. Madison: University of Wisconsin Press.

Richardson, Louise. 2006. *What Terrorists Want: Understanding the Enemy, Containing the Threat.* New York: Random House.

Robinson, Geoffrey. 2010. *"If You Leave Us Here, We Will Die": How Genocide Was Stopped in East Timor.* Princeton, NJ: Princeton University Press.

Roche, Christian. 1985. *Histoire de la Casamance: Conquête et résistance: 1850–1920.* Paris: Karthala.

——. 2006. *Léopold Sédar Senghor: Le président humaniste.* Toulouse: Éditions Privat.

Rosenbaum, Alan, ed. 1996. *Is the Holocaust Unique? Perspectives on Comparative Genocide.* Boulder, CO: Westview Press.

Ross, Marc Howard. 1993. *The Culture of Conflict: Interpretations and Interests in Comparative Perspective.* New Haven, CT: Yale University Press.

——. 1997. "Culture and Identity in Comparative Political Analysis." In *Comparative Politics: Rationality, Culture, and Structure,* ed. Mark Irving Lichbach and Alan Zuckerman, 42–80. New York: Cambridge University Press.

Ross, Michael. 2004. "How Does Natural Resource Wealth Influence Civil War?" *International Organization* 58:35–67.

Rowland, Jacky. 1992. "The Tuareg Rebellion." *Africa Report* 37 (4): 43–45.

Ruf, François. 2007. "The Cocoa Sector." Overseas Development Institute, Background Note. Available at www.odi.org.uk/resources/docs/586.pdf, accessed November 30, 2011.

Ruf, François, and Jean-Luc Agkpo. 2008. "Etude sur les revenues et les investissements des producteurs de café et de cacao en Côte d'Ivoire." Afrisystems Consortium.

Rule, James. 1988. *Theories of Civil Violence.* Berkeley and Los Angeles: University of California Press.

Rumiya, Jean Gualbert. 1991. "La révolution socio-politique de 1959." In *Les relations interethniques au Rwanda à la lumière de l'aggression d'Octobre 1990,* ed. F. X. Bangamwabo et al., 139–208. Ruhengeri: Editions Universitaires du Rwanda.

Rummel, Rudolph. 1994. *Death by Government.* New Brunswick, NJ: Transaction.

Samatar, Said. 1991. *Somalia: A Nation in Turmoil.* London: Minority Rights Group.

Sambanis, Nicholas. 2004a. "Using Case Studies to Expand Economic Models of Civil War." *Perspectives on Politics* 2 (2): 259–79.

——. 2004b. "What Is Civil War? Conceptual and Empirical Complexities of an Operational Definition." *Journal of Conflict Resolution* 48 (6): 814–58.

Sanín, Francisco Gutiérrez, and Elisabeth Jean Wood. 2014. "Ideology in Civil War: Instrumental Adoption and Beyond." *Journal of Peace Research* 51 (2): 213–26.

Schabas, William. 2000. *Genocide in International Law: The Crime of Crime.* Cambridge, U.K.: Cambridge University Press.

——. 2006. "The 'Odious Scourge': Evolving Interpretations of the Crime of Genocide." *Genocide Studies and Prevention* 1 (2): 93–106.

Schaller, Dominik. 2008. "From Conquest to Genocide: Colonial Rule in German Southwest Africa and German East Africa." In *Empire, Colony, Genocide: Conquest, Occupation, and Subaltern Resistance in World History,* ed. A. Dirk Moses, 296–324. Oxford: Bergahn Books.

Schaller, Dominik, and Jürgen Zimmerer. 2009. *The Origins of Genocide: Raphael Lemkin as a Historian of Mass Violence.* London: Routledge.

Schatzberg, Michael. 2001. *Political Legitimacy in Middle Africa: Father, Family, Food.* Bloomington: Indiana University Press.

Schelling, Thomas. 1960. *The Strategy of Conflict.* Cambridge, MA: Harvard University Press.

——. 1966. *Arms and Influence.* New Haven, CT: Yale University Press.

Schulz, Dorothea. 1997. "Praise without Enchantment: Griots, Broadcast Media, and the Politics of Tradition in Mali." *Africa Today* 44 (4): 443–64.

Schwartz, Alfred. 2000. "Le conflit foncier entre Krou et Burkinabé à la lumière de l'"institution krouman."" *Afrique Contemporaine* 193:56–66.

Seawright, Jason, and John Gerring. 2008. "Case Selection Techniques in Case Study Research: A Menu of Qualitative and Quantitative Options." *Political Research Quarterly* 61 (2): 294–308.

Sémelin, Jacques. 2007. *Purify and Destroy: Political Uses of Massacres and Genocide.* New York: Columbia University Press.

Sen, Amartya. 2008. "Violence, Identity, and Poverty." *Journal of Peace Research* 45 (1): 5–15.

Senghor, Léopold Sédar. 1964. *Liberté 1: Négritude et Humanisme.* Paris: L'Éditions du Seuil.

———. 1971. *Liberté 2: Nation et Voie Africaine du Socialism.* Paris: L'Éditions du Seuil.

———. 1977. *Liberté 3: Négritude et Civilisation de l'Universel.* Paris: L'Éditions du Seuil.

———. 1983. *Liberté 4: Socialisme et Planification* Paris: L'Éditions du Seuil.

———. 1988. *Ce Que Je Crois: Négritude, Francité, et Civilisation de l'Universel.* Paris: Bernard Grasset.

———. 1993. *Liberté 5: Le Dialogue des Cultures.* Paris: L'Éditions du Seuil.

Shaw, Martin. 2003. *War and Genocide: Organized Killing in Modern Society.* Oxford: Polity Press.

———. 2007. *What is Genocide?* Cambridge, U.K.: Polity.

Shimamungu, Eugène. 2006. "Ethnicity, Regionalism, and Powers in Rwanda: Discourse and Political Action. Expert's Report in the Trial of 'Prosecutor versus Bagosora, Nsengiyumva, Kabiligi, and Ntabakuze.'" ICTR-98-41-T 24-05-2006.

Sibomana, André. 1999. *Hope for Rwanda: Conversations with Laure Guilbert and Hervé Deguine.* Trans. Carina Tertsakian. London: Pluto Press.

Sikainga, Ahmad Alawad. 1993. "Northern Sudanese Political Parties and the Civil War." In *Civil War in the Sudan,* ed. M. W. Daly and Ahmad Alawad Sikainga, 78–96. London: British Academic Press.

Sikkink, Kathryn. 1991. *Ideas and Institutions: Developmentalism in Brazil and Argentina.* Ithaca: Cornell University Press.

Slater, Dan, and Daniel Ziblatt. 2013. "The Enduring Indispensability of the Controlled Comparison." *Comparative Political Studies* 46 (10): 1301–27.

Smith, David Livingstone. 2011. *Less Than Human: Why We Demean, Enslave, and Exterminate Others.* New York: St. Martin's Press.

Smith, Etienne. 2010a. *Des arts de faire société: Parentés à plaisanteries et constructions identitaires en Afrique de l'Ouest (Sénégal).* PhD dissertation, Sciences Po, Paris.

———. 2010b. "The 'Informal' Politics of Linguistic Pluralism: The Case of Senegal." In *Language and Politics in Africa: Contemporary Issues,* ed. Ochieng Orwenjo and Obiero Ogone, 271–93. Newcastle, U.K.: Cambridge Scholars Publishing.

Smith, Robert S. 1976. *Warfare and Diplomacy in Pre-Colonial West Africa.* Madison: University of Wisconsin Press.

Smith, Stephen. 2002. "En Côte d'Ivoire, le Spectre du Rwanda." *Le Monde,* October 24.

Societe de Consulting et d'Application. 2008. "Projet de recensement des producteurs de cade-cacao de Côte d'Ivoire: Rapport d'activites." Abidjan, February.

Solonari, Vladimir. 2010. *Purifying the Nation: Population Exchange and Ethnic Cleansing in Nazi-Allied Romania.* Washington, DC, and Baltimore: Woodrow Wilson Center Press/Johns Hopkins University Press.

Soudan, François. 2010. "Laurent Gbagbo: L'interview vérité." *Jeune Afrique,* October 1.

Staub, Ervin. 1989. *The Roots of Evil: The Origins of Genocide and Other Group Violence.* New York: Cambridge University Press.

———. 2003. *The Psychology of Good and Evil: Why Children, Adults, and Groups Help and Harm Others.* New York: Cambridge University Press.

Stearns, Jason. 2011. *Dancing in the Glory of Monsters: The Collapse of the Congo and the Great War of Africa.* New York: PublicAffairs.

Stearns, Jason, and Federico Borello. 2011. "Bad Karma: Accountability for Rwandan Crimes in the Congo." In *Remaking Rwanda: State Building and Human Rights after Mass Violence,* ed. Scott Straus and Lars Waldorf, 152–69. Madison: University of Wisconsin Press.

Steele, Abbey. 2009. "Seeking Safety: Avoiding Displacement and Choosing Destinations in Civil Wars." *Journal of Peace Research* 46 (3): 419–29.

Stein, Janice. 2013. "Threat Perception in International Relations." In *The Oxford Handbook of Political Psychology,* 2d ed., ed. Leonie Huddy, David Sears, and Jack Levy, 364–94. Oxford: Oxford University Press.

Steinmetz, George. 2007. *The Devil's Handwriting: Precoloniality and the German Colonial State in Qindao, Samoa, and Southwest Africa.* Chicago: University of Chicago Press.

Straus, Scott. 2001. "Contested Meanings and Conflicting Imperatives: A Conceptual Analysis of Genocide." *Journal of Genocide Research* 3 (3): 349–75.

———. 2005. "Darfur and the Genocide Debate." *Foreign Affairs* 84 (1): 123–33.

———. 2006a. "Darfur and Rwanda: A Comparative Analysis." *Genocide Studies and Prevention* 1 (1): 41–56.

———. 2006b. *The Order of Genocide: Race, Power, and War in Rwanda.* Ithaca, NY: Cornell University Press.

———. 2007. "Second-Generation Comparative Research on Genocide." *World Politics* 59 (3): 476–501.

———. 2011a. "From 'Rescue' to Violence: Overcoming Local Opposition to Genocide in Rwanda." In *Resisting Genocide: The Multiple Forms of Rescue,* trans. Emma Bentley and Cynthia Schoch, ed. Jacques Sémelin, Claire Andrieu, and Sarah Gensburger, 331–44. London: Hurst.

———. 2011b. "'It's Sheer Horror Here': Patterns of Violence during the First Four Months of Côte d'Ivoire's Post-Electoral Crisis." *African Affairs* 110 (140): 481–89.

———. 2012a. "'Destroy Them to Save Us': Theories of Genocide and Logics of Political Violence." *Terrorism and Political Violence* 24 (4): 544–60.

———. 2012b. "Retreating from the Brink: Theorizing Mass Violence and the Dynamics of Restraint." *Perspectives on Politics* 10 (2): 343–62.

———. 2012c. "Wars Do End! Changing Patterns of Political Violence in sub-Saharan Africa." *African Affairs* 111 (443): 179–201.

Straus, Scott, and Lars Waldorf, eds. 2011. *Remaking Rwanda: State Building and Human Rights after Mass Violence.* Madison: University of Wisconsin Press.

Sullivan, Christopher. 2012. "Blood in the Village: A Local-Level Investigation of State Massacres." *Conflict Management and Peace Science* 29 (4): 373–96.

Sunseri, Thaddeus. 2003. "Reinterpreting a Colonial Rebellion: Forestry and Social Control in German East Africa, 1874–1915." *Environmental History* 8 (3): 430–51.

Suny, Ronald Grigor. 2011. "Writing Genocide: The Fate of the Ottoman Armenians." In *A Question of Genocide: Armenians and Turks at the End of the Ottoman Empire,* ed. Ronald Grigor Suny, Fatma Muge Goçek, and Norman Naimark, 15–41. Oxford: Oxford University Press.

Swidler, Ann. 1986. "Culture in Action: Symbols and Strategies." *American Sociological Review* 51 (2): 273–86.

Tambadou, Moustapha. 1996. *Les convergences culturelles au sein de la nation sénégalaise: actes du colloque de Kaolack, 8–13 juin 1994.* Dakar: Ministère de la culture.

Tareke, Gebru. 2009. *The Ethiopian Revolution: War in the Horn of Africa.* New Haven, CT: Yale University Press.

Tarrow, Sidney. 2007. "Inside Insurgencies: Politics and Violence in an Age of War." *Perspectives on Politics* 5 (3): 587–600.

Tatz, Colin, Peter Arnold, and Sandra Tatz, eds. 2006. *Genocide Perspectives III: Essays on the Holocaust and other Genocides.* Sydney: Brandl and Schlesinger.

Taylor, Christopher C. *Sacrifice as Terror: The Rwandan Genocide of 1994.* Oxford: Berg, 1999.

Thomas-Lake, Hillary. 2010. *Keeping Promises: Building Peace after the Peace Accords.* PhD dissertation, Johns Hopkins University.

Tomz, Michael, and Jessica Weeks. 2013. "Public Opinion and the Democratic Peace." *American Political Science Review* 107 (4): 849–65.

Totten, Samuel, and Williams Parsons, eds. 2009. *Century of Genocide: Critical Essays and Eyewitness Accounts.* 3d ed. New York: Routledge.

Truth and Reconciliation Commission of Liberia. *Final Report.* 2009.

Tubiana, Jérôme. 2005. "Le Darfour, un conflit identitaire?" *Afrique contemporaine* 214 (2): 165–206.

——. 2007. "Darfur: A War for Land?" In *War in Darfur and the Search for Peace,* ed. Alex de Waal, 68–91. Cambridge, MA: Global Equity Initiative/Harvard University.

Tubiana, Marie-José. 2006. *Carnets de Route au Dar For, 1965–1970.* Saint Maure des Fossés, France: Éditions Sepia.

Turner, Matthew. 2004. "Political Ecology and the Moral Dimensions of 'Resource Conflicts': The Case of Farmer-Herder Conflicts in the Sahel." *Political Geography* 23 (7): 863–89.

Ulfelder, Jay. 2011. "Making a Case for (Imperfect) Statistical Modeling as the Basis for Genocide Early Warning." United States Holocaust Memorial Museum, October 5. Available at www.ushmm.org/genocide/analysis/details/2011-10-05/Jay%20Ulfelder%20Early%20Warning%20Final%20Paper.pdf, accessed June 23, 2014.

Ulfelder, Jay, and Benjamin Valentino. 2008. "Assessing the Risks of State-Sponsored Mass Killing." Political Instability Task Force, Washington, D.C., available at http://papers.ssrn.com/sol3/papers.cfm?abstract_id=1703426.

Umutesi, Marie Béatrice. 2004. *Surviving the Slaughter: The Ordeal of a Rwandan Refugee in Zaire.* Trans. Julia Emerson. Madison, WI: University of Wisconsin Press.

Ungor, Ugor. 2006. "When Persecution Bleeds into Mass Murder: The Processive Nature of Genocide." *Genocide Studies and Prevention* 1 (2): 173–76.

United Nations. *Report of the Independent Inquiry into the Actions of the United Nations during the 1994 Genocide in Rwanda.* December 15, 1999.

United Nations Commission on Human Rights. 2004. "Report of the Special Rapporteur on Contemporary forms of Racism, Racial Discrimination, Xenophobia and Related Intolerance, Mr Doudou Diène, on his Mission to Côte d'Ivoire from 9 to 21 February 2004." December 22.

———. 2005. "Report of the United Nations High Commissioner for Human Rights and Follow-Up to the World Conference on Human Rights: Situation of Human Rights in the Darfur Region of the Sudan." E/CN.4/2005/3, May 7.

United Nations High Commissioner for Human Rights (UNHCHR). 2003. "Report of an Urgent Human Rights Mission to Côte d'Ivoire." S/2003/90, Geneva.

———. 2004a. *Report of the Commission of Inquiry on the Events Connected with the March Planned for 25 March 2004 in Abidjan.* Geneva.

———. 2004b. *Commission d'enquête internationale sur les allegations de violations des droits de l'homme en Côte d'Ivoire (CEI). 2004. Rapport sur la situation des droits de l'homme en République de Côte d'Ivoire depuis le 19 septembre 2002 jusqu'au 15 octobre 2004 confromément aux dispositions de l'annexe VI de l'Accord de Linas-Marcoussis et à la Déclaration du Président du conseil de Sécurité du 25 Mai 2004.* PRST/2004/17, Geneva.

———. 2010. *Democratic Republic of Congo, 1993–2003: Report of the Mapping Exercise Documenting the Most Serious Violations of Human Rights and International Humanitarian Law Committed within the Territory of the Democratic Republic of the Congo between March 1993 and June 2003.* Geneva: UNHCHR. August. Available at www.ohchr.org/Documents/Countries/ZR/DRC_MAPPING_REPORT_FINAL_EN.pdf, accessed June 23, 2014.

United Nations Human Rights Council (UNHRC). 2011a. "Report of the High Commissioner for Human Rights on the Situation of Human Rights in Côte d'Ivoire." February 15.

———. 2011b. "Report of the High Commissioner for Human Rights on the Situation of Human Rights in Côte d'Ivoire." June 14.

———. 2011c. "Report of the Independent, International Commission of Inquiry on Côte d'Ivoire." June 9.

United Nations Office of the UN Resident and Humanitarian Coordinator for the Sudan. 2004. "Darfur Humanitarian Profile No. 6." Khartoum, Sudan, September 1.

United Nations Office of the Special Advisor on the Prevention of Genocide. 2004. "Statement by the Special Advisor on the Prevention of Genocide." November 15.

United Nations Operation in Côte d'Ivoire (UNOCI). 2005a. "Rapport sur la Situation des Droits de l'Homme en Côte d'Ivoire, Janvier-Février 2005." Division des Droits de l'Homme, Abidjan, March 2005.

———. 2005b. "Rapport sur la Situation des Droits de l'Homme en Côte d'Ivoire, Mars-Avril 2005." Division des Droits de l'Homme, Abidjan, May.

———. 2006a. "Rapport sur la Situation des Droits de l'Homme en Côte d'Ivoire, Rapport No. 4, Aout-Septembre-Octobre-Novembre-Decembre 2005, Division des Droits de l'Homme." Abidjan, February.

———. 2006b. "Rapport sur la Situation des Droits de l'Homme en Côte d'Ivoire, Rapport No. 5, Janvier-Fevrier-Mars-Avril 2006." Abidjan, June.

———. 2007a. "Rapport sur la Situation des Droits de l'Homme en Côte d'Ivoire, Rapport No. 6, Mai-Juin-Juillet-Aout 2006." Abidjan, March.

——. 2007b. "Rapport sur la Situation des Droits de l'Homme en Côte d'Ivoire, Rapport No. 7, Septembre-Octobre-Novembre-Decembre 2006." Abidjan.

——. 2007c. "Rapport sur la Situation des Droits de l'Homme en Côte d'Ivoire, Rapport No. 8, Janvier-Fevrier-Mars-Avril-Mai-Juin 2007." Abidjan.

United Nations News Service. 2011. "UN Warns Deadly Shelling of Ivoirian Market May Be Crime against Humanity." March 18.

United Nations Visiting Mission (UNVM) to Trust Territories in East Africa, 1957. 1958. *Report on Ruanda-Urundi.* New York: Trusteeship Council.

United States Department of State Human Rights Practices. 1994–2011. Senegal. Available at www.state.gov/www/global/human_rights/hrp_reports_mainhp.html and www.state.gov/j/drl/rls/hrrpt/, accessed June 23, 2014.

United States Department of State. 2004. "Documenting Atrocities in Darfur." September 21. Available at www.state.gov/g/drl/rls/36028.htm, accessed June 23, 2014.

——. 2005. "Sudan: Death Toll in Darfur." State Department, March 25, 2005. Available at www.state.gov/s/inr/rls/fs/2005/45105.htm, accessed June 23, 2014.

Uppsala Conflict Data Program and International Peace Research Institute. 2006. UCDP/PRIO Armed Conflict Dataset and Codebook, Version 4-2006. Available at www.pcr.uu.se/publications/ucdp_pub/conflictlist1946-2006, accessed June 23, 2014.

Uvin, Peter. 1998. *Aiding Violence: The Development Enterprise in Rwanda.* West Hartford, CT: Kumarian Press.

Uwizeyimana, Laurien. 1991. "La politique d'équilibre ethnique et régional dans l'emploi." In *Les relations interethniques au Rwanda à la lumière de l'aggression d'Octobre 1990,* F. X. Bangamwabo et al., 308–22. Ruhengeri: Editions Universitaires du Rwanda.

Valentino, Benjamin. 2004. *Final Solutions: Mass Killing and Genocide in the Twentieth Century.* Ithaca: Cornell University Press.

Valentino, Benjamin, Paul Huth, and Dylan Balch-Lindsay. 2004. "'Draining the Sea': Mass Killing and Guerrilla Warfare." *International Organization* 58 (1): 375–407.

Valentino, Benjamin, Paul Huth, and Sarah Croco. 2006. "Covenants without Swords: International Law and the Protection of Civilians in Times of War." *World Politics* 58:339–77.

Valentino, Benjamin and Chad Hazlett. 2012. "Revisiting Forecasting Models for State Sponsored Mass Killing, 1957–2012." Working Paper.

Vansina, Jan. 2001. *Le Rwanda ancien: Le royaume nyiginya.* Paris: Karthala.

Varshney, Ashutosh. 2002. *Ethnic Conflict and Civic Life: Hindus and Muslims in India.* New Haven, CT: Yale University Press.

Verdeja, Ernesto. 2012. "The Political Science of Genocide: Outlines of an Emerging Research Agenda." *Perspectives on Politics* 10 (2): 307–21.

Verwimp, Philip. 2006. "Peasant Ideology and Genocide in Rwanda under Habyarimana." In *Genocide in Cambodia and Rwanda: New Perspectives,* ed. Susan Cook, 1–40. New Brunswick, NJ: Transaction.

Villalón, Leonardo. 1995. *Islamic Society and State Power in Senegal: Disciples and Citizens in Fatick.* New York: Cambridge University Press.

Villalón, Leonardo, and Abdourahmane Idrissa. 2005. "The Tribulations of a Successful Transition: Institutional Dynamics and Elite Rivalry in Mali." In Leonardo Villalón and Peter VonDoepp, eds., 49–74. *The Fate of Africa's Democratic Experiments*. Bloomington: Indiana University Press.

Waller, James. 2002. *Becoming Evil: How Ordinary People Commit Genocide and Mass Killing*. Oxford: Oxford University Press.

Walter, Barbara. 2002. *Committing to Peace: The Successful Settlement of Civil Wars*. Princeton, NJ: Princeton University Press.

Warburg, Gabriel. 2003. *Islam, Sectarianism, and Politics in Sudan since the Mahdiyya*. Madison: University of Wisconsin Press.

Waugh, Auderon, and Suzanne Cronjé. 1969. *Biafra: Britain's Shame*. London: Michael Joseph.

Wayman, Frank, and Atsushi Tago. 2010. "Explaining the Onset of Mass Killing, 1949–1987." *Journal of Peace Research* 47 (1): 3–13.

Wedeen, Lisa. 2002. "Conceptualizing Culture: Possibilities for Political Science." *American Political Science Review* 96 (4): 713–28.

Weiss-Wendt, Anton. 2009. *Murder without Hatred: Estonians and the Holocaust*. Syracuse, NY: Syracuse University Press.

———. 2010. "The State and Genocide." In *The Oxford Handbook of Genocide Studies*, ed. Donald Bloxham and A. Dirk Moses, pp. 81–101. Oxford: Oxford University Press.

Weitz, Eric. 2003. *A Century of Genocide: Utopias of Race and Nation*. Princeton, NJ: Princeton University Press.

Weinstein, Jeremy. 2007. *Inside Rebellion: The Politics of Insurgent Violence*. New York: Cambridge University Press.

Wilkinson, Steven. 2004. *Votes and Violence: Electoral Competition and Ethnic Riots in India*. New York: Cambridge University Press.

Williams, Paul. 2011. *War and Conflict in Africa*. Cambridge, U.K.: Polity.

Wilshire, Bruce. 2005. *Get 'Em all! Kill 'Em! Genocide, Terrorism, Righteous Communities*. Lanham, MD: Lexington Books.

Wimmer, Andreas. 2002. *Nationalist Exclusion and Ethnic Conflict: Shadows of Modernity*. Cambridge, U.K.: Cambridge University Press.

Wing, Susanna. 2008. *Constructing Democracy in Transitioning Societies of Africa: Constitutionalism and Deliberation in Mali*. New York: Palgrave Macmillan.

Wood, Elisabeth Jean. 2003. *Insurgent Collective Action and Civil War in El Salvador*. New York: Cambridge University Press.

———. 2006. "Variation of Sexual Violence during War." *Politics and Society* 34 (3): 307–41.

Woodward, Peter. 1990. *Sudan, 1898–1989: The Unstable State*. Boulder, CO: Lynne Rienner.

Woodward, Susan. 1995. *Balkan Tragedy: Chaos and Dissolution after the Cold War*. Washington, DC: Brookings Institute.

World Bank. 2011. *Conflict, Security, and Development: World Development Report 2011*. Washington, DC: The World Bank Group.

Young, Crawford. 1994. *The African Colonial State in Comparative Perspective*. New Haven, CT: Yale University Press.

———. 2012. *The Postcolonial State in Africa: Fifty Years of Independence, 1960–2010*. Madison: University of Wisconsin Press.

Young, John. 1997. *Peasant Revolution in Ethiopia: The Tigray People's Liberation Front, 1975–1991*. New York: Cambridge University Press.

Zartman, I. William. 2010. "Preventing Identity Conflicts Leading to Genocide and Mass Killings." New York: International Peace Institute.

Zimmerer, Jürgen. 2008a. "The Model Colony?" In *Genocide in South-West Africa: The Colonial War of 1904–1908 and Its Aftermath*, trans. E. J. Neather, ed. Jürgen Zimmerer and Joachim Zeller. Monmouth, U.K.: Merlin Press.

——. 2008b. "War, Concentration Camps, and Genocide in South-West Africa: The First German Genocide." In *Genocide in South-West Africa: The Colonial War of 1904–1908 and Its Aftermath*, trans. E. J. Neather, ed. Jürgen Zimmerer and Joachim Zeller, 41–63. Monmouth, U.K.: Merlin Press.

Zimmerman, Andrew. 2006. "'What Do You Really Want in German East Africa, Herr Professor?' Counterinsurgency and the Science Effect in Colonial Tanzania." *Comparative Study of Society and History* 48 (2), 419–61.

Zolberg, Aristide. 1969. *One-Party Government in the Ivory Coast*. Rev. ed. Princeton, NJ: Princeton University Press.

Zuccarelli, François. 1987. *La vie politique Sénégalaise (1940–1988)*. Paris: Le Centre des Hautes Etudes sur l'Afrique et l'Asie Modernes.

Speeches

The texts of the speeches listed in this section, as well as other speeches consulted for the research for the book, are available at: http://users.polisci.wisc.edu/straus/speech/

Abbud, Ibrahim. 1959. "Premier Abbud Speaks on Anniversary." Foreign Broadcast Information Service, November 17.

Al-Bashir, Omar. 1989a. "Al-Bashir Praises Military in Speech." Foreign Broadcast Information Service, July 4.

——. 1989b. "Al-Bashir Addresses Rally in Al-Kabbashi." Foreign Broadcast Information Service, August 27.

——. 1989c. "Al-Bashir's 27 Nov Martyrs' Day Speech Broadcast." Foreign Broadcast Information Service, November 27.

——. 1989d. "Al-Bashir's Speech at Khartoum Rally 3 Dec." Foreign Broadcast Information Service, December 3.

——. 1990. "Al-Bashir Addresses Residents." Foreign Broadcast Information Service, February 11.

——. 1992a. "Al-Bashir Addresses National Assembly Session." Foreign Broadcast Information Service, February 24.

——. 1992b. "Al-Bashir Delivers Address." Foreign Broadcast Information Service, July 6.

——. 1993. "Al-Bashir Addresses National Assembly." Foreign Broadcast Information Service, October 25.

——. 1995a. "Al-Bashir urges election of strong candidates." Foreign Broadcast Information Service, January 18.

——. 1995b. "Al-Bashir on Eritrean, Egyptian, UK 'Enmity.'" Foreign Broadcast Information Service, June 30.

——. 2000. "Sudan's Al-Bashir on Arab Tour, Peace." Foreign Broadcast Information Service, March 5.

——. 2003. "Sudan's Bashir Pledges to Invite Rebels into Government during Transition." Foreign Broadcast Information Service, October 8.

Al-Mahdi, Al-Sadiq. 1986a. "Omdurman Radio Reports Premier's Address to Assembly." Foreign Broadcast Information Service, July 7.

——. 1986b. "Prime Minister's Statement on Armed Forces Changes." Foreign Broadcast Information Service, September 4.

——. 1987. "Al-Sadiq al-Mahdi Gives Speech on IMF, Islam." Foreign Broadcast Information Service, October 20.

BBC Monitoring of Radio Rwanda. 1990a. "Rwandan President Outlines Stance on Conflict." October 29. Accessed from Lexis-Nexis, March 2013.

——. 1990b. "Rwandan President Briefs Central Committee on Political and Military Situation." December 3. Accessed from Lexis-Nexis, March 2013.

——. 1991. "Rwanda: Habyarimana Addresses Extraordinary Congress." April 28. Accessed from Lexis-Nexis, March 2013.

——. 1992a. "Rwanda President Habyarimana on Political Situation, Negotiations with RPF." August 17. Accessed from Lexis-Nexis, March 2013.

——. 1992b. "Report on Interview with President RPF and Army, Political Reforms." September 12. Accessed from Lexis-Nexis, March 2013.

——. 1992c. "President Habyarimana's Army Day Speech Calls for Unity and Vigilance." October 28. Accessed from Lexis-Nexis, March 2013.

——. 1993a. "Rwanda: Habyarimana 'Shocked' by Gapyisi's Murder." May 24. Accessed from Lexis-Nexis, March 2013.

——. 1993b. "Rwandan Peace Accord Ceremony in Arusha; Speech by President Habyarimana." August 4. Accessed from Lexis-Nexis, March 2013.

Bédié, Henri Konan. 1990. "Speaker Bédié Addresses National Assembly." Foreign Broadcast Information Service, April 26.

Biloa, Marie-Roger. 1989. "Juvénale Habyarimana: les quatre vérités d'un homme tranquille." *Jeune Afrique* 1471, pp. 4–12.

Diagouraga, Mahamadou. 1994. "Les convictions de Mahamadou Diagouraga." *L'Essor*, October 8–9, p. 3.

Dieng, Amadou Abdoulaye. 1990. "Le general Dieng gouverneur de Ziguinchor: 'Je serais disponible mais ferme.'" *Le Soleil*, June 7, pp. 1, 7.

Diouf, Abdou. 1984. "Les souhaits du President de la Republique: 1984, année de la fraternité retrouvée." *Le Soleil*, January 2, pp. 1, 6.

——. 1987. "Le Chef de l'Etat: 'Le sursaut national est une attitude positive face aux defies.'" *Le Soleil*, January 2, pp. 2, 6.

——. 1988a. "Persévérance et vigilance: Message a la nation." *Le Soleil*, January 4, pp. 1, 10–11.

——. 1988b. "Le changement pour le meilleur: Le message a la nation." *Le Soleil*, April 5, pp. 1, 5.

——. 1988c. "Diouf Lifts State of Emergency; To Meet Wade." Foreign Broadcast Information Service, May 17.

——. 1990a. "Conformité aux ideaux de paix et de solidarité." *Le Soleil*, May 8, p. 4.

——. 1990b. "Diouf: Aid for Islamic Media." Foreign Broadcast Information Service, June 15, p. 6.

——. 1996. "L'addresse du chef de l'Etat." *Le Soleil*, January 2, pp. 1, 4–5.

Gasana, Anastase. 1990. "Interview Granted by Anastase Gasana to Bamwanga, a Journalist at Radio Rwanda, October 21, available at Radio Rwanda Transcripts." Montreal Institute For Genocide and Human Rights Studies, transcript available at http://migs.concordia.ca/links/Rwandan_Radio_Transcripts_RadioRwanda.htm.

Gbagbo, Laurent. 2002a. "L'heure du patriotism a sonné." *Fraternité Matin*, September 21–22.

———. 2002b. "Le discours de S.E.M. Laurent Gbagbo à la Nation." abidjan.net, October 8.

Habyarimana, Juvénal. 1974. "Message du président de la République à l'occasion du nouvel an 1974." *Rwanda: Carrefoure de'Afrique,* No. 26, January 7–13, pp. 1–4.

———. 1977. *Discours et Entretiens.* Présidence de la République Rwandaise. Kigali, Rwanda.

———. 1981a. *Discours, Messages et Entretiens: 5 Juillet 1973–Décembre 1974.* Présidence de la République Rwandaise. Kigali, Rwanda.

———. 1981b. *Discours, Messages et Entretiens Durant l'année 1981.* Présidence de la République Rwandaise. Kigali, Rwanda.

———. 1982. *Discours, Messages et Entretiens.* Présidence de la République Rwandaise. Kigali, Rwanda.

———. 1987. *Discours, Messages et Entretiens 1987.* Présidence de la République Rwandaise. Kigali, Rwanda.

———. 1990. "Discours du President Habyarimana du 07.12.1990." Exhibit Number 224, ICTR-98-44-T. Admitted October 26, 2005.

———. 1992a. "Habyarimana Speaks on Independence Day." Foreign Broadcast Information Service, July 7.

———. 1992b. "15.11.1992: Habyarimana speech in Ruhengeri." Exhibit Number DN28B, ICTR-98-44-T. Admitted October 14, 2005.

———. 1992c. "President on Arusha Negotiations, Security." Foreign Broadcast Information Service, December 1.

———. 1993a. "Habyarimana Urges Understanding Within Government." Foreign Broadcast Information Service, January 25.

———. 1993b. "President on Talks with Rebels, Reconciliation." Interview. Foreign Broadcast Information Service, April 30.

———. 1993c. "President on National Situation, Peace Talks." Interview. Foreign Broadcast Information Service, May 13.

———. 1993d. "President Habyarimana Hails Accord." Foreign Broadcast Information Service, August 5.

Houphouët-Boigny, Felix. 1966. "Le message à la nation du Chef de l'État." *Fraternité Matin*, August 6.

———. 1967. "Le message du Chef de l'État." *Fraternité Matin*, August 9.

———. 1985. "Faire germer ces grains de paix, d'amour, de justice, et de liberté." *Fraternité Matin*, August 12.

———. 1990. "President Accepts Nomination." Foreign Broadcast Information Service, October 6.

Kayibanda, Grégoire. 1965. "Points principaux du message du Président G. Kayibanda, à l'occasion du nouvel an." *Rwanda Carrefour d'Afrique.*

Keita, Cheikh. 1990a. "Le général Dieng gouverneur de Ziguinchor 'Je Serais Disponible Mais Ferme.'" *Le Soleil*, June 7, pp. 1, 7.

———. 1990b. "Ziguinchor: le gouverneur aux jeunes: 'Ne cédez pas aus pressions.'" *Le Soleil*, June 21, p. 13.

Konaré, Alpha Oumar. 1993a. "La democratie doit etre percue comme le cadre ideal d'une participation constructive." *L'Essor*, January 9–10, p. 2.

———. 1993b. "Fête de l'armée: Les exigencies d'une nouvelle identité militaire." *L'Essor*, January 23–24, p. 1.

———. 1993c. "La democratie est la seule chance du Mali." *L'Essor*, April 17–18, p. 2.

———. 1993d. "Sans craindre l'effort, sans sacrifier à la facilité, sans céder au désespoir." *L'Essor*, September 25–26, p. 2.

———. 1994a. "Les temps sont difficiles, mais l'avenir n'est pas somber." *L'Essor*, January 8–9, p. 2.

———. 1994b. "L'incommunicabilité ne doit pas render inaccessibles les idéaux de lutte." *L'Essor*, April 1–2, p. 2.

———. 1994c. "Les acquis, les attentes, les perspectives." *L'Essor*, June 11–12, pp. 1, 3.

Numayri, Ja'far Muhammad. 1970a. "An-Numayri Address Marks 25 May Anniversary." Foreign Broadcast Information Service, May 25.

———. 1970b. "An-Numayri on RCC Changes, Perils to Revolution." Foreign Broadcast Information Service, November 23.

———. 1974. "Numayri Threatens Retaliation for Internal Interference." Foreign Broadcast Information Service, May 24.

———. 1975. "President Numayri's Speech to New Cabinet." Foreign Broadcast Information Service, January 28.

———. 1979. "President Numayri Addresses National Action Leaders." Foreign Broadcast Information Service, August 18.

———. 1980. "Suna: President Numayri Addresses Sudanese Nation." Foreign Broadcast Information Service, May 5.

———. 1981. "Numayri Speaks on Relations with Egypt 25 May." Foreign Broadcast Information Service, May 24.

———. 1982. "Numayri Addressses Nation on Armed Forces Day." Foreign Broadcast Information Service, August 13.

———. 1983. "Numayri, Mubarak Addresses Nile Valley Parliament." Foreign Broadcast Information Service. May 25.

———. 1984. "President Numayri Speech Marks 'Id Festival." Foreign Broadcast Information Service, June 29.

Touré, Amadou Toumani. 1991a. "Une vigilance permanente et une solidarité sans faille pour préserver l'acquis du 26 Mars." *L'Essor*, May 4–5, p. 6.

———. 1991b. "Aussi originale et belle que la victoire du 26 Mars." *L'Essor*, July 3–4, p. 2.

———. 1991c. "ATT lance un appel à la mobilization et à la defense des acquis démocratiques." *L'Essor*, July 20–21, p. 2.

———. 1991d. "Transition: La reussite au boutde l'adhesion aux valeurs varies de democratie." *L'Essor*, September 28–29, p. 2.

———. 1991e. "Sa reussite exigeait ce delai supplementaire." *L'Essor*, November 16–17, p. 2.

———. 1994. "ATT, au pas de charge." *L'Essor*, August 20–21, p. 4.

Wade, Abdoulaye. 2001. "Nouvel an: Wade appellee au travail." *Le Soleil*, January 2, pp. 1–2.

———. 2002. "'Le Sénégal qui gagne, notre credo, engrangera chaque jour de nou-velles victoires.'" *Le Soleil,* January 2, p. 3.

———. 2003. "Message à la nation à l'occasion de la celebration du 43e anniversaire de l'Indépendance." www.gouv.sn. April 3. Accessed February 1, 2012.

———. 2004. "Message à la Nation du chef de l'Etat à l'occasion du 44e anniversaire de l'Indépendance." www.gouv.sn. July 4. Accessed February 1, 2012.

———. 2005. "Message à la Nation du chef de l'Etat à l'occasion du 45e anniversaire de l'Indépendance." www.gouv.sn/. April 4. Accessed February 1, 2012.

INDEX

Page numbers followed by *f* and *t* indicate figures and tables.